The Knight-Monks of Vichy France

The Knight-Monks
of Vichy France

Uriage, 1940–1945

JOHN HELLMAN

McGill-Queen's University Press
Montreal & Kingston • London • Buffalo

To Christophe

© McGill-Queen's University Press 1993
ISBN 0-7735-0973-9

Legal deposit second quarter 1993
Bibliothèque nationale du Québec

Printed in Canada on acid-free paper

This book has been published with the help of a
grant from the Canadian Federation for the
Humanities, using funds provided by the Social
Sciences and Humanities Research Council of Canada.
Publication has also been supported by the Canada
Council through its block grant program.

Canadian Cataloguing in Publication Data

Hellman, John, 1940–
    The knight-monks of Vichy France: Uriage,
    1940–1945
    Includes bibiographical references and index.
    ISBN 0-7735-0973-9
    1. École nationale supérieure des cadres d'Uriage.
    2. Uriage-les-Bains (France) – Intellectual life.
    3. France – Intellectual life – 20th century. 4. France –
    Politics and government – 1940–1945. I. Title.
    DC397.H44 1993   944'.99   C93-090055-3

Typeset in Baskerville 10/12
by Caractéra production graphique inc., Quebec City

Photograph of Pierre Dunoyer de Segonzac on jacket
appears courtesy of Louise-Marie Lozac'hmeur and
Antoine Delestre.

Contents

Preface

One of the most controversial elements of the *non-lieu* verdict in the Touvier case in early 1992 was its pronouncement that the Vichy government "cannot, without falsifying the least questionable historical facts, be described as a State that was practising a policy of ideological hegemony" (*Le Monde*, 15 April 1992). The judgment implied that the Pétain regime was neither fascist nor totalitarian and should not be confused with its nefarious neighbours. Consequently, an employee who, like *milicien* Paul Touvier, had hunted down resisters and Jews, was a devout Catholic anti-Communist, as he claimed, and not a Nazi or a Fascist. The Touvier verdict has since been denounced as part of a concerted effort to forget the fascist or "New Order" aspects of the Pétain regime, an effort encouraged by the collapse of Soviet communism with its attendant questioning of the allied understanding of World War II and of allied war aims. In the Touvier pardon "it is the fascist – not only the dictatorial – nature of the Vichy government that seemed to benefit from clemency, even absolution" (Maurice Caveing, "Vichy et l'Humanité," *Raison présente*, no.103 (1992): 3–5).

The three judges of the Touvier case would benefit from reading Claude Singer's *Vichy, l'université et les juifs* (Paris: Éd. Les Belles Lettres, 1992), which carefully documents the drastic policies of racialism and exclusion pursued by the governmental and educational establishments of the Pétain regime. The Touvier case has revealed not only the complicity of Church officials in hiding the fugitive from justice for so many years after the war, but also the reluctance of many French Catholics to admit that the Pétainist militia was serving international fascism, working for a regime representing authority and exclusion, a government with a new kind of

"State Culture" (Fumaroli) seeking a place for France in the European New Order.

The Touvier verdict contradicts the contemporary scholarship that suggests the Vichy regime was neither an accident nor an imposition from the outside, but rather the culmination of decades of *French racialism* (cf. Ralph Schor, *L'antisémitisme en France pendant les années trente* [Brussels: Éditions Complexe, 1992]) and authoritarian anti-republicanism, of a distinctive French rebellion against liberal democracy. This book will argue that the École Nationale des Cadres d'Uriage, with its "knight-monks," was an important representative of such a rebellion against France's republican and democratic heritage.

Since this manuscript was written, Marc Fumaroli has argued that the Uriage group, in concert with the Vichy cultural association *Jeune France*, invented an original notion of culture, one quite antithetical to the values of liberal democracy (*L'État culturel. Une religion moderne* [Paris: Éditions de Fallois, 1992]). For him Uriage/*Jeune France* gave birth to the idea of a "cultural state" that sought to impose a "modern religion" of culture in France, analogous to the *Opera Nazionale Dopo Lavoro* (O.N.D.) of Fascist Italy or the Hitlerite *Kraft durch Freude*. For Fumaroli the influence of *Jeune France*/Uriage was "disproportionate to its brief life and the relative modesty of its resources," for this milieu refined the notion of "culture" in the official sense that it took during de Gaulle's Fifth Republic, and outlined plans for a Ministry of Culture.

The "official" historian of Uriage has reacted with characteristic vehemence (*Le Débat*, Summer 1992), claiming that Fumaroli's distortions are only equalled by the "caricatural and deforming" approach of historians such as the author. Here again the friends of Uriage try to avoid the fact that the school served a militant, totalitarian regime of exclusion. While no longer denying the Pétainism of Uriage, they play down the milieu's manifestations of sympathy for the European New Order, its anti-liberalism and anti-Americanism, while stressing incidents of hostility toward the German occupant. There is a reluctance to face the anti-semitic, anti-communist, and anti-masonic activities of the Uriage group, and to admit that the "State Culture" they embraced was profoundly – if not always openly – authoritarian, intolerant, anti-liberal, anti-democratic and, at least to some degree, racialist. As soon as the Vichy regime was in place, that government set into motion a revolutionary program that groups like Uriage legitimized and sought to implement. The "knight-monks" of Uriage are hesitant to admit that the Uriage school created and represented a Pétainist ideology, or, for that matter, that Vichy had an ideology. This book argues that the Uriage experience, the Uriage synthesis, *was* the Vichy ideology – at least for some of the "best and the brightest," most faithful servants of that state – and it was of greater historical importance than the school's alumni have wanted to believe.

Memorable encounters over the last twenty-five years with former "knight-monks" of Uriage, their friends, and their admirers precipitated this book. While the Uriage school was supposed to represent one of the most important and proudest experiences of their lives, the subject proved a veritable minefield of potential misunderstandings. When detractors were mentioned, Uriage alumni and their friends reacted with remarkable ferocity. Why should a school that functioned a half-century ago still provoke such strong feelings, such fierce invective? In North America (save Quebec) there is no great outrage, no daunting censorial pressures, when scholars describe the pro-fascism, the anti-semitism, the militant anti-communism of sections of the population, such as Catholics, in the nineteen-thirties and during the war. In France the situation is quite different.

Among those with whom this subject was discussed, particular gratitude is due, first of all, to the late Hubert Beuve-Méry, and to Oscar Arnal, Shirley and Gregory Baum, François Bédarida, Albrecht Betz, Pierre Birnbaum, Marie-Dominique Chenu, o.p., Bernard Comte, Antonio Costa Pinto, Cardinal Jean Daniélou, s.j. Antoine Delestre (who was very generous in sharing documents and photographs), Jean-Marie Domenach, Henry W. Ehrmann, Paul and Simone Fraisse, Bertram Gordon, Elisabeth Guyon, Georges Hourdin, William Irvine, Jean Lacroix, Paul de la Taille, Daniel Lindenberg, Cardinal Henri de Lubac, s.j., Alexandre Marc, Henri-Irénée Marrou, Paulette Emmanuel Mounier, Francis Murphy, Jean Onimus, Denis Pelletier, Monique Pichoff, Denis de Rougemont, Christian Roy, Maurice Schumann, Pierre de Senarclens, David Shalk, Zeev Sternhell, the Templeton family, René Thoreval, and Michel Trebitsch.

Research for this manuscript was much facilitated by the hospitality, generosity, and intellectual stimulation of the various branches of the Onimus clan – at Bourg-la-Reine, St-Cloud, Collonges-au-Mt. d'Or, le Tour, Valbonne – particularly above 3000 metres during alpine expeditions. Robert, Joanna, and Alice were kindly hospitable during research excursions to Washington, D.C., and the *Institut d'Histoire du Temps Présent* and the "Murs Blancs" community of Chatenay-Malabry during séjours in Paris. Particular thanks is also due to those who read the manuscript and offered their comments and suggestions, including Shirley Baum, Robert Hellman, Odile

Hellman, Patrice Higonnet, Christian Roy, and, above all, Janet Shorten. Susanne McAdam, Joan McGilvray, and Philip Cercone of McGill-Queen's were a great help, and the sshrc of Canada and the graduate faculty of McGill University provided indispensable support for research and publication.

Marshal Pétain, on his first official visit outside of Vichy, greets Pierre Dunoyer de Segonzac and the "Marshal Pétain cohort" of the École Nationale des Cadres on the baptismal day of the latter at the Chateau de la Faulconnière (20 October 1940).

The "Chateau Bayard" at Uriage.

The two "Vieux Chefs" and fellow instructors in front of the Chateau Bayard. *Left to right:* Gilles Souriau (mostly hidden), Eric Audemard d'Alançon, Jacques Lochard, Paul de la Taille, Pierre Dunoyer de Segonzac. (Photo: Jean-Gabriel Seruzyer.)

"Hébertisme" in practice: a group of Chantiers de la Jeunesse climb a rock face.

Right Father Marcel-Denys Forestier, o.p., saying Mass for a youth group.

Below Emmanuel Mounier, director of *Esprit* and personalist philosopher.

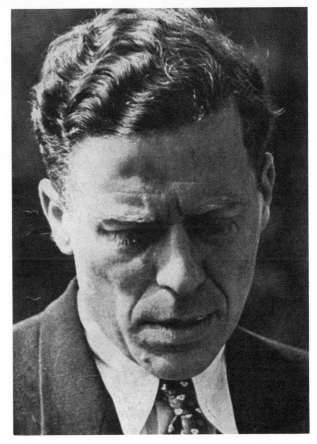

JEUNESSE....FRANCE !

ORGANE DE L'ECOLE NATIONALE DES CADRES D'URIAGE

Directeur : P. DUNOYER DE SEGONZAC. — Chef de l'Ecole Nationale des Cadres —

22 MARS 1941

Première année : N° 9 — Prix : 1 franc — Parait le 4 et le 22 de chaque mois. —

Liberté ?

L'indiscipline des Français est notoire. Elle peut toucher à la bêtise la plus sombre dans certains cas; on a vu, il y a quelques mois, dans les gares, à un moment de presse dans les chemins de fer, des groupes rester en équilibre aux portières des wagons, les uns voulant monter et les autres descendre avec une résolution également obtuse. Des hommes de bien essayaient de s'entremettre et prêchaient sur le ton de la conciliation d'excellents principes de circulation; peine perdue. L'heure du départ approchant on finissait par souhaiter avec une ferveur grandissante l'arrivée d'un représentant de l'ordre, autant que possible fort, expéditif et s'il le fallait brutal qui appliquerait les principes d'une discipline que les hommes vraiment libres connaissent et mettent en exécution tout seuls. On est parfois tenté de se demander si les Français ont encore assez l'intelligence de la vraie liberté et de la vraie discipline pour être laissés à eux-mêmes ?

Liberté était devenu synonyme de licence. On utilisait de plus en plus une telle liberté à se dégager de toutes sortes de liens jugés ennuyeux ou périmés. Au nom de cette liberté les jeunes contestaient l'autorité de parents qui pour les mêmes raisons renonçaient à l'exercice de leurs devoirs familiaux; au nom de cette liberté les maris négligeaient leurs femmes. L'usage de cette liberté ne tendait qu'à supprimer des devoirs sans même en examiner le fondement; il suffisait qu'ils fussent gênants. Et pourtant comme le disait M. Jean Lacroix, parlant de la vraie liberté dans un article récent : « L'observation la plus superficielle montre combien la liberté est pour l'homme source des plus hautes douleurs. Etre spirituellement libre, c'est avoir la responsabilité de soi-même, c'est-à-dire vraiment répondre de soi, se prendre en charge: est-il plus lourd fardeau ? »

Renoncer à supporter le lourd fardeau de soi-même c'est le confier, si on veut vivre, à d'autres, c'est-à-dire tomber en esclavage. Il ne paraît pas que les Français d'une certaine génération aient assez de tonus moral et physique pour faire cet effort considérable d'être vis-à-vis d'eux-mêmes vraiment des hommes libres; ils sont déformés par l'usage de trop longues erreurs ou usés ou simplement apathiques. D'autres effrayés par les difficultés à vaincre, découragés par leur propre faiblesse ont abandonné avant la lutte. Les uns et les autres sont promis à une servitude dont ils ne souffriront même pas et que beaucoup appellent de leurs vœux consciemment ou inconsciemment. Car ils éprouvent depuis longtemps l'insupportable malaise d'impuissants à qui on propose l'exécution d'actes personnels et libérateurs dont ils sont incapables; tout, plutôt que cela.

Le problème pour les jeunes est de savoir s'ils accepteront un esclavage ou plutôt s'ils ont en eux les ressources profondes qui leur permettraient d'y échapper, ce qui n'est pas certain.

UN EMOUVANT PORTRAIT DU MARECHAL, FAIT A URIAGE, PAR LA FEMME D'UN INSTRUCTEUR, MADAME MALESPINA.

Q. O. 14.979

Paroles du Maréchal

— Pour que les vieilles générations puissent vivre dans le repos, il est nécessaire que les jeunes générations s'adonnent à un travail obstiné.

— Solidarité des âges, puisque ce sont les jeunes générations qui cotisent pour les vieilles.

— Travailleurs, depuis que j'apprends à vous connaître, j'ai le sentiment de vous mieux comprendre et de m'attacher à vous de plus en plus. Restons les uns et les autres au coude à coude. Les plus beaux espoirs nous seront permis.

(15 MARS 1941)

The title page of Uriage's paper *Jeunesse ... France!* from the issue of 22 March 1941.

A party celebrating a marriage at Uriage. *Left to right:* Henry Ripert, two uniden-
tified women, Charles Muller, Maurice Daroux, Joffre Dumazedier, André Boisard,
Jacques Lochard, Paul de la Taille (with glasses), Olivier Hussenot (with guitar),
Louberob, Pierre Geny, Gilles Souriau, Claude Toulemonde (with accordion),
Henri Lavorel, Maurice Berthet, Hubert Beuve-Méry, Charles Henry-Amar,
Pierre Cazenavette.

Right   Pierre Dunoyer de
Segonzac at a Uriage festival.
Left to right: two women in folk
costumes, Anne-Marie Hussenot,
Pierre Dunoyer de Segonzac.

Le Baptême de la Promotion
"Verdun"
à Uriage, le Ier août 1942

La démonstration d'une leçon d'hébertisme sur le plateau du stade

Les équipes régionales installent leur camp

Visite des chalets où les élèves viennent de passer les six mois de leur stage

Les anciens élèves de l'Ecole montent vers le château

Pages 1 and 2 of the brochure published for the celebration of the "baptism" of the

Les équipes régionales d'anciens élèves de l'École nationale des Cadres se sont réunies à Uriage le 31 juillet et le 1er Août à l'occasion du baptème de la promotion "Verdun" cloturant le premier stage de formation de six mois.

a gauche: Le lever des couleurs au mât de l'École

chef de Segonzac baptise promotion "Verdun"

La veillée au théâtre de verdure

Verdun cohort (six-month training group) at Uriage on 31 July–1 August 1942.

Hubert Beuve-Méry in the Resistance, 1944 (Photo: Louise-Marie Lozac'hmeur)

The Knight-Monks of Vichy France

Introduction: French Catholic Intellectuals and the Ideological Origins of the Vichy Regime

Was there a "French fascism"? Once this would have been a lunatic fringe question, but recent monographs have suggested not only that there was a distinctive French fascism but that fascism itself, far from being a somewhat ephemeral Italian or German import, actually originated in France.[1] Beyond that, contemporary historians have been suggesting that French support for *Pétainisme,* if not for outright fascism, though marginal according to the accepted view in France since the Liberation, was in fact widespread. Acceptance of the new view of France's relationship with fascism/*Pétainisme* requires a rethinking of several aspects of the history of modern France. This may be part of the reason why it has been non-French revisionist historians for the most part who have initiated this radical reappraisal of much of the French past.[2] The debate is not so much over whether the conservative and authoritarian Pétain regime was or was not "fascist," but rather how Pétain's *Révolution Nationale* was established with such ease and why so many of the French came to embrace authoritarian, anti-liberal, and anti-democratic ideas.

It is the contention of this book that an important new understanding of the role of intellectuals in pre-war years must grow out of this new perspective on French fascism and the Vichy regime. This new grasp of the relationship between the extreme Right and the French, in turn, will foster a new understanding of the way in which certain intellectuals shaped attitudes and *mentalités* in this century. We will come to see the hitherto hidden role of the principal figures of the "French Catholic Renaissance" of the late nineteenth century – Maritain, Claudel, Péguy, Bernanos, Blondel, Sangnier, and the rest – in the germination of anti-liberal and anti-democratic movements. With this perspective, we may develop some understanding of the role of the intelligentsia in carefully and thoughtfully laying the groundwork in the 1930s for what would become the "National Revolution" of the Vichy regime, and what was most original and distinctive in the initiatives of that regime as embodied by institutions such as the École Nationale des Cadres d'Uriage.

The literature on the role of Catholics in the Vichy regime, almost all of it by Catholic sympathizers,[3] suggests that their coreligionists were met with a *fait accompli* in the form of the Révolution Nationale, with its peculiar youth organizations and unprecedented vision for the transformation of the country. But while we have some relatively incisive studies of Catholics under the Vichy regime, we are only beginning to have studies of those movements of ideas, organizations, networks of students, Catholic laymen, military officers, and intellectuals who resolutely set the stage for a period in which, in the words of one historian, "France changed more in a few months than at any other time in her history since 1789."[4]

We know a great deal about the colourful, though relatively marginal, pro-Nazis and pro-fascists in France in the interwar period, but very little about the mainstream movements of ideas among the intelligentsia (many of whom were Catholics), who, although sometimes explicitly pro-Franco or pro-Mussolini, seemed intent on creating the guidelines for a distinctively communitarian, hierarchical, and spiritual France in the post-liberal, post-individualistic age that was assumed to be dawning.

If we have a dearth of studies on the "underground" anti-liberal and anti-republican movements among intellectuals in the 1930s, we know even less about the role of these men and women at Vichy and their work on setting the guidelines of the Révolution Nationale. Their role and that of institutions in which they were markedly active such as Uriage, notwithstanding some later Resistance heroism, were often primary in the advancement of "a Vichy that might have been," a sort of "conservative revolution" outlined in the early pronouncements of the Révolution Nationale, which, after some months of heady illusions, began to turn sour – only to return underground and resurface, in different forms, after the war.

We need balanced studies of French intellectual and religious life during the late 1930s and the Second World War that take this perspective into account. Histories covering these years have tended to centre on certain individuals, often unknown at the time, who figure retrospectively as early Resistance heroes. Such studies emphasize the growth of the Resistance, especially from the occupation of all of France in late 1942. But Catholic resisters seemed "few and far between" during the first years of the occupation when places like the École Nationale des Cadres d'Uriage were flourishing. Further, in the opinion of an authoritative student of the French Church in this period, the established French Catholic forces – political and social, cultural and spiritual – were "poorly represented," and led in a markedly unenlightened way, during the entire four years of the Vichy regime.[5] He might have added that the role of the Catholic intellectuals was particularly questionable.

But the myth of the Resistance still prevails in writings about French Catholic intellectuals during the occupation, so much so that although Catholics played a far more prominent participatory role in Vichy than in the faltering governments of the pre-war Third Republic, we still have an incomplete picture of their place during the first two years of the occupation regime. The Vichy of 1940–42, as the Uriage school vividly illustrates, was distinctive, "an exceptional phenomenon," even flourishing for a time, before the onset of the progressive disintegration that characterized the years 1942–44. After 1942 the coherence progressively eroded until in its last stages – as the early regime's most original achievements, such as the Uriage experiment, disintegrated – Vichy became "no more than the politics of opportunism, drawn toward highly derivative, Nazi-style solutions, but with no coherent ideology, and no fundamental class basis."[6]

In order to better understand the efforts of thinkers to shape a conservative revolution in the 1930s, and to gain a more accurate portrait of the intellectuals in institutions such as Vichy's leadership school network, we must put aside sympathies and smug historical hindsight to get at the facts. Even in the case of a single institution such as Uriage that has proved a tall order. The stakes of praise and blame remain high even today.

BACKGROUND: THE 1930S AND THEIR ANTECEDENTS

An overview of pre-war thinking in France shows that the themes that later prevailed in Pétain's Révolution Nationale in general, and in settings like Uriage in particular, had already been advanced by a host of organizations. For decades there had been a particularly zealous promotion of new, pure, even heroic, communities – unsullied by the "politics," liberalism, "individualism," money, materialism, or permissiveness of the Third Republic. There was the important notion of an impending "new Middle Ages," of a Europe-wide "youth revolution" – a generation's quest for purity, innocence, and "meaning," the dream of recapturing a lost brotherhood. The Young Christian Workers, the Scouts, Catholic Action, the Young Catholic Students, and the Catholic youth hostel movements had all been promoting such goals. A sympathetic attitude toward European youth movements, notably those in Germany and Portugal, was noticeable among French intellectuals. All of this would reach its apotheosis in the Uriage experiment.

Various innovative economic, social, and pedagogical projects sprang up in religious circles – and several among them sought to break down the barriers between the classes without giving in to the "sin" of class struggle. There were also dreams of a new knighthood, a chivalrous order of the young, who would exercise leadership, embody and spread these ideals: shock troops, as it were, of the spirit. The Uriage school and most of the other leadership schools at Vichy grew directly out of these idealistic ventures for, in the early stages at least, Vichy often meant "Catholics in power," and many of the National Revolution's ideals seemed close to those the Catholics had been nurturing through the 1920s and 1930s (if not since the mid–nineteenth century).

Several pre-war movements – the Jeunesse ouvrière chrétienne (JOC), Association catholique de la jeunesse (ACJF), Scouts, Auberges de la Jeunesse – provided young people with values, an altruistic life-style, and a sense of community and collective identity that afforded high-minded and self-righteous alternatives to the "self-indulgent" individualism of Republican France. The large adults' organizations – Catholic Action, the Catholic trade unions and farmers organizations, the Équipes sociales, the veterans' organizations – promoted a similar set of values backed by a quantity of serious literature that advocated a drastic conservative and authoritarian transformation of France and dramatic spiritual renewal. The vision of the future these groups then passed on to people such as the Uriage cadets was of "a new Middle Ages" (Berdyaev), of communities of spiritual elites fostering a "True Humanism" (Maritain), of a society valuing the "social role of the officer" (Lyautey) and of the engineer (Lamirand), as "The Social Dimension of Catholic Dogma" (Henri de Lubac) would finally receive its due. The new society would see the birth of "a communitarian personalism" (Mounier), ending years of selfish materialism and experiencing the "primacy of the spiritual" (Maritain).

Such sanguine hopes, expressed in a common, if sometimes vague, idiom, characterized the publications of various pre-war popular movements, some mass-circulation religiously oriented publications, essays by high-profile intellectuals in the popular press, and (in a more recondite form) small-circulation reviews (such as *La Vie Intellectuelle, Études, Ordre Nouveau, Esprit, Temps présent*). A wave of enthusiasm seems to have touched some school teachers, army officers, priests, and a certain segment of the bourgeoisie nurtured by the "religious revival" that had been flourishing among the intelligentsia in France since the late nineteenth century. In the sermons of curés, or the courses of Catholic teachers, in trade union meetings, study groups, scout camps, prayer groups, the Catholic schools – in the whole self-conscious larger Catholic community with its common concerns and frame of reference – an ambitious, coherent, intellectual counter-culture was being created with the help of the writings of Péguy and the later Bergson, Maritain and Berdyaev, Perroux and Henri de Man, Chenu and Congar, Psichari and Lyautey, Le Bret and Carrel, De Lubac, and even, in mimeographed form, Teilhard de Chardin. These writers tended to position themselves squarely against a world in an advanced state of decadence. The ardent Uriage community tried to bring all of this together into a viable synthesis.

A number of 1930s French intellectuals devoted considerable energy to planning a "community of communities" to succeed the Third Republic. By 1940 their insistent, even strident, criticism of liberalism, scorn for democracy, attacks on individualism, fear of communism, ridicule of parliamentary institutions, alarm over sexual liberties, condemnation of materialism, criticisms of capitalist economics, and disdain for Protestant Anglo-Saxon cultures had done much to set the stage for the disappearance of the Third Republic. When the collapse came, many of these people felt their predictions had been confirmed, and saw the disappearance of the old institutions as inevitable, and perhaps even fortuitous.

A number of pre-war French Catholic leaders did not so much consciously undertake anti-democratic, anti-parliamentary strategies as celebrate their own religious culture's authoritarianism, dogma, discipline, doctrinal coherence, and dedicated, celibate clergy-elites and sense of community. Many Catholics came to consider these characteristics precious advantages as Catholicism formed an indispensable barrier against godless communism. Thus these qualities were celebrated in the various organizations in which Catholic participation was strong (Scouts, JOC, ACJF, Jeunesses Patriotes, Croix de Feu, Action Française). Whether in an Arles scout troop camping in the mountains of Provence, a prayer confraternity for women textile workers in Lyon, a veterans' organization in Rennes, or a support group for a Catholic publication in Dijon,[7] there was present a sense of community, a sense of sharing distinctive and "healthy" attitudes, a common culture or *mentalité* different from that officially encouraged during the Third Republic.

The fact that fascists advocated at least some "Catholic" qualities encouraged certain Catholics to feel comfortable with at least some forms of fascism, or at least with the moralistic Pétainism of 1940. To French people shaped by an authoritarian and dogmatic religious culture, who had grown up with a coherent and, in some respects totalitarian, collective mentality, Pétain's "Revolution" – particularly when it vaunted the elitist and communitarian spiritual values of places like the "Château de l'Âme" at Uriage – could seem familiar and even attractive. So Vichy was able to stimulate an enthusiasm on the part of some Catholics that baffled liberals or republicans untouched by the Catholic experience. A number of traditionalist intellectuals had been prophesying the collapse of modern society for decades; in 1940 they seemed vindicated by events.

1940: THE *RÉVOLUTION NATIONALE* AND ITS "SPIRITUAL UNIVERSITY"

There was an extensive fraternal network of Catholic organizations or communities with a well-defined program in 1940 France. Partly because the members of several of these groups had felt so alienated in the pre-war years, they had come to bond with each other, both professionally and socially, through mutual friends, by the good offices of *curés* or dedicated laymen involved with one or several religiously oriented movements, organizations, institutions, or publications. Certain visionary elites – the men who shaped Uriage are an example – had reached a consensus on the priorities of a post-Republican regime: create communities that would neutralize the poisons of permissive liberalism, rampant individualism, communism, and the erosion of spiritual values; restore prestige and influence to a Church and to teachings that had refused to accept the revolution of 1789. The Church, in France and in Rome, had often served as a refuge for those who had lost their privileges, who hated anti-clericalism and the enemies of religion. It was only natural that certain Catholics began dreaming of reshaping young people through vigorous spiritual and moral indoctrination and physical training, of purging the government, and the educational and cultural establishments, of nefarious influences. Thus conservative revolutionaries wanted authoritative leadership, hierarchy, and deference to traditional values in the society, and they laid plans for institutional expressions of the social teachings of the Church and explored ways of promoting Catholic notions of sexual morality, support for the family, and community.

In the end, some of the most daring and original thinking on transforming France came together at the romantic Château d'Uriage, in the efforts of Vichy's École Nationale des Cadres. This remarkable institution – which was even envisaged by some of its promoters as offering a kind of a spiritualized and virile substitute for the old École Normale Supérieure – was meant to provide new leaders for a new kind of France. It soon belied its medieval trappings by becoming, at least for its sympathizers, not only an avant-garde community living what it described as "the style of the twentieth century" but also the most innovative and prestigious think-tank of the National Revolution. Vichy's Secrétariat Général de la Jeunesse went so far as to characterize it as "the spiritual university" of French youth.

Much of the French Catholic hierarchy, apparently taking their wishes for realities, exercised poor judgment in assessing the situation in 1940, and so did many of the bright young men who gathered in the Study Bureau at the Vichy leadership school at Uriage. Like the churchmen, these promising young philosophers, historians, journalists, and army officers bore the legacy of deeply anti-democratic traditions. Many of them were ready to write off human liberty and cultural pluralism in the name of the "new Middle Ages" that was supposed to be supplanting the Republican heritage. While it is true that the roots of this brand of anti-modernism go back at least to the counter-reformation, several reactionary impulses had been powerfully reinforced by the theorists, writers, and artists of the Catholic intellectual revival in the late nineteenth century. There had been the influence of the crypto-Catholic reactionary Charles Maurras and his Action Française and, beyond that, of the important Catholic thinkers (Maritain, Sangnier, Bloy, Péguy, Claudel, Psichari) who valued the Catholic community's "style," its deference to authority and anti-liberalism, and fixed upon these qualities as essential to national renewal.

A Uriage alumnus reflected the mindset of many at the École Nationale Supérieure des Cadres, as well as, he thought, of a good number of his countrymen at large, when he recalled in 1940:

I was completely fed up with the kind of parliamentary democracy we had had, with that circus of governments that broke a longevity record if they lasted two weeks! It made one sick. And rather than being astonished at the defeat, I was, on the contrary, prepared for it. Uriage, for me, represented a radical questioning of society on the level of fundamental structural reform:

I was looking for a sort of "October 1917." The challenge was quite simply to create a society other than the one we had known ... We had to totally change society. Our priority was to live in another society.[8]

This "other society" of Uriage was not, however, to be the egalitarian and progressive one promised by the united Left of the Popular Front in 1936. The sorts of people who flocked to the Uriage school were different: they had an anti-liberal agenda, a consensus to create an antithetical society, an aspiration they were gratified to find shared by others. With France on her knees, humiliated, two-thirds occupied, with the repression of liberties and a new racism reinforcing the persecution of dissidents, masons, Jews, and other minorities, the first priority for many of the first resisters was, quite logically, the restoration of the rule of law, liberties, and freedoms. The Uriage group, however, had a different mentality and a different focus as they began to create the guidelines of, and the leaders for, a post-liberal and post-Republican society. Ominously, however, French partisans of a nazified "New Order" were also in favour of abandoning the parliamentary regime and democratic institutions.

To what extent were "fascist" or "national socialist" themes to dominate French national renewal? Vichy authorities soon discovered that the occupying forces and their French sympathizers could sneer at the "choir boys" and "tender-minded dreamers" and fight for their own, tougher sort of French national reconstruction.

An anti-Republican Uriage cadet was not unique in 1940 France, as a host of people with similar attitudes were at that time committing themselves to Révolution Nationale projects. Several Catholic and other anti-modern thinkers bore considerable responsibility for this. Ever since the late nineteenth century the Catholic intelligentsia had been celebrating the values of the past while decrying the modern world – in particular, setting authority against libertinism, doctrinal coherence against free-thinking, communitarian values against self-fulfillment, family values against sexual pleasure, "spirituality" against "materialism." Like our Uriage cadet, they expected the collapse of a regime that they believed (a belief often held since they were children) to be fatally flawed. By 1940, a considerable proportion of the Catholic intelligentsia was in favour of some sort of conservative revolution, and so it is not surprising that Dunoyer de Segonzac, the young commander of the Uriage school, could not recall ever having heard – either among the instructors or the trainees, or among the visitors to the Uriage school – a single word in defence of the Third Republic.[9]

Several of the key figures at Uriage, considering themselves vindicated by the Republic's demise, were not so much bent on resisting tyranny and fighting to restore liberties as they were fired by a passion to create that "other community" they had dreamt about for years. Their attitude reveals that it was not a specific idea or organized movement that fostered the Révolution Nationale so much as a predisposition toward change. A number of academics, writers, social organizers, trade unionists, "new" theologians, and Church functionaries had been creating this sort of mentality throughout the whole multifaceted network of French Catholic institutions. The case of Uriage shows how this cast of mind had made people susceptible to entering such a collective effort with ease, naturalness, and even enthusiasm.

The important role certain collective undertakings and brilliant or charismatic personalities played in the background to Vichy's National Revolution remains little known: in the first place, in the light of the complexities of Resistance experiences or possible postwar recriminations, a generation of the major figures exercised a collective silence. This selective recall of the past then blurred comprehension of some crucial years. The distorted story was supported in a rather clandestine way by an academic and publishing hegemony exercised by certain important personalities at places such as Uriage.[10]

But there is no hiding the intellectual and artistic efforts of the French Catholic leadership in the 1930s. Their common undertaking in political thinking, social theory, philosophical speculation, and theological reflection resulted, by the late 1930s, in a fairly drastic "conservative revolutionary" blueprint, with militant, organized supporters. By the end of that decade men and women taken with a "Catholic alternative" for France believed they were sharing the experience of a remarkable – perhaps unprecedented – intellectual, artistic, and literary community. Uriage may be seen as a continuation of this movement.

The Vichy regime marked the triumph, and the tragedy, of considerable collective effort. In certain governmental creations, such as the early École Nationale des Cadres d'Uriage, *Pétainisme* seemed to signify the success of years of hard and dedicated theoretical and practical work. From being a marginal and eccentric species, threatened with extinction at the beginning of the Third Republic, militantly Catholic men (and a few women) rose to some central positions in officially sanctioned institutions committed to radically changing their country by transforming French elites and French youth. The question, of course, would be, what kind of change? The answer would dash their hopes to the point that they would one day deny ever having had them.

Several intellectuals who were, from near or afar, enthusiastic participants in the Uriage experience have been reluctant to discuss the affair with any save certified admirers of Uriage. Something of a collective amnesia has been imposed over those traumatic, crucial Uriage years. Yet as we become more and more knowledgeable about the role of institutions such as the Uriage school within the Vichy regime, it is inevitable that we will have to revise our understanding of, among other things, this last century of French intellectual life: this is equally true for the literary and philosophical revivals of the late nineteenth century, the bold projects and optimism of the thirties, the traumas of Vichy and triumphs of the Resistance, and the decisive French role in the intellectual origins of the Second Vatican Council – not to mention the origins of phenomena such as Liberation Theology. A balanced study of institutions such as Vichy's École Nationale des Cadres de la Jeunesse d'Uriage will help us to better understand the forces that transformed French experience in this century. The school institutionalized all the strengths and weaknesses of the ascendant French anti-liberal conservative revolutionaries. While they can revise their roles and contest their place in the Vichy story, the school cannot be wished away. It mirrors the illusions and delusions of its ruling spirits, however much they may be reluctant or unwilling to face them today.

At the conference celebrating the fiftieth anniversary of the review *Esprit*, in the fall of 1982, I spoke on the history of the relationship between personalism and fascism, arguing that Vichy's national leadership school, the École Nationale des Cadres de la Jeunesse d'Uriage, where personalism was the unofficial doctrine, was crucial to the debate as to the nature of the ideology of the Vichy regime and the debate as to whether or not there had in fact been a French fascism. In the heated discussion that followed it was alleged that the final publication of Professor Bernard Comte's doctoral thesis, on which he had been working for many years – with exclusive access to many sources and the full support and co-operation of many Uriage alumni – would refute the main contentions of my presentation.[11] In spring 1988 M. Comte was kind enough to lend me a copy of the two volumes of his rich and generously documented, just-completed, Doctorat d'Histoire on the history of the Uriage school from 1940 to 1942.[12] In the preface to the abridged version,

which was subsequently published, René Rémond announced it to
be "a definitive work ... which, one hopes, will end the controversies
and still the arguments." Comte's study, Rémond concluded, not only
restored a chapter in French history but did even more by "giving
us grounds for not being ashamed of our elders."[13] Professor Comte,
frankly admitting his great sympathy for the Uriage community, the
Uriage "style" and experience, did not seem as optimistic as his
mentor about the thesis putting an end to the controversy: he published a vast quantity of documents in his work so that others with a
different cast of mind from his own could form their own judg-
ments.[14] For that we must remain in his debt as, in the end, Professor
Comte's study suggested that not only was Uriage not "fascist" but it
could hardly be accused of having been *"pétainiste"* either: it was an
institution that hid behind a general declaration of loyalty to the
person and thinking of Pétain in order to ignore the government
and its policies and work toward the liberation of France from the
occupant, "without even hiding their intention of preparing to
resume hostilities from the trainees."[15]

Within a few months of the completion of Comte's thesis two
monographs appeared by authors (Professors Pierre Bitoun and
Antoine Delestre) who had not read Comte's work but were both also
sympathetic to the Uriage school and had important contributions
of their own to make on the subject (which they both carried on
beyond the year 1942). I am particularly grateful to Professors Comte
and Delestre for their generosity and assistance.[16]

Most recently Pierre Giolitto's history of French youth in the Vichy
regime has situated Uriage in a larger context. In his concluding
chapter (which is devoted to Uriage), Professor Giolitto suggests that
while the school was clearly *"pétainiste"* in inspiration one must bear
in mind that there was "a *Pétainisme* of the Right and a *Pétainisme* of
the Left," and that Uriage demonstrated what the Vichy regime could
have been had it been led by more visionary leaders. He concluded
that if there was one thing worth keeping from the whole Vichy
experience, "in our view, it would be, without a shadow of a doubt,
that 'other Vichy' that Uriage represented."[17]

Given the importance of this new information, Professor Daniel
Lindenberg's effort to place Uriage in the larger perspective of the
history of French ideas in the period from 1937 to 1947 has been
particularly timely. Lindenberg argues that, given the general pre-
occupation with discovering a new sense of community, Uriage was
at the very centre of what was, in retrospect, significant in French
intellectual life in that decade. He describes the school as basically
pétainiste and surprisingly unrepentant about it afterwards, and

asserts that it was the fruit of years of "underground" intellectual effort at thinking out new forms of community life (Catholic and non-Catholic) before the war. He isolates what he considers to be key aspects of the Uriage story (which are ignored by Comte): that Uriage formed an Order that not only worked against the political influence of, but was to explicitly exclude, Jews; that the first elite school in the Uriage chateau was succeeded by another, run by Catholic fascists of the *Milice*; and that the postwar trumpeting of the school's discovery of the "style of the twentieth century" entailed a remarkable fidelity to several of the National Revolution hopes of 1942. He also describes it as having contributed directly or indirectly to many significant movements having a "communitarian personalist" orientation that followed, such as *Économie et Humanisme*, *Jeunesse de l'Église*, *Esprit*, *Vie Nouvelle*, and the "Third World" orientation of the French Catholic Church; these, with several other groups, he saw as leading up to the Second Vatican Council.[18] After Lindenberg's bold analysis, Professor Rémond's hope for the end of any hint of controversy, much less of shame, over the record of the knight-monks of Uriage is unlikely to be realized.

This book is the result of what what has been learned from these new studies, from materials accumulated over the years, and from research in the extensive, soon to be accessible, Uriage archives.[19] It is the first study of the École Nationale des Cadres d'Uriage in English, and the first in any language that, by focusing on the social thought, "life-style," and mentality of the school, tries to demonstrate that it was a more significant institution than has been assumed: that it was, in fact, the purveyor of seductive and original ideas – a Uriage "style for the twentieth century," a special kind of "communitarian personalism" – that had solid, if "underground," roots in pre-war France, matured and even flourished during the war, and subsequently came to enjoy an enduring influence in France and beyond. This book also tries to demonstrate that this institution's ideas were not as marginal and "non-conformist" as has been claimed, but were, rather, central to what was lively and original – and durable – in the intellectual, artistic, and cultural life before the war, under Pétain, and in the postwar period.

CHAPTER ONE

Beginnings

Against the stirring spectacle of European young people leading movements for freedom and democracy in the late 1980s, it is doubly difficult to imagine how easily European regimes just a half-century earlier set about transforming their societies through a totalitarian remoulding of their young people. Yet after the terrible shocks of defeat and occupation in 1940, the newly created authoritarian government of unoccupied France undertook just such an indoctrination. Marshal Pétain declared the transformation of youth essential to France's "National Revolution," and earmarked revolutionized young people to be the key agents for the remaking of their peers.

A peculiarity of the youth revolution in France was its religious style: many of the young men and women who came forward to help take French youth in hand were ardent Christians who had been involved with youth and family organizations before the war. The Secrétariat d'État à la Famille et à la Jeunesse post (created on 12 July 1940) was given, initially, to Jean Ybarnégary, vice-president of the Catholic war-hero Colonel de la Rocque's old Parti social français (PSF), a party in which Catholics had been strongly influential. Ybarnégary, in turn, picked a number of Catholics connected with youth movements to help him. For several reasons, the effort to transform French young people was, and would remain, strongly Christian and spiritual in orientation.

Why was there such a religious cast to the youth policies of the new regime in a republican country that had been so determinedly secular since the 1870s? Some attention to the men who came to power in 1940 is revealing in this regard. We now know that there was a strong interest in reshaping youth among various influential figures of Pétain's first governments, including, for example, Paul Baudouin, polytechnician and "inspecteur des Finances" who became Minister of Foreign Affairs. Baudouin, a "convinced Catholic," like many Catholics of the time considered himself "non-political" although he had been a committed member of the militant nationalist movement Action Française.[1] He had also been a Catholic scout leader in the years just prior to the war and had written a notable exhortation to young Christians for the *Revue des jeunes*. That journal was an influential Catholic youth movements publication co-directed by Father Forestier, a pre-war Scouts leader who would become an important figure in the youth initiatives of Vichy's National Revolution. From Pétain's rise to power in June until December 1940, Paul Baudouin was one of the civilian members of the government most attentive to the rising generation; his cabinet and entourage inspired a host of new programs for the regime, as he drew upon his Catholic scout or *Revue des jeunes* contacts. Soon this young technocrat appeared to be the centre of a Catholic/Action Française cohort set on re-educating French young people.[2]

Other high-minded Catholic social activists also surfaced at Vichy, such as the charismatic Robert Garric, president-founder of the high-minded social action group for young bourgeois, the Équipes sociales.[3] Garric took as his hero the legendary Marshal Lyautey, visionary French colonial administrator of Morocco, as did Garric's vice-president at the Équipes sociales, engineer Georges Lamirand, who would be named to run Vichy's youth ministry. The goal of the Équipes sociales had been to bring middle-class school and university people together with rank and file proletarians. Garric's *Le message de Lyautey* (Spes, 1935) had been an important inspiration for the circles that had trumpeted a call for the moral renewal of France in the *Revue des jeunes*,[4] and thus, at least indirectly, for the prime movers of the National Revolution.

The Catholic Scouts were also an important part of the background of the National Revolution. During the tumultuous pre-war years, Fathers Forestier and Doncoeur had taught the scouts to be both militantly patriotic and devoutly Catholic. Straightforwardly authoritarian if not reactionary, frankly opposed to laicism, "materialism," and liberal and democratic values, scout leaders had exhorted pre-war young people to surmount the class antagonisms, secularization, and demoralization of modern urban society. Like other Catholic movements, the scouts proudly claimed to be above mere politics, but their movement's firm anti-republican bias was clearly understood in the strained political climate of 1930s France.

Father Paul Doncoeur was one of the most zealous, striking leaders of the flourishing interwar scout movement, having started his "Cadets" in 1923 – an organization that eventually fancied itself as a sort of chivalric order, with its members getting together in nomadic summer camps. The Cadets employed German youth movement techniques – particularly their linking of ascetical training with supreme physical effort – in their dream of restoring Christianity in France; for, in the words of their motto, there was "Un pays à refaire, une race à ranimer, une écrasante mission à soutenir dans le monde."[5] Doncoeur, like his compatriot Father Forestier, hailed the advent of Marshal Pétain as providential, allowing the moral elite of a new generation to assume leadership in a country that finally acknowledged the importance of values and ideas that the Republic had ignored.

In the Marshal's immediate entourage there were several figures both sympathetic to the scouts and attuned to the liveliest Action Française and Catholic intellectual life. For example, the Marshal seems to have assigned the writer Henri Massis, high-profile convert to Catholicism and old friend of Marshal Lyautey (as well as of the prominent figures of the Catholic intellectual revival such as Jacques Maritain and Charles Péguy), to elaborate youth doctrine for him.[6] While the articulate Massis was close to Charles Maurras, even serving as a sort of censor over Vichy youth policies for the latter's newly influential Action Française,[7] he also thought himself a disciple of the pre-1914 national populism of Péguy[8] and open to innovative Catholic thought.

Another Pétain speech-writer and "idea man" who would promote Vichy's elite schools was René Gillouin, a well-known Protestant and nationalist writer who had become an open admirer of fascism.[9] Gillouin had frequented avant-garde "non-conformist" circles in Paris in the early 1930s: his apartment had served as a meeting place for the alumni of the Franco-German youth camps organized into the "Club du Moulin-Vert," as well as for early meetings of the Ordre Nouveau group. At Vichy, he was assigned by Raphael Alibert, the ardent Catholic convert who was now Minister of Justice, to compose a brief for Pétain on university reform. As we shall see, Gillouin would become a champion of the Uriage school.[10]

Vichy's elite schools were created at a time when the Vichy government was not interested simply in revitalizing the youth of the country but also in furnishing "new men" to replace the "old elites" that the regime considered decadent, and Raphael Alibert's activities at this time should be seen in the context of his larger effort to exclude masons and Jews from French life. As Minister of Justice, Alibert instituted a review of all naturalizations since 1927, which made stateless some 15,000 people, including 6,000 Jews. In October he promulgated the first *Statut des Juifs*, which excluded Jews from certain civil service posts and presaged action against those in the liberal professions. Alibert's other target was Freemasonry; he employed the law of August 1940 that abolished secret organizations. He was aided in this project by other devout Catholics, notably Bernard Fay, administrator of the Bibliothèque Nationale (who set his trained personnel to work on the *fiches* necessary to that task), and Robert Vallery-Radot, the writer friend of Bernanos. Their task was to root out about 15,000 masonic dignitaries from public life.[11] This seemed to be part of an effort by militant right-wing Christians to displace, while taking revenge on, their "secularizing" enemies.

In September 1940, important openings emerged for Catholic social activists when the government, under the aegis of the Secrétaire d'État à l'Instruction Publique et à la Jeunesse (Georges Ripert), created a Secrétariat Général à la Jeunesse (SGJ) and named the devout young Catholic engineer Georges Lamirand, of the Équipes sociales, as general secretary, effectively giving the youth movements a new autonomy. Chosen by Pétain himself, Lamirand was a former personnel director at the Hachette company who had risen to the post of director of the Renault factories in 1940. He was known in Catholic circles for his uplifting book *Rôle social de l'ingénieur* and his admiration for Marshal Lyautey.[12] Convinced of the beneficial effects of the kind of collaboration of classes that the Équipes sociales had encouraged, Lamirand became an enthusiastic advocate of Catholic participation in the youth projects of the National Revolution.

The *Jeune France* "cultural association" was an early Vichy institution that seemed close to Lamirand's ideal of National Revolution, since it had grown directly out of the pre-war activities of ardent Catholic laymen. In 1938 Paul Flamand and Pierre Schaeffer had created the Éditions du Seuil publishing house and the magazine *Départ* as instruments of their "post-capitalist commune," the Société de St. Louis,[13] which was working toward the creation of a completely "new Christian temporal order."[14] Jeune France claimed to be a "private association" but it was actually under the jurisdiction of the Secrétariat Général à la Jeunesse which subsidized it. The administrative council of Jeune France, designed in the statutes, included three representative of the SGJ and six members of the association. In fact, the first three were founders of the association: Pierre Schaeffer (head of the "Show and radio propaganda" service of the SGJ), vice-president; Paul Flamand (assistant head of this same service), secretary and administrator in the occupied zone; and Albert Ollivier (director of Radio-Jeunesse). All of these men had been involved with avant-garde Catholic or "spiritual" movements before the war: Flamand and Schaeffer in the Société de St. Louis and Éditions du Seuil, Ollivier in the heady theorizing of the Ordre Nouveau movement. The Catholic personalist philosopher Emmanuel Mounier, director of the review *Esprit*, would soon help create the ideology of the Uriage school and play an active role at Jeune France. The association then drew artists, poets, musicians, and theatre people (and would organize the youth assemblies that marked Lamirand's tour of visits to the cities of the southern zone in 1941).[15]

Another vivid personality of Vichy's early national revolution was the dashing young cavalry officer, Pierre Dunoyer de Segonzac, who was, by the late summer of 1940, in command of the regime's flagship leadership school. Born in 1906, Dunoyer de Segonzac came from that firmly traditionalist provincial Catholic nobility who were still proud to have a great many children.[16] He believed in the virtues of a hard and athletic education and, like many provincial Catholics from a "good family" at the time, conveniently combined a relative lack of financial resources with a contempt for money. Segonzac and his kind valued authority, loyalty, obedience, "good taste," and humanistic culture. Like Charles de Gaulle, Segonzac was an army officer with a special interest in mechanized warfare (tanks in particular) and (also like de Gaulle) was attracted by the innovative Catholic social and religious thinking of the interwar period, especially that expressed in the lively Dominican reviews *Sept* and *Temps présent*. Segonzac became directly involved with Catholic Action circles and visited the avant-garde Dominicans in their convent on the Boulevard Latour-Maubourg near the Invalides. (A few of the order would later play important roles in his projects.) Dunoyer de Segonzac, with his strongly religious sense of the human condition, felt that there was a gross misunderstanding of human nature in liberal and republican France and, like Garric and Lamirand, was impressed by the apparent success of Marshal Lyautey in promoting traditional French values in Morocco. He admired the call for a new relationship between action and contemplation put forward in books like Denis de Rougemont's *Penser avec les mains* (1936).[17] By the late 1930s Segonzac was committed to working for radical change in his country.

The sudden French military collapse in 1940 dealt Segonzac a powerful setback: in May and June, at the head of his squadron of tanks, he participated in the battle for France. On 18 May his squadron of tanks was sent to close a breach in the Ardennes front. It was the battle of Jolimetz, a confused and tragic encounter in which Captain Dunoyer de Segonzac was forced to run from one tank to the other to convey his orders to his men. By the end of the battle he found himself commanding a tank with an immobilized turret and damaged engine while nineteen of his twenty tanks (the French army possessed 3,000 at the time) were out of combat and seven of his officers had been killed. He found that after this humiliation he could no longer look his subordinates in the eye.[18] After the armistice Dunoyer de Segonzac left his dishevelled troops for Vichy where Commander de la Chapelle (founder of the pre-war "cercle social d'officiers" to which Segonzac had belonged)[19] had, it seemed, invited him. La Chapelle had been sent from the General Staff of the army to the new Secrétariat d'État à la Jeunesse established on 1 August 1940, which was being temporarily run by a former director of the *scoutisme-routier* organization[20] (one of those religiously oriented youth groupings that was favoured by military officers from provincial noble families) until Georges Lamirand took charge on 27 September.[21]

Years later, in his memoirs, Segonzac remembered spontaneously asking for a "congé d'armistice" and going off on his own to Vichy to find ways of boldly plotting revenge against the Germans under Vichy's very nose.[22] This tale became part of the Uriage school legend. In fact, however, Commander de la Chapelle, head of the Chantiers de la Jeunesse, sent an invitation to Segonzac at Mussidon; Segonzac responded enthusiastically, and then headed straight down to the headquarters of the youth services at Vichy that the commander was organizing.[23] By the end of July Segonzac had his own office in the "Youth Bureau" at Vichy alongside de la Chapelle's. While Segonzac later seemed to recall having come up with the idea for a leadership school himself, it is likely that de la Chapelle had some part in the original conceptualization.

The project was described, from the outset, as an "École des Chefs."[24] Appropriately, Segonzac's second in the project was another young Catholic officer from a distinguished noble family, "an old and dear friend" of his, Eric Audemard d'Alançon. He had also been summoned to Vichy by Commander de la Chapelle.[25]

The new Vichy government's reasons for founding a leadership school seem to have been relatively down-to-earth: faced with the massive unemployment and aimlessness of young people, and an attendant risk of social problems, the regime's planners responded with measures under the rubric *Entraide Nationale des Jeunes* (ENJ) in an effort to both put youth to work and provide them with some moral and political indoctrination. The youth movements were requested to train leaders for these new youth "chantiers" (work-sites) in specialized centres and camp-schools, and to see that these *chefs* participated in a *stage* (training course). A new school, set up in the impressive Château de la Faulconnière near Vichy to oversee this training course, provisionally became the Higher Centre for the training of leaders of the General Youth Secretariat at Vichy. Thus the original overriding concern of the instructors of la Faulconnière was to provide leaders who could instill a sense of order and purpose in the mass of French young people left shocked and demoralized by the defeat.[26]

Captain Pierre Dunoyer de Segonzac, Captain Eric d'Alençon, Lieutenant Jean Devictor – as well as several other prominent leadership school personalities – came from patriotic Catholic families in which professional military service was a proud family heritage and the ideas of Marshal Lyautey were held to be of some importance. Convinced young traditionalists had been encouraged by the apparent successes at social transformation of Lyautey in the French colonies, and read and meditated on the ideas for transforming society in Lyautey's famous book *Le Rôle social de l'officier*.

In fact Hubert Lyautey had written "The Social Role of the Officer in Universal Military Service" (a translation of its complete title) before becoming the pacifier of Morocco. Taking into account the "democratic fact," this right-wing monarchist pointed out that *universal* suffrage, *universal* education, and *universal* military service were all leading to a redefinition of the role of elites – a redefinition that, he thought, should be recognized by what he called "cultivated youth" of all political families. Every intellectual history of the period must take into account what Daniel Lindenberg has called "the Lyautey moment" as Marshal Lyautey "shaped the concept of the Leader peculiar to all the reform movements that flourished in the milieux trained in social catholicism, whether in Vichy, London, or Algiers, not to mention the Resistance inside France".[27]

During the 1930s some young Lyautey disciples like Segonzac had lamented the communication barriers between the army and the French populace. They joined the new-style communities such as "les cercles sociaux d'officiers" established by Captains de la Chapelle and de Virieu,[28] to try to gain an understanding of the social backgrounds and politics of civilian recruits from whom they had long been isolated by their own antiquated family backgrounds and *esprit de corps*. These men of *l'ancienne France* might have seemed outdated, patronizing, even ridiculous, but at least they had tried to communicate with their men across the social barriers.[29] Their spirit was passed on to the leaders of the Vichy youth movements.

Thus Captain de Segonzac found a grand setting near Vichy placed at his disposal in the form of the Louis XIII–era Château de la Faulconnière, near the village of Gannat. The castle, with its massive towers and park terrace overlooking the valley and village, was requisitioned from its lawyer proprietor[30] (who had lent the property to his friend, the former right-wing youth leader Philippe Lamour who was intent on participating in a Vichy "return-to-the-land" program).[31] Lamour was living in the outbuildings and had been trying to restore the fallow lands on the castle farm in the context of the Vichy project when, he sardonically recalled, he was "invaded" by the pretentious Segonzac and his men:

One afternoon a young officer with a gazelle-like head arrived at la Faulconnière. With courtly apologies he explained that the château had been requisitioned for the Chantiers de la Jeunesse. He was really sorry but ... in short he threw us out.

I know that after the war he was celebrated as a sort of guide for youth, a herald of new times, and a bit of a resistant on top of everything else. Perhaps ... [but] when I knew him, he seemed to be a pure Pétainist and accompanied by a gang of phoneys and cranks to boot ... Each morning the troop was called to the foot of a pole on which Dunoyer de Segonzac would hoist the colours, shouting in a falsetto voice: "Jeunesse de France, toujours ... " to those jokers responding in choir, "*Prêts!*".[32]

Even to the former Fascist youth leader Lamour the new school had comic-opera qualities:

There was a slightly wacky major. He had the recruits eating vegetable peels – the only healthy and nourishing thing, in his view, to fortify them for marching in step chanting, axes on their shoulders, to go off and massacre some poor trees that had not done them any harm. They burned entire trunks in the Château chimney, during *soirées* in which, between scout anthems, they venerated the Marshal.

That carnival ended with a handsome chimney blaze that roused the firemen from the whole area; and then those *messieurs* marched off to ply their vocal talents in another château in the Dauphiné area.[33]

But despite Lamour's poor impression, there is evidence that Segonzac soon attracted some remarkably talented and competent people to his staff. While most of the Château de la Faulconnière instructors had middle-class Catholic backgrounds and educations,[34] the two directing officers quickly gave a distinctly military and religious flavour to the operation. Although it was soon vaunted as the "spiritual university" of French youth by Vichy's youth ministry, an intellectual tone did not, at first, predominate at the school, the only "intellectuals" being the ethnologist Paul-Henri Chombart de Lauwe and the social-activist chaplain, the Abbé René de Naurois from the Catholic faculty of Toulouse. Both of these men, however, would play important roles: Chombart de Lauwe had studied under the distinguished cultural anthropologist Marcel Mauss while participating in the class-mixing efforts of Robert Garric and Georges Lamirand's Équipes sociales.[35] The Abbé de Naurois had been a militant in the *Jeune République*, as well as in that street-fighting offshoot of the journal *Esprit*, the *Troisième Force* of Georges Izard.[36] Like Chombart de Lauwe, who had begun a project to study German (and Italian) youth, de Naurois considered himself an authority on Nazi Germany, having studied German philosophy and having spent considerable time in that country since 1933. His interest in the kind of training received by the most promising members of the young Nazi elite in the Ordensburgen (Order-castles) had led him, before the war, to escort an Esprit group tour of Germany, where they visited the Ordensburg of Sonthofen in Bavaria.[37] This vigorous lover of the outdoors recalled hearing of the projected French leadership school through alpinist friends, before he went to Vichy to see Segonzac, who hired him on the spot.[38]

The high-level support that the Château de la Faulconnière project enjoyed by September 1940 was demonstrated when Segonzac asked that the government requisition of the Château de la Faulconnière be extended to the farm and estate around it. Philippe Lamour vociferously protested (citing, perhaps with tongue in cheek, the government's rhetorical priority of putting land back into cultivation), but the Youth Secretariat unreservedly supported this expansion.[39] The quest for volunteer trainees led Segonzac to search out personalities interested in becoming leaders of youth groups among the demobilized officer cadets and non-commissioned officers in a battalion stationed in the Vichy region. But among ninety-five cadets recruited, very many were students, most of them between twenty and twenty-five years of age, all of whom were outfitted in a school uniform of light-coloured riding breeches and a grey shirt. There were ten seminarians and a Cistercian monk in this number.

These religious inductees graphically illustrated the new importance given to Catholics in the National Revolution: before the war it would have been unimaginable to have any seminarians or monks, much less over ten per cent, in a republican national elite school, such as the old École Normale Supérieure. But Dunoyer de Segonzac and his fellow-officers shared the dreams of Catholic visionaries such as the Latour-Maubourg Dominicans. The first class, "New France," arrived at la Faulconnière castle on 19 September and stayed two weeks, having been divided into teams of fifteen men. Each team was directed by a leader who slept in the same tent with his group and shared their daily life, in an effort to provide them with a concrete example of morality and discipline in the service of the community.[40]

By the time the second cohort arrived on 5 October 1940, there had been a fundamental change in the role envisaged for the school. It was no longer to be simply a leadership school for the Chantiers de la Jeunesse; it now claimed to be a "Centre supérieur de formation des chefs" for the country as a whole, with the dramatic, even grandiose, ambition of constituting a new sort of French leadership school, which in turn would profoundly change France by creating a new breed of French elite.[41]

In terms of its original purpose, Segonzac's school was a disappointment to the Chantiers de la Jeunesse, since it furnished them only with about 200 middle-level functionaries (assistants, group leaders, and team leaders) despite the fact that the organization needed, and would eventually employ, several thousand young men for these tasks. There was soon bad blood between Segonzac and the imperious head of the Chantiers program, General Joseph de La Porte du Theil, an older man (then in his fifties), who as a veteran artillery officer and leader of the scout movement could not help finding young Captain Segonzac cavalier and pretentious.

The general wanted the "École des chefs" to stay in line and do its job for the Chantiers, and he resented the school's growing sense that it had a distinct ideology and a special mission.[42] De La Porte du Theil received support in this from another well-known scout personality, Père Marcel-Denys Forestier, now chaplain of the Chantiers, who levelled a public warning against the religious "neutrality" of a "certain école des cadres" in the *Revue des jeunes* (15 December 1940). Even apart from Segonzac's immoderate ambitions, then, there was also uneasiness among some of the more conservative Catholics over the avant-garde "spiritualism" promoted at the school by men like the intense Abbé de Naurois. General de La Porte du Theil fought to sever the ties between the Chantiers and Segonzac's elite school, until, in October 1940, the two institutions in fact separated. At that point, back at Vichy, Commander de la Chapelle, who had helped start both institutions, went along with the Chantiers, taking command of one of their regional schools under General de La Porte du Theil's orders. Some of the trainees of the first cohort at la Faulconnière seem to have shared the reservations of the old scouts La Porte du Theil and Forestier, some seem to have simply been indifferent to their two weeks under Segonzac, but a substantial number of the rest were enthusiastic about the experience and declared themselves committed to the ideals of the school.[43]

By the time of the break with the Chantiers, the "Centre de la Faulconnière" was described at the SGJ as the mother-house of future regional centres, directed by "an elite of leaders of men," while the "bureau des cadres" at Vichy referred to Segonzac's school as an "École Normale des chefs supérieures de la Jeunesse." Soon the "Vieux Chef" (as Segonzac was being called by his slightly younger trainees) began claiming responsibility for the reshaping of French young people for the National Revolution, and his staff began publishing a series of thoughtful short monographs at the Presses Universitaires de France along those lines. The school's second cohort, larger than the first, numbered 150 young men split into nine "teams." Most of them, again, were twenty to twenty-five years old (though some were over thirty), and many came from the scouts, but there were also fifteen "Jocistes" (members of the Young Christian Workers' Movement), fifteen Éclaireurs unionistes (non-Catholic scouts), three navy officers, a few professors, and, again, "a strong group of seminarians." But this time all of the trainees were hand-picked, having been singled out as leaders in their respective circles beforehand.[44]

Among the high points of the second course at La Faulconnière was a visit of Catholic activist Robert Garric, who had become supportive of his former colleague Lamirand's efforts (and was himself active at that time in the military "École des Cadres" created by General de Lattre de Tassigny near the general's chateau at Opmé). The highest point, however, was the solemn baptism of the newly formed "Marshal Pétain" cohort on October 20 – in the presence of a beaming Georges Lamirand, new General Secretary for Youth, of Georges Ripert (former autocratic dean of the Paris Law Faculty, now authoritarian Minister of Education), and Marshal Pétain himself. This was, in fact, the old Marshal's first official visit outside of Vichy and it seems to have been considered a great success, and to have given him much pleasure.[45] In a ceremony that mixed the old ways of religious orders and scouts with New Right choreography, the graduates took a vow:

"In the name of my team, and for France, I vow to lead and serve with all my heart and strength until death."

Several members of that select Pétain class became dedicated instructors at the school.[46] And it seems that by this time not only Segonzac but also some of the highest governmental authorities envisaged this "École Normale des chefs supérieurs de la Jeunesse" playing a key role in the transformation of all French young people – in both the free and the occupied zones.[47] Segonzac's "Marshal Pétain class" was symbolically linked to the one baptized a few days earlier (and also given the name "Marshal Pétain class") at the elite school at Sillery just outside of Paris in the occupied zone (the "École des Cadres de l'Île de France").[48] Whatever the spirit at the Sillery school,[49] at la Faulconnière, alongside Vichy, there was one basic emotional focus, as one of the head instructors in those early days, Jean Devictor, recalled: "It must be said: we were all completely devoted to Marshal Pétain. We sang 'Maréchal, nous voilà' ... We really idolized Marshal Pétain."[50]

MOVING UP:
THE CHÂTEAU D'URIAGE
(NOVEMBER 1940–
JANUARY 1941)

In the late fall of 1940 a dramatic new backdrop was abruptly requisitioned[51] for the French national elite school: the historic Alleman family's impressive "Château Bayard" and its surrounding grounds, romantically set high in the Alps that overlook Grenoble from the east. The basic structures of this impressive seventy-room castle, which is perched on the top of a massive rock on the edge of a plateau above the mountain village of Uriage, dated from the twelfth century. The great knight-hero Bayard was said to have spent time there as a boy since it had belonged to his mother's family. The main floor was constructed around a central courtyard-terrace dominating the valley. This opened onto a great hall which would become the dining room of the instructors (who called it "*le grand carré*"), and among the other rooms on that level were the kitchens, a chapel, and what became the "Marshal Pétain" meeting room – which was dominated by an outsized colour portrait of the Marshal painted by Line Malespina, wife of the school's resident artist.[52] The Pétain room was the only modern-looking one in a building replete with the Alleman family's valuable antique furniture and often attractively decorated in seventeenth-century style, or with remarkable wood carving. On the second floor, to which one ascended by small winding stairways in the castle towers, were the school's offices, and from there one could still ascend several flights of stairs to a host of other rooms in the castle towers.[53] A gently climbing path from the main castle entrance led to a vast terrace-like plateau overlooking the alpine valley, which became the school playing field. Also scattered on the Uriage plateau were a group of chalets which had been requisitioned, or rented, for Segonzac and the other married instructors.[54] The Château d'Uriage was an inspiring and somewhat dreamlike setting for what had become an ambitious, though slightly unrealistic, enterprise.

In contrast to the makeshift improvisations at la Faulconnière castle, the school now became a structured institution made up of a core "team" of nineteen members, supported by auxiliary personnel. Soon the establishment was employing at least fifty persons,[55] and its financial resources were increased to two million francs (437,000 for personnel and 1,450,000 for other expenses), or about four per cent of the ordinary budget of the SGJ. But the salaries of the faculty and staff at the school were relatively modest,[56] and the instructors at the school were now dressed in a simple, distinctive costume: light-coloured riding breeches, a grey smock, and mountain shoes. The trainees were outfitted in a blue shirt and smock, trousers of black flecked cloth or blue golf pants, a grey tie, a beret, and spats.[57] They were expected to be not only neat but even "elegant" and, typically, the effect was simultaneously romantic, military, and monastic.

Daily life at the Uriage school was also a mixture of the soldierly and the contemplative. The trumpet summoned the men at seven in the morning to the first, pre-breakfast session of what would be a total of one and one-half hours of vigorous physical exercise (although on some days this became as many as three). Beyond that there would be two to three hours of manual labour on one of the construction projects set out by the instructors on the plateau or in the surrounding mountains. The day also had a place for "spiritual nourishment." Mass was said every morning at eight o'clock,[58] and there was one hour of strict monastic-like silence after lunch. In the midst of all this austerity, as at La Faulconnière castle, the high point of the day was the after-dinner gathering, the *veillée*, in front of the wood fire blazing in a massive castle fireplace. These get-togethers came to involve singing, plays, talks, readings, and a sort of homily by the Vieux Chef himself who, as the school evolved, became more and more the elegant, imposing, much-admired embodiment of its "style." Each day, too, the "chef de l'École" reunited his "chefs' council" where all listened in silence to whomever was designated to speak.

Besides the daily masses, and the periods of silence, the monastic element was also evident in the oath of the trainees, which remained the same as it had been for the Marshal Pétain cohort of 20 October at the Château de la Faulconnière. (The question was posed: "Are you prepared to do your duty as leaders?" Response: "Yes." The *Chef* then responded: "I consecrate you ["Je vous sacre ... "],[59] the ... ['Pétain,' 'Bayard,' 'Lyautey,' or whatever]" class.) This blending of the martial and the religious characterized the school, and, to a certain extent, the times.

The military, patrician, and clerical bent of the new Uriage school might have seemed rather narrow for an institution that purported to form leaders for the nation as a whole. But in fact one of the earliest preoccupations of the young aristocrats who ran the place was the question of how France's new elites would deal with the French working class. One of the first significant visiting experts from Vichy to the school was the former trade union (CGT) leader M. Courrière, head of the staff of the Minister of Labour René Belin. While talking of trade unionism in his lecture on 17 October Courrière termed class struggle "an artificial construction of the mind" and sketched out a vision of the future industrial corporation in which the organization committees would include "the better workers" and unceremoniously abolish the "moribund trade union confederations." (In fact, the union central offices would be dissolved by the government a few weeks later, on 9 November 1940.) In sum, Courrière's was a firmly anti-Communist talk, geared toward rooting Communists out of French trade unionism and dismissing the "illusory" notion of class conflict.[60]

A series of lectures to the "Lyautey" class by the well-known Catholic labour leader Marcel Montcel (national president of the JOC [Young Christian Workers] from 1937) were on "La psychologie ouvrière" (The workers' mind). They, too, reflected an attempt by Catholics and other anti-Marxists (such as the *normalienne* mystic and social thinker Simone Weil, who herself worked in factories in this effort)[61] to "understand" labouring people so as to reconcile the French proletariat with religion, or break down the communication barriers between working-class army conscripts and their officers.[62] The new thinking about class relationships at Vichy was also evident in the talk by Robert Bothereau, another prominent non-Communist trade union leader. Bothereau had been administrative secretary of the CGT from 1933, assistant secretary of the reunited CGT from 1936, and a friend of the prominent CGT leader Léon Jouhaux. Although he had been a severe critic of Jouhaux's successor René Belin, and of the "pacifists" after Munich, he had, in September

1939, agreed with their position of suppressing the Communists from France for defending the Nazi-Soviet pact. While keeping his distance from Belin, now Minister of Labour in the new regime, Bothereau declared himself "expectant" and hopeful regarding the National Revolution.[63] In short, Uriage trainees were given the general impression that the various factions of the French trade union movement were agreed in abolishing the Communist Party, and supportive of the Vichy government's efforts to replace the trade unions with alternative structures.

How did French union leaders, for their part, react to the new social philosophy stressing the importance of hierarchy and leadership that the new national elite school represented? As far as Uriage's ideas were concerned, Robert Bothereau discreetly admitted to some scepticism on the part of working people regarding the meaning of newly popular terms such as "la Personne" ("can they be expected to understand what phrases like the 'gift of the person' mean?"), or "*chefs*" ("Is it a question of those one chooses, or of those who are imposed upon you?").[64] While most Uriage instructors seemed untroubled by any lack of comprehension of their ideals among the French working class, invitations to men like Bothereau demonstrated an effort to get to know those who knew the proletarians, and wisely so, for the school's "*chefs*'" relative lack of contacts in, and ability to communicate with, that milieu remained flagrant – a source of concern for at least a few of its founders.

At this point hostile observers might portray Uriage as part of a bald-faced effort by French reactionaries to profit from the confusion of the defeat. Under a cloak of patriotism they could be seen as trying to re-establish the hegemony of those bourgeois and aristocratic Catholic families who had been shut out of power and influence during the Third Republic (and it is true that there was a remarkable frequency of the "de" particle among the *chefs* and lecturers at the school). But this would be to belittle the conscious motivations and intentions of the men of Uriage. It was not that simple.

Of considerable importance in the early life of the school was an inspiring talk by the *normalien* philosophy graduate Robert Garric, who had created the Équipes sociales in 1919 in a high-minded effort to bring bourgeois students together with young workers in a new sort of community experience – study circles distinguished by a serious pedagogical program. In 1940 Garric was running the Secours National organization (a variety of French Red Cross) for the southern zone from Gannat, quite close to Uriage.[65]

Garric's Équipes sociales directly inspired the "cercles d'études" created under Segonzac's direction, which became one of Uriage's pedagogical structures.[66] The Uriage chaplain, the Abbé de Naurois, later remembered the Équipes sociales communities as having had much to do with his going to Uriage: "[in the Équipes sociales ...] we organized meetings, study circles, between students and workers, without ever raising metaphysical or religious questions, and we had discussions with anarchists as well as with communists, socialists, and freemasons. There were very good results ... a transcending of ideologies."[67]

During the interwar period, then, Robert Garric's altruistic grouping taught Catholic leaders how to counter divisive class and ideological factors by fostering "dialogue," understanding, and fraternal feelings across class and ideological lines. In 1940 a new French government suddenly gave Catholic youth leaders extensive opportunities to share their values with "de-Christianized" segments of the French population from whom they had been cut off for generations. The Uriage school would try to find ways to seize this opportunity.

At the beginning, the lectures of Chaplain René de Naurois, replete with ideas he had picked up in "progressive" Catholic circles, were an important source of new thinking at Uriage, particularly on how the school could foster an appetite for change among younger working people. In the early 1930s, as a seminarian, he had seconded Toulouse University librarian André Déléage's efforts to turn the supporters of the personalist review *Esprit* (which Déléage had co-founded with Emmanuel Mounier, and with which de Naurois had been involved from early in its life)[68] into a disciplined, insurrectionist, extra-parliamentary political group. When the philosophers Jacques Maritain and Nicholas Berdyaev, the best-known backers of and contributors to *Esprit*, forced Mounier to block the review's involvement in what they saw as ill-advised hot-headedness, Déléage and de Naurois joined another politicized *Esprit* founder, Georges Izard, in organizing a band of street-fighters called the "Third Force."[69] This "Third Force" soon fused with (while furnishing several leaders for) the "Parti Frontiste" of the up-and-coming young "neo-Radical" Gaston Bergery. Soon Bergery and these ex-*Esprit* leaders were employing extravagant anti-capitalist rhetoric in a peculiar political configuration that began to display a "fascism of the Left" style.[70]

Father de Naurois had other connections and interests beyond the *Esprit* group and the "Third Force"; while a member of the Catholic faculty at Toulouse, he was a self-styled disciple of Father Bernadot, the Dominican priest behind a range of Catholic publications full of avant-garde ideas (such as the reviews *La Vie Intellectuelle, La Vie Spirituelle*, and *Sept*). After his experiences as vicar of the French parish in Berlin he considered himself, like his friend André Déléage, something of an authority on German politics, and particularly on the German youth movement.[71] Before the war Paul-Henri Chombart de Lauwe, the only other self-conscious "intellectual" present at the beginnings of the Uriage school (and another member of the Équipes sociales) had shared de Naurois's interest in German youth, visiting him in Berlin to hear his views on the situation there.[72]

In an ingenuous effort at opening the staff of the new French national leadership school to the French working class, de Naurois introduced "a true worker," Bénigno Cacérès, to Uriage. In presenting the Toulouse carpenter to the school, the chaplain called attention to Cacérès' workingman's hands as certifying his social status, and said it was important "not to keep the great family of workers outside of the National Revolution" lest it run the danger of becoming a "class" revolution. Cacérès then spoke on his "love of work" to a school that listened "in religious silence" until, afterwards, Segonzac stepped forward and "very naturally" shook his hand. The Toulouse carpenter was introduced into a world of books, ideas, and grandiose social theorizing that would change his life.[73]

De Naurois' contacts with radical youth movements in France and Germany had, he later recalled, made him sharply critical of a soft French society:

There are things that condense an entire mentality. The fact, for example, that after the war of 1914–1918, there were French newspapers called ... *Le Petit Méridional, Le Petit Journal, Le Petit Dauphinois, Le Petit Parisien,* ... culminating in the *Petit Écho de la mode*. The little Frenchman, his little wife, in his little house ... was a whole psychology, the antithesis to expansion, risk-taking.

While Uriage's chaplain did not later remember himself as uncompromisingly anti-Republican in 1940, he did admit to having had serious doubts about "the system" in France:

So, even if I had regularly defended the Third [Republic] in a democratic and republican spirit, why had we lost in 1940? Why had we been crushed, rolled over, knocked into moral disarray by the defeat? Because we were not capable of producing ... an efficacious army, competent military leaders – lucid men, of a high intellectual level, capable of seeing the weakness in our own defences, of seizing on how one might neutralize the enemy or at least stop him.

It was this context of decadence and defeat, de Naurois recalled, that fuelled the national-revolutionary impetus at Uriage:

We wanted to remake the social fabric, multiply the number of social group-ings ... And we thought that required an individual probity, a moral integrity, a devotion to work, a high sense of professional duty, and a commitment to the national cause. Also the ideal of not having enemies, of not ignoring one's fellow countryman on the pretext that he was of a different social class.[74]

Like several other men who would serve under Dunoyer de Segonzac, René de Naurois had returned from Nazi Germany con-vinced that France could only stand up to a vigorous Germany after effecting her own sort of youth revolution, and this was his agenda at the Château Bayard. These efforts were soon known well beyond the Uriage plateau because the school began to self-consciously take on the role of avant-garde laboratory of the National Revolution, describing its community experience in a host of publications addressed to those working to transform the younger generation in France.

Prominent among the school's publishing and propaganda efforts was *Jeunesse ... France!*, a new bi-monthly periodical published at Uriage from the late 1940s, and soon lauded by the Vichy authorities as "a propaganda journal for French youth, even for those overseas," and "the official organ of the Ministry of Youth." It seemed a great success and was, by January 1941, publishing 25,000 copies per issue. Its front page displayed a celebrated quotation from Pétain on edu-cation (from his essay in the *Revue des Deux Mondes*, 15 August 1940): "The school of tomorrow will teach respect for the human person ... Life is not neutral ... between France and anti-France one must choose ... ," and so on. This "personalist" declaration was thought, at Uriage, to have been written for Pétain by Gaston Bergery, a frequenter of "personalists" before the war, and now considered a Uriage sympathizer.[75] In displaying the range of Uriage's ideas *Jeu-nesse ... France!* was a rich source of new ideas and initiatives for Vichy's youth ministry, even representing a whole blueprint for a French National Revolution, what historians years later would call the "Vichy that might have been."

The basic purpose of the new École Nationale des Cadres d'Uriage was outlined by "Chef" Paul-Henri Chombart de Lauwe in a com-parative analysis of youth movements in Europe, where the erudite young ethnologist called for the invention of a French experience distinct from those of the Italians and the Germans.[76] In fact,

Chombart de Lauwe's idea of France creating its own, original youth revolution was similar to a recurrent aspiration of the 1930s peculiar to Catholics, or to those non-religious advocates of a spiritual revolution who called themselves Personalists. The young personalists of the Ordre Nouveau movement had written a popular and prescient book predicting a European youth revolution – *Jeune Europe* – in 1933 and thus had been among the first to put forward this notion.[77]

From the very beginning Uriage did not pretend to be strikingly original on the level of ideas. Initially the school, like the SGJ at Vichy, cited traditionalist writers as inspiration: the SGJ study bureau publications made frequent reference to the major reactionary thinkers of the nineteenth century, especially Joseph de Maistre, or to contemporary conservatives such as Charles Maurras, or General Weygand. There was also mention of the authors of the Catholic revival (venerated heroes like Charles Péguy, but also men still in their prime such as Jacques Maritain, Père Doncoeur, Nicholas Berdyaev, or younger thinkers such as economist François Perroux or Emmanuel Mounier). These discussions centred on issues such as the desirability of a "purely French" youth experience, or a "Catholic order."[78] Indeed Uriage was meant to be just the beginning: the law of December 1940 created two Écoles Nationales des Cadres de la Jeunesse, one for boys at Uriage and the other for girls at Ecully. Not long after that, Georges Lamirand would announce that France was dotted with regional leadership schools.[79]

By the end of 1940 there were three "cohorts" at Uriage, each made up of about 125 trainees: the "C" ("Bayard") had been there from 4 to 19 November, and the "D" ("Lyautey") from 8 to 29 December – this latter being the first of the new, longer, three-week training courses. Among these trainees there had been only twenty of those "chefs" of the Chantiers de la Jeunesse that the school had originally been set up to train, and those twenty had been sent to Uriage on the orders of the SGJ (and probably to the displeasure of General de La Porte du Theil and other Chantiers authorities).

Soon Uriage was consciously husbanding a distinctive style and keeping files on the qualities of individual cadets in an effort to single out potential leaders particularly taken with the school's unique spirit but these dossiers also included criticisms of such things as a lack of generosity, "an excess of critical spirit" ("esprit dissolvant"), or a "civil servant mentality".[80] On 29 December 1940 Lamirand proudly told a youth festival in his home town of Toulouse that Uriage (which was called the "spiritual university of French youth" in an official publication) was special, the apple of his eye, "at the head of all the schools," and he wished everyone could be present at a Uriage *veillée*, as he had done a few days earlier: "There, two hundred young people under thirty-five, including engineers, foremen, workers, peasants, students, are grouped together around Chef Segonzac and his team of instructors." Lamirand also announced that he had created almost sixty other "écoles des cadres," which "rivalled one another for ardour and enthusiasm."[81]

One of the better known individuals who were already active on the Uriage staff during this time was the thirty-five-year-old philosophy *agrégé* and editor of the personalist review *Esprit*, Emmanuel Mounier. Mounier, like his *Esprit* friend and fellow personalist philosopher Jean Lacroix, who accompanied him there,[82] had been a favourite student of the austere, black-clad, Catholic mystic Jacques Chevalier, Bergsonian philosopher and dean of the University of Grenoble (and a Pétain godson and confidant who was Vichy education minister in the period when the school was established).

Both Mounier and Lacroix seem to have been brought to the school by their friend the Abbé de Naurois,[83] and both quickly felt quite at home there. Mounier expressed a growing sympathy both for Segonzac and for the school in general in his diary. Mounier then brought de Naurois to meet the well-travelled journalist Hubert Beuve-Méry, a powerful personality who would soon play a decisive role at the school.[84] Mounier's diary records a memorable, euphoric *réveillon* at Uriage, on 31 December 1940, when Mounier spoke with Segonzac and de Naurois of the community's grandiose projects,[85] and soon his own communitarian personalism was having a major impact there.

Even Mounier, who as the editor of one of France's most important Catholic-oriented journals was used to being around priests, was surprised to find what he thought were too many curés in the Uriage school's courses. And alongside the young curés and seminarians at the school there were also nationally famous leaders of youth movements such as Father Paul Doncoeur, whom Mounier described as delighted with the spirit of the young men at the château: "leading little folk dances during which his soutane would fly in the air ... reciting verses of Péguy with his thin, energetic mouth during the initial evening *veillée* in front of the wood fire."[86] Mounier was somewhat taken aback to discover that Dunoyer de Segonzac wanted even more clerics in his courses, but relieved that this idea was opposed by the Catholic hierarchy.[87] Despite the personal piety of the Vieux Chef and of most of his key aides, French Church leaders would, for several reasons, never wax enthusiastic about the Uriage experiment.

An important Church official who had regular contact with Uriage was Msgr Émile Guerry who, as the general secretary of the permanent commission of the Assembly of Cardinals and Arch-bishops of France, was one of the few French clergymen with regular contact with all of the country's hierarchy, effectively serving, in Mounier's words, as the "secretary of the Church of France."[88] Guerry was also the auxiliary to Msgr Chollet, the Archbishop of Cambrai who was responsible for co-ordinating the various Catholic Action movements in the country. In 1925 Mounier had been an enthusiastic member of a small community directed by Guerry in a poor neigh-bourhood of Grenoble that sought, like the Équipes sociales, to intro-duce middle-class students to working people and the poor. By 1940 Guerry was known for his publications on Catholic social doctrine and was invited to lecture on this subject at Uriage.[89]

Given Msgr Guerry's long friendship with Mounier, he might have been expected to be sympathetic to a school in which Mounier's ideas seemed to blossom. But Guerry's responsibilities for the Catholic Action movements made him apprehensive about the possibility of their being co-opted by a state-directed, totalitarian youth organi-zation.[90] He privately complained to Mounier that government offi-cials were beginning to act in a high-handed way with groups like the Young Christian Workers (JOC) – sending them out in the streets to sell portraits of Pétain on a Sunday when they were scheduled to do something else that they had been planning for a long time.[91]

Mounier may have been disappointed with the blandness of his old mentor's talk at Uriage (which he described in his diary as deplorably "episcopal and scholastic"), and he privately pleaded with him to urge the Church to profit from the opportunities offered by the new youth movements.[92] In fact, however, Guerry merely reflected the thinking of much of the French Catholic hierarchy when he kept some distance from even the most Catholic-oriented of Vichy's youth organizations or institutions. While a man like Mounier might dismiss the Catholic authorities as self-centred or timorous, their fears for the autonomy of their organizations were not groundless.

By the end of 1940, the École Nationale des Cadres d'Uriage had plans that soared far beyond its original mission of training personnel for the Chantiers de la Jeunesse. In their remarks at the first *veillée* of the December cohort, Segonzac and de Naurois shared their dream "that all men occupying whatever post of command in the society, whether civil servants or engineers, professors or lawyers, take a course at Uriage." By early 1941 Uriage's leaders seem to have envisaged the eventual transformation of all of France through the new kinds of elites that the school would produce.[93] Lest it be thought that the young captain and his friends were suffering from delusions of grandeur, we must recall that not only did Segonzac seem to believe he could have direct access to Marshal Pétain in emergencies, but he also knew and liked several important people in the Marshal's entourage.[94] In sum, Segonzac was fully convinced that Uriage was the right school, in the right place, at the right time, to change the destiny of France.

However well connected Segonzac was, there were still some important problems with his vast ambitions of Christmastime 1940. For one thing, Mounier and Lacroix's celebration of "the person" or "communitarian personalism" may have inspired much of the Uriage community, but such high-minded concepts often seem to have dumbfounded the trade-unionists – thus suggesting a certain weakness in the school's hope of leading the whole nation beyond the recondite and ingrown intellectualism represented by the old École Normale Supérieure. Soon there was a conscious effort to recruit beyond that peculiar milieu of Catholic philosophers, clerics, and young officers from old families that made up its inner circle. There was also a serious and ambitious attempt to situate Uriage philosophically within the context of France's National Revolution, the war, and the great historical changes that faced twentieth-century man. Bringing such ideas down to earth, however, would not be easy.

By early 1941 Uriage increasingly claimed to be a think-tank for the SGJ, if not for the whole National Revolution. After attending a meeting organized by Mounier in Lyon in December, at which a leader of the Compagnons spoke to the Catholic intelligentsia on "the spirit of the youth movement,"[95] Chaplain de Naurois invited Mounier, Jean Lacroix, and a young Jesuit close to them, Father Henri de Lubac, to lecture during the Uriage study days on the doctrine of the National Revolution.[96]

The tall, blond Mounier, a native *Grenoblois* with a strong literary and mystic bent, called for "a French humanism of the person and the community" that would value the community-oriented *personne* over against the pernicious "individualism" of the defunct Republic. Mounier envisioned an end to the self-centredness that had flowed from the Renaissance, and he predicted a dramatic personalist and communitarian revolution in France.[97] His ideas struck a responsive chord in a school that was in search of a doctrine suited to its hierarchical community style, and his talk was, by all accounts, the most popular presentation of the colloquium. In the ensuing debate over "the future of French youth," Mounier's "communitarian personalism" seemed the most popular among the ideologies presented to the school.[98] In short order the personalist thinker emerged from relative obscurity to become a vital philosophical guide to what had been called the "spiritual university" of Vichy's National Revolution, an ideologue shaping an ambitious project for the transformation of French youth.

After the major study days, Mounier, Lacroix, de Lubac – as well as Professor Jean-Jacques Chevallier of Grenoble – became increasingly involved with Uriage. Segonzac asked the SGJ for the means to establish a serious research facility at Uriage, and planned to have Mounier as one of the five or six men of the permanent staff running this Study Bureau ("Bureau d'études permanent").[99] Mounier declined membership on Uriage's permanent staff, however, preferring to contribute to the school "tangentially" – as he was already doing with the Jeune France cultural movement. He did not want to be considered a man of one political configuration or one organization.[100] As events would later confirm, Mounier was justified in his wariness of his critics in responsible positions at Vichy.[101] The "Study Bureau" would soon be taken in hand by one of Mounier and Father de Naurois's friends – a remarkably willful, brilliant, demanding, and rather cantankerous personality – the law professor and journalist Hubert Beuve-Méry.

A MASTER OF NOVICES: HUBERT BEUVE-MÉRY

Early in 1941 the Abbé de Naurois brought Hubert Beuve-Méry to Uriage. While teaching law and economics in the French Institute in Prague, Beuve-Méry had become known for his informed descriptions of the rise to power of the Nazis in eastern Europe for Le Temps, France's leading newspaper. He had resigned from the paper over its flaccid, business-as-usual reaction to the Munich crisis. De Naurois had been quite impressed on meeting "Beuve" for the first time. There had been a discussion on youth movements at Jean Lacroix's house in Lyon and the strapping professor/journalist had arrived without a coat (despite a glacial fog and cold in the city), improbably dressed in riding breeches with strips of cloth wound round his legs to serve as makeshift gaiters.[102]

Hubert Beuve-Méry would soon become very influential at Uriage, and his unusual background helps explain the decisive cast he would give to Uriage (and later to his newspaper, Le Monde). The journalist had had a hard life: his father had deserted his mother, and the boy saw him only when he was eight years old – laid out in a Parisian morgue. Young Hubert's mother became dependent on the Catholic clergy, and the child literally grew up in the shadow of the cathedral of Notre Dame – in a world of attentive women and priests whom he admired.[103]

The boy showed precocious intelligence and an ascetic bent, and the clergy, in turn, provided him with a free education. While still their boarding student he imposed penitential mortifications on himself, spreading holly in his sheets, forcing himself to pray when the wooden bar of the kneeler was cutting into his knees. He decided to consecrate himself to God, wear a soutane, and lead a life of prayer and contemplation. During Easter 1920 young Beuve-Méry heard the lenten sermons of the famous preacher Father Albert-Marie Janvier, a sixty-three-year-old Dominican who had been prior of Saulchoir, one of the centres of the order since 1904. When Beuve-Méry went to see him, Father Janvier was much taken with the younger man, and made something of a protégé of him. Although not explicitly "political," Janvier was much influenced by the Action Française and numbered among his closest friends intelligentsia then close to the movement, such as Jacques Maritain, Henri Massis, and Léon Daudet. Young Beuve-Méry was brought along to their discussions.[104]

By 1925 Beuve-Méry had been directly involved in a militant right-wing, even proto-fascist, youth movement.[105] He was also showing that passion for journalism that would help make him the most influential journalist of postwar France. Disgusted by the reporting in Paris's five major dailies, he took to reading Georges Valois's *Nouveau Siècle*, which was promoting the ideas of Le Faisceau, the first Fascist movement in France. It also (like Uriage later) called for an "anti-bourgeois" revolution. Valois's rejection of both capitalism and communism fascinated Beuve-Méry, who met some impressive people, such as the young writer Paul Nizan, at the movement's headquarters on the rue d'Aguesseau.[106]

As they would at the Château Bayard years later, world-historical concerns tended to displace Beuve-Méry's penchant for contemplative prayer. His plans to become a priest had been postponed by the late 1920s, but he did join the Dominicans' Third Order, which included a number of devout intellectuals.[107] This commitment was made under the paternal authority of Father Janvier, who summoned together, once a month, for intense discussions, a small group that included Maritain (then considered the most important younger philosopher of the Action Française school) as well as the prestigious Moldavian mystic Prince Vladimir Ghika.[108]

Beuve-Méry found journalistic work in a Dominican enterprise when finishing his doctoral thesis in law.[109] By 1924 he was an attentive reader of Nicolas Berdyaev, author of the famous *Un nouveau Moyen-Âge*, and studying medieval philosophy with Étienne Gilson at the Sorbonne.[110] The young law student's fascination for the Middle Ages would become an important factor in the training of the men of Uriage.

Like other Uriage leaders, Beuve-Méry had moralistic attitudes toward the modern world, puritanical perceptions of sexual relationships, and very negative attitudes toward divorce and free love.[111] He continued to feel most comfortable with Catholic intellectuals and writers, and after his posting to a position teaching law for the French Ministry of Foreign Affairs in Prague, a review in which many of them were active, *Politique*,[112] began publishing his essays. Although *Politique* had less than one thousand subscribers, it was, like the progressive Catholic journal *Esprit*, which would publish some of the same people, known for its sophistication and originality. Beuve-Méry met a supportive community, a veritable "family," around the review, whom he visited each time he came to Paris. In the same years, but in Jacques Maritain's circle, he met Emmanuel Mounier, whose journal *Esprit* would appear in 1932. He agreed with Mounier's aims of struggling against the "reign of money," denouncing the political bankruptcy of the Third Republic (in the style of Proudhon and Péguy), and taking a critical attitude toward America.[113]

His interest in foreign policy issues heightened by his Prague experiences, Beuve-Méry made a long, attentive visit to the Soviet Union. There he discovered a society favouring "the primacy of the material over the spiritual," as "insidious propaganda" transformed that "mystically oriented, primitive people" into simple-minded fanatics.[114] Beuve-Méry would communicate his profound antipathy for the Soviet Union to the Uriage school.

But Beuve-Méry's *Politique* analyses were not liberal-democratic in tone, as was shown, for example, by his reaction to the rise of anti-semitism. Noting that Hitlerism progressed in areas of Europe where anti-Jewish feeling was rife and that Christians were obliged to show religious tolerance, he nevertheless described anti-semitism in Hungary as a rather understandable reaction "against the grasp on business by Israelites who held almost all business, and all finance."[115]

In fact, the pre-war essays of Beuve-Méry displayed relatively little concern over the wholesale abandonment of liberal democracy in Europe and saw Hitlerism more as twentieth-century German expansionism than as a deadly assault on humanistic values. While the Nazis' racism and fanatical nationalism were clearly unacceptable, "it was not enough to reject a system outright ... a fact that, for better or worse, one was obliged to accept."[116] For Beuve-Méry, as later for the Uriage school, Nazism was neither an ephemeral, nor intrinsically perverse, phenomenon.

Beuve-Méry would figure as the leading ideologist of Uriage because he had a fairly clear idea of an authoritarian, but newly Christian, France that could be created in a Europe dominated by Hitler's Germany. From 1936, setting himself over against "the mass of tepid Catholics," he called for a return to a world of true faith, and of "a civilization which while not completely synonymous with Christianity would be formed and permeated by it,"[117] and in concluding his book *Vers la plus grande Allemagne* which appeared in February 1939 Beuve-Méry claimed that despite the elements of disorder and violence, "the elements of a new synthesis remained ... And it is not too late to prepare, beyond the ... dreams of Chancellor Hitler, the coming of a more united and more just Europe." The future director of Uriage's study group wanted to join a modified form of democracy and a new concern for order, the "primacy of the person" and efficacy, a concern for morality and action. This book caught the attention of diplomatic and political milieux not only in France but also in Berlin – where, invited to a dinner, he was seated across from Goebbels and Himmler.[118]

Beuve-Méry's ideas were, after all, more realistic than those of politically marginal admirers of Hitler like Jean Luchaire or Alphonse de Chateaubriant; the young law professor and foreign correspondent had wide connections with, and a potential support group in, the Catholic elites. After the Munich agreements in the fall of 1938, in the evenings following hikes in the Alps in the Arêches region, Beuve-Méry pored over Henry de Montherlant's *L'Équinoxe de septembre*; here was another bellicose *anti-Munichois* attacking the spinelessness of the French.[119]

After the German invasion forced him to leave Prague in July 1939 Beuve-Méry was hired by the new Commissariat général à l'Information established by Daladier on the very eve of the war and directed by the playwright Jean Giraudoux, a high-profile advocate of Franco-German rapprochement.[120] Giraudoux's *La Guerre de Troie n'aura pas lieu* had been a moving plea for the avoidance of a Franco-German conflict and he employed men who saw things like Beuve-Méry such as Louis Joxe, who had published the former's *Vers la plus grande Allemagne*, Emmanuel Mounier, and future Pétain speech writer René Gillouin, in his effort to create a French propaganda office.[121] For whatever reason, this immediate pre-war Giraudoux information service drew people who favoured adaptation to, rather than confrontation with, a European New Order directed by Germany, including several future architects of Pétain's National Revolution.[122] For Bernard-Henri Lévy Giraudoux was one of the most prominent examples of cultured and aesthetic fascism, of a "fascisme doux" entertained in the best circles on the eve of the war.[123]

When war was declared Beuve-Méry went from Giraudoux's service to work for the central service of the Deuxième Bureau at Nancy, whose assignment was counter-espionage.[124] After the French army collapsed and the armistice was declared, he went down to Lyon in the unoccupied zone to renew his contacts with Catholic publishing circles, notably his friends, such as Mounier and Stanislas Fumet of *Temps présent*, who were trying to find their way in the new situation. Beuve-Méry helped Fumet start *L'Hebdomadaire du Temps Nouveau* (contributing the "Sirius" column) and published several tracts in what would later be seen as the *Le Monde* style: they compared, successively, the virtues of communism, the Christian tradition, and Nazism, juxtaposing their virtues and their faults. While Nazism brought "enthusiasm for the construction of a New Order" it had to be admitted that "every human person was being crushed in it." Communism may have provoked an admirable dream of worker fraternity and universal justice but a long series of crimes had been perpetrated in its name. Despite the fact that one owed two thousand years of civilization to Christianity, "the triumph of communism, fascism, and national socialism would have been unimaginable without the deliquescence of too many Christians." Although accepting "a merited defeat," and rejecting all appeals to "bloody and ruinous revenge," Beuve-Méry called for a precipitate burst of energy, a "human order," a new sort of "French community" that would have a higher moral tone than what had preceded. He did not lament the republicanism, liberalism, or parliamentary democracy of the Third Republic.[125]

In March 1941 Beuve-Méry's essay "Révolutions nationales, Révolutions humaines" in *Esprit* talked of the new revolution:

The most pertinent, the youngest revolution, the one that simultaneously transcends Marxism and nationalism, postulates a spiritual exigency as *sine qua non*: the restoration of the primacy of man, in the plenitude of his being and his vocation, the primacy of the person ...

An exigency of the heart: the discovery of a style of life inspired by the oldest French traditions and the better qualities of the race ...

It is not a question of projecting some sort of nostalgia for the past as our dream of the future. It is a question of giving to man that "extra spirit" that the sudden collapse of an over-mechanized civilization requires. There results a revolution that is as much human as national, and that cannot remain isolated. It admits, it even postulates, an audacious rationalization of Europe,

which the Versailles Treaty had ridiculously compartmentalized ... That is
to say that the principles that were the bases of Europe for a long time – the
absolute sovereignty of small or large states, the European equilibrium, the
right of neutrality – must cede their place to a more orderly arrangement
of the continent.[126]

During the winter of 1940–41, just when Segonzac wanted to start
a Study Bureau/Research Department to situate Uriage's efforts in a
larger context, the well-informed and impressive Beuve-Méry not
only published these distinctive essays but he also came to the school
to give some memorable lectures on "The Europe of Yesterday and
Tomorrow."[127] Then the professor/journalist went off to Portugal
under the aegis of the French Ministry of Foreign Affairs to lecture
to the leading Portuguese universities on the prospects for national
transformation in France. From there he returned on permanent
assignment to Uriage in June 1941.[128]

Beuve-Méry was thirty-eight, older than most of the Uriage community, when he came to the Château Bayard for the first time.
Because of his intelligence, maturity, and worldly experience he soon
held sway over others at the school. Although too cynical and taciturn
to be a charismatic leader in the usual sense of the term, he soon
showed that he could inspire a strong sense of fraternal affection
and loyalty. Vigorous, demanding of himself and others, he was a
brooding, often anti-clerical, Catholic and a serious alpinist and seen
as one of "the best and the brightest" of his generation; he seemed
to feel immediately at home in the rigorous military/monastic atmosphere of the alpine castle community.

"Beuve" had already achieved some notoriety with his distinctive
perspective on France's situation vis-à-vis Nazi Germany. Earlier, in
his analysis of National Socialism, Beuve-Méry had seen a bright
side:

against the deprivations of intellectualism, individualism, liberalism, capitalism, against the dulling qualities and compromises of Christianity ...
before degenerating and falling into deception, corruption, and cruelty, it
[National Socialism] contributed to giving men ... a taste for life and the
courage for sacrifice, the feeling of a certain solidarity and of a certain
grandeur.[129]

Like de Naurois and Mounier, Beuve-Méry was convinced by his
firsthand experience that the Nazis would dominate France and

Europe for a long time, and so, he felt, a realistic response was demanded. He successfully imposed this particular perspective toward Nazi Germany upon the school – with, as we shall see, serious consequences.

In that reflective essay, in the March 1941 *Esprit*, Beuve-Méry was not optimistic about the prospects for transforming France. He warned of a certain void in the country: "The National Revolution in France can be neither radical nor rapid for several reasons. A revolution needs a leader, *cadres*, troops, a faith or a myth."[130] But, on the other hand, in the 25 January 1941 *Le Figaro* he had described his very favourable impression on visiting the Uriage community, where he had met "generous and resolute men" for whom "it sufficed to know that no effort is ever lost whatever might happen, [and it is exhilarating] to live around a leader worthy to command them, through the joyous gift of self. The search for true and virile friendship [is] one of the handsomest of human adventures." He concluded that the Uriage community was "a power centre, a central laboratory, a source of life ... perhaps the first sketch of the new university."[131]

By the end of 1940 the national "École des Chefs" had fixed upon a quasi-monastic "Règle de communauté des chefs." It declared that "the team ... is ruled by the idea of, and absolute loyalty to, the person of Marshal Pétain, head of the French State," and required, rather singularly, both "a total submission to the order of the Marshal" and a "total obedience to the two 'vieux chefs.'"[132] Beyond that, the rule noted that "a meticulous cleanliness is required of everyone, even a certain elegance," and that "a total frankness, an absolute sincerity toward oneself and toward others is essential." As far as daily life was concerned, the rule noted that "at the beginning of each meal all present sing in chorus ... At the end of the meal a team member, chosen in turn, reads a high-quality text listened to by everyone in silence, with respect. That reading is never to be given by an outsider."[133]

The community rules reflected the peculiar ideals and quirks in the mentality of a closely knit group of army officers, teachers, journalists, priests, and civil servants, who, if they were not strong Catholics, at least shared sympathy for "the spiritual dimension" of community life and were disenchanted with "individualism," liberalism, and democracy. With the support of Pétain or at least of his entourage,[134] this group began to contend for influence over French youth with the more orthodox Catholics and Maurrassians of the

Action Française, represented at Vichy by men like Henri Massis, as well as with the Paris-based collaborationist elements. For the next several years the loyalties of French young people would be courted by competing, often mutually hostile, institutions and organizations, by several branches of Catholic Action, and wartime versions of other pre-war youth groupings as well.[135] The ideals were lofty, but the stakes were even higher. There was no shortage of programs to save young people from decadence and defeat, or to seduce youth for their own good.

CHAPTER TWO

Beuve-Méry, the Research Department, and the Knightly Order

THE "URIAGE SPIRIT"

By early 1941 France's national leadership school was much taken up with the new idea of a communitarian personalist revolution. It was, however, publicly cautious about this: the uniqueness of Uriage, its faculty said, was "the Uriage Spirit," not any doctrine peculiar to it, and Dunoyer de Segonzac insisted that his school never had "a doctrine other than that contained in the speeches of the Marshal."[1] Indeed, from its earliest days the École Nationale des Cadres exhorted "an absolute loyalty" and a "total submission" to Marshal Pétain on the part of its instructors, and an official objective of the school was "to spread the principles of the Marshal," as the trainees were quickly made to recognize.[2] Uriage edited the *Message aux Français* of the head of state, publishing them at the end of 1942,[3] thus assuming the role of quasi-official purveyor of the Marshal's vision of the National Revolution, until as late as the German occupation of the free zone in late 1942. It even appeared that the Marshal had chosen Uriage to express his thinking, just as, before the war, he had chosen as ghost writer the brilliant young military theorist Charles de Gaulle.[4] Further, Uriage did not merely regurgitate official speeches but urged its trainees to live out the Marshal's moralistic injunctions.

The pillar of *Pétainisme* at Uriage was certainly the Vieux Chef Pierre Dunoyer de Segonzac, who would display a total, unshakeable confidence in the Marshal (despite the doubts of instructors such as the cynical Beuve-Méry), at least until the invasion of the free zone by the Germans in November 1942. In a message broadcast by Radio-Jeunesse on 11 May 1941 the head of Uriage declaimed that:

Jeanne d'Arc, long ago, accomplished the marvel of suddenly reanimating a national community that was unconscious of itself or dispersed.

We in France have the unique good fortune of having the Marshal. Thanks to him our community will emerge with strength once there will be enough true men in France to compose it.

We wish to work toward that at Uriage.[5]

From 1940 until 1942 Segonzac would see and speak with Pétain several times, for what he later recalled to be short intervals. While not particularly informed about the activities of Uriage, Segonzac thought, the Marshal never had anything but encouragement for the unknown young captain, and Segonzac always found firm support from Pétain's inner circle.[6] It seems that for Segonzac Pétain was no mere patron in trying circumstances but rather a sort of great Christian prince offering hope for the nation to make a recovery from the defeat, and from those pernicious effects of republican and secular institutions that had done so much to bring about the national disaster. The Vieux Chef would be granted the prestigious Francisque – an insignia created in 1941 by Pétain and distributed, in his name, to reward and encourage the devotedness of his faithful.[7] During the heyday of Uriage, Segonzac was among the most selfless, loyal, and constant of the Marshal's faithful.

The largely uncritical faith that Segonzac and his compatriots placed in Pétain was rooted in their Catholic-patriarchal cultural background and was coupled with a sense that the great historical lesson of 1940 was the superiority of authoritarian and disciplined societies over individualistic and liberal ones.[8] Segonzac cultivated a fervent, principled, personal veneration for the grandfatherly old Marshal, just as the Uriage students began to apotheosize the handsome, enthusiastic, elegant Segonzac himself. Such an emphasis on deference to authority, as well as romantic tales of great nobles and mystics who had saved France in the past, encouraged a suspension of normal judgment and common sense in favour of a quasi-religious faith in "the leadership principle" and hence, unfortunately, in men who would ultimately prove unworthy of the trust placed in them.

Pétain's speeches and writings soon proved a rather unsubstantial foundation on which to build a sophisticated educational institution, much less transform an entire country. Accordingly, new ideas were constantly germinating and being clarified in the 1941 Uriage school, and circulated beyond it. The École Nationale des Cadres began publishing a mass-circulation periodical, *Jeunesse ... France!*, which supplied follow-up documentation to the different schools to which their graduates went to teach. Uriage sought to bring its key ideas together into a charter, using the ambitious speculative work of the Study Bureau and feedback from the new "École Nationale d'Uriage" alumni network.[9] And while all of this was done in the name of the Marshal, it began to develop a momentum of its own.

Until Hubert Beuve-Méry's return from Portugal in June 1941, the Uriage study group had been directed by the traditionalist Catholic Louis Lallement who, usually on the first or last day of each course, gave long presentations on "The Mission of France." Displaying a strongly "providentialist" philosophy of history, Lallement presented a vast historical panorama in which the monarchical and Christian contributions to France since the Baptism of Clovis were idealized, the Napoleonic period celebrated, but the preceding bourgeois, industrial, and parliamentary century strongly deprecated.[10]

Joffre Dumazedier, who was also invited by Segonzac to work with the Study Bureau of the school, was, as a self-styled atheist and man of the Left, a striking contrast to the Catholics and royalists of Uriage. A former member of the *ajiste* youth hostel movement, Dumazedier had been an enthusiastic member of the "Marshal Pétain" cohort at the Château de la Faulconnière and had been assigned to direct one of the first centres for unemployed workers at Saint-Étienne. He was then summoned by Segonzac to direct the "Social Studies and Pedagogical Section" of the new Study Bureau, while Lallement was to deal with spirituality, and Beuve-Méry with international relations.[11] Dumazedier, influenced by the writings of Jean Guéhenno and the spiritualist socialism of Henri de Man, had been impressed by the meetings between workers and intellectuals during the Popular Front, and by the flourishing youth hostel movement with its promotion of vacations in the open air.[12] Dumazedier's atheism would always make him see things a bit differently from most of the staff, but he was interested in dialogue with Christians and sensitive to the spiritual dimension of life, and coupled this with a special interest in "psychopédagogie," as well as in popular and physical education, on which he would become a recognized expert.[13]

Already by February 1941, the imperious Beuve-Méry was trying to assure that a permanent "Study Bureau" be accepted as an integrated, essential part of the school.[14] "Beuve" wanted to include Mounier and Jean Lacroix, since these personalists had outshone the other outside lecturers who had come to address the Uriage school. It did not hurt also that Mounier was unreserved in his admiration for Segonzac and for Uriage,[15] sketching a flattering portrait of the Vieux Chef for the public in *Esprit*.[16] During the first semester of

1941 *Esprit*'s eloquent young editor spoke to almost every training session, usually on "The End of Bourgeois Man."[17] Jean Lacroix, for his part, described "the revolution of the twentieth century" within which France could only live "by integrating healthy elements of that revolution, by transcending it and inventing something new."[18]

The Bureau's interests were not confined to philosophy. It put in a request to the sGJ for a young economist; the well-known economic theorist François Perroux, an expert on corporatism who had worked with Mounier and *Esprit* before the war, was asked to recommend someone "in his line of thinking." Perroux (1903–1987) was the most influential French economist of this century and played a definite role in the life of the Uriage group, but we still have no biography of him. We do know that in 1934 he had entered into contact with the *Esprit* group through Jean Lacroix, who was then professor of *khagne* in the Lycée du Parc at Lyon (where he also numbered the devout young Catholics Louis Althusser and Jean-Marie Domenach among his students). Lacroix, who in that period was no democrat, led a *Cercle Joseph de Maistre*. Perroux, for his part, was a resolute anti-parliamentarian interested in authoritarian economic and political solutions. Besides *Esprit*, he had collaborated with *La Flèche* of Gaston Bergery and even with the radical right-wing *Je suis partout* published by Robert Brasillach and other dissident Maurrassians. He had been a candid French admirer of the "conservative revolution" in Germany and, in 1940, committed himself to Marshal Pétain and the National Revolution in a far less reserved way than did his good friend at Uriage, Emmanuel Mounier, soon reproaching his friends in the Château Bayard for "not having broken with 1789." Perroux was a friend in an influential (if still not clarified) role in the inner circles of the Vichy government.[19]

In 1941 Paul Reuter, professor of international law, gave a series of lectures, followed by a seminar the next year, on the "trusts" that he described as dominating the pre-war French economy. Reuter's courses gave a sophisticated critique of Marx's analysis of the problem of the nefarious role of trusts and his courses demonstrated how Beuve-Méry's Study Bureau was becoming less concerned with setting out basic principles – "these had been affirmed, notably with Mounier, during the first months of 1941" – than with finding their applications and implications in several areas and at several levels. Although disclaiming all pretence of being an intellectual himself, Segonzac began to affirm his own idea of a "personalist and communitarian" revolution – one inspired by Péguy. Thus despite his claims to being indifferent to ideology, Segonzac seemed to feel more and more comfortable with personalist ideas and language.[20]

Among the colourful personalities who influenced the early period of the school was strapping Jean-Jacques Chevallier, professor of law and of the history of ideas at the University of Grenoble. A former university track champion and excellent cross-country skier, Chevallier delighted Segonzac, and impressed the students, by bicycling the steep, winding, thirteen kilometres up through the heavily wooded valley to the Château from Grenoble to give his courses. An eloquent orator who extolled the French "ordre viril" – himself held up by Segonzac as a model of "the new man" the school was trying to create – Chevallier explained "the sense of action" to the trainees. In this he drew from both his athletic career and his experiences as a citizen and soldier of 1940 who had known defeat and humiliation.

In his lecture during the Uriage study days on "Liberal Democracies and Totalitarian Regimes" – which was a classic subsequently repeated on the eve of the departure from the school of each *stage* – Chevallier showed how totalitarian regimes were inevitably more efficacious than democratic ones, and he warned that "every inefficacious community that respects the person will be conquered and absorbed by an efficacious community that does not respect him." He rather harshly suggested that inefficacious civilizations on that level deserved to disappear. Hence his appeal for a new manliness in France, one that healthy women would welcome because, "if she is not spoiled by false ideas, conventions, or snobbishness, what she wants of a man, first of all, is to be a man. And the more and the better she is a woman, the more she harbours contempt for the womanish man. In that she is more than correct." The law professor described the virile order as a manner of being, a tone that characterizes the exterior attitude, the allure of the body, the cast of the face – the very bearing of the man. His prose style carries the same virile quality. He even suggested that the great authors of the past in that special tradition, beginning with Péguy's soldier-mystic friend Ernest Psichari, reflected the special quality (which would later be incarnated by the Uriage Order, and was already being talked about at the school). Perhaps a bit carried away by enthusiasm, Chevallier lumped together fervent believers with atheists, cynics with romantics: "The writers in that line, from Montherlant to Saint-Exupéry, nobly traverse the waves of literature in the great wake of Psichari: they recognize one another, and we recognize them. They form an Order."

Chevallier proposed a method of character training that would combine alpinism, with its "pleasure at searched-out, and conquered, difficulty," with Uriage physical educationist Vuillemin's famous morning shape-up (*décrassage*) and with *Hébertisme*. Men developed in this way, Chevallier claimed, would have a taste for risk and effort, a love for work well done (Péguy), the habit of dressing neatly (the "gentleman"), and a general attitude of "authenticity" that would be antithetical to all artifice. It all came together in his almost "macho" notion of "the virile order" ("You will be obliged, *chefs*, to restore a male order, a virile order"); in the last courses of the semester, Chevallier's new order would be inspired by a Christianity that would allow the new spirit of masculinity to predominate. While it was true that "virility was opposed to femininity" because "the woman has her proper order, which is complementary to the virile order," respecting the different orders was not meant to cast aspersions on "the eternal feminine, eternally necessary to man."[21]

As the professor coasted on his bicycle back down through the forest to Grenoble, no one back in the castle seems to have made light of his notion of a virile order. For his part, Segonzac was beset with Nietzschean anxieties over whether or not Christianity had "de-virilized" men. Years later veterans of Uriage would admit that misogyny was an early, and unresolved, problem at the school. We shall turn to the question of the place of women at Uriage in the next chapter but at this point we may, perhaps, be mindful of Wil-helm Reich's views about the woman-hating that religiously inspired male "orders" seemed inevitably to foster.[22]

While Chevallier's idea of a virile order lived on at Uriage, the he-man law professor himself departed. In June 1941, he was invited by ex–world tennis champion Jean Borotra, now the "Commissaire Général à l'Éducation générale et aux Sports" at Vichy, to take charge of the organization of "l'éducation générale et sportive" in the French school system (i.e., to help transform both the bodies and the char-acters of French young people). Chevallier accepted in order to be, in Segonzac's words, a bit of "Uriage at Vichy."[23] His involvement in Vichy's bureaucracy illustrated Uriage's policy of encouraging its men to take positions in the higher echelons of the National Revolution,[24] just as the rough and ultra-masculine *Hébertisme* that, under Vuil-lemin, had become an essential part of the Uriage experience was made the standard approach to physical education in all of France.

The loss of Chevallier was lessened by the brilliant, somewhat maverick Jesuit theologian Henri de Lubac, who also gave some significant lectures at Uriage during the early period.[25] In 1938 Father de Lubac, rising star in the Jesuit seminary of Fourvière, published a classic study that had been much encouraged by the thinking of the personalist milieu around him: *Catholicisme, aspects sociaux du dogme*. Along with another classic that had appeared in 1936, Jacques Maritain's *Humanisme intégral*, it encouraged those inclined or who felt a need to live in community to do so. The communitarian aspiration, according to Maritain and Father de Lubac, did not necessarily lead one to neo-monasticism; it was not a question of going into the desert, or withdrawing from the world, but of going out to meet it.

Father de Lubac was unusual among priest-intellectuals of the period for his interest in modern atheistic thinkers such as Proudhon, Nietzsche, and Marx – as well as suspect Catholics such as Maurice Blondel – and for his notion of the existence of an "atheistic humanism" (on which he wrote a popular book in this period). He also remained close to his fellow-Jesuit Pierre Teilhard de Chardin who was, during this period, in a form of unofficial exile in China for his theological speculations. Father de Lubac aided the diffusion of the evolutionary theological ideas of the Jesuit paleontologist and evolutionist at Uriage, where they were circulated in mimeographed form (as they had been in the *Esprit* group in the 1930s) and had a significant influence on the world-historical perspective of individuals such as Beuve-Méry.

In his lecture on "A Christian Explanation for Our Times," Father de Lubac criticized contemporary myths, calling, in his conclusion, for the development of a truly "Catholic" spirit after centuries of individualistic and rationalistic deviation – the "human revolution." De Lubac described the "Catholic renaissance" that was an element in "the present work of reconstruction" and, citing Beuve-Méry's *Esprit* article "Révolutions nationales, révolutions humaines,"[26] de Lubac articulated his "dream" of "a generation of young Frenchmen who would take Christianity seriously."[27] Like his friend Father Teilhard, Father de Lubac also envisaged the Second World War, in a larger context, as marking the passage of the modern man from an epoch of bourgeois individualism to one of personalist community.[28] Partly due to de Lubac's influence, Uriage soon had a vision of the important role it might play in the transformation of Catholicism in France. It must be said, however, that the Jesuit seemed noticeably less enthusiastic about Pétain than were other visitors to the school.[29] His focus was more on ideas than personality cults.

Indeed, ideas had their place and the French Catholic intellectual revival was an important inspiration to the SGJ. For at the SGJ a "Catholic order" was the ideal, "with its dogma, doctors ... magisterial teaching, definitions, universalism ... the sacred ... transcendence ... the theological virtues ... obedience ... fidelity ... obligatory respect for the person ... hierarchy ... parishes ... monasteries."[30] So it was not surprising that a Catholic spokesman suggested that the new French national leadership school formally acknowledge "that French and Christian civilization" that Péguy, too, after years of republican and socialist enthusiasms, had finally come to recognize, and that the school should make certain that Péguy be bedside reading for students there.[31] At the early Uriage, Bernard Comte has written, "the heirs of Péguy, of Blondel, and of Maritain, passionate for a spiritually inspired total revolution, met the heirs of Lyautey, who craved a patriotic synthesis, and a disciplined and efficacious form of education that would be geared toward action." And then, too: "The philosophers of personalism, in developing their affirmations at Uriage, added stability to the work of Segonzac and furnished him with an intellectually coherent language suited to the expression of his experience, and the verbalization of his convictions and his spontaneous inclinations."[32] A chemistry developed between the Catholic revival, the inspiring catch phrases of Mounier and his friends, and the combined scoutist vigour, group-singing, authoritarianism, venturesome theology, spiritual bonding, and spartanism of the school. Something unique had been created; the question was how it would be put to use.

There were several signs during the first months of 1941 that the higher authorities at Vichy had important plans for the École Nationale des Cadres. At 7:15 A.M. on 9 March 1941, for example, Youth Secretary Lamirand came "as a friend" to inspect the institution, which had become the apple of his eye, and to encourage its director. After attending a mass said by the Abbé de Naurois in the castle chapel, Lamirand gave a talk to the instructors in which he said that the school should begin to think beyond simply forming leaders of the youth movements. He stressed the "always more important part the school should play in the conquest of young people and of all those who would have a leadership role in the nation ... The mission of reuniting, in a spirit of collaboration, the elites of all the milieux that ought to participate in the common work of rehabilitation was to be confided to the Uriage school."[33]

The formal upgrading of Uriage's status would be announced only a few weeks later, with great ceremony, by the head of the government, Admiral Darlan.

On 2 June 1941, in torrential rains, Admiral Darlan arrived in a special train at the station at Voiron for his official visit to inspect the Uriage school.[34] This official call proved to be an important event for the institution because, for whatever reason, Darlan was impressed. He would assure its promotion within the institutions of the National Revolution.[35] As if by magic, important long-awaited supplies suddenly appeared, a million francs were promised to launch a weekly publication, and the 15-million-franc debt accumulated by the school was erased overnight. Darlan had even decided to require a session at the École Nationale des Cadres for all future high government functionaries (as determined by the recruiting examinations), as well as for the students of the *grandes écoles* and diverse military officers. No longer simply a school to train leaders for the sGJ, Uriage had become obligatory for the future leaders of all of France.[36] It was a significant step that would change the school in unforeseen ways.

The measures that followed Darlan's June visit resulted in new types of people attending Uriage, different from those "volunteers" scouted out by the Uriage network: there would be special sessions for students of the *grandes écoles* such as Polytechnique and the École de l'Air, and for the Saint-Cyriens of Aix-en-Provence. From a relatively unimportant school to train instructors for the Chantiers de la Jeunesse, Dunoyer de Segonzac's institution had graduated to a force that would guide France's elite.

The new importance of the Uriage school resulted in a tightening of ideological reins there, and the expulsion of some prominent personalities. René de Naurois had been not only chaplain but recruiter of personnel, middle-man of ideas, and even, on at least one occasion, "Chef d'équipe."[37] But the Toulouse priest was "too much to the Left" for Segonzac, and his outspokenness and swash-buckling style irritated Beuve-Méry[38] (who at one point directly told him, "*You* are not the chaplain that we need").[39] In any case, when Vichy official Louis Garrone (considered a friend of Uriage) wanted the chaplain out,[40] Segonzac complied. He had de Naurois replaced in July by the ascetic Dominican intellectual Jean Maydieu.[41]

Another victim of the heightened profile of the school was Emmanuel Mounier. There had been Vichy pressure on Uriage to do without Mounier's services (coming from, Mounier thought, his old critic, now sGJ adviser, Henri Massis), which Segonzac had resisted. But, in July, as the government upgraded the school and increased its subsidies, it flatly forbade Mounier's lecturing there.[42] Apparently Mounier was faulted at the sGJ (as well as by directors of the scouts and Chantiers) for "talking politics" rather than simply preaching fidelity to the Marshal.[43] In an effort to console the disappointed Mounier, Segonzac apologetically remarked that Darlan did not "have the sense of the spiritual";[44] both de Naurois and Mounier, however, had noted that Darlan had been quite successful in turning a few heads at the school.[45] In any case, these expulsions led to Uriage's publishing its distinctive positions under the less rhetorical, more down-to-earth Hubert Beuve-Méry.[46]

After Mounier's departure, his personalism was still very well represented at Uriage by his philosophical alter ego Jean Lacroix, and also by, among others, the multifaceted Bertrand d'Astorg who joined the Study Bureau in July 1941 on the invitation of Segonzac.[47] Curiously, d'Astorg came from the same radical Catholic and personalist circle as the dismissed Abbé de Naurois, having encountered the Esprit group as a law student in Toulouse in the person of the free spirit André Déléage, then correspondent of *Esprit* for south-western France. D'Astorg had become, in his words, "very attached" to the journal and to early personalists such as Mounier, Arnaud Dandieu of the Ordre Nouveau, the Swiss personalists Denis de Rougemont and Albert Béguin, and poet Pierre Emmanuel, among whom he was moved to find "contempt for politics and politicians" and a "tragic sense of the powerlessness of the state."[48]

D'Astorg had then participated in the work of the Collège de sociologie and lived, for several years, in the company of the Catholic utopians – and future Vichy-era culture activists – Paul Flamand and Pierre Schaeffer in their Poitvins community (which was then creating the future Éditions du Seuil[49] in the form of an anti-capitalist and co-operative *librairie* inspired by ideals close to those of *Esprit*.)[50] D'Astorg had befriended Catholic revival writers and poets like Francis Jammes and Pierre Emmanuel, and had won several literary prizes of his own in the pre-war period while achieving both a license-es-lettres and a doctorate in law with his thesis "Le Réveil de la neutralité dans la crise de la Société des Nations." After joining Air France in January 1939 at twenty-five years of age, d'Astorg fought in the battle for France, was captured by the Germans in 1940, escaped, and rejoined the headquarters of the national airline in the southern zone, at Marseille. Sent to Uriage for a training session as a representative of Air France in February 1941, he had found the radical Catholic atmosphere to his liking and accepted Segonzac's invitation to come back to the school and stay on. Despite coming to be known as "the poet of Uriage," d'Astorg "looked like a cavalry officer" and was "an unusual mixture of inspired unease, and military and aristocratic pride."[51]

The Abbé de Naurois's absence, meanwhile, was filled by a young Dominican who had the angular and austere features of a Zurbaran monk, Jean Maydieu.[52] Maydieu, originally from Bordeaux, was a former member of the extreme right nationalist movement the Camelots du Roi ("newsvendors of the King") and had been trained as a mining engineer (like SGJ secretary Lamirand whom Maydieu had come to know well). After military service in the artillery, he had entered the Dominican seminary of Saulchoir, emerging as an important figure by publishing the burgeoning Dominican publications. First, as director of *La Vie Intellectuelle*, contributor to *Sept* (and leader of the "Amis de *Sept*"), and then, when *Sept* was silenced, as "chaplain" of the "Amis du *Temps présent*"[53] (the support group for *Sept*'s laymen-run successor), Maydieu had become one of France's best-travelled and best-known younger priest-intellectuals.[54] He knew Pierre Dunoyer de Segonzac from the latter's visits to the Dominican convent of Latour- Maubourg in Paris, through the *Esprit* group, and particularly through that great friend of the Dominicans who was Hubert Beuve-Méry. Father Maydieu's influence on the school, and on the Vieux Chef, would prove to be very important. Some years later, Segonzac would recall Maydieu's unique role:

A difference of temperament surfaced [among the staff of the Uriage school] ... On the one hand there were men of action, down to earth and perhaps somewhat abrupt, oriented toward simple solutions; on the other hand there were thinkers looking for doctrinal clarification, theorists a bit on the abstract side. We lacked the unfindable man who had the qualities of both yet had enough superiority, naturally or given by grace, to be above question. It was then that Father Maydieu appeared.[55]

Beuve-Méry later admitted that he had worked to have Maydieu come to the Château Bayard to counter the influence of the Abbé de Naurois;[56] accordingly, the Dominican's arrival was another sign of Beuve-Méry's growing moral and intellectual ascendancy over Uriage. Back at Vichy, Lamirand and Garrone seemed to have hoped that the Abbé de Naurois's replacement would be a dedicated but docile, middle-of-the-road Pétainist; if so, they may have been disappointed by the high-profile priest-intellectual Maydieu who, like Bertrand d'Astorg, soon revealed himself to be a supporter of the most ambitious and original ideas of Beuve-Méry and of Segonzac.[57]

By the summer of 1941, when its role within the National Revolution was dramatically upgraded, Segonzac's school – which had not been particularly intellectually oriented at the outset -began to exert a special fascination for the rising stars of France's younger Catholic intellectual elite. Uriage had attracted, in the person of Henri de Lubac, a man who would become one of France's best-known post-war theologians and a cardinal of the Roman Catholic Church; in

Beuve-Méry France's most influential postwar journalist, founder of
Le Monde, France's greatest newspaper; in Mounier the man who
would be celebrated as the founder of personalism and director of
one of France's most prominent postwar intellectual publications; in
Lacroix one of France's most renowned postwar philosophers; and in
Maydieu the director of one of France's most significant theological
journals and a central figure in the lively intellectual ferment within
the Dominican order. And these men were only among the best
known of the instructors or lecturers who would play outstanding
roles in French political, intellectual, and religious life after the war.

It is worth noting, too, that these energetic, intelligent, capable,
and articulate men were put together in highly unusual and challenging circumstances – they were ensconced in a chateau up in the
mountains with a commission to completely rethink and transform
the way France educated its young people. Many of them had been
thinking about how to rejuvenate their country, train adolescents, or
promote religious renewal before the war. Now they had their chance.
The heady atmosphere was recalled with evident nostalgia, years
later, by Segonzac:

Ceci se passait autrefois en des temps plus misérables que ceux d'aujourd'hui,
mais plus riches d'espoir.

Comme nous étions beaucoup plus jeunes, et même vraiment jeunes, nous
avons choisi de refaire le monde, entre nous, dans une sorte de monastère
qui avait abrité des chevaliers authentiques, au Moyen-Age, puis des touristes
équivoques, au XXe siècle, et qui cachait enfin notre détresse d'enfants
trahis ...

Il fallait donc retrouver des raisons de vivre ...

La base de départ était bonne, puisque nous rassemblions des clients de
toutes les paroisses, les uns et les autres pleins d'idées préconçues, très
variées, mais pas encore cristallisées dans une opposition réciproque.

Et dès l'abord le sentiment grisant qu'une sorte d'unité spirituelle pourrait
s'établir entre nous, malgré nos différences aussi accusées qu'elles puissent
être, nous avait saisis."[58]

The influence of the Uriage men within the National Revolution
might be resisted and, eventually, apparently, opposed and undone.
But their longer-term influence, particularly in the rise of certain
Catholic elites in post-war France, would be remarkable.[59]

BEUVE-MÉRY'S PROJECTS

When Beuve-Méry returned to Uriage in June 1941 he dreamed of
creating a "communitarian order" to struggle against "anarchic

individualism" and "the reign of money." He wanted a more authoritarian state offset by revitalized intermediary bodies (such as families, professional organizations, youth movements, and "écoles des
cadres"). Accordingly, he was very interested in the "Planist" economics of Henri de Man, as well as in reorganizing production units
into the "communautés de travail" proposed by economist François
Perroux.[60] He also thought that the French nation should reintroduce
"Dieu à l'école et dans la cité" and, in the circumstances, lead an
austere and laborious life "inspired by the better traditions and qualities of the race."[61]

On a somewhat more practical level, Beuve-Méry envisioned creating lay "Order" communities, committed to spiritual values. These
were intended to save civilization, for he foresaw an impending collapse when, as he confided to Mounier, "everything would end up in
a general collapse and a return to the land-clearing monks."[62] This
pessimistic analysis was seconded by a distinguished historian in the
Esprit group, Henri-Irénée Marrou, who saw striking analogies
between the present and his special period of study, the late Roman
Empire.

The imminent demise of "liberalism" and "individualism" was tac-
itly assumed among many personalists,[63] and this historical deter-
minism dissuaded Beuve-Méry from frontal attacks on the new
authoritarianism in Europe (although he endorsed the idea of a
Europe-wide return to the ancient provinces, on the Swiss model, as
an antidote to centralized tyranny). At Uriage a *völkisch* federalism,
similar to that nurtured in groups like the Ordre Nouveau circle
before the war, shone in contrast to the concern for the fundamental
liberal and democratic values that others considered essential to the
resistance against world totalitarianism and fascism. Still, Beuve-
Méry came out publicly against collaboration with Germany in the
circumstances, since "the liberation of [French] territory is a *sine qua
non* condition for all national revolution and for all sincere collaboration."[64]

Beuve-Méry's intellectual ascendancy over the École Nationale des
Cadres was not immediately apparent: in his (very favourable) report
on his Uriage course in summer 1941, trainee Paul Delouvrier noted
that the school, in the view of several trainees, seemed to lack clear
doctrines and direction.[65] And in his long description of Uriage in
Temps nouveau, in August,[66] Beuve-Méry simply echoed Segonzac's
line that the Uriage community need not elaborate their ideas
because they were all contained in the speeches of the head of state
and that it was the school's "method, its spirit" that constituted its
celebrated originality.[67] In reality, however, the key men of Uriage

had every intention of clarifying and fleshing out the method and spirit they had discovered.

THE CHARTER

In the next months, under Beuve-Méry's direction, the Uriage study group produced the Uriage Charter, "L'esprit d'Uriage," a "rule of life of a community." It was intended for internal use, and references to "collective experience" tended to eclipse references to the Marshal or the National Revolution. This Charter described a fundamental commitment in the community to "the sense and service of the spiritual." While only "a religious faith" would give "full value to that affirmation," in the absence of a religious faith, the aspiration of "a man of good will," determined to "transcend himself" while striving toward the ideal, would be recognized as nurturing an authentic interior life.[68]

While historian Bernard Comte found that the first chapter of the Charter of Uriage displayed very much "the vocabulary and structures of thought familiar to the readers of Jacques Maritain,"[69] the bulk of the document showed no special deference to Maritain or to anyone else. Rather it described a pluralistic convergence, in Péguyist style, of all the "mystiques" of the country "in a unity of heart and of action under the sign of France." It recommended that the country "in its own style and according to its own traditions ... promote a new order serving the accomplishment of the human person."

The community also endorsed a special series of virtues as particularly suitable for the circumstances: the "sense of honour," loyalty, generosity, sense of justice, sense of grandeur in simplicity, taste for commitment, just sense of strength, fidelity, a taste for enterprise "carried out to the point of adventure and of risk, without vain bravado but not without a certain *panache*." There was a striking insistence that men be brave, athletic, etcetera, with "elegance," and there was a noticeable lack of references to the Marshal.[70]

The Uriage Charter was at the same time a communitarian and an unashamedly elitist document. While avoiding the "capital sin of caste spirit," the community recognized that the first condition for national renewal was the "determining and putting in place of authentic elites" (implicitly, this meant replacing the old liberal, Jewish, masonic elites with new men). Building upon the legacy of the Catholic intellectual revival, and with authoritarian backing, the community intended to replace "republican" elites with "spiritualist" elites (who were not anti-religious, Jewish, *normaliens*, foreigners, egoists, or sensualists).[71]

For the men of Uriage, individualism, feminism, trade unions, republican and democratic instincts, mainstream parliamentarianism, money, pleasure-seeking, unbridled intellectual inquiry were all unhealthy forces, and thus they became determined to extirpate the "individual" in each trainee in order that his better part, his "person," might flourish. The indissoluble links tying individual destinies together were described in lyrical Claudelian imagery: "Economic ties, carnal ties, spiritual ties weave the stuff of human communities on a triple chain; the threads of individual destinies are woven in an indissoluble solidarity."[72] There were also the demands of "social construction": "authority, hierarchy, organization, interdependence, limitation of liberty. And above all the sacrifice of individual goods for the common good in everything temporal."[73] It was lofty, romantic talk, well suited to a lofty, romantic place. It is remarkable that the enthusiasm reflected here could have been fostered in a humiliated and war-torn country venerating "a vapid old man whose mind was known to be frustratingly ordinary by those associated closely with him (and whose life was itself somewhat less than beyond reproach)."

"L'Esprit d'Uriage" was succeeded, toward the end of January 1942, by *La Charte de la communauté*, which was adopted for the new, extended, six-month leadership class. Citing the Marshal, and the need for authority and discipline, Segonzac wrote, "the school community is a veritable national community in miniature, and perhaps the only place where it is possible to do healthy thinking about the problems of the hour," and he asserted that the community had its "statement to make." In this new "community" charter, Segonzac described the mission of Uriage as the forming of "a youth elite" for future tasks, in making them "as complete as possible, Frenchmen of good race, leaders equally prepared to serve and to command."[74]

A striking part of the new charter was a definition of the "spiritual dimension" so important to the community: "the profound aspiration of man for invisible realities that transcend him, give his life its *raison d'être*, its meaning and its value." The community would nurture the spiritual aspect of life:

That aspiration, which is always of a religious nature, is the divine part of man. It allows him to attain unity of conscience or spirit, to ordain all his life to a vocation, to assure the fidelity of his *témoignage*, in a word to be a person. That does not necessarily imply adhesion to a specific religion: believers and non-believers are, in France, sufficiently impregnated with Christianity that the better among them could meet, beyond revelations and dogmas, at the level of the communion of persons, in the same quest for truth, justice, love.[75]

This text evidences the direct personalist *Esprit* inspiration, and perhaps the mysticism of Henri Bergson as filtered through *Esprit* down to the Uriage Study Bureau. It is worth pointing out also that this reforming of men and reforming of Christianity was being nurtured among *men* living a manly life-style "with panache" in an ascetic, quasi-monastic community of the chosen and the "pure."

Although the École Nationale des Cadres d'Uriage was supposed to be a "national" elite school, its Catholic style was evident in the community charter. The strong Catholic backgrounds of most of the instructors[76] help to explain the growing monastic bearing of a school whose charter's rules resembled those of a religious community. For example, entry into the "community" passed through the four stages of the "call" defined by the Vieux Chef. Punishments included open confession of one's faults by the accused, and penalties ranged from moral reprimand to public reproach. In all of this the sense of honour figured as a very important sanction. The community charter required obedience, "entire in spirit and in fact," to the Vieux Chef and, while praising "initiative," it stressed the virtues of "total frankness, absolute sincerity" and, perhaps to sweeten the pill, "gaiety."[77] Not surprisingly, the school's critics were soon deriding the quasi-religious and totalitarian side of "the spirit of Uriage."

The emphasis on authority at Uriage came partly from the consensus among many Catholics and the military that weak leadership had accelerated French decadence in the 1930s and precipitated the collapse of France in 1940. The guides of Uriage considered education for leadership the most important way to change things.[78] Therefore, they abandoned the idea of an anonymous, purely intellectual selection system, such as that in use for candidates to the *grandes écoles* before the war, in favour of a selection process in which the national leadership school would choose candidates, from the graduates of France's foremost professional schools, who had been distinguished for their "leadership abilities." These could then be combined with other young people "coming from everywhere and remarkable simply for their aptitude to command."[79]

In the school itself, Segonzac enjoyed an absolute "authority without appeal" that seems never to have been seriously challenged. Segonzac tried to make no distinction between Catholic and non-Catholic trainees, but he did assert that religious training was one of the goals of Uriage[80] and he showed that he felt he represented Catholic religious discipline (e.g., in reproaching a group of Catholic members of the *équipe* who went skiing on a Sunday morning instead of attending mass).[81]

This imperious "Uriage style" was not to everyone's taste, and there were predictable tensions between the ex-scouts or military men at

Uriage and the "intellectuals" who, the former felt, behaved patron-izingly toward them. Nonetheless, Beuve-Méry was able to impose his views, even on those critical of his cynical ways – what they called his "negativism," or "intellectually anarchist" ways.[82] One former trainee recalled his own growing discomfort in "that improvised 'com-munity' that imitated both regiment and monastery, without allowing its members either the inward liberty that army discipline allowed soldiers or the personal space that the rule of monastic silence afforded."[83] And then there were regular debates over the compati-bility of Christian values with the Uriage style: the sort of *force* (strength) the school should nurture was regularly set against the "Nietzschean sense" of *force*.[84] The intelligentsia at the school were much concerned with the relationship between traditional religious values and what they perceived as "the Revolution of the twentieth century."[85] Beuve-Méry performed a remarkable balancing act in keeping the Uriage coalition together.

THE IDEA OF AN ORDER

The idea of creating an Order at Uriage occurred early in the life of the school.[86] Orders of dedicated laymen were fairly common in French Catholic circles by the late 1930s,[87] and Beuve-Méry had alluded to the possibility of an Order in his essay on "A Personalist and Communitarian Revolution." This was another area in which Uriage was the heir of decades of efforts by participants in the Catholic intellectual revival and non-Marxist revolutionary thinkers to create alternate institutions. Ever since the 1920s, Father Doncoeur had trumpeted the chivalric spirit of Joan of Arc as essential to Christian reconstruction, the defence of the *patrie*, and the formation of the elites required for these tasks. Indeed Catholic scout law, in contrast to that of its Protestant rivals (which required simple cour-tesy), included an obligation to be "chivalrous."[88]

The 1920s had also witnessed Jacques Maritain's call for the "pri-macy of the spiritual," and Berdyaev's prediction of *Un nouveau Moyen Âge* (Paris, 1927). That same year Belgian socialist Hendrik de Man's *Au-delà du marxisme* (1927) had called for the spiritual renewal of the socialist movement through an elite who would provide a living example of their own interior transformation before going out to propagate their ideas.

Later, in early 1933, Henri Daniel-Rops, a high-profile convert to Catholicism and member of the Ordre Nouveau movement, suggested a *corps franc* of chivalries, and an Order.[89] In 1933–34 Mounier and Maritain were interested in the efforts of the young Belgian Esprit and Ordre Nouveau contact, Raymond de Becker, to try to create an Order out of his movement Communauté. Some of the most distinguished Trappist reformers in France had participated in that effort.

De Becker's "order" was to be explicitly Catholic, dedicated to the spiritual purification of its members, while also engaging in political or social action.[90] In fact, a young man who would be a future member of the Uriage team, Paul Thisse, was one of those who had met with de Becker and his Belgian friends at the French Cistercian abbey of Tamié in this period to prepare for the creation of an "order."[91] De Becker's partner of the time, Emmanuel Mounier, basing his analysis on a questionnaire that *Esprit* had sent out, reflected in 1935: "There is today a common desire to create a sort of 'lay order' where tools such as those we have set out here ... will generate honour-based commitments, and, given their public nature, exert considerable attraction."[92]

In 1938 Catholic youth leader Georges Bidault (a future Resistance leader) envisioned a "new chivalry to be founded against the new barbarians," and there followed in 1938–39 the "Order of the Companions of Péguy."[93] In 1939, too, future Vichy Foreign Minister Paul Baudouin called for "the renaissance, in the humble form of a lay-men's order, of the chivalry of old times" to defend the spiritual patrimony of the Christian West.[94] Years later French Catholic writer Jean Guitton waxed nostalgic in recalling all of those bold projects of the 1930s, when zealous Christians dreamed of founding new orders, a bit like the monks of the West, like the Franciscan or Dominican order, or, better still, like chivalry in the Middle Ages – to promote a "laymen's Order for the new times," to prepare the "new Middle Ages":

Est-ce que les réunions maçonniques, ces clubs qui ont précédé ceux des jacobins, les premiers soviets n'étaient pas aussi des ensemencements? Est-ce qu'on ne pourrait pas reprendre sous une autre forme accomodée à notre temps, cet effort pour transformer une société en y insinuant une sorte de noblesse dépouillée, un "petit reste" comme en Israël, prophétique et laïc?[95]

Many of those pre-war efforts to create a new chivalry, to revivify France, celebrated by Guitton, were essentially opposed to contemporary sexual permissiveness, critical of "americanized" women, even opposed to the whole egalitarian, liberal, and democratic heritage of 1789. Uriage's heavy inheritance of cultural pessimism was behind the school's effort to institutionalize the "Uriage spirit" in the form of an Order.

The idea of creating an Order at Uriage also grew from the instructors' perceptions of the apocalyptic implications of the 1940 defeat. For example, during his first conference at Uriage in early 1941, Jean Lacroix had the prospect of a long domination of Nazism over continental Europe, or, failing that, a destruction of German military power by fire and blood in a ruined Europe given over to anarchy.[96] Emmanuel Mounier, for his part, envisaged the disappearance of institutional Christianity,[97] and approvingly cited Beuve-Méry's belief that "everything would finish in a general destruction, with a return to the land-clearer monks".[98] So it was that Uriage, like several other Catholic-oriented communities of the time, tended to believe that liberty might disappear from Europe for a long time. Thus the school joined fervently religious communitarian-style enterprises – such as that recently begun by the young Protestant intellectual Roger Shutz at Taizé, ten kilometres from the ruins of the ancient abbey of Cluny[99] – in adopting a mystical perspective that encouraged men to band together for mutual support like those monks of the late Roman Empire who laid the foundations for a new culture in a Europe overrun by the barbarians. Brother Roger's Taizé set out to create a community built upon the dream of a *Humanisme intégral*, joining young Catholics and Protestants – and even Christians and non-Christians, believers and non-believers – in living and practising a quasi-monastic communitarian life, a "new Christianity," in what has proved an inspiring experience for young people from all over Europe – and the world – to this day.

In contrast to the more ecumenical, strictly spiritual thrust of Taizé, the monastic style of Uriage contained the promise of a kind of idealistic communism that, as in the great orders of the Middle Ages, could transcend not only Christian theological differences but social class and ideological conflicts. A contributor to *Jeunesse ... France!* contrasted "the deplorable spirit of the pre-war years ... with its class antagonisms" to the school's "frankness and simplicity" and its teamwork, which constituted "a sort of retreat in common," encouraging the realization that the "qualities of the race are found in all of the different milieux" and "the confrontation of different points of view, which until then vainly confronted one another ... now, most often, proved reconcilable."[100] Georges Lamirand underlined this point on a visit to Uriage, saying "the Uriage school is entrusted with the mission of bringing together the elites from all of the groups that ought to participate in the common task of reconstruction in the same spirit of collaboration."[101]

The school had done very well by the end of its first year of existence, having taught, during the first fifteen months of its activity (September 1940–November 1941), around a thousand students in ten regular three-week sessions, and six hundred in special sessions.[102] It had created an attractive, even charismatic, community in a prestigious setting,[103] formed a network of affiliates, and was playing a respectable and valued social role in forming leaders for the government according to its own original method.

The school enjoyed political and church support, and nationwide supportive contacts. Through the offices of the Prefect of l'Isère, it took measures to legalize the fait accompli and legally expropriated, from November 1940, not only the chateau and dependent buildings, with eight hectares (c. twenty acres) of grounds, but also a sixteen-hectare farm and the "chalet Reymond" (recently built by a Grenoble industrialist) as a residence for the Segonzac family. Besides the twenty instructors, the Uriage school soon had fifteen employees (gardeners, kitchen help, a telephone operator, two chauffeurs, etc.) and, by the end of 1941, it would be employing a dozen secretaries for its various publications, its "Équipe nationale d'Uriage" (alumni network), and several other projects. The ten "team chalets" (with twenty students per chalet) had been named after many of the same heroes of national, colonial, or Christian legend as the cohorts of the school: Joan of Arc, Foucauld, Mermoz, Bayard, Lyautey, Saint-Louis, Roland, Guynemer, Chatellus, d'Alançon.[104] In a humiliated, demoralized, and impoverished France, the new elites of Uriage were relatively well appointed and full of hope for the future.[105]

In that summer of 1941, the General Secretary of the Youth Secretariat was delighted with Segonzac's school: on visiting Uriage, the rather naively enthusiastic Lamirand made a great point of shaking hands warmly, looking everyone in the eye. (A postwar story has it that as a joke one after the other of the Uriage class climbed out of the window and went down a drain pipe, to reappear at the door and then shake his hand again – only to receive, again, the same "personal" attention).[106]

Back at Vichy the devout Catholic Louis Garrone, a close ally of the travelling Lamirand and of Uriage, was, for one year, the "true head of the youth policy in the southern zone." Professor of philosophy at the elite École des Roches at Verneuil,[107] Garrone had been named by Jacques Chevalier to the new sgj (youth secretariat) as a senior official.[108] Garrone himself had tended to hire young Catholic *agrégés* or graduates of "Sciences Po" who were tuned in to avant-garde reviews such as *Esprit* rather than the reactionary *Action Fran-çaise* or the more cautious publications of the Christian Democrats. Predictably, Henri Massis, "conseiller technique" to the sgj and watchdog for the Action Française, was kept at arm's length by Garrone, who was soon faulted by Massis as too susceptible to Christian Democrat and personalist influences.

In July 1941 Garrone held a special meeting in the Château Bayard for the personnel of his "Direction de la Formation des jeunes," calling for a transcending of divisive ideologies and the "restoration of the French Community" by wedding personalism with total fidelity to Pétain. During that summer Garrone saw Uriage as a model institution, thanks to the dedication and faith of its founders, and affirmed his belief that it would create a youth elite that would transform the country.[109] In fact Uriage had become vital to the government's leadership training program for, as an official SGJ communication put it: "One school dominates the others, the École Nationale d'Uriage, a veritable Mother-school; its program and spirit serve as a model, and it has furnished the instructors for the regional schools."[110]

Uriage seemed to embody the post-liberal and post-capitalist ideal community that had been "in the air" in certain Catholic circles for some time. Uriage was only a beginning for men like Beuve-Méry's close friend and contributor to the same Catholic reviews, Georges Hourdin. In 1942 Hourdin sketched the dream[111] of having even contemporary scholars and artists live in community like the ancient monks and create a new culture: "Les foyers culturels de demain et les revues de position même politiques ne traceront les grandes lignes de l'*ordre* nouveau après lequel le monde aspire que si, se référant à l'expérience monastique, ils constituent d'abord eux-mêmes, dans leur lieu de travail, une sorte d'ordre nouveau."[112]

More and more, journalists began referring to the men of Uriage as *moines chevaliers* ("knight-monks"),[113] and the symbols on the Château Bayard's publications – a knight, mounted and armed from head to foot, his face entirely hidden, and a cross on his shield – encouraged this idea. For these men, fired by romantic oratory and literature, knighthood exemplified the virtues of honour and generosity over against the individualism and materialism of the bourgeois and urbanized modern era.

Austere, ascetic, virile, visionary, romantic, Uriage captured the imagination of observers such as the New Right writer Alfred Fabre-Luce, who found a kind of Order when he visited in fall 1941:

The select youth of Uriage are like the first cell of a new world introduced into a worn-out one ... From a union of young and ardent young men, in a sublime setting *from which women are excluded* [emphasis mine], an enduring force is coming to birth. Beyond the France of Pétain will survive, if necessary, an Order of Knights of Uriage.[114]

Twenty years later Fabre-Luce again, more briefly, recalled his visit to Uriage and concluded, "On that hill, I dreamed for a time of an

Order of Knights who would maintain lofty values in the vulgarized twentieth-century world."[115] Thus the Vieux Chef was not a solitary dreamer. A man like Fabre-Luce, whose intuitive efforts to sketch out the future France of the New Order were widely read, immediately recognized that Dunoyer de Segonzac's school was a powerful symbol of a very different kind of France.

Pétain and his circle did not represent the total spectrum of political power in occupied France, and at the end of their first year, the knight-monks of Uriage encountered other elements competing for the loyalties of French youth, particularly those in the occupied zone. On 15 June 1941, "French youth meetings" organized by the "Jeunesse France" committee and the weekly journal *Jeunesse* were held at the Salle Wagram in Paris. The diminutive, white-haired *académicien* Abel Bonnard – perennial candidate of committed collaborationists to head the education ministry at Vichy – was prominent.[116] This Wagram show took place in a "style close to fascism," where Georges Lamirand and his fascist-leaning deputy Georges Pelorson (who had been assigned to Lamirand by Bonnard) gave the most memorable speeches.[117] Lamirand could, apparently, look more than one group squarely in the eye.

Georges Pelorson, who had been placed in charge of youth propaganda in the SGJ in early 1941, used much the same chivalrous language but was in fact a curious foil to the high-minded, carefully Catholic Louis Garrone back at Vichy. Pelorson, a *normalien* and writer, was director of his own innovative private school and a firm anti-clerical. Founder of the avant-garde review *Volontés* (for which Pierre Prévost of Ordre Nouveau wrote, and which had ties with Georges Bataille's Collège de sociologie) and close friend of absurdist playwright Samuel Beckett, Pelorson also presented a vivid contrast to the devout and devoted Pétainist Lamirand (who was spending much of his time travelling the country giving uplifting orations).[118]

At the Wagram meeting, the officious Pelorson proved noticeably more *fascisant* than Lamirand, calling for "an absolute communion in the same faith, under the same flag, under the authority of the same leader," with mere lip-service to "the spiritual diversity of persons." As Chief of Youth Propaganda he subsequently addressed a Catholic public, employing personalist terminology but also vaunting the "mystique du chef," opposing individualism while respecting "the human spiritual person." But the totalitarian-style meetings and personalist language of Pelorson deviated widely from Lamirand's gatherings in the south, where Compagnons and scouts were making frequent, if somewhat ritualistic, references to the Marshal and his sayings.[119]

Still, notwithstanding competing efforts such as Pelorson's, the École Nationale de Cadres d'Uriage was a remarkable, successful, more and more distinctive institution by the summer of 1941. But as the existence of rival movements suggests, the efforts of the Uriage staff were based upon certain questionable assumptions – some regarding the course of the war, human nature, and the German occupation; others regarding Marshal Pétain and his government. Soon the Uriage enterprise would face some serious challenges to its most firmly held assumptions and ambitions.

CHAPTER THREE

The Uriage Experience

AT THE HEIGHT OF ITS GLORY

During the second half of 1941 the École Nationale des Cadres d'Uriage was, for its admirers, the flagship of the National Revolution, the first school in the land, the training centre of France's new elites. But was Uriage during its heyday in fact the truly national institution its title implied? Who was studying and teaching there? What was their daily life, and their real relationship with the Vichy government? What was the actual agenda of Dunoyer de Segonzac and his staff – for example, with regard to Vichy's youth movements, or toward modern women? How should history judge the Uriage experience?

Admiral Darlan's new policy of requiring the students of France's most selective and prestigious schools to take a course at Uriage could hardly fail to flatter Segonzac, who perhaps even negotiated it with the head of the government. But from July 1941 the school had to deal with an influx of young civil servants who had had the course imposed on them, after being selected according to criteria very different from those applied to the previous hand-picked candidates for the school. Thus during the final months of 1941 those "special sessions" were set up for the graduates of the *grandes écoles* such as Polytechnique, or the École de l'Air, or the Saint-Cyriens of Aix-en-Provence, who attended the special sessions with regular army officers.[1]

Segonzac was no longer preaching just to the converted, but also to the ambitious.

Social Background of the School

There was a persistent problem in finding a place for the less favoured classes in French society at Uriage. We have seen how

Bénigno Cacérès, a Toulouse carpenter, was engaged as an instructor to give at least token representation to the urban working class. Cacérès' own account of his reception at the school by *chef* Joffre Dumazedier reveals a mixture of embarrassment, naive good will, and a rather patronizing curiosity:

Dumazedier asked me a multitude of questions. He asked me what I read, how I read it, what interested or struck me. And he oriented me along certain lines. In fact, I was a kind of guinea pig. I was the authentic "prolo" on whom he wanted to perfect his method of mental training, of understanding proletarian structures of thought. But I ought to give him [Dumazedier] credit. It was done with dignity, without paternalism. The others were paternalistic, unconsciously. Not Dumazedier. He even had a tendency to overvalue. When you left an interview with him, you took yourself for Jesus Christ![2]

Despite the best intentions and efforts of Segonzac, Dumazedier, and their like, only 6 to 8 per cent of the trainees (most in their twenties) in the more important training sessions at the school could be described as "workers," while there might be more than four times as many "personnel from industry," and three or four times as many "students."[3]

But if proletarians were noticeable for their relative rarity in the school, the number of peasants was almost non-existent, making up less than 1 per cent of the trainees.[4] Peasants seemed even more out of place in Uriage, with its estheticism and aristocratic panache, than they had been in the scouts.[5] This was illustrated by the strained relationship, even mutual contempt, between the Uriage school and the local population, which was noticed by many observers of the school.

"Old Uriage had something aristocratic and antipathetic that didn't make me happy, any more than it did the peasants of St. Martin d'Uriage," a former trainee turned instructor recalled.[6] There were even people in the village who "detested" Segonzac's school, and this had practical consequences given the difficulty of acquiring food in those stark days: farmers in the surrounding countryside refused to sell anything to Uriage, even preferring to vend their produce on the black market rather than let it get into the hands of those *chefs* who had taken the Château Bayard from the heirs of the Alleman family.[7] The local peasants may also have had something to do with the lurid stories about the school that filtered down to the city of Grenoble and set tongues wagging: the "knight-monks" were spoken of rather ironically, and it was alleged they kept beds in their offices and swam naked with their secretaries in the castle swimming pool. (This despite the fact that the only open water in the area, the castle pond, was overrun with weeds, and the *chefs* were distant to the point of rigidity toward the secretaries, as we shall see.)[8]

In short, working peoples' aversion toward Uriage's elitism undermined the school's claim to better the pre-war republican elites schools in representing the nation as a whole.[9] It was a serious shortcoming in a school that already excluded many social elements on the basis of ideology.

The enthusiastic candidates for Uriage came from the kind of people who frequented the high-powered circles of the Catholic intelligentsia (such as the Latour-Maubourg Dominicans or the Jacques Maritain *salon* at Meudon) before the war: from the army, ministries, the law, universities, the church, and, to a certain extent, industry. The school could therefore be faulted for reinforcing the pre-war French social pyramid and for complacently equating "elite" status with the competence and confidence that comes from education, family background, and previous "connections." In fact, the "new elites," the "true leaders" the school was to help to claim their just place in the nation, were still young men,[10] most of them in their mid-twenties (although nearly one-third were over thirty) and most from milieux favoured by birth or education.[11]

Thus the school was in danger of being accused of reaffirming traditional power relationships and social hierarchies, particularly the historical authority and privileges of the old aristocracy or bourgeoisie. Actually, the religious image of the school was pronounced: eight of the ten most prominent intellectuals associated with the school were of firm Catholic background – Hubert Beuve-Méry, Jean-Jacques Chevallier, Paul Reuter, Emmanuel Mounier, Jean Lacroix, Bertrand d'Astorg, Jean-Marie Domenach, and Paul-Henri Chombart de Lauwe (and this did not include the chaplains René de Naurois, Maydieu, and des Alleux, or prominent visiting lecturers such as Henri de Lubac). Only two of the Uriage intellectuals, Joffre Dumazedier and Gilbert Gadoffre,[12] came from other sorts of backgrounds: and both of them, like the "non-believers" who frequented Esprit circles, tended to think of the spiritual dimension of life as an invisible reality. An admiring historian of the school made the rather cavalier remark: "Certainly it [Uriage] was predominantly Catholic and Christian, but so is France."[13] It is crucial, however, to recall that Uriage was hoping to impose conformity, of a religiously inspired sort, on all of France, and, whatever certain Uriage members thought, most French people of the time were definitely not

"Catholic" as in the Uriage ideal. Such lofty medievalism was anathema to many, and pious nonsense to others.

There were always some who envisaged the school breaking down social classes, as in the original agenda of the German National Socialists. (At one point Segonzac put a stop to a Vichy film project on Uriage because "he didn't appreciate the simplistic exaltation of the decor and the exterior gestures envisaged by the film maker. The film would have illustrated, in his view, a mythology of the leader 'in the Ordensburgen style' rather than in the spirit of Uriage.")[14]

At any rate, Uriage did not really break down social classes the way revolutionary youth movements or leadership schools in other European countries had apparently been able to do. Dunoyer de Segonzac, summing up a major effort with the school's special six-month training session in the summer of 1942, perceived a failure of the school, and of the entire National Revolution, in this area:

Our six-month stagiares are coming back from the factories where they have spent a few days working as manual labourers. They confirmed what we have already learned from the representatives of the industrial world who have passed through Uriage; not only are workers in their totality not integrated into *the national community* [emphasis my own] but they are taking their distance from it, and that distancing, already larger than before the war, is continuing to grow.[15]

It is interesting to note that the people represented at Uriage simply assumed that they themselves were, as leaders, the ones best suited to measure the degree of integration of working people into the new "national community." The school's distant relationship with the nearby villagers was symptomatic of a national malady.

Daily Life

Daily life at Uriage had some striking features. Everyone was roused by a trumpet at seven in the morning, and there were five minutes to gather in shorts in front of the Château Bayard, so the physical education specialist Roger Vuillemin could lead the trainees across the grounds. (This ritual warm-up was not obligatory, but how could one abstain when all of the instructors, Segonzac at the head of them, participated?) For twenty minutes, there were exercises of various kinds, then jogging and running at full speed, and finally, upon regaining their wind, a brisk march to the château, chanting and in step, all the time being prodded by the dynamic physical education instructor with exhortations like "Allons garçons!" "Secouons-nous!" That merely began the days, for each of which every student had a page divided into quarter-hours, with particular activities marked by special colours.[16] The instructor known for his lectures on "the virile order," Jean-Jacques Chevallier, had special praise for the virtues of this morning warm-up:

A direct blow to that passivity that is our principal enemy at wake-up time in a freezing sunrise, it assures the victory, at the beginning of the day and perhaps for the whole day, of the *best part* of ourselves – the better, the active, alert, diligent, virile part – over the other, the *bad part* – the flabby, the passive, the lazy, the pleasure-loving, the negative – in a word, the destructive.[17]

What our age would find to be the rather awkward "macho" or sexist imagery of Hébert's "natural method" was in fact an important, if not universally popular, part of the Uriage "style."

Some differing views over the rough physical training imposed on the trainees at Uriage reveal some interesting things both about the school and the temper of the times in France. Despite the silence in the ranks, opinions were, in fact, quite varied about that famous morning *décrassage*:

For thirty minutes one ran across the countryside, jumped across little rivers several metres wide. And he [Vuillemin] spent his time bawling us out. Sometimes he would have us slow down so he could run up ahead to close a pasture gate so the men would have to jump over it. That determination to look for an obstacle at any cost always seemed very symbolic to me.

For Bénigno Cacérès, the only authentic proletarian on the staff, this *décrassage* was an uncomfortable and unnecessary conceit for men who had enjoyed more comfortable lives than his had been:

Vuillemin was a strong man, a bit of a brute, but likeable. An intellectual and he were cut of different cloth. One had to wake at the sound of a 6:30 trumpet to go out and roll in the snow, run, climb. I did the "warm-up" like everyone else, but I found it idiotic. Why get up at dawn when one could rest peacefully in bed? Everyone found that marvellous, but not me. And I told Vuillemin, "I have gotten up at five in the morning all of my life. For once when breakfast is at eight, because the courses only begin at nine, why should I warm up? And from what?"

The demanding physical efforts of the *décrassage* were succeeded, later in the day, by a thirty- or forty-minute session more explicitly based on the so-called "natural method" developed at the beginning of the century by Georges Hébert, a former naval officer turned physical education theorist. "Hébertisme" came to represent an ideology that was not universally popular, as was illustrated by Vuillemin's conduct at the afore-mentioned pasture gates. Lochard commented: "I still see Vuillemin closing the pasture gates with the troop behind him that he was continually scolding. Sometimes he made very strong negative remarks about intellectuals. That made me uncomfortable, particularly when he made them in a humourless way."

Chef Joffre Dumazedier, years later, saw it as a question of differing approaches between Vuillemin's hero – General Georges Hébert – and Pierre de Coubertin, founder of the Olympic games:

Vuillemin was a teacher of *décrassage* quite convinced of the value of the Hébert method. Between us there was always that old quarrel between Hébert and Coubertin. In the natural method climbing, walking, jumping, living like an animal, sufficed for developing the man. But for Coubertin, that was impossible, it was too primitive. [Coubertin thought] that gestures should reach their full potential – handsome, altruistic, efficacious. It was essential to cultivate them. Training in sports was necessary. It was important to confront groups with the body, to co-operate, to compete according to the rules.

Dumazedier later recalled the more "civilized" conception of physical education as alien to Uriage's rough coach: [Coubertin] was "another world. Vuillemin had doubts about all of that. A whole philosophy of 'sweat,' 'suffer' ... to be 'a man' marked Vuillemin's notion of physical education and of the role of the Uriage school."

Chaplain de Naurois also had some negative memories of that aspect of Uriage training:

I thought a lot about that aspect. There was a domineering emphasis which didn't agree with me ... the emphasis placed on physical energy, bodily dynamism. They were all younger than me and capable of physical efforts impossible for me. Moreover, I felt myself having both a pastoral responsibility and [an] intellectual and moral one.[18]

Thus even the priest-alpinist expressed retrospective reservations about the punishing, at times overtly anti-intellectual, physical regimen to which these young men – many of them after years of study and in their mid-twenties – were subjected.

While Vuillemin was making the "natural method" synonymous with Uriage, General Hébert himself, in 1942, published a third edition of his *L'éducation physique, virile et morale par la méthode naturelle* and in the preface made admiring remarks about "a foreign nation" that had been more perspicacious than France during the interwar period about the way in which physical education could be employed "to 'forge' a race." While in France "the time had been spent in discussions as to whether doctors or psychologists ought to direct the physical education of youth," other nations were forging men with an "intense and virile" program. Hébert called for the creation of a "virile culture by means of violent and dangerous exercises" and "of a moral culture celebrating noble sentiments."[19]

Thus not only *Hébertisme*, but Hébert himself, seemed to fit very well with a certain notion of the National Revolution and of a specifically French response to the European New Order. Hébert's natural method prevailed against its critics at Uriage and, at least partly because of Uriage's guiding role, it was also imposed as the official system of physical education on France as a whole. Physical education was not completely apolitical in Vichy France and, not surprisingly, there would be a strong reaction against *Hébertisme* after the liberation.

Of course the Uriage experience involved much more than a struggle for virility, and different people found different things to appreciate there. For example, law professor Paul Reuter came to the school in August 1941 with a wooden table that he had just crafted in a village in the Hautes-Alpes, and which he exhibited during his talk on manual labour. Reuter recalled Uriage as having offered "a partial and temporary experience of lay monasticism."[20]

Pierre Dunoyer de Segonzac, with his military and aristocratic ways, did much to shape the Uriage style. The Vieux Chef required strict punctuality from everyone, and the cohorts were required to go everywhere outside the chateau in step (not as a sign of militarization, Segonzac insisted, but because, in his words, "to go from one point to the other in order and in rhythmic step is the best way to move quickly, harmoniously, buoyantly"; he thought society as a whole could profit from this sort of discipline).[21] A person late for a meal (even when on an errand for a member of staff) had to sing through one of the school anthems before being allowed to sit down.[22]

Besides being a stickler for promptness, the head of Uriage also valued direct, "personal" contact: he met each individual trainee on his arrival and "with his clear look and patient voice assessed his intentions."[23] Each new potential instructor was also met by Segonzac, who asked about his goals and convictions, promised to respect them, and assured him that he would be clearly told "what was not working," and that the same frankness would, in turn, be expected from him.[24]

Like many other provincial Catholics of his class and generation, Segonzac was a rigorous anti-materialist affecting a veritable contempt for money.[25] (An anecdote recounted by several of the alumni: "Greeting a very promising candidate, with several academic degrees, for a position on the staff, Segonzac suddenly broke off the interview and showed him the door; the young man had wanted to know, first of all, what his monthly salary would be.")[26]

Among the other controversial characteristics of the school were the emphasis on hierarchy, the cults of leadership and personality, and the anti-republicanism that prevailed. Paul Grillet, an alumnus of the six-month training session, recalled a rather oppressive pecking order:

What bothered me was the separation between the leaders, the lesser leaders, the lesser-lesser leaders, the almost leaders, and the not-at-all leaders! There was a hierarchy that came from I don't know where, from before 1789, which was super-irritating. The central team were gods. Below there were people who were affiliated but not really part of them. And then the group apart, the *stagiaires*; they were "small beer." Finally the others, the civilians, were mere tourists! It was a very elitist hierarchy.[27]

And although Uriage claimed to be above mere politics, it had a deeply anti-Republican cast – shown by the fact that no one seems to have spoken a single word in favour of the defunct Republic during the entire life of the Uriage school. Recalling that fact years later, Dunoyer de Segonzac simply thought the school reflected the attitude of the whole country: "The Uriage school did not pronounce itself firmly on the strictly political plane. However, I never heard the Third Republic defended, either by the team or by the *stagiaires* or the numerous visitors. It seemed that it had been condemned by all of the French."[28] The tendency of these young men with Catholic backgrounds to consider themselves "above politics" while maintaining a visceral hostility to republican institutions would orient their conduct during the war. Already by the summer of 1941 there were many men of Uriage who would brook no compromise with the Republican past but, as firm "Pétainists," were determined to resist the encroachment of the German occupant.[29]

The particular ways, the special "style," of the École Nationale des Cadres could hardly please everyone. The stiff and "offended" bridling of several future foreign service officers during the Uriage experience became common knowledge in the youth movements circles and was even reported in the press. Some newly minted degree-holders, unhappy to be cut off from the intellectual life they had known, disliked having to submit to tests of obedience, physical prowess, and leadership abilities. Some detested the austere living conditions, or living cheek to jowl in community with people of very different ages and backgrounds, and feelings of mutual hostility occasionally surfaced.

For other trainees, already committed to working with one youth movement or another, Uriage was simply a pleasant and useful complement, with "familiar vocabulary and ways." Some of the older trainees found selected aspects of the training useful (e.g., pedagogical methods, the notions of civic virtues), but never thought of committing themselves to the movement the school was beginning to represent.

Among the more enthusiastic adherents to the spirit of Uriage, at least a few – as even the instructors admitted – were very naive politically, displaying more "revolutionary" fervour than critical sense. Certain trainees of the first sessions saw no more in the "spirit of Uriage" than conformity to the directives of Lamirand: faith in the National Revolution and devotion to its leader, determination to create something new while abolishing the heritage of the "old regime" – a basically moral, if not moralizing, notion of the problems of the nation and of its youth. But while attitudes among the trainees toward the Uriage experience varied considerably, it is clear that for a good number of them Uriage was "a decisive experience," even "a veritable turning point in their lives."[30] Whether pleasant or unpleasant to the initiate, it was unique.

Vichy Relations

The Uriage school would not have risen to a position of some prominence and influence without highly placed sympathizers at Vichy. Among these, in addition to the government bureaucrats we have mentioned, were several intellectuals in the Marshal's immediate entourage, such as the Protestant writer René Gillouin. An authoritarian traditionalist linked to Abel Bonnard and General Weygand before the war, Gillouin was a special adviser to Pétain, for whom he wrote many speeches and texts. One of the principal inspirers of the philosophy of the regime, he was, at the same time, an anti-German and anti-Nazi patriot as hostile to the collaboration of Darlan as to that of Laval, and opposed to the anti-semitic measures of the government.[31] Gillouin had a sympathetic interest in personalism that went back to the old "Moulin-Vert" discussion group in the early 1930s and the founding of the Ordre Nouveau group. He related his very favourable impression of his visit to Uriage to the Marshal, who registered his "profound satisfaction."[32] Thus it is not surprising that after the regime's banning of the personalist journal *Esprit*, Mounier had a long conversation with Gillouin, whom he found very indignant and sincerely sympathetic, and he received "an astonishingly courageous" letter of support from him.[33]

Gillouin's strong support for Mounier was in line with his own "personalism"[34] and is indicative of the thinking of the "Vichy that might have been" in the entourage of the Marshal. Men like Gillouin envisaged Pétain less as a shield against the enemy than as the patron of a distinctly French national revolution that would make a place for their country, distinct from that of the Germans, in a new, authoritarian (German-dominated) kind of Europe.

Another writer from the Pétain circle was the biographer of Pétain, René Benjamin, a member of the Académie française and well-known author of novels glorifying the virtues of life in the countryside and traditional values.[35] Benjamin made a lyrical announcement, in a headline article of the newspaper *Candide*, of his visit of discovery to what he called the "Château de l'Âme" at Uriage – one of the places (like the Chantiers de la Jeunesse) where France was "rediscovering her soul." He even claimed to recognize at Uriage the peculiar and particular spirit that his hero, the Marshal, was trying to transmit to their countrymen:[36]

It is a sublime poet's notion [Benjamin wrote] to envisage moulding leaders high in the mountains, in a castle where Bayard had lived. But what might only be a poet's dream is, in fact, a reality.

The "Ecole des cadres" installed by M. Dunoyer de Segonzac in the Château d'Uriage on a marvellous rock that towers above the valley, where ordinary men live with day-to-day problems, is a school that is not only existing but prospering.

Forming leaders is a noble ambition! This people almost died because it was no longer being led. And it is a moving notion to literally elevate someone who is to be perfected; to raise him, materially, to isolate him in the pure air, on the heights. It's more than symbolic. Things act strongly upon the spirit. M. Dunoyer de Segonzac saw all of this correctly ...

Benjamin felt that Uriage personified a special, new mood that was beginning to sweep France, one in which the individualism and selfishness of the past were being replaced by something else:

When I keep saying that times have changed, am I wrong? A great inspiration is traversing France, that of the spirit. I feel sorry for the insensitive who don't feel it. Why couldn't they visit Uriage with me? They would have encountered a majestic phenomenon! Souls full of the ideal, penetrated with the mystery that is the drama of *living*, trying to banish egotism and inculcate generosity in cultivated young men, well-bred in appearance, but still obsessed by the central problem of *society*.

One begins by removing their city clothes, by exposing them to the rays of the sun, and praying that lush star to ripen them and prepare them for the warmth of disinterested words ...

For the writer, the striking details of daily life in the "Château de l'Âme," with its monastery-like mixture of beauty and noble gestures, captured the genius of the place:

In the morning, after the salute to the flag, which had made [the trainees] hold their heads straight and their eyes wide open, a young Chef, energetic and calm – as calm as the dawning day and who one sensed as being powerfully energetic, quietly explained, in the courtyard of the chateau before the panorama of the valley, that *one never gave oneself enough*. Life is short: a tragic fate; [but] it could be prodigious, there is its beauty! ... As he spoke one saw the last mists of morning pass away. Nature beckoned. And he was speaking with open hands, as if to say: "Offer yourselves too! Don't stay turned in on your own precious persons."

Benjamin recalled various telling vignettes:

During the ... morning, on the mountainside, under the mighty chestnut trees whose shadows, on the edge of a field bursting with sunlight, enticed one to meditation, a young man glowing with zeal told of returning from a Chantier de la Jeunesse, where the most beautiful hopes were possible. In a luminous voice, with eloquent eyes, he told them of his great joy at having been able to make the gift of his person to young boys who asked only to be helped.

"If you only knew," he exclaimed, "how receptive they are!"

Benjamin did warn, however, that the intensity of the Uriage experience was such that the instructors soon risked burning out:

The young orator told them that the role of chef, in the most beautiful camp in the world, could not be maintained for long. You wear yourself out; you spend yourself. One would soon be obliged to resign. "But ... isn't that magnificent!" he added. The recruits would not have it any other way, and neither would the ... *chefs*.

The writer also noted, and approved, a special Uriage attitude toward the intellectual life:

During the hot part of the afternoon ... in a cool room at the castle discussing "the social role of the intellectual," a pretentious speaker put forward the three names of Gide, Proust, and Valéry, thinking that they would impress, like three jewels ... [But] The man who was leading the debate pinned them up like three butterflies from a curé's garden! He put forward an engaging viewpoint, embellished with neither Proustian nor Gidian imagery. He showed the danger of intelligence unsupported by the soul, the nullity of the intellectual devoid of interior life, the superiority of the truly great artist – from whom one can learn everything, without his ever having to give a single lesson.

A bit before dinner, Benjamin went to interview the Vieux Chef in his study "encompassed by thick walls that shielded him from coarseness." He found Segonzac a bit morose, sensitive to the criticism that Uriage didn't yet have a fixed doctrine, and explaining that they were trying to learn, "while teaching, clarifying our thoughts, formulating them bit by bit. The unfortunate thing is that society has sunk so low. The machine has demeaned everything, even heroism! Men have to be immersed in nature, and left there a long time, a long time ... Alas! We have them only three weeks!" But Pétain's apostle had been impressed and he reassured the Vieux Chef: "It's a handsome beginning. It's a foot in the stirrup. Be happy. Those observing you are moved."

The end of that memorable day brought the most poignant moments for the writer: "At twilight, a *chef* who looked like a monk, serious and warm-hearted at the same time, sat down encircled by his students on the low courtyard wall. They were facing the valley laid before them under a golden, angelic sky, and he began to speak of 'the Mission of France.'" The instructor spoke about Péguy, "of course," and was followed by Benjamin himself on the Marshal. Descending from the mountain, under a starry sky, his visit at an end, the writer was surprised to hear running footsteps, and have an elegiac poem on Pétain, "le sauveur de la France" pressed upon him by the writer, a timid but ardent young poet from the school. "So tomorrow," Benjamin concluded, France could be optimistic, for she would find that "there will not only be *chefs* to act, but poets to celebrate them!"[37]

For René Benjamin, who had studied the Marshal more than anyone else, and from close range, and who was thought to understand his thinking as well as anyone, the École Nationale des Cadres d'Uriage was an almost miraculous embodiment of Pétain's ideas and values. The school seemed, to him at least, one of the finest flowerings of the Marshal's vision of what the Révolution Nationale could and should be.

A rather different personality from Benjamin, François Poncet, member of Vichy's youth commission and one-time ambassador to Berlin, made lecture-visits to Uriage several times – to condemn both "the spirit of resignation" and "the spirit of revolt" and to advocate "collaborating with the occupant – in the sense the Marshal gives to that word: in honour and dignity. Bend the body, do not bend the soul – keep it intact".[38]

For several Pétainist intellectuals, then, the École Nationale des Cadres seemed to be one of the most important and hopeful achievements of the new regime. Uriage had some solid friends at Vichy.

Peripheral Organizations

The situation of students from the French colonies at the Ecole Nationale des Cadres was an interesting reflection of the mentality of the place. A self-assured imperial pride characterized Uriage's publication *Jeunesse ... France!*,[39] and particularly its special number consecrated to the empire (8 July 1941). But this issue was not mindless propaganda. Besides Dunoyer de Segonzac's rather tender-minded assertion that the French empire had built upon a certain spirituality "inimitable et inimitée" and that the "spiritual vocation of France" was understood and appreciated by the colonized peoples,[40] the issue also contained Patrick Heidsieck's essay on "The Spirit of the Leader According to Lyautey," which stimulated critical reflection. This essay showed the persistent determination at the school to take an intelligent, distinctive, position on important issues.[41]

A number of the colonials came to the Château Bayard via a sort of "personalist network." For example, Jules Belpeer, director of the Foyer des Étudiants africains et asiatiques in Marseille (and active member of the "friends of *Esprit*" there), came with three of his students. His organization offered material and moral help, a place for exchanges and contacts with natives of French colonies arriving as students in Marseille, and was being subsidized by both the chamber of commerce and the archdiocese. Inspired by both Christian humanism and a sense of service to the French community, Belpeer's Foyer tried to promote friendship through a tolerant intercommunication of cultural and spiritual traditions; it thereby offered another illustration of the Esprit group's Bergsonian inspiration fostering contacts between spiritual "persons" from different cultures. Not surprisingly, Belpeer and his charges immediately felt at home with the "personalism" reigning at Uriage.[42]

At the École Nationale des Cadres, Belpeer and his colonial students were established as a team with two chalets of their own, their own morning exercises, Hébertisme and manual work projects. They attended a few of the larger "doctrinal" lectures with the other trainees ("Mission of France," "The Sense of Honour," "the Spirit of the Team"), but the remainder of their labour consisted of their own study sessions, with their own themes for reflection. These were set up with the aid of Beuve-Méry and Lallement. The colonials were given talks on the empire and its resources (Belpeer, Baumel), and on the mystic and missionary Charles de Foucauld (Follereau), while participating in study sessions on colonial youth, Islam, Buddhism, and Confucianism organized by volunteers from among their own group.[43] Finally, seven lectures were given by the colonial cadets themselves, on subjects such as North Africa, Islam, Senegal, and Indochinese youth, to the French mainland cadets. The usual *veillées*, mountain hikes, and Deffontaines excursions completed the program.[44]

We do not know what the "colonials" really thought about their experience at Uriage but, according to their instructors, the Uriage school seemed "to have been a real revelation for them." Besides the sense of voluntary discipline and effort, they perceived "the true bases of the French character for the first time" and Belpeer was delighted to see a bond formed "between the community of Uriage and the community of Marseille."[45] As would be the case in several quite different situations in later years, personalism proved useful to Catholic leaders trying to bring men of different religious traditions together "in the spirit" in a divisive cultural situation in which Catholics were struggling to exercise supreme political authority.[46]

URIAGE IDEAS

Pierre Dunoyer de Segonzac and His Ideas

The Vieux Chef was the dominant personality at Uriage, and seems to have made a strong impression – favourable or unfavourable – on practically everyone he met. Writer Roger Stéphane described his reception by Dunoyer de Segonzac on arriving at the school for the first time, on 17 November 1942:

After a quarter-hour's wait, I was introduced into a large, but dark, room where Taride maps sharply contrasted with a Louis XIV desk. A tall man with grey, slightly wavy hair stood holding out his hand. I introduced myself, a bit ill at ease at his calm, his reserve ... His extreme cordiality, his obligingness ... an imperceptibly distant politeness, put me at ease. His blue eyes, his striking uniform – blue shirt, beige riding breeches, white stockings, low black shoes – disconcerted me and added to the aura emanating from his person.[47]

A general reading of the testimonials of the former instructors suggests that most of them were captivated by Segonzac. "He was the boss," Charles Müller recalled, [and] "on top of that everyone agreed that he had a charmer side, a mysterious and mystical side."[48] "The whole personage of the Vieux Chef impressed me," wrote carpenter Cacérès:

His handsome, impenetrable face was marked by two fixed creases. One would have said that nothing could surprise that man, master as he was of all his reactions. With his slow intonations, it was as if he were always searching for his words, and wanted to speak to each one of us, and yet beyond. The Vieux Chef seemed to be descended from some Saracen (his classmate and friend at St-Cyr, Henri Frenay, future founder of Combat, nicknamed him "the negro"); he had a bit of the look of those old noble families of the south-west from which he came. Such confidence, such natural authority, such greatness, emanated from his personality that we would have, at his order, followed him anywhere at all.[49]

For chef-instructor Gilles Ferry, "Segonzac was a sort of great lord, a charismatic personage, simultaneously energetic and gentle, at the same time a military man and whimsical.[50] All of the instructors appear to give the impression of having had a special relationship with Segonzac. Or, in the words of Jean Le Veugle: "His prestige on his own team [was] so considerable, that some people seemed almost to be under his spell."[51] Jean-Louis Lévy's retrospective view of the Vieux Chef was also favourable, but stressed the ecumenical side:

He was an intransigent, but not a narrow nationalist, and not an Action Française type at all: an open nationalist. A seductive man – physically seductive – he was sensitive but solid at the same time. A very refined, firmly rooted man, very loyal to where he had come from. Simultaneously faithful to his roots, to his background, and open ... He could form friendly relations, on the spiritual plane, with Protestants, Catholic, Jews, Moslems, agnostics. That was not a problem for him. He preferred [rooted] people – not exactly like himself, evidently, but [people] in their own setting, in their own culture. I don't think he appreciated people who were too indecisive or uncertain.[52]

Dunoyer de Segonzac was immensely charismatic at a time when many French young people had been badly disillusioned and were looking for direction. In assessing the peculiar attractiveness of the Uriage school, it is important to stress the vividness of Segonzac's personality and his determination to instill the leadership principle, while beguiling and developing his charges in the name of absolute obedience to the Marshal. The captain's deeply rooted Catholicism did much to encourage this founder-of-a-religious-order tendency. And personalism served him well, as a philosophical support for the effort to suppress the "individual" while letting the "person" flourish in the womb of his authoritarian and hierarchical school. The Uriage community had certain obvious similarities to a Catholic religious order, where everyone was encouraged to obey, admire, even love, the superior, while the Catholic superior, in turn, loved and obeyed the pope, as Segonzac venerated the Marshal. Critical thinking regarding the precepts or personalities was discouraged in both the Uriage and the Catholic hierarchical relationships.

The Vieux Chef was straightforward with the school about his ideas and beliefs: "For my part, concerned with being frank, I declared myself a monarchist. This avowal provoked consternation among most of my comrades."[53] Segonzac's rather ambiguous attitude toward philosophical reflection, intellectuals, and the whole academic life reflected educational priorities very different from those of the pre-war pedagogues whom he blamed for France's defeat. According to Segonzac, the National Revolution needed men who were not only accomplished, resolute masters of themselves, but who knew how to lead people. For example, a true *chef* should know how to utilize collective recreation as a "powerful means (for) inculcating in his men that style of common, non-uniform life that, while respecting legitimate divergences, expresses a profound unity of souls." [54]

Segonzac extolled the sense of responsibility and of collective discipline found in organizations such as the army, against what he described as a "superstitious" French bridling against any effort to make their lives orderly, rhythmic, or punctual.[55] In fact, he attacked "individualism" and excessive liberty with such virulence that it almost appeared that he considered them the chief problems of occupied France, and of Europe at war. His conclusion on how the Uriage community should pick intellectuals was characteristic: "we should immediately select the intellectuals of the National Revolution, select them preferentially in good physical condition, good fathers of families, and capable of jumping onto a moving streetcar".[56] And in fact instructors at the Uriage school seem to have been chosen with these criteria in mind, as much as for their erudition or eloquence. They went Plato one better: they were philosopher-kings in fighting trim.

A rather romantic approach to the problems of the army was also taken by Segonzac, since he deplored the rupture between the army and the country that had poisoned France since the Dreyfus case: he envisaged a solution in the form of the armistice army. This was to be a corps of volunteers, for which officers "with a vocation" could be recruited and trained in "an exemplary community" that was united in a cult of honour and a concern for setting an example, with an understanding of "the social question." Segonzac envisioned military schools becoming true "écoles des cadres" capable of forming "not only military heroes, but great men such as the Marshal".[57] For Segonzac, elites charged with spirituality were essential to national renewal; he thus fused his veneration for Pétain, and Pétain's notion of national renewal, with his own Catholic religiosity. In the speech to Radio-Jeunesse (11 May 1941), we have noted that Segonzac compared the role of Joan of Arc to that of the Marshal in accomplishing "that marvel of giving life all at once to a national community that was unconscious of itself or dispersed."[58] For Segonzac, Pétain was not only a great man but a providential figure as well.

During the first evening *veillée* of each class, amid songs, the reading of texts, and periods of silence, Segonzac would introduce the school and its history and program. Then his close brother-in-arms, Eric Audemard d'Alançon, archetypal "soldier-monk" (and father of sixteen children), would read a text from Péguy on the idea of "work well done," known as the "chair cross-bar" text, which came to be often cited at the school:[59]

We have known the honour of work exactly like that which governed hand and heart in the Middle Ages ... We have known that solicitude carried to perfection ... We have known that piety of *work well done* ... These workers ... worked. Their honour was absolute, as is characteristic of honour. It was imperative that a chair cross-bar be well done ... A tradition that came, welled up, from the deepest profundity of the race, a history, an absolute, an honour wanted that that chair cross-bar be well done. Every part, in the chair, that could not be seen, was exactly as perfectly done as those one saw. That was the very principle of the cathedrals."[60]

This call for an integrated, total sense of French communal purpose was followed by J-J. Chevallier's extolling of virile energy, the gift for decision, and the sense of what is real – all of these neglected by the university – of a people become "civilized to the point of decadence" in the interwar period.[61] As we mentioned earlier, the question of a "virile order" would be taken up again by Segonzac as well as by Père de Lubac in his 1942 lecture "Ordre viril, ordre chrétien."[62] Father de Lubac had begun by reflecting on Catholicism and gone on to study "atheistic humanism," particularly Nietzsche and Proudhon, at least partially in an effort to "virilize" Christianity.

The Other Instructors

Aside from Segonzac, Chevallier, and Père de Lubac, there were several others lecturing at the school who deserve our attention. At the beginning of courses, to set the tone, Mounier or Jean Lacroix, or both, would give formal lectures on civilization, the national community, or personalist humanism. After that there could be a whole range of invited speakers: in addition to Lacroix, Melle Fouché, and other regulars, the "Richelieu" session for the *grands corps* trainees heard a succession of visitors such as playwright Paul Claudel, Msgr Bruno de Solages, historian Joseph Hours,[63] philosopher Charles Blondel, Vichy youth official Louis Garrone, Pierre Deffontaines, René Benjamin, Louis Salleron, the "doyen" Garraud, the diplomat Fouques-Duparc, and the *compagnon* Jean Bernard.[64] Uriage appeared as a beacon of French intelligence and culture in those dark years, and many of the most distinguished men in Vichy France seemed honoured to be asked to lecture there.[65]

Despite the approval that Uriage enjoyed at Vichy and Segonzac's fidelity to the Marshal, the school seemed to keep a certain distance from unreflective Pétainists. René Benjamin, for example, as high priest of the cult of the head of state, had spoken to the "Richelieu" cohort on "the personality of the Marshal."[66] But despite a warm reception for Benjamin's talk and his subsequent fulsome praise for the school he was apparently not invited back.[67] Of the lectures given by visitors in the above series, only that of the Vichy official Louis Salleron seems to have been reproduced and circulated by the school.[68] Thus the Uriage staff seemed to take an approach vis-à-vis the European political situation that avoided that uncritical, unreflective enthusiasm for the National Revolution and the European New Order displayed by other youth movement leaders, such as the scout leader Père Doncoeur.[69]

Communism was one issue on which Uriage took a particularly distinctive line. According to Alfred Fabre-Luce, who visited Uriage in October 1941, Segonzac had "during that year of 1941 gauged the rise of the Communist menace better than anyone else."[70] Jean Lacroix's course claimed to entail a scientific, literal study of Marx's thought, but one based upon the aptness of Berdyaev's 1920s prophecy that Marx and Nietzsche were in the process of dividing up the twentieth century, or, more precisely, "each twentieth-century man." This gave some foundation to the notion of a world-historical background to the French National Revolution of the twentieth century.[71]

Dunoyer de Segonzac regularly referred to "our revolution," which he juxtaposed with the national or the socialist revolutions, which were "communitarian but not personalist." A personalist revolution, whether directly inspired by Christianity or not, was founded on the respect for the human person and his liberty. Personalism demanded an education that established an equilibrium between the physical and moral, the quest for strength and disinterested civic courage. But "our revolution will be communitarian too," he added; to the reform of individuals it couples the quest for a "a certain order," "the order necessary to community survival."[72]

Segonzac and his staff assumed they had a clear and particular alternative to communist revolution, a vision one could devote one's life to promoting, and which was far more humane, modern, and realistic – more harmonious with French national and spiritual traditions – than that put forward by Marx or the communists.

Besides the narrowness and "obsolescence" of communism, another regular theme at Uriage was contempt for the bourgeoisie who were thought to have dominated the defunct Third Republic; Segonzac would denounce the "bourgeois spirit" and the "bons jeunes gens, fils à papa ou petits prétentieux" who do not merit a place among the true elites.[73] This anti-bourgeois rhetoric (in a school that was, as we have seen, largely made up of the sons of the bourgeoisie) seems to have been inherited from those avant-garde Catholic movements and publications of the 1930s that had influenced some of the key figures at the school.

Aside from personalism, the Uriage trainees were also exposed to a whole range of new issues and subjects for reflection. For example,

Joseph Hours, professor of history in the *khâgne* of Lyon, in his lecture on "The Permanence of French Traditions since 1870," showed how the constants and themes of the past illuminated the present. He discussed the meaning of the state and of the national interest, the recovery by the popular and working classes of certain valuable traditions (such as that of "work well done") that first the aristocracy, and then the bourgeoisie, had abandoned. Hours' reflections on issues and themes in the *histoire des mentalités* fit in well with the sweeping world-historical approach encouraged at Uriage, and with the openness to the generalist approach to history encouraged by the National Revolution as a whole.[74]

A different but complementary perspective was provided by Paul-Henri Chombart de Lauwe's rethinking of his approach to ethnology. He told the cadets that the intellectual method of historical, geographical, and sociological endeavour had to be accompanied by an opening of the heart and a more conscious adhesion to the French national community.[75] Vichy youth official Louis Garrone was also interested in ethnographic issues and on several occasions spoke to the trainees on what he called "the national problem": the need to "rediscover, experientially, an earthly fatherland ... to recreate the sense of being a people, a race." But he also recommended "pluralism" in the organization of young people, "without temporal domination [exercised by the state] over consciences."[76]

The Issue of Pluralism

The issue as to whether there were to be several or just one French youth movement was very important for the École Nationale des Cadres d'Uriage. The school's creativity, distinctness, influence, and prestige, as well as the high-level government support it received, created concern in some quarters over its long-term role: would a single *pétainiste* youth movement swallow up all the others? To help offset the idea that a National Revolution inevitably brought with it totalitarian control over young people, Hubert Beuve-Méry praised the youth situation in a country such as Portugal where, while adhesion to the Salazar-sponsored youth movement was obligatory, private movements, (though not encouraged) were not suppressed. Forced recruitment in Portugal, Uriage's director of studies suggested, was moderate in that the objective was educational rather than directly political; the Portuguese regime renounced its original totalitarian ambitions and initiated co-operatives without pretending to impose an "absolute," or a "religion," on the population. Beuve-Méry explained how the compulsory state movement which intended to direct "the total education and training of youth" nevertheless tolerated the existence of private and independent movements, and "at least the task it has fixed for Portuguese young people, and the methods it has employed, are healthy."

Segonzac, for his part, argued that there should be no exclusive French youth movement (the national socialist system was no model in this area), but neither should pluralism be allowed to degenerate into anarchy. He recommended that the government "leave a certain liberty to young Frenchmen" while preserving four or five large movements.[77] This seemed to be another situation in which the Uriage Study Bureau was trying to refine and distill the "revolutionary" projects of France's neighbours in order to adapt them to the French situation.

But although it supported youth-group pluralism, the role of the national leadership school in Pétainist, authoritarian France remained suspect. Catholic leaders feared the zealous "ecumenism" of Uriage, its insistence on bringing together men with different "mystiques" while affecting a "manly" impatience with clericalism, dogma, and the orthodox.

On the other hand, as we shall see, government officials and collaborationists deplored Uriage's tolerance of and concessions to the democratic spirit. By March 1942 there was a sense of crisis in the Secrétariat de la Jeunesse as a pro-government newspaper noted that 80 per cent of young people did not participate in any youth movement at all, and argued that there was an obvious need to *co-ordinate* the private youth movements – without, of course, suppressing them. It was argued that French youth had to be brought into a truly national movement, to be truly united, by means of more authority than was presently being demonstrated by the secrétariat.[78]

Psychology, Women, and the Family

Uriage's faculty were much concerned with providing psychological and moral training for the future leaders in their charge. Jean Lacroix was important in this effort for his original, and rather puritanical, reflections on adolescent psychology. It was "dangerous," he argued, to see the crisis of adolescence as simply a question of sexual development, for "in a sense adolescence is the age of enthusiasm, of the spiritual, of contempt for the carnal." After going on to cite Dostoevsky and August Comte in support of his views, the personalist philosopher declared that over against the spirit of self-indulgence and sexual liberty, "Claudel is certainly the one who knew how to seize, the most profoundly, in a phrase, the essence of youth:

'Adolescence', he said, 'is not made for pleasure, but for heroism' ...
In any case, one can always galvanize the young by proposing an
ideal of purity, one demanding the greatest sacrifices of them."[79]
Lacroix also put forward his notion of a "family humanism" as a
major element of the "complete humanism" that should be juxtaposed against the double threat of individualism and of totalitarianism.[80] A study group was proposed on "the woman and marriage"
and a text by a woman working in the Uriage milieu, Anne-Marie
Hussenot, was circulated for this purpose.

Mme Hussenot explained how the traditional virtues demanded
by the "woman's *métier*" (where "strength" and "simplicity in giving
oneself" count for as much as tenderness and femininity) should be
supplemented in 1941, at a time of mobilization for national renewal,
with "the sense of teamwork and the sense of danger." She saw the
essence of a woman's role, whether she worked in a profession or not,
as "gravitating between two poles, the child and the man. The woman
is the companion of the man, and the mother of his children." She
should know how to "limit herself to her *métier* of being a woman,
which is, however, immense." She should never forget that if there
had been a Joan of Arc or other heroines of that sort, "throughout
the exceptional mission that was confided to them, they first of all
performed humbly and simply their woman's role":

Let woman limit her efforts to her own sphere, knowing that if each one did
as much the renewal that we want would be accomplished. Let us try to
render the little corner of earth where we are living strong, peaceful, and
fertile.

Let us do this simply, without anxiety, and with much wisdom.[81]

Uriage wanted a new breed of men, but preferred relatively old-
fashioned women.

Despite their humanistic language, Lacroix's and Hussenot's
defences of the family, while less heavy-handedly moralistic than most
National Revolution rhetoric on the subject, were clearly against
feminism and opposed to anything substantially altering the sub-
missive attitude of women in French society. In general, this "community of men" seemed decidedly uncomfortable with this issue and,
according to Bernard Comte, their "very traditional" vision of the
role of the woman testifies to the little attention given by the Uriage
team to these problems.[82] But it could also be argued that a hidden
fear of modern women was evidenced by this huge effort to create
a patriarchal and authoritarian society that would keep them in their
traditional roles.

The bleak situation of the women who lived and worked at Uriage illustrates this point. The girls who were hired from the surrounding area or from Grenoble to do secretarial work at the Uriage school, like the wives of the instructors, generally came from "good families" and were delighted to work at the chateau because they shared its ideals. But they soon discovered that they were going to be treated very differently from the men, and not in a particularly chivalrous way. While three of the secretaries lived with the parents of one of them, the others were given rooms in an annex of the convent in the village of St. Martin, below. To their displeasure, or disgust, they discovered that at the school, during the day, they were to eat in a dining room completely apart, and things were arranged so that they would not even see the instructors. Save for the *veillées*, and certain community get-togethers to which everyone was invited, they were not asked to school functions. "We were dying of hunger," one of them later recalled, "and very badly fed because we didn't have meat tickets like the men, who had the right to ninety grams of it because they did sports and physical work."[83]

In November 1941, a twenty-four-year-old archivist, Lucette Massaloux, the only woman admitted to the institution's elite Conseil des Chefs, arrived at the school. "My role," she recalled, "was very mute. I felt myself humbled by all those *chefs* (very respectful toward me on the whole) who impressed me very much, and above all by personalities like Beuve-Méry. He was very demanding. Sometimes I spent the whole night preparing *cahiers de cycle*. Time didn't matter ... From time to time we were invited by their families, but very rarely."[84] Summing up her experience, Massaloux said: "There was a problem in regard to women. [The leaders of Uriage] were all warriors, all *chefs*. It was a rather sexist school. But it could not have been anything else in that period."[85]

The men of Uriage were not only warriors but warriors of a special puritanical and Christian variety. Segonzac took upon himself a certain sacerdotal role, even regarding the wives and children of his instructors. For example, the wife of instructor Charles Müller, having just given birth to a son, recalled having an abrupt and unannounced visit in her bedroom from the imperious Vieux Chef and his chaplain:

It was the Abbé de Naurois who baptized my oldest son, by force or nearly so ... We were practically ruled by the rod there. Segonzac came into my room with the abbé and then they baptized him, whether anyone liked it or not. Personally I didn't much appreciate that kind of thing because I think it is a personal matter. I had intended to baptize my son when I wished.[86]

A memorable exception to the austere life the secretaries led in the alpine chateau came on the occasion of a major religious feast in 1942, as one of them recalled:

Chombart de Lauwe, who was kindness itself, said one day: "Those girls whom we brought here, who in spite of *their good background* [emphasis mine] lead an infinitely austere life. We hold them apart. Their lives are rather monastic."

Then on 4 April 1942, an Easter Saturday, Chombart said: "This evening we are going to eat in the *grand carré* [the *chefs'* dining hall], with the secretaries and the unmarried, because we have to make their lives a bit more pleasant." That was greatly appreciated. We were dumbfounded and said to one another: "What's happening to us?"[87]

But nothing much happened to them thereafter, and following that singular gesture the puritanical routine for the women at the Château Bayard went on much as before – worlds apart from that easy equality with men some of them would discover later in clandestine Resistance organizations. In a general way, women seemed to be considered a potentially troublesome presence at the school, tolerated at best, and this attitude would be set down in black and white in the rules of the Uriage order, as we shall see. In the thinking of the school's leadership, "liberated" French women seemed to have had some responsibility for pre-war French decadence and hence the French defeat; the "virile order" at the school was going to correct that situation.

Most Uriage veterans who later reflected on the situation of the Uriage women, while they often tried to justify it as understandable at the time, recognized it as a serious problem, or potential problem, for the school. "Life at the École Nationale des Cadres," Yvonne Jacquot later mused, "is difficult to explain to other generations. If one wanted, one could stress ... a rather "macho" aspect understandable in a men's school and almost inevitable if one takes into account the mood of the time." "As *stagiaires*, we did not speak about women," Paul Grillet remembered. "Indeed there were other human beings who were not dressed like us, who one assumed were women, but we didn't have any contact with them!" "During the two years of the existence of the community women were treated in a rather cavalier way," former instructor Gilles Souriau admitted. "They were only very rarely consulted and the problem would probably have been serious if the community had continued to exist."[88]

Some of this Uriage sexism was due to the quasi-monastic and military style of the place. The traditionalist religious background and peculiar anti-feminine, anti-decadence outlook of men like

Segonzac, Beuve-Méry, and J.-J. Chevallier also seems to have discouraged egalitarian contacts with women. In any case, for whatever reasons, most leaders of the school seemed to prefer the company of men, and believe that the future would be determined by them.[89]

Uriage Ideas: New or Old?

Visiting lecturers at the École Nationale des Cadres were often of very high quality. Distinguished Catholic writers such as Paul Claudel (who lectured on "the gesture and the word," with readings from his *Jeanne au bucher*) were not unusual. Members of French Catholic intellectual and artistic circles seemed to think that the school had great promise. Péguy was the author most often cited in these lectures, followed by Vigny, Montherlant, Saint-Exupéry, Malraux, Pascal, Dostoevsky. Georges Bernanos, who had been touted as "the French Dostoevsky" by the French Right before becoming a prominent anti-fascist, anti-Vichy polemicist was not mentioned at all,[90] but Jacques Maritain, who was beginning to write resistance tracts in New York, was cited for his pre-war defence of the "primacy of the spiritual" and a "true humanism."[91]

While there was an impressive array of literary, theological, psychological, and philosophical references in Uriage lectures, there were also some rather notable absences: contemporary scientific thought was not mentioned at all, any more than the questions it posed about the place of modern man in the universe. In *Jeunesse ... France!*, under the rubric "books," Study Bureau member Gilles Ferry might signal an important new book by Silone, Montherlant, or Copeau, but the major publishing project of Uriage, the "Le Chef et ses Jeunes" series, was very *ancienne France* – heavy on military or colonial heroism and Catholic morality, with few references to contemporary thought, or even to the whole post-1789 world.

The first volume of the new series "For a National Revolution"[92] published study group outlines worked out by the school: "Qualities of the young Frenchman; Work; Marriage; Family; Role of the leader; Vie Intérieure; Patrie." What seemed to give coherence to the pedagogical enterprise of the school was the formula in which the community summarized their convictions at the end of 1941: primacy of the spiritual (a concept apparently derived from Jacques Maritain's book of that name), the cult of the fatherland, a sense of humour and of team spirit.[93] But as basic as community was elite leadership, and that still meant, at Uriage, the cult of the absolute authority of, and obedience to, the Vieux Chef – and, of course, to Marshal Pétain. There were some things that were very new, but much that was very old, about the Uriage experience.

CHAPTER FOUR

Uriage Influence:
Jeunesse ... France,
Marche, and
the Regional Schools

As the École Nationale des Cadres d'Uriage prospered, some of the
more senior military officers involved with Vichy's youth training
began to bristle at young Captain Pierre Dunoyer de Segonzac's
pretentions, his independence, and the centrality of his personality
in the school. The Study Bureau had attracted other high-profile
personalities to Uriage – lively, sometimes controversial, young Catholic intellectuals such as Mounier, Lacroix, Beuve-Méry, de Lubac,
and Maydieu. It was becoming clearer that Uriage was the focal point
of a collective effort to orient the National Revolution in a certain
direction as the school tried to reach the country with publications
ranging from the popular to the erudite to nurture the new leaders
of a new kind of France. Could this be accomplished under the
determined thumb of Segonzac?

JEUNESSE ... FRANCE!

Uriage wanted to shape and orient the National Revolution by both
teaching select individuals in the school and influencing others
through example, and especially by publishing the fruits of Uriage
reflections and pedagogical experiences. *Jeunesse ... France!*, a lively,
illustrated, mass circulation bi-weekly appeared at the end of 1940
as the Uriage staff sought to clarify their distinctive approach to the
psychological and moral forming of future leaders. In the lead editorials of Segonzac, as well as in the essays by his principal aides,[1]
Jeunesse ... France! alerted a wider audience to the ideas and activities
of the school – circulation figures grew steadily during the first six
months of 1941, attaining a regular printing of nearly 30,000 copies,[2]
considerably more than pre-war circulation of those personalist journals that inspired its philosophical conceptions.[3] *Jeunesse ... France!*

also helped to maintain communications between the mother-school and its graduates, as well as the ties between Uriage and the whole elite school network that looked to Uriage for leadership.[4] It made the recondite world-historical speculations and personalist psychologizing of the school more accessible, while also conveying the Uriage team's reaction to the major new foreign policy issues that began to divide the French.

As far as literature was concerned, *Jeunesse ... France!* published "belles pages" citing nineteenth- and twentieth-century writers who celebrated old-fashioned values and Christian humanism, authors such as Péguy, Malègue, Lyautey, Pierre Termier, Alain-Fournier, Kipling, Mistral, Pierre de Coubertin, Pourrat. More modern thinkers such as the visionary architect Le Corbusier and Hyacinthe Dubreuil were also cited for their reflections on the problems of work, the machine, and technology, and there was a special appreciation for the writings of Henry de Montherlant on sport, and of Ernest Psichari on contemplation. Psichari, grandson of the great sceptic Renan, had, in converting to Catholicism on the eve of World War I, generated an original kind of Catholic- patriotic-chivalrous mysticism before World War I. The soldier-monk community at the Château Bayard would have been the fulfillment of his dreams.[5]

Jeunesse ... France! seemed to want to steer an independent, eclectic course among the various ideologies, or models, of national transformation competing for the attention of French young people. Two of the most important thinkers at Uriage, Paul-Henri Chombart de Lauwe and Hubert Beuve-Méry, analyzed foreign youth movements for *Jeunesse ... France!* – de Lauwe, the Italian and German movements; Beuve-Méry, the Portuguese. Their informed, sophisticated expositions were based on firsthand observations that were intended to help the men of Uriage discern the valuable ideas as well as the errors in the experiences of other countries, just as the school formed its own Study Bureau to set out the guidelines for the youth revolution in France.

In December 1940, Chombart de Lauwe rendered a detached, generally positive, assessment of Italian Fascist youth, although he recognized that there was a certain tension in Italian Fascism "between the theories of the equality of individuals confronted by the all-powerful state on the one hand, and the search for an elite on the other." Although Italian sociologists had tried to set out guidelines on how the elites could be renewed from below, and in principle young Italians were accepted into organizations without any distinctions made as to origin, the original Fascist partisans maintained a preponderant influence. He noted, in conclusion, that the Fascists had abolished the Young Christian Workers (JOC) and the scouts (albeit with Vatican acquiescence), and there had been tensions between the Fascists and the Catholic Church. But the Catholic Youth Organization was still flourishing and, when differences arose between the Catholics and the Fascist leaders, "the Duce himself intervened, and, it seems, rendered an equitable judgment."[6]

The Hitlerjugend were the object of special attention in *Jeunesse ... France!*, and the school's attitude toward that organization is worthy of extended analysis if we are to grasp what was unique to Uriage. In a series of long, illustrated articles on the Hitlerjugend which began in January 1941, Chombart de Lauwe went into greater detail and precision than he had in his discussion of the Italians. He began by noting that the German youth movement had its roots in the famous meeting of the free spirits of the Wandervögel, "an intellectual and philosophical elite" who met on the Hohen Meissner mountain peak in Hessen, in 1913, but that the ranks of the "wandering birds" were subsequently swelled by a generation of young veterans shaped by the experience of life at the front. Baldur von Shirach's Hitler Youth came from this double heritage and put forward a total philosophy for transforming the education of German young people, and through youth, the country as a whole:

The main lines of the education revolution are simple: they begin with a small number of general rules. Certain of these [rules] are not specifically national-socialist: the need for a physically active life and fresh air, the necessity for the fusion of classes, the development of political education; others claim to be more original: the guidance of youth by young people themselves, the imposition of a "Weltschang" [sic] or "conception of the world," the leader or "führer princip" [sic].

The Uriage instructor went on to explain how these general principles functioned practically, and saw at least one that could be useful to the French since it did not seem far from what Uriage was trying to implement:

The leading of youth by the young corresponds to one of the special characteristics of the German mentality which a saying of the Führer ("Die Jugend müsse durch die Jugend geführt werden" [Youth ought to be led by youth]) crystallized in a simple phrase. In many organizations before Hitlerism, which we have described, this ideal was put in practice, since the founder, and the leaders, of most of them were very young boys. Now the maxim has been changed into an absolute rule, and almost all of the gymnastics lessons, almost all of the study circles, are directed by monitors barely older than their comrades. This system has advantages: it develops the sense of responsibility, makes the lessons more lively. But it is not, as we said, particular to Germany and the benefits that one can draw from it have not been missed by educators in foreign countries.[7]

The following month, Chombart de Lauwe went on to describe the relationship between this transformation of German youth and the maintenance of social services, and the remarkable way in which youth could be employed in social rehabilitation:

The Social Service is responsible for professional career counselling, for the control of the apprenticeship. It has a medical section, organizes vacations, creates housekeeping courses for girls, et cetera. To re-adapt errant youth, or at least those who are accused of minor crimes, one assigns them to comrades responsible for seeing to their keep. This is the most radical application we have seen of the principle of the efficacy of the young taking charge of the young. To discern the *elite of young people*, the social service organizes centres in each little town, centres charged with aiding young people who merit escape from their [disadvantaged] backgrounds.

Uriage had, as we have seen, tried to act as a pioneer in a new notion of the relationship between physical and intellectual training, and in trying to bridge the gap between social classes, and Chombart de Lauwe was particularly impressed by the way this problem was confronted in the Hitler Youth. He visited various offices of that organization, discussed this question with specialists, and observed organizations for young workers firsthand:

"Kultur" of the body and "Kultur" of the Spirit

While the services centring on physical training are separate from those dealing with intellectual questions, the organizers' approach tends to meld these two sorts of activities: "Leibes Kultur" and "Geistige Kultur." The instructors seek that ideal equilibrium perennially sought between the development of body and of that of spirit. One finds in the structures of the "Hitler Youth" the classical equilibrium for each age group between "sport" and "Schulung" (teaching in the larger sense).

In the area of physical culture itself, the Germans insist on the distinction between gymnastics (which is a state-ordained duty) and sport, which completes it by adding play and the risk-taking dimension. We do not believe, we repeat, that those programs, albeit very well conceived, have anything essentially original in them; what is noteworthy is their systematic application.

Chombart de Lauwe also drew attention to the Hitler Youth's "Kultur Amt" (the Intellectual Culture Office) whose officials told him of their projects for music, literature, fine arts, theatre, and popular festivals (which varied according to whether they were for centres in the cities or for outdoor camps). And, again, he found much that was understandable – including the Hitler Youth struggle against the influence of "Jewish" art:

In the area of fine arts the leaders of the "Kultur Amt" propose a teaching method that seems excellent: to create works of art more accessible to children and young people, they decided to make such works themselves. Simple critical study is not enough; every veritable amateur ought to be capable in their view of "creating something" (schaffen), however awkward. The principal goal of the fine arts section is to discover a style, a manner, that would be typical of the present German spirit. In fact the conceptions of the architects of the Third Reich have sometimes given some happy results, of which we have been able to see an interesting example in the Paris exposition of 1937 (due to the young head architect of the Reich, Sparr [sic]). Moreover, while one might readily envisage the "search for a style" in architecture or in decoration, in painting or sculpture, it is a dangerous tendency. Young Germans seem to have, in part, understood that pitfall; what they want, they say, is to struggle against "Jewish" art, which lacks sincerity.

Over against the decadence of "Jewish" art, the Hitler Youth wanted to follow the Führer's lead toward recreating an art more rooted in folk traditions, but they were not, Chombart de Lauwe thought, spectacularly successful: "They want the 'primitive' or 'spontaneous' but, rather than seeing anything new that they have created, one sees expositions of the 'academic' or the 'well-crafted.' Chancellor Hitler, whose personal influence on the evolution of art is considerable, prefers that sort of work to the works of modern French artists, which he does not want exposed in Germany because he judges them too immoral."

As far as theatre was concerned, Chombart de Lauwe found Hitler Youth works quite similar to those mounted by the new theatrical groups that had been established in the shadow of Uriage. He stressed how the Hitler regime involved young people in its activities as much as possible: in the city of Weimar there were festivals to introduce the works of young playwrights, and in the countryside there were efforts to make theatrical works accessible, much like those of the "Quatre Saisons" troop of Xavier de Lignac (of the Ordre Nouveau group) in France. He singled out a new association founded by a young assistant director of the "Kultur Amt," the "*gemeinschaft*

jungeschaffen," which brought "young creators" together into meetings
or special camps: "This manner of struggling against excessive com-
partmentalization can give the leaders of the budding German youth
cultural movement more strength and confidence in themselves." But
for the Uriage instructor the *gemeinschaft jungeschaffen* had had analogies in France that were at least as successful, such as the Catholic
movement *Départ,* which grouped together technicians, literary
people, and artists of all kinds into work teams. While in Germany,
Chombart de Lauwe also observed something like a Hitler Youth
version of the *veillée*:

"Heim abend" ... take place in the evening. They are organized following
the directions given by the leaders of the movement in the monthly illustrated
bulletins. The group leaders find plans for lectures and detailed methods
for physical, moral, intellectual and, of course, political education. The liberty
allowed young people following the principle "youth should be led by youth"
is thus tempered by precise instructions.

Chombart de Lauwe also described, matter-of-factly and without
much comment, some of the racialist measures taken by the Hitler
Youth, concluding his exposition with a global assessment. There
were, he said, significant differences in mentality to be considered:

German passivity in obeying orders, their static conception of discipline,
always surprises the French. We have a tendency to believe that such an
attitude corresponds to an identity of thinking in individuals because our
critical spirit generally prevents us from following a man or becoming enthusiastic about an idea without having discussed the qualities or the consequences involved. That difference in mentality falsifies our judgment. Since
the National Socialists attach much importance to the "gemeinschaft" we
tend to think that in Germany the collectivity is everything but the individual
counts for nothing.
    ... National-Socialist law is founded on five principal bases: race, land,
work, honour, and the Reich. The theories that justify all of the actions of
the government are elaborated on these bases.

The ethnologist warned that apparent German collectivism should
not be exaggerated:

These juridical conceptions do not enlighten us as to the internal attitude of
the Germans, and notably of the young people, who are our interest in this
study. In spite of the mass movements of the crowds or the military parades,
the German remains isolated in his dream. He is one hundred times more

individualist than the Frenchman but on another level; he doesn't discuss the politics of the local village with such pungency in the café du Commerce, but in front of his beer stein he dreams of his music and faraway places. Germany has produced philosophers and mystics, the kind of searchers who work in solitude and who figure among its greatest glories. One should not be surprised to see the young Hitlerite, who marched in the ranks of his "Ban" chanting the party hymn, take out his harmonica and leave for a solitary walk far from his university in search of the first signs of spring.

In conclusion, the Uriage instructor remarked that the Germans, in contrast to the French, did not find a way to separate temporal and religious questions, and for the Germans "a political revolution is incomplete if unaccompanied by a spiritual revolution":

One often remarks that the mentality of the young Germans is disconcerting to our minds, formed as they have been by Latin sources; we might say that it is even more disconcerting when one tries to follow its twists and turns more carefully. The social and spiritual problems to which we have alluded are very far from our present preoccupations, at least in the form that our neighbours present them.[8]

Chombart de Lauwe's general analysis of the Hitler Youth is best described as guardedly sympathetic. Certainly the Hitler Youth had several characteristics that were incomprehensible, or unattractive, to the French, but they had taken some bold initiatives and were clearly living an interesting experiment. While he did not seem to find the racism of the Hitler Youth attractive, it was not horrifying to him either. Neither did he appear to be deeply troubled by what we would consider to be the totalitarian, anti-intellectual, brainwashing tendencies of the organization, nor by the effect of all of this mass militarization and indoctrination. Rather, he seemed to imagine a world-historical youth movement in which all peoples would be obliged to engage their sons and daughters sooner or later. In this light, the German youth revolution was the Germans doing "their thing" and it was up to his countrymen to create their own distinctively French youth experience.

Chombart de Lauwe's articles were followed by a sympathetic exposition by Beuve-Méry on the authoritarian (but not totalitarian) organization of youth in Portugal:

Portuguese students still wear those long black capes that have covered them to the ankles for centuries. Coimbra is a university town as still exists nowhere else in Europe. Lovers still woo, evenings, underneath the balcony of a more or less cloistered beauty. The languorous nostalgia of the "fados" still attracts a public of young people suffering from the Portugese disease of melancholy ... [But] in five years, the national organization of the *Mocidade portuguesa* (Portuguese youth) has created a new sort of young person, more open, more virile, more conscious of his responsibilities in the necessary rebuilding of the society.

Beuve-Méry noted that the *Mocidade*, though devoid of immediate political objectives, did have a lofty political goal, as its educational work aimed at the total development and training of youth. It tended to form "men, soldiers, citizens ... thriving, disciplined personalities in the service of the national collectivity." The meaning of Portuguese youth's efforts, the Uriage director of studies concluded, could be summed up by Dr. Oliveira Salazar's statement on the nature of Portuguese nationalism:

One day it will be recognized that Portugal is governed by an original system, suited to her history and her geography, both of which are very different from those of other countries; we hope that then it will be finally understood that we have not rejected liberalism and false democracy simply to embrace other, perhaps even worse, errors and vices. We have rejected them, rather, to render our country robust and vigorous – aided by the principles of authority, order, and national tradition, allied to those eternal truths that are, happily, the patrimony and the privilege of Christian civilization.[9]

This statement could be transposed into an excellent summary of what Beuve-Méry saw in the Portuguese experience that could be imported into France.

After these relatively favourable expositions on Italian, German, and Portugese youth movements, *Jeunesse ... France!* put forward certain themes that would not have been out of place in any of one of these. The publication praised the *Corporation agricole* and celebrated the soil that nourished "a robust and strong race" and "the French fatherland, the result of two thousand years of Christian peasantry." It also took to task pre-war writers for the decadence that had brought France down – and, in fact, did so with such vehemence that Emmanuel Mounier, no friend of the Third Republic, protested that the journal was going too far.[10] In spite of this the priest-scholar Father Carré, after granting the evident faults of "French intelligence" that had been made all too evident by the defeat, declared that Uriage crystallized some of the best thinking in the National Revolution, and had become one of those "pinnacles ... [where] one proposed an integrated education to the young ... in an absolute and exigent fidelity to the 'sense of man' that, on the theoretical level, sets us apart."[11]

Jeunesse ... France! published not only Catholic, or traditionalist, moralists but also thinkers who have been described, in retrospect, as among the most important theorists of a "French Fascism."[12] An essay by Thierry Maulnier, *normalien* and precocious authority on Nietzsche, was reprinted and cited as "defining with intelligence the principles of a French order" in its juxtaposing of totalitarianism, founded on the supremacy of a single intransigent, absolute principle, and the French tradition of equilibrium. For Maulnier there could be an acceptable French "totalitarianism" only if it were to be a superior one, integrating the various aspirations and forces that had gone to make up the soul of French society; the present world struggle, he thought, would not result in the total victory of the ideology of one of the contending camps, but rather in a new synthesis, in which French diversity would play a role.[13] In autumn Beuve-Méry cited this Maulnier article, the gist of which was that the only acceptable totalitarianism for France would be a distinctively French and spiritual one, as Uriage's director of studies tried to sketch out the present and future prospects of France.[14]

Maulnier, one of the non-Catholic originators of "Personalism" in the early 1930s, could be seen as upholding the French spiritualist totalitarianism being established under personalism's banner. A few years earlier, the young Belgian personalist youth leader Raymond de Becker had remarked: "Only Catholicism has the right to be totalitarian." Because of their Catholic sensibilities the men of Uriage could, like Salazar's Portugese elites, promote totalitarianism with a good conscience. Despite their claim of having exclusively moral and religious preoccupations, therefore, the Uriage team could not avoid endorsing certain kinds of politics. Otherwise, as Paul Nizan had earlier warned, they would run the risk of being perceived as a naive French "spiritualist" intelligentsia "distilling the thick foreign currents" of Fascism or National Socialism for French youth being formed for the French National Revolution as part of a European New Order.[15]

Jeunesse ... France! presented texts from the regime, such as the one in personalist language on "the respect for the person and authority," while giving its own, sometimes ambiguous, interpretations of the "new principles" that were to be substituted for the "old trilogy" Liberty, Equality, Fraternity: Discipline ("harmoniously conjugated with liberty"), Responsibility, Elites (in all of the classes). "No unfavourable prejudice will affect a Frenchman because of his social origins, on condition that he integrate himself into the new France with unreserved co-operation." (8 February 1941)[16] Michel Dupouey evoked the place of young people in the Révolution Nationale in a series of articles: this bureaucrat at the SGJ, and director of the Compagnons movement after it had been forcibly reorganized by his office, wrote for *Jeunesse ... France!* in the tone of a friendly regular of the school, rather than as an administrator of the SGJ.[17]

Jeunesse ... France! did not discuss most day-to-day foreign policy issues, and the many articles on the collapse of 1939–40 did not cast sole blame upon England. But when the combined Free French and British attacked Vichy forces in Syria in June 1941 there was a severe critique of the anglo-gaullists.[18] The 8 July 1941 issue described the naval battle at Suffren against the English fleet, depicting "our navy called to defend our empire against blows from whatever quarter." A later issue vividly described Vichy aviation's underdog struggle "against the enemy" and the wounds inflicted on Frenchmen in Syria by American Curtiss P40 aircraft.[19] In an October talk to Uriage alumni Segonzac was hard on the Gaullists in Syria, arguing that French officers who agreed to fight at the side of a foreign government against other Frenchmen "have, in a way, lost their sense of honour."[20]

But however disappointing Uriage's *Jeunesse ... France!* line might have been to the Gaullists, it also attracted some criticism at Vichy. By the end of 1941, there was concern at Vichy over "a certain orientation," an improper politicization, in the publication, and it was recommended that a new chaplain be appointed to the school.[21] But whatever the private reservations of some Vichy officials about Uriage's publications, they did not prevent the regime's giving the school even greater means to further its views.

On 15 January 1942 *Jeunesse ... France!* announced that it was suspending publication in its current form but that this would be replaced by a monthly review with more limited circulation, available only by subscription (which appeared in March 1942).[22] Certain signs had anticipated a turn toward a wider public: in the fall of 1942, the publication had replaced its second issue for October with a larger November issue – 16 pages, a press run of 45,000 copies – "a special issue consecrated to the new youth institutions," which gave much space to the official literature of the heads of the diverse organs of the SGJ.[23] So at the beginning of 1942, a new, more house-oriented, review *Jeunesse ... France. Cahiers d'Uriage*, replaced the old one, accompanied by two new publications: an internal publication for the alumni movement, "Équipe nationale d'Uriage," and, for a larger public, *Marche*, a magazine officially and generously supported by the SGJ and edited by Segonzac (discreetly – his name was not on the masthead).[24]

MARCHE

The idea of publishing a mass-circulation magazine had been in the air at Uriage for months. Roger Radisson, a pre-war member of the avant-garde Left-Catholic publishing circles, proposed to M. Pfimlin, Le Chef de la Propagande, Secrétariat Général de la Jeunesse, Secrétariat d'État à l'Instruction Publique, the creation of a journal bringing together the different youth movements in a way that could rival the magazine *Signal* in mass appeal for the young – notably by drawing upon the combined talents of both Uriage and of the Compagnons.[25] Contributors would include the leading Catholic or "spiritual" writers such as Massis, Saint-Exupéry, Deffontaines, Mounier, Beuve-Méry, Doncoeur, and so on. The magazine was to be directed by Segonzac, but the editor-in-chief would be Philippe Gaussot of the Compagnons. The sub-editors were to be Charles Müller, Chombart de Lauwe, Ollier de Marichard (of Uriage), and Oudinot (of the Compagnons). Contributors would include various individuals involved with "Jeunesses féminine," the scouts, the Équipes sociales (Garric), the Compagnons (Cruziat), the Auberges de la Jeunesse (Magnant, Auclair), Jeune-France, Jeunesse maritime, the Chantiers de la Jeunesse, the Union Nationale des Étudiants, the étudiants coloniaux, as well as the Maisons de Jeunes (Dumazedier).

Marche, le magazine français, with its generous government subsidy of one million francs and intention to publish ten times as many copies as had *Jeunesse ... France!* (200,000 copies were to be sold at two francs a copy),[26] was a clear demonstration that Dunoyer de Segonzac, in concert with the Compagnons, was determined to play a leading role in the Révolution Nationale. Uriage not only wanted to form elites but also to draw a larger public into the work of national transformation via mass propaganda. For as the Vieux Chef put it: "Uriage is an act of faith in the National Revolution. It is a part of that revolution, and its fate is tied to the success or failure of that vast enterprise of renewal."[27]

Marche, like *Jeunesse ... France!*, was immediately noticeable for its love for mountains: there were romantic photos of the French Alps, detailed expositions of such subjects as the folk traditions of Saint-Véran (the highest village in Europe) and articles on the activities of the "Jeunesse et Montagne" youth movement. Mountain scenes adorned descriptions of heroic individual exploits in travel, aviation, and the wilds of French colonies. There were numerous stylized illustrations of young men in bathing suits or shorts engaged in collective effort (such as balancing a huge log in the air), or of healthy, strapping, bare-limbed young girls. From time to time a flattering portrait of Pétain would appear.

Marche reflected much the same literary tastes as Uriage: there was thinly veiled contempt demonstrated for "Le disciple de Monsieur [André] Gide" (timorous, unable to "*take*" a woman),[28] and there were reservations about the cynicism and egoism of "Le disciple de Monsieur [Henri] de Montherlant".[29] Both writers were a sorry contrast to someone with the "right stuff" – Paul Claudel, *meneur de jeux*.[30]

In March, the first article signed by the magazine's director Segonzac (who was not identified as the head of Uriage) was a flattering description (illustrated by pictures of Henri Massis and General de La Porte du Theil) of the wise and well-meaning elders of the *Conseil national* at Vichy before whom Segonzac had reported on his school:

There are several university professors among the counsellors but not the ponderous, pontificating, bearded and big-bellied professor type with whom we are familiar. One is a tennis champion ... and the president ... M. Gidel looks more his role of part-time Colonel of Artillery than rector of the Law Faculty of Paris. He is, moreover, a perfect example of a Frenchman of good stock. It is surely thanks to his firm and intelligent stimulus that the Conseil National's projects are so rich in results.

Segonzac also had some appreciative words for the presence on the Conseil of that "old friend of young people" Gaston Bergery, the former *enfant terrible* of the Radical Party, who, strikingly dressed completely in black, with his blue eyes and crew-cut, looked like "a mixture of professional officer and Cocteau"![31] Segonzac's subsequent exhortation on "Building the National Community" called for unity and a public spirit in a tone characteristic of the magazine in general.[32]

Marche devoted special attention to the military situation in the world, with maps of the progress of the various fronts and analyses of the different fighting forces. Edited as it was by a French cavalry officer, one might have expected some sense that the fortunes of the war were changing with the disastrous German invasion of the Soviet Union, and the entry of the United States on the side of the allies. Some weeks after Pearl Harbour, in early 1942, there were articles on the United States, rather unflattering commentaries on American

political, economic, and especially military power. The clear implication was that the strength of the German submarine fleet was such
that America was cut off and could hardly figure importantly in the
European conflict for some time to come, if at all.[33] Although in
April there had been some good words for the elite British commando brigades, England was now described as a poor match for a
powerful Germany which, fortunately for unprepared England, was
preparing a massive offensive against Russia.[34] In June, it was suggested that the German offensive in the Caucasus faced difficulties,
but it was implied that Hitler's forces would likely succeed.[35]

By the end of the summer of 1942, when Segonzac and some of
his friends had apparently withdrawn as editorial directors, *Marche*[36]
published a special issue, *L'Aviation Française*, consistent with its general perspective on the evolution of the war: the Germans – excel-
lently trained and equipped as they were – would probably win; the
Americans – however wealthy and likeable – were inept; the British
– poorly prepared for war – continued to act dishonourably. The
periodical illustrated the cruel allied bombing of Paris, and recalled
that in June 1941, the allies had "dishonourably" attacked the planes
of heroic Vichy French aviators in Syria on the ground.[37] Even at the
end of 1942, as the magazine was about to cease publication and the
Uriage school was about to close, *Marche* insisted on the power of
the vast German submarine fleet which, it was suggested, would
inevitably demoralize the British, who continued to be much weaker
than the axis forces (despite the unmentioned disastrous situation of
the German forces in Russia by this time).[38]

Whatever the private intentions of Segonzac in publishing *Marche*
for several months,[39] the magazine always looked very much like a
relatively smooth and high-class propaganda tool for the Marshal (Pierre
Laval was not mentioned); its insistence on German strength and allied
weaknesses would certainly have demoralized potential resisters. The
publication regularly encouraged participation in National Revolution
organizations close to Uriage like the Chantiers, Compagnons, and
Jeunesse et Montagne and, to the end, called for national unity
through support for *Le Chef*.[40] Its final issues predicted that French
prisoners would return from the Reich with a great and well-merited
affection for, and loyalty to, the Marshal, full of "Faith, Confidence"
in him for his noble sacrifice of his person for the country.[41]

URIAGE'S REGIONAL SCHOOLS

A particularly important means of spreading the ideas and influence
of the École Nationale des Cadres d'Uriage was the proliferation of
"mini-Uriages" which sprang up across the country. Regional Écoles

des cadres were created during 1941 from the fourteen centre/schools set up by Vichy's youth movements during the fall of 1940. These regional schools were directed by men who had, for the most part, been trained by the École Nationale des Cadres in the second cohort at the Château de la Faulconnière and the charter of these new institutions assigned their "spiritual direction" to Uriage, their mother school. The first sessions of the regional schools, even more makeshift than those of the Château de la Faulconnière which they imitated, sought to quickly mould their trainees by "bolstering" them morally, while also helping to provide the practical skills they needed for their jobs as youth leaders. The talks given by the instructors at these schools (according to a trainee at one of them) seem to have been drawn from lectures that the new instructors had heard at la Faulconnière or at Uriage, from articles in *Jeunesse ... France*, or from literature circulated by the youth movements. The spirit common to these regional schools was largely that of the scouts modified by la Faulconnière training[42] – even if not all scouts approved.

When the government established these regional Écoles des Cadres, the two large Catholic youth movements, the Scouts of France and the JOC, insisted on maintaining their independence and specificity. Several vignettes will illustrate why they did so, and what sort of problem the Écoles des Cadres posed for these groups.

In one instance the national president of the JOC passed on to the SGJ the complaint made by Abbé Folliet, federal chaplain of the Young Christian Workers in Haute-Savoie, who had seen a deplorable transformation in five unemployed young men on their return from the regional elite school at St. Étienne. Returning puffed up with pretensions at having become certified full-fledged leaders, they insisted on being addressed in the "vous" form and exempted from manual work, and, in general, displayed the mentality "of 1,200-francs-a-month bureaucrats." They began to be out of touch with the masses, ignored the Jocist badge, imposed saluting of the flag on others, and kept pushing ideas that were alien to the movement.[43]

An unemployed young man from Marseille lodged a similar complaint about his course at the Marseille-La Blancarde school, which had entailed what he called *embourgeoisement*, the fostering of a mentality of *petit-chef* who wanted to be "vouvoyé," an unlearning of class solidarity and of the distinctive style of the Young Christian Workers' movement.[44] Thus there is evidence that the elitism of Uriage made at least some unemployed young working-men into "high-hats," convinced of their superiority over the despiritualized masses.

The French scouts, for their part, were more troubled by the religious than the class attitudes fostered by Uriage. A meeting at the general headquarters of the *chefs d'écoles* of the Scouts de France in January 1941 focussed on "the religious question." In the presence of Father Forestier, general chaplain of the Scouts, there was much concern expressed about the religious "neutrality" of the École des cadres, after all of the *chefs* had read Father Carré's article from the *Revue des jeunes* on that subject.[45] The scouts were specifically preoccupied with Uriage:

> One must not be neutral. But we must concede that there has been a clear evolution at Uriage on that point since its beginnings at la Faulconnière. There are now special sessions for Catholics at Uriage.[46]
> It is vital that all our Catholicism not have to have a secretive air about it ...

The scouts' leaders thought the religious situation at the leadership schools could be improved by appointing a chaplain for each school, and having special lectures for the Catholic trainees.[47] The leaders were delighted to note that at the school at La Vareinne where "the scout spirit unselfconsciously prevails" both leaders and trainees, members of the Scouts de France, were participating in group prayer every evening.

Unlike the Catholic scouts, the two "Éclaireurs" associations (Éclaireurs Unionistes and Éclaireurs de France, Protestant and secular respectively) did not seem to have this distrust of the regional leadership schools, but regularly reported on regional school activities in their publications.[48] The secular EDF (Éclaireurs de France) were particularly relaxed about their schools – one of those it founded caught the attention of the authorities because the manager, Jacques Lang, was Jewish![49] The ecumenical thrust in Uriage's spiritualist personalism seemed to threaten traditional Catholics much more than it did the Protestants or the "seculars."

Louis Garrone, staunch friend of Uriage in the SGJ, presided over the opening meeting of a conference on the "Regional Schools" at Uriage in July 1941, describing the role of the SGJ and the place of these new institutions within its plans. This event consecrated the Uriage school and bestowed upon it the role of guide, or mother-school. Many of the younger delegates at the "regionals" meeting were Uriage graduates (almost all of the instructors of the regional schools came from the Château de la Faulconnière ["Pétain" cohort], or the first cohorts of Uriage) so it was almost an alumni reunion. Garrone confirmed the École Nationale des Cadres spiritual director's role within the National Revolution and a declaration at the end of the session announced that "the unity of doctrine and spiritual inspiration of the schools would be drawn from Uriage," even more than had been the case in the past.[50] So whatever reservations had been expressed about Uriage's snobbishness, ecumenism, or ties with fuzzy-minded ideologists like Mounier, the school clearly commanded the loyalty of many in Vichy's youth movements, as the youth director recognized.[51]

Uriage's relationship with the regional schools was illustrated by its ties with the École des Cadres de Gascogne, the high-profile "Uzos school" near Pau in the Pyrénées. The town had not had a happy experience with its elite schools: in June 1941, a regional youth delegation from Pau asked Uriage to send new instructors capable of giving it a second wind. The first chef of the École de Lascazères, André Tiberghien (a graduate of the Marshal Pétain cohort from la Faulconnière) had been fired in December 1940 by Louis Garrone, then regional representative at Pau, for using excessively brutal methods.[52] In response to the appeal, Uriage sent Alain Desforges, then editor-in-chief of *Jeunesse ... France!*.

In the summer of 1941, Desforges transferred the establishment to a romantic site reminiscent of Uriage, the beautiful Château-Chazal at Uzos on a crest dominating the Gave river valley, with a magnificent view of the Pyrénées. It combined the convenience of having the regional capital of Pau nearby with the advantages of a large thirty-acre property. As at Uriage, the nine-man core of the team was made up of accomplished and well-educated men, with token proletarian representation: two had "played an active social role in industry," two were engineers who had graduated from the *grandes écoles*, there was one doctor in law who had graduated from *Sciences Politiques*, one bachelor of law, one bachelor of science, one university professor, and one professional metalworker. The majestic setting created a special "climate": it seemed a sort of "retreat centre."

Desforges had been strongly marked by his time at Uriage; among all of the heads of the regional schools in France, he was the only *chef* directly sent out from a senior position on the Uriage team. He made it clear that he intended to achieve a "strong and living community" with a clearly established functional hierarchy and a common ideal, represented by a demanding "rule of life" beyond anything then in place at Uriage:

A favorable geographical setting was by itself insufficient to our needs. The "place" itself had to be exceptionally beautiful, so as to create a psychological shock. The school's furnishings, too, were to create a certain climate: elegance, rusticity, order, and scrupulous cleanliness ... The instructors' rooms will be furnished by them according to individual tastes ... only the bed must be the same as that of the trainees. The instructor, who is called to spend one or several years at Uzos, ought to be able to feel at home in his little chamber.

... To teach the Révolution Nationale to others is, in the end, relatively easy; to live it personally is certainly more difficult ... Our rule of life is summarized in two words: example and selflessness.[53]

The members of the community were obliged to make a firm commitment to give a full, renewable, year of their life to the common task. In fact their principles of example and selflessness were strictly applied: they made "the *chef* everywhere the first and the best" and instituted a rule of poverty with a common treasury favouring married instructors, and then donated their surplus to projects involving young people. Spiritual life at Pau was marked by a few days of common retreat, every semester at least, assembling the team around a visiting personality known for his charismatic spirituality.

Desforges carried the ideas of a new "virile order" further than Uriage had. Only the celibate instructors were detailed to the "fighting positions" in the community, leaving sedentary tasks to married people. The school's training stressed "the development of virility" over all else, and each training course began with a major physical ordeal: in the summer of 1941, for example, it began with a four- or five-day mountain climbing expedition. Each team (christened a "*cordée*," a roped party of alpinists) had to set off on its own expedition, envisaged as a proof of endurance from which the trainees and their *chef* would emerge forged together and tempered. During this trial the *chef* was to judge the value of each one of his men and immediately eliminate those judged inept. During the winter this initiation ritual was transformed into hikes in the countryside, including improvised voyages of exploration in the region, surprise tests such as having exhausted trainees (with their newly blistered feet) suddenly rising in the middle of the night to go off on a supplemental excursion, and games of chase between teams.[54]

Desforges encountered considerable scepticism over his approach at the Uzos Château but this did not prevent him from continuing his experience "*quand-même*" ("all the same"), which expression he made the motto of the school. In fact Uzos, with its veritable cult of the virile ordeal and community life, was revealing of the Uriage mentality and the possible spin-offs of the Hébertisme side of Segonzac's school. The Uzos monthly bulletin, *Joie*, imitated *Jeunesse ... France!*, to the point of including "le mot du chef" signed by Desforges.[55]

The Uriage and the Uzos elite schools were not alone in having a strong religious dimension to their activities. The Languedoc-Roussillon regional school even staged a colourful session for priests[56]

(directors of Catholic diocesan programs) in what had been a Protestant school: the thirty-two trainees, all chosen by their bishops,
spent three days living what was basically the life of a normal école
des cadres and were informed on the activities of the SGJ, the new
youth organizations, and the training of cadres.[57]

Another regional elite school with a strong religious slant was the
one at the Château de Mercuès, near Cahors (Lot). The first ten-day
session, organized in consultation with Segonzac, began in July 1941
with the ambitious intellectual program of rediscovering "the originality of the French nation." In a spirit of resistance "against the
powerful influences coming from the east," trainees studied "the
French ethnic group" and its Christianized greco-latin heritage; there
was a solemn oath of fidelity to the land and to the dead (another
instance of a peculiar national and synthetic, but Christian, religious-
ness growing up in the orbit of Uriage). Several people associated
with other movements were involved with the Mercuès school's efforts
and it was widely and favourably reported in Catholic publications.[58]

Two regional schools, Bobigneux and Marseille, made a special
effort to reach working people. The instructors claimed they had
faced, but overcome, an instinctive mistrust; the young workers came
to accept collective discipline, including marching in step, very well.
The enthusiastic directors of these schools stressed the importance
of their experience, while admitting that there had been tensions
between their pedagogical approach and their moralism, and what
they called the "individualism" or "petit-bourgeois scepticism" of
their charges. Certain trainees had even hinted at being opposed to
the regime and to all the ideas associated with the Révolution
Nationale. Was this working-class hostility toward Vichy's national
renewal schemes fostered by a critical sense, by class consciousness,
by political convictions? The directors of the Bobigneux and Marseille schools made no distinction between these diverse attitudes.[59]
What these schools demonstrated (once again) was that there was
little room in Uriage's orbit for urban working people. The mother
school's directors always seemed uncomfortable with proletarians,
settling for a largely symbolic representation of manual workers.

Another example of Uriage's influence was the Centre-jeunesse,
annexed to the École Nationale Professionnelle of Saint-Étienne, and
directed by administrators trained at the École Nationale des Cadres.
"They devoted an hour every evening to reviewing the day's activities,
and the conversation terminated in silent meditation." The devout
young Protestant professor in charge of the Centre d'apprentissage,
Jean Le Veugle,[60] kept a decisive contact with his alma mater Uriage,
and felt a profound, life-long commitment to Segonzac and his team.[61]

The French youth hostel movement (Auberges Françaises de la Jeunesse) also began to imitate the example of Uriage in their training methods, from morning *décrassage* to study circles. And individuals who played central roles in other organizations, such as Ollier de Marichard, founder of the "Camarades de la Route," also kept in regular contact with Segonzac's school.[62] In short, the influence of the École Nationale des Cadres over French youth movements extended from one end of the country to the other.

The ties between the Château Bayard and its alumni directing the regional schools were rich and complex: a good number of these former Uriage trainees kept in close touch with the school, confiding their difficulties or their plans to an instructor they knew, recommending someone for a course, requesting help in changing a job, or describing their efforts to adapt the Uriage style to the particular group of young people in their charge.[63] Uriage's responsibilities were formalized by government measures on 1 October 1941: the different movements were no longer to be held responsible for the various schools they had created; rather, all of these schools, supported by their various regional associations, were to be directed pedagogically and "spiritually" by Uriage.

As its responsibilities in the youth movements grew, Uriage maintained ever closer ties with its graduates. The Uriage reunion of the "Pétain" cohort of la Faulconnière from 19 to 21 October 1941 (the first anniversary of their baptism in the presence of the Marshal) served as a pretext to constitute an alumni association, with formal statutes and directors. The eighty regional school instructors were divided into sections: the thirteen school directors met with Vieux Chef Segonzac, those concerned with ideology or study programs with Hubert Beuve-Méry, and so on, as part of a more general discussion of the role of the regional schools in the light of the directives of the mother school. These meetings boosted the *esprit de corps* of the cadres of the schools, and encouraged adhesion to Uriage's political line.[64] It was becoming ever clearer that the École Nationale des Cadres was struggling to orient itself within the country's Révolution Nationale.

The tightening of the links with Uriage, "ardently desired" by the heads of the schools, was to involve regular supplies of documents and information, and more frequent visits and lectures by Uriage *chefs* or study team members. A Hébertisme lesson from Vuillemin, or the baptism of a cohort in the presence of the Vieux Chef, were particularly sought after.[65] Segonzac told the regional school leaders that "the three basics valued at Uriage were: primacy of the spiritual, the sense of honour, the cult of the Patrie," but he also remarked that: "It is understood that the Christian spirit remains the foundation of our civilization and this impels us to underline our independence vis-à-vis foreign ideologies".[66] While Segonzac asked the schools to undertake "more and more an interior and exterior adaptation to the soul and to the customs of the region where they are located," he resisted what he considered to be the exaggerations of regionalists like Vichy official Garrone.[67]

Uriage influence was also notable at the school founded in Algeria at the end of the summer of 1940. Director Rouher ("one of the better *chefs d'école*") of the Lapalisse school was succeeded by his local *adjoint*, Bernard, as the school that would soon benefit from the attentive solicitude of the Algerian authorities, was set up in the *domaine* of El Riath, at Birmandreis.[68]

The youth delegations, though more strictly dependent than the regional schools on the sgj (of which they were the effective representatives in the regions and the departments), also had important ties with Uriage, since most of their officials had passed through the mother school. (In June 1941, thirty-six of the sixty functioning delegates were Uriage graduates.)[69] Thus Segonzac's school had had direct influence on the majority of the directing personnel of a segment of Vichy's youth ministry, and, for that reason, was a force to be reckoned with in the Vichy youth movements.

There was also a discreet leadership school for women tied to Uriage. Initial legislation[70] in fact created two écoles nationales des cadres de la jeunesse, one for men, the other for women, giving them the same juridical status and, in theory, the same resources and personnel. Despite some important differences in objectives and style, they shared common civic and "spiritual" orientations.[71] In establishing a policy toward young women the sgj at Vichy turned, once again, to Catholic social activists – in this case, naming the foundress of the women's branch of the Young Christian Workers movement (jocf), Jeanne Aubert.[72] Putting aside her pre-war post of permanent administrator in the jocf national office, Aubert began to direct the women's programs of the sgj. As part of the sgj's effort to organize young unemployed women an "école de formation des cadres féminins" was opened on 15 October 1940, at Ecully near Lyon.[73]

The Ecully-les-Lyon school held three-week sessions for classes of fifty young women destined to be the directors of regional training schools. Three regional schools for women were soon created: at Saint-Galmier (Loire), at Marseille (in the Château de Belmont, at Saint-Jérôme), and at l'école de Pau (villa Saint-Basile), where five sessions were organized from January to September 1941.[74] The Ecully school was first directed by Marie-Madeleine Bureau, former director of the family auxiliaries created under the aegis of the Jesuit Father Desbuquois's L'Action Populaire movement. She was succeeded by Elisabeth Guyon, wife of Bernard Guyon, a well-known young Catholic specialist on Balzac and Péguy who had been active in the Esprit group but was then in prison in Germany.

This leadership school for women was shaped, intellectually and politically, by Uriage. The visits and talks of Beuve-Méry, particularly, made a strong impression on the Ecully team, along with those of Lyonnais intellectuals such as historian and folk-musicologist Henri-Irénée Marrou of the Esprit group.[75] The women's school seemed to adopt a girl-scout style compatible with the "virile" image of the male organizations, and with Uriage's rather old-fashioned ideas about a woman's role.

Leadership schools were also created in the occupied zone, and their relationship to Uriage is of considerable interest. Pastor Jean Joussellin, representative of the Protestant scout organization (Éclaireurs Unionistes) in the occupied zone, opened the first school for the training of cadres there in October 1941 in the Château de Sillery at Épinay-sur-Orge (Seine-et-Oise) for one hundred students, most of them from the youth movements. They formed the first cohort of this "École des Cadres de l'Île de France" and were baptized in the name of Marshal Pétain a few days before the ceremony for the "Pétain" class at the Château de la Faulconnière in the south.[76] Joussellin also directed what was officially called the "Centre de formation des Cadres supérieurs" in the Château de Charaintru (Seine-et-Oise), where he selected and trained the future instructors for the centre-schools that were being created, as well as personnel such as regional representatives, or central administration bureaucrats, for the SGJ in the occupied zone.

Thus the Charaintru school was to perform the same function in the occupied zone as Uriage for the free zone (but without the same legal status). The officials of the SGJ, fearing that this leadership school might escape their control, then envisaged the creation in the occupied zone of a formal annex of the men's École Nationale, and this was in fact legislated on 11 August 1941. By February 1942 Joussellin, with the official title of Regional Representative for Youth, was directing a network of seventeen centre-schools.[77] In a talk on 1 March 1941 at the Faculty of "Sciences Po" (École libre des Sciences Politiques) in Paris, Joussellin spoke of trying to develop a new "lived civism" that would be translated into "a commitment of the person." His "Christian and Humanist notion of a leader," and his vocabulary, showed that the influence of personalism had leaped the demarcation line to affect people in the occupied zone.[78]

The monitors at Sillery had to face conflicting tendencies among young people in occupied Paris as their trainees ranged from former left-wingers of the Faucons rouges to self-styled national socialists and former Camelots du roi.[79] Joussellin's Christian humanism proved contemptible to many fascists in the occupied zone, where there was more collaborationism and German influence than in the south. Jacques Bousquet (the Parisian teacher who had begun the successful school-pupils' movement Les Jeunes du Maréchal in the Lycée Voltaire, and called himself nationalist, socialist, and "European") then brusquely took over, moved, and reoriented the national school. This was part of a larger power struggle within the National Revolution: Bousquet, like Georges Pelorson, became one of the right-hand men of Georges Lamirand's "pagan" rival Abel Bonnard in the effort to make French young people more open to collaboration.[80] In fact, Bousquet's appointment to head the national "leadership school" in the northern zone in October 1941 was approved by the occupation authorities as "corresponding to the German interest."[81] He then put together a new team of instructors, and took over the "Château Madrid" at La Chapelle-en-Serval (Oise), a property confiscated from a wealthy Jewish family. (Before the war the Éclaireurs Israélites had held their camp-schools for training leaders, called "Montserval," there.) A vacillating Lamirand inaugurated it in January 1942.[82]

Although the La Chapelle-en-Serval school seemed to be modelled after Uriage, there were soon tensions between Uriage itself and Bousquet's group. In a letter on 21 January 1942, Segonzac warned his ally at Vichy, Louis Garrone, about the La Chapelle-en-Serval school and not long after having visited it, recalled its directors as being "hare-brained illuminati."[83] Yet Bousquet's school seemed to be thriving, planning to create and maintain sixteen regional schools, including five for the Île de France area alone.[84] The La Chapelle school, however, acquired an unsavoury reputation, as Bousquet shocked the locals by instituting the Nazi salute and having spade-bearing men mount the guard at the school in palpable imitation of the German labour service, the Reicharbeitdienst. (Bonnard explained this away to Pierre Laval by claiming it was a way of honouring agriculture!) The trainees also acquired a bad reputation for petty thievery, and a church dignitary, visiting the school at Easter 1942, was scandalized to hear the strains of the "Internationale" rising in the distance from a group of primary school teachers on a course. Vichy soon learned that Bousquet was firing staff for not being sufficiently "*hitlérien*."[85]

There were also efforts, some involving Uriage, to set up leadership schools for women in the north. Four "centres de formation de monitrices" began in October 1940 to train classes of sixty potential "chefs d'équipe" in three-week sessions: they were then assigned to direct teams of ten young women in the centres for young female workers. Thus three of the centres were functioning in the occupied zone, another in the "forbidden" zone, in which women led "a mixture of the military and the monastic" life. Of the sixty to seventy trainees who would take their rigorous program, the leaders would then select about twenty-five to thirty future monitrices, and *chefs*, for the different centres.

Perhaps because the crypto-fascists and collaborators such as Pelorson and Bousquet tended to focus primarily on training of young men, these women's schools attracted as lecturers Catholic intelligentsia interested in guiding young women – men like Beuve-Méry's friend and fellow journalist Georges Hourdin, pre-war scout leader Pierre Goutet,[86] or historians from the Catholic personalist milieu Jacques Madaule and Daniel-Rops. The goal of these schools was, in Daniel-Rops words, to recreate the French community – to break down social classes, "egoisms," routines, in what constituted "a unique opportunity" to "radically change the rapports of social classes with one another."[87]

That so many Catholics were involved in running the regional schools was not surprising because the Vichy government sought out professionals – people involved in the pre-war social services or youth movements, or intellectuals who had demonstrated an interest in the problems of the young – and Catholics were disproportionately represented in those categories. Many of these Catholics already knew one another and the government tried to broaden their views by getting them to work in movements based upon a non-confessional syncretism. It was also evident that the delegation of a project to an experienced, rather than an inexperienced, person (to men such as Segonzac, Joussellin, or Melle Aubert) would result in the development of a viable and durable institution.[88]

The success of *Jeunesse ... France!* and of the network of regional schools nurtured by Uriage demonstrated the leadership qualities of Dunoyer de Segonzac and the originality and attractiveness of the inspiration of his school. The competing leadership schools that took shape were disquieting to Vichy authorities for various reasons. Segonzac had founded more than a school and a community: he was behind a particular vision of the National Revolution and of Vichy France, one that seemed to enjoy a certain support, particularly among the young. Uriage was also providing Vichy – whether it wanted it or not – with its very own young shock troops, albeit of the spirit.

The Uriage Network, 1941: The Équipe nationale, Économie et Humanisme, the Scouts and Compagnons

THE ÉQUIPE NATIONALE D'URIAGE AND THE *ÉCONOMIE ET HUMANISME* MOVEMENT

An organized association of Uriage graduates, an "Équipe nationale d'Uriage," was already envisaged by early 1941. It was thought that for the good of the alumni,

The school would remain the fixed point to which they could return to recharge their spiritual batteries when they were badly treated by life's realities. They would think healthily again, and see things simply; once again they would shed the egotism and cupidity of modern life and experience that same state of spirit in which, at the end of their course, they had taken their oath at the foot of the flag.[1]

Thus in creating the Équipe nationale d'Uriage, Segonzac wanted to create more than just an alumni association – a community of deeply committed men, limited in number at the outset. He would require discipline and solidarity of them (a more or less solemn commitment – a renewal of the "Uriage oath," which would express their profound attachment to "the spirit of Uriage"). To find the right men the school provided each instructor-leader of a team with a list of all of his new trainees to confidentially rate their suitability for the "Équipe nationale." The leaders of the school also approached instructors who had left for their opinions of their trainees. What had been announced by the SGJ as a sort of friendly society of alumni became, in effect, an inner circle for which the founders co-opted the members.[2] The Uriage school wanted to bring together under Segonzac's leadership the cream of the faithful from across the country.

The creation of an association for the various regional leadership schools (the ERC) was planned for the meeting of directors and instructors from the regional schools organized for 20–21 October 1941 at Uriage to commemorate the anniversary of the visit of Marshal Pétain to la Faulconnière.[3] Jean Stouff, the head of the ERC of Bobigneux, had just confided some secret information to his trusted friends: the militant collaborationists of the PPF (the Parti populaire français of Jacques Doriot) were going to try to take power at Vichy, and take over the SGJ: "Garrone would be fired. Uriage would be closed for three months. The *chefs* would go work in a mine ... The regional schools would be threatened." He concluded: "The position of the Marshal is not known. We are prepared to defend the Uriage doctrine whatever the cost, by every means."[4] Clearly the men of Uriage were preparing to fight for their kind of Révolution Nationale, one directed by those leaders who had a sure "sense of the spiritual."

The École Nationale des Cadres d'Uriage was frankly and unashamedly elitist and the Équipe nationale faithfully reflected this characteristic. The new ENU consciously set out to gather "an elite" in accordance with Segonzac's vision: "to group the best for a task ... bring together the people in whom we have confidence."

In his speech to the general meeting of 21 October 1941 Segonzac said of the ENU:

We are operating on a national level ... above parties ... even above movements; we are working for the Marshal; we know what is healthy in the nation and what is not; we want to guide people in healthy directions ... the only movements we can [presently] support and toward which we can orient our boys are the confessional movements and the Compagnons ... The Compagnons movement has had a serious crisis; [but] it has a worthy doctrine and a good leader: it is better than certain other movements that are new and that, no doubt will eventually fall apart in a ghastly mess; nothing is invented in life and the essential thing is to begin with a doctrine, and solid *cadres* ... we ... represent the Marshal's thinking; perhaps that sounds ambitious, but we believe it.

Segonzac's stubborn belief that Uriage represented the thinking of Pétain required a largely uncritical loyalty to the person of the Marshal that set Uriage over against the Gaullists and de Gaulle. Later he said:

We have always argued that young Frenchmen should not fall into the wake of a foreign power. So we have always condemned Gaullism. If you took the

training course at Uriage you would have had a chance to see the officers
who returned from Syria [where they fought against the English and the
Free French]. They said that the French who have gone into General de
Gaulle's service have, it seems, lost their sense of honour in a way, while the
people who fought [against the allied forces] saved honour.

But who did Segonzac really hope would win the war? He went on
to insist on certain distinctions, to reflect on the meaning of certain
terms:

The word "collaboration" has been abused; unfortunately, we are indeed
obliged for better or for worse to accept a certain co-ordination of efforts
that allows us ... to live ... and that also permits the Germans to continue
the war. There is a reciprocity that is built into the situation that we have
not been able to avoid. [But] we are waiting for only one thing: that the
[national] territory be liberated ...

Lest there be any misunderstanding about his attitude toward
Nazism, Segonzac once again insisted that it was difficult to reconcile
Hitlerism with the spiritual values of Uriage, and that, in any case,
Germany might not be invincible after all:

national socialism is completely opposed to Christian civilization, so there
can be no equivocation ... a certain number of things are working in our
favour: there is the war in Russia which is solving many problems; in constituting an "Équipe nationale d'Uriage," we are not set on doing something
extraordinary, we simply want an elite, at the service of the nation, at the
service of others.[5]

In sum, like Marshal Pétain (the Pétain imagined by Segonzac), the
Vieux Chef seemed committed to a proud, independent France ...
but one adapted to the New European Order. Within the ENU
Segonzac envisaged a tight unity of purpose, a co-ordination of
responses to crises: "Granted you might need a signal from Uriage
on one problem or another that might arise. I ask you, each time
that happens, to inform us right away; we might not have the solution, but we will give you our opinion on the issues you put to us,
and as sincerely as possible."[6]

Segonzac's declaration was a clear moral condemnation of the
Gaullist action in Syria, and a claim to represent integral fidelity to
"the policy of the Marshal" (which he seemed to distinguish from
that of the government).[7] In this, Segonzac displayed an unshakeable,
quasi-mystical faith in the Marshal, and proud confidence in his own

capacity to guide the politics of the ENU without a balanced, open discussion of what was becoming, for the French, a crucial episode in the war.

An important article in *Jeunesse ... France!* a few weeks later (apparently written by Chombart de Lauwe)[8] credited the ENU with leading French young people away from the temptations of collaborationism or resistance and toward revolutionizing France, since the ENU represented new elites who would take power and transform the country "from above":

In expanding the activities of the École Nationale des Cadres and the Écoles régionales, the purpose of the Équipe nationale d'Uriage (Association des anciens élèves) is to form among the young, in the largest sense of that word, a self-conscious French elite capable of rebuilding the country from above ...

As Marshal Pétain said, the first revolution to be accomplished is a personal one ... the team holds that none of us can pretend to act on other levels if he has not begun to reform himself ... The association will only be comprised of trainees who, during their course or after leaving the school, have demonstrated their worth.

... The French elite will not have a soul if its body cannot develop. ... [this project] involves forming teams, by region or municipality, for periodic meetings, comparing notes, a little athletics, a few practical projects, and social action.[9]

The directors of the mother-school would play a central role here: "Some precise tasks will be set out by the Central Committee and passed on to the leaders of the regional sections for execution, to the extent to which their circumstances permit. The section heads will [also] propose to the Central Committee projects that might be undertaken [by the regional sections]."

In a France divided between partisans of France's closer collaboration with Germany in the construction of a European New Order, and those supporting the allies and de Gaulle, the Équipe was to strive, above all, for French unity under the Marshal:

We have to place the maintaining of unity among the most urgent tasks ... the French Community, and ... the defence of our spiritual patrimony based in Christian civilization. Above and beyond the divisions imposed by the armistice, a partisan spirit still surfaces in diverse forms. Opposition between the sympathizers of one or another foreign power, rivalry among the movements, et cetera, must completely disappear from the heart of the team and then, through us, from all of the groups, organisms, and social milieux in which the members exert their influence.

As far as the ENU's relationship with the government's youth office was concerned,

The Équipe is the best guarantee on a private level of the liaisons between diverse groups that the various governmental organisms are trying to establish on the official level …

Members of the Équipe will encourage, in all the areas to which they can extend their activities, the development of state-recognized youth movements and help with their recruitment and publicity … attaching particular attention to the task of the recruiting of trainees for the Écoles Régionales des Cadres and for Uriage.

And if the ENU would be a supporter for Vichy youth projects it would also play a special role in regard to Frenchmen in the prison camps back in Germany: while providing material and moral support they would "try to acquaint them with reassuring achievements (Écoles des Cadres, Chantiers de Jeunesse, the creation of movements, the organization of the Commissariat aux Sports, of the Commissariat au Travail des Jeunes), showing them that certain groups do not simply echo the National Revolution in their speeches or writings." In sum:

The essential mission of the team member is to act in his family, his profession, his milieu, his movement, his region … to truly appear as leader there. That task is difficult because he will be pulled from all sides and could quickly fall back into a routine or mediocrity. The Équipe is there to help reassure him that he is not alone, that he is part of an elite and that he must keep up the same standards as his comrades.[10]

In short, the ENU was to form an elite within the elites who ran the government youth movements. Like the Jesuits, they were to be a chosen, disciplined, committed, and selfless cohort, united in their spiritual ideal and bound by a special bond to their leader, the Vieux Chef (who, in turn, offered unshakeable fealty to the Marshal). The chosen of the ENU, exploiting the Pétain government's organizations, could reconstruct the country along new lines. But the document enunciating the guiding principles of the ENU was not overly optimistic as it recalled that the country was "defeated and crippled," that it was a time "when everything should be questioned" and it was "necessary to defend, inch by inch, what remained, and rebuild what was destroyed": "The future is uncertain and [young people] ought to be ready for ever greater sacrifices, and, if necessary, the sacrifice of their lives".[11] It was not always clear, however, who the ENU might be asked to give their lives defending their country against: they were warned, successively, of the Germans, the collaborators, the Communists, the allies, and the Gaullists.

Segonzac's insistence that the ENU accept discipline and direction was rooted in an aristocratic cavalry officer's contempt for pre-war political bickering and discord, and in an early newsletter Segonzac charged the team never to forget its prime directives:

That our activity is inspired by the precepts of Christian civilization.

That we recognize no pre-war political party, and even want to obliterate the spirit of parties.

That our politics is the Marshal's, that we are certain of following his line more faithfully than anyone else. The ENU is a team of elites at the service of France, the French, and the Marshal. Devoid of personal ambition, it should provide the most solid support ever seen for the healthiest French institutions and for Frenchmen worthy of the name.[12]

An ENU committee made up of the Council and the *chefs* d'Alançon, Beuve-Méry, and Vuillemin began meeting monthly at Uriage. Chombart de Lauwe and Lavorel took charge of the secrétariat of what became a permanent "service ENU" of the school. At the end of October 1941, 200 alumni were approached about entering the ENU, among whom were 105 who had been at Uriage during the October days. Besides the instructors of the regional schools, and members of the "Pétain" cohort of la Faulconnière, only a small number of former trainees were invited in the first round; the others would be sounded out if they "passed their tests."[13]

Examination before acceptance to the Uriage inner circle apparently involved proving that one had a "spirituality" compatible with that of the rest of the team. If this was missing then one did not qualify as one of the "happy few" – those new elites whose advance within the structures of the nation the Uriage team was supporting.

In any case, by the end of 1941 the Équipe nationale d'Uriage was demanding a total commitment of its members. A Uriage alumnus recorded a discussion that took place in December 1941: "At Terrenoire, Stouff spoke to us of the ENU. It is to be a knighthood. Only people prepared to die for our cause. Meeting of the regional directing committee. A reading by Stouff of the directives of the Vieux Chef."[14] Back at Vichy, Louis Garrone wrote Segonzac that he was worried that the ENU might get out of hand and young people think there were two different youth programs "when, after all, these programs were identical in their goals."[15] And toward the end of October 1941 Chombart de Lauwe met with Cardinal Gerlier who "clearly showed his reticence about the alumni movements – whether that of Uriage or of the Chantiers – fearing they would turn young people from participation in Catholic Action."[16]

In order to head off further difficulties the secrétariat of the ENC made a list of "persons to see" to prevent misunderstandings. These included the cream of the French Catholic elite at the time: Cardinal Gerlier, Robert Garric, Valentin (director general of the ex-serviceman's organization the Légion des combattants), Father Doncoeur, Dary (Scouts de France), Gortais (secretary-general of the ACJF), Dubois (JOC), l'Amicale des Chantiers, Msgr Courbe, the Compagnons de Péguy, and the key economist, social thinker, and Pétain adviser François Perroux – all of them key figures in the "Catholic mafia," or official Catholicism, at Vichy. A discreet but systematic effort was made to recuperate sympathizers of the schools in the regional military command posts as well as in the governmental ministries. At Vichy, Lebrec, who worked in the Youth services, headed a team of Uriage people that included young officials from several offices.[17]

Chombart de Lauwe also contacted Perroux's high-powered "Économie et Humanisme" think-tank at Marseille. In January its founder, Father Louis Lebret, had spent several days at Uriage, marking the beginning of the *Économie et Humanisme* intellectual collaboration with the study group of the school. This organization is, in retrospect, of some historical importance and although only in its beginnings in 1942 it would prove to be a useful ally to the Uriage group. Its story in the light of the Uriage experience is instructive for several reasons.

Father Louis Lebret, the founder of *Économie et Humanisme*, had been a navy officer, and his traditionalist Breton background gave him much in common with Vieux Chef Segonzac of Uriage. He entered the Dominican order without abandoning his concern for social issues and, in the wave of popular evangelism at the end of the 1920s, had founded the Jeunesse maritime chrétienne, a new cousin to the JOC and JAC (Jeunesse agricole chrétienne). When the Depression had hit the Breton docks in 1933, he had worked to organize the sailors into a community, a "corporation," to defend their interests.

In 1940 Father Lebret initially had reservations about Pétain, but his aversion to republican France had led him to accept the National

Revolution with enthusiasm. He was one of those many communitarians who were out to fight capitalism in the name of social justice without giving in to class struggle. This last imperative, by itself, explains the initial fidelity of people like Lebret to the National Revolution and to Marshal Pétain. But Lebret's ideas at the time concerning the means of achieving social justice were still vague. In the first edition of his *Mystique d'un monde nouveau (découvert du bien commun)*, replete with references to the Marshal, National-Socialist Germany was held up as an example.

In early 1942, Lebret joined Dominican Father Jacques Loew (another individual with worldly experience – he had been a lawyer in Nice before joining the Dominicans) in founding the Centre d'étude des complexes sociaux (*Économie et Humanisme*) at Marseille with the help of François Perroux and Gustave Thibon (as well as René Moreux, Alexandre Dubois, Jean-Marius Gatheron, and Edmond Laulhère). The Économie et Humanisme movement proposed, like Uriage, a Third Way between "capitalist chaos" and "socialist statism," between "the capitalist myth of profit" and "the socialist myth of equality" (as in their *Économie et Humanisme*, special issue of February–March 1942). Some impressive new thinking and new experiences resulted from the initiative.

Father Jacques Loew, who pioneered a new "style of life" by labouring alongside Marseille dockworkers, became the first "worker priest" – and a cahier of *Économie et Humanisme* described his "proletarian" experience. The movement's *Manifeste d'Ecully*, published at the beginning of 1944, called for a "style of life" that would be "really revolutionary," employing a language very similar to that of Uriage.

While later, for nearly forty years, the Économie et Humanisme group would exert great influence through their attention to the problems of the Third World, during the years 1942–1947 Lebret, Loew, Henri Desroches, and other "communitarian" Dominicans – at first inspired by a certain *pétainisme* – essentially attacked the proletarian condition. The Christian personalists of all the groups engaged in action (Économie et Humanisme, Jeunesse de l'Église, Esprit, the Routiers) agreed that Christianity had to be "re-virilized." A whole "neo-franciscan" ambience prevailed (Francois Perroux, for one, had a special devotion to his patron saint), from the Chantiers of Vichy to the *maquis*, and via Uriage and the first "communautés de travail," the principles of Father Lebret (whose lectures at Uriage celebrated the beauty of nature and the holiness of work) were applied. It was symptomatic that the major priority of Économie et Humanisme was, like that of Uriage, the "forming" of leaders. Pedagogical concerns, in the largest sense, took precedence over all the projects of rebuilding society from above, supported, of course, by the new studies of "the human phenomenon" that were concocted in the study groups or among the intelligentsia of the *chantiers*. For Father Lebret's group, as for the Uriage community, 1942 marked a turning point in which the Catholic milieu in Lyon in 1942–43, strongly influenced by the Resistance and avant-garde Jesuits and Dominicans, played an important role. These latter were trying to transfer certain values of the National Revolution to patriotic groups struggling against the nazis, and that concern led to the promotion of contacts between elements of the Resistance (Henri Frenay, Viannay) and elements of Vichy that were supposed, rightly or wrongly, to be salvageable. Father Maydieu and the Uriage community took part in these activities; Économie et Humanisme, now at l'Abresle, also participated. That reorganization led to some quarrels – with Gustave Thibon, unshakeably faithful to Pétain, and with a reproachful François Perroux.

Économie et Humanisme eventually became an important movement, which would lead the Le Play generation of economists and social thinkers to a variety of reforms, left-wing political engagements, and even flirtation with communism, It would promote, above all, *tiers-mondisme*, leading to the concern for the Third World that seems to be an essential component of Catholic identity in today's France. Louis Lebret became, in Daniel Lindenberg's words, "objectively speaking, one of the greatest 'revolutionaries' of the twentieth century."[18]

The Économie et Humanisme connection demonstrated that some first-rate minds with a *mystique* not so different from Uriage could work alongside the school – that the Uriage "style of life" could extend far beyond the Château Bayard. Beyond that the Équipe nationale d'Uriage provided the organizational framework for the formidable network of elite school graduates, with a mandate from the mother-school (and, presumably, the Marshal) to extend its influence as much as possible. By the end of 1941 the men of Uriage had become a power to be reckoned with in the National Revolution.

URIAGE, THE SCOUTS, AND THE CATHOLIC YOUTH ORGANIZATIONS

Christian youth organizations soon noticed that their most promising young people could be drawn off by the Uriage school. Of all the youth organizations, it was the Catholic scouts that had displayed the most spontaneous enthusiasm for Vichy's initial youth programs,[19] but it was the École Nationale des Cadres, not the scouts, that were summoned by the youth ministry to bring together all of the movements of French young people through their "personalism." The SGJ youth movements office announced that: "The principle for unity among youth ought to be the construction of our national community in a more authentically French direction – that is, in respect for the person."[20]

On 7 April 1941 the "Conseil national de la jeunesse," an organization set up by the SGJ to co-ordinate the youth movements, held its first meeting. Georges Lamirand had named seven members to meet regularly for one year – four directors of movements (the Scouts, the ACJF, the Jeunesse ouvrière chrétienne féminine (JOCF), and the "Jeunesses Paysannes" of Dorgères) and three men involved with Vichy's youth programs (sometime Uriage instructor Jean-Jacques Chevallier, Hyacinthe Dubreuil, and Doctor Biot, author of a cahier in Daniel-Rops' *Présence* series in the 1930s). Also present, ex officio, as consultants, were Directeur de la Jeunesse Louis Garrone, and Pierre Dunoyer de Segonzac as the head of the École Nationale des Cadres. In the spring of 1941, then, the Uriage school became Louis Garrone's accomplice in the SGJ scheme of combining the independent French youth movements, and high-level ties were established between Uriage and the directors of the whole spectrum of French youth movements, strengthened by Uriage's hosting of a discussion on the question. The school had a particularly warm response from the Protestant movements, judging by the abundance of ensuing communications.

The Uriage group had considerable input into the discussions about the harmonizing of youth movements. In fact, Beuve-Méry, in opening the meeting at Uriage to discuss this issue, established its agenda and perhaps its vocabulary. The school began to play a role in tandem with the SGJ, defending a communitarian but "pluralistic" ideal for Vichy's youth movement.[21] The role was evident in a symptomatic book *Jeunesse et communauté nationale*,[22] published in the Dominicans' "Rencontres" series, which had two Uriage intellectuals, Lallement and Reuter, join Father Pie Duployé (an authority on Péguy) in an invitation to Catholic youth movement activists to transcend their particularities and take on the "national task" (an agenda described as patriotic, not political). In the same book Thomist philosopher Étienne Borne presented an acceptable "Christian heroism" that would promote physical vigour, strength, and the communitarian life, over against suspect German notions of courage based on distorted conceptions of vitality and the will to power. A friend of Beuve-Méry, the brilliant young Dominican historian and theologian Marie-

Dominique Chenu, published a monograph in François Perroux's "Bibliothèque du Peuple" series at the Presses Universitaires de France calling for a new "community of work," *Pour être heureux travaillons ensemble* (Paris, 1942), which also became an important book in Uriage training. Thus many of the Catholic intelligentsia could agree on the most positive aspects of the Révolution Nationale, thereby showing their common aversion to liberalism and individualism. But as they tried to define and refine the Révolution Nationale, some of their traditional values collided with some of the new ideas and impulses generated by the New Order.

The Catholic hierarchy, for their part, seemed most interested in keeping control over and conserving the religious specificity in the Catholic Action movements; the bishops demanded a *droit de regard* on what was going on in the Écoles des Cadres, the Auberges de Jeunesse, and other "national" institutions.[23] But as the bishops temporized, Garrone showed the importance of Uriage for the French National Revolution by announcing: "No one can be director of an affiliated association if he has not passed a course either at the École nationale or at an École régionale de cadres du secrétariat général à la Jeunesse".[24]

The synthesizing impetus of Uriage, its effort to draw disparate young people into a personalist community of the spirit, was vital to the new government youth organizations such as the Compagnons de France or the associations of youth hostels that developed in co-operation with Uriage and relied on its support.[25] Uriage, to them, represented the "cutting edge" of the National Revolution; it would lead the "old" movements to share in a unique community experience. Such a Uriage *mystique* could hardly fail to worry some Catholic leaders, or make them jealous.

Among the pre-war Catholic youth leaders, those who were most open to the National Revolution seem to have had the most sympathy for Uriage. Prominent among these was Scout leader Father Paul Doncoeur, a man genuinely if naively enthusiastic not only about Pétain but about the general New Order in Europe. Doncoeur's perception of occupied France was distorted by his lifelong nostalgia for a simultaneously spiritual and temporal unified order; he had devoted his life to encouraging his disciples to participate in his dream of the eventual heroic convergence of all of the higher energies. In 1940 he thought he saw, after decades of indifference or hostility, a political power favourable to the Church and to the values he had served so selflessly. The outspoken priest was quick to denounce slackers and to call spiritual and political resistance either culpable or blind. Some Doncoeur arguments were repeated by others, and Garrone even used them, in his own way, to oppose Emmanuel Mounier's idiosyncratic influence on youth organizations and Uriage.[26]

Another priest with a high profile in the National Revolution was Father Marcel-Denys Forestier, founder of the Rover scout movement which had flourished in some *grandes écoles* before the war. As chaplain-general of the Scouts de France and a faithful follower of Pétain, Forestier soon played an important role in "re-educating" French youth, particularly as chaplain to Vichy's first youth organization, the Chantiers de la Jeunesse.[27] In his first doctrinal declaration in fall 1940, entitled "A New Middle Ages," Forestier called all the scouts and *routiers* to a heroic effort to create islands of "luminous Christianity" in preparation for "the renewal of France, the reconstruction stone by stone of a Christendom of Europe".[28] By 1940 generations of *routiers* had been so impregnated with notions of knighthood and Christian reconstruction that they were fertile material for the National Revolution and the mentality that flourished at the Château Bayard.[29] Scout leaders like Fathers Forestier and Doncoeur appreciated Uriage when it was resolutely toeing the government line, dutifully doing its part in the national effort to transform the young.

Among the leaders of the scouts who became special friends of Uriage was André Cruziat, a close collaborator of Père Forestier. Cruziat was a director of the Compagnons and headed, from spring 1941, the new "Amitiés scoutes" movement made up of fraternities of married couples, drawing from civic and professional action groups. Unlike some of his colleagues in the scouts, Cruziat was particularly interested in, and appreciative of, Uriage's search for a distinctive approach.[30] Segonzac valued the scout movement and men like Cruziat but felt that Uriage could definitely effect improvements. The Vieux Chef granted that the famous *veillées* of Uriage had been "borrowed from the scout movement," but he insisted that the men of Uriage had found it "necessary to differentiate them from scoutism by making them more manly," thus aiding the trainees by "making them more accessible to your public."[31] The École Nationale des Cadres was confident it could add an extra something to the scouts – temper them, make them more mature, virile, open to other ideals and *mystiques,* and broader-minded.

While scout leaders tended to sympathize with Uriage, other Catholic groups were explicit about their reservations. Uriage's cultivation of Mounier and *Esprit*'s ecumenism, and its intention to unite its trainees in a mystique that transcended class differences in what some even saw as its "national socialism," ran directly against the thinking of some Catholic groups. Gortais, secretary-general of the Catholic youth organization ACJF, clarified the position of his group to a meeting of the federal and diocesan directors of the ACJF at Lyon: "Methodically mixing the young belonging to different milieux, however pleasant ... in no way solves a fundamental problem. Even if this mixing fosters reciprocal ties of esteem and friendship, the fact remains that after such more or less extended get-togethers, the bourgeois's son finds himself a bourgeois again, and the worker's son, a worker."

According to Gortais the ACJF intended to help reconstruct the French community in making young people discover "not only the meaning of their vocation of being French persons, but above all – to escape from disappointing abstractions and to be realist as life itself demands – the meaning of their vocation of French worker, French peasant, or French bourgeois."[32] In other words, Gortais found the heady vision of transcending classes not very Catholic, and good reason for a cool ACJF attitude toward the École Nationale des Cadres. In short, Uriage could be appreciated by the "independent" youth leaders if it did not excessively intrude upon their activities or ideas but was content to moderately complement them.[33]

The Young Christian Workers' Movement (JOC) was worried that a "youth mystique" might supplant its own worker mystique. But it was not Uriage, but the Compagnons, with their ambition of mobilizing the great mass of young people, using laic and revolutionary vocabulary, that provoked their mistrust.[34] And the Young Christian Students, Jeunesse étudiante chrétienne (JEC) had a position similar to that of the JOC on this issue as, according to one of its directors,[35] it was wary of Vichy trying to create one unified Pétainist youth movement, a "jeunesse unique."[36] While JEC leaders had some ties with the Uriage school, and assumed it hostile to the Nazis, Catholic traditionalists among them feared the Pétainist, spiritualist, and "personalist" thrust of Vichy youth movements. They judged it difficult to manage and possibly anti-Catholic or anti-Christian, and hence potentially totalitarian.

Given the Christian-Knight ambience at Uriage one might have expected reticence about the school from the Protestant, Jewish, and independent scouts. In fact, however, the spiritualist and personalist synthesis of the school seemed to offer them room to manoeuvre in the midst of the heavy-handed clericalism of Pétain's regime. At Easter 1941 there was a course at the school with a good number of Protestants in attendance; André Dumas (a future pastor) recorded favourable impressions in his magazine. After noting that "intellectually the influence of the *Esprit* group is primary at Uriage," he concluded by citing, approvingly, some words of the Vieux Chef: "'We have the ... strong feeling that there are specific and primary French values. The two principles of the National Revolution are therefore respect for the person and desire to live in community'."[37]

The independent "Éclaireurs de France" seemed the most enthusiastic of all the different scout movements about the different youth organizations meeting at Uriage, and particularly about the ecumenical tone of the gathering. As one of their leaders put it: "Here we are members of a great team, diversified in a particularly French way, each working according to his temperament, his specialty, his spirituality."[38] The Éclaireurs de France, like the *chefs* at Uriage, held certain basic values as self-evident but claimed to be above disputatious ideologies and orthodoxies: although "neutral" and "laïc" they eschewed scepticism, respected all beliefs, and even encouraged the deepening of individual religious commitments.

By 1939 the Fédération des associations d'Éclaireurs de France seem to have been well integrated into the Republican regime and the secular school system – without abandoning either the Christian motivations of a number of its directors, or the pedagogical and moral principles of Baden-Powell that inspired their condemnation of the individualism and egoism of a lax and dissolute society.[39] But even an innocuous scout movement like the Éclaireurs de France encouraged a moralistic contempt for the "softness" and lack of spirituality of the city-dwellers, and for "sceptics," which, in the 1930s, had anti-Republican implications. Something similar to the synthesizing Scout mentality of the Éclaireurs de France, reinforced by the philosophy of Bergson, seemed central to Uriage and to the National Revolution ("Life is not neutral") and, when it was carried to extremes, promoted a kind of spiritualist totalitarianism: one was "free" to believe what one wanted, as long as one (strongly) believed in something. The Uriage school and the Éclaireurs de France had the same sorts of ideological preoccupations and responded to them in similar ways, so the affinity between the two was not surprising.[40]

THE COMPAGNONS AND THE TOTALITARIANS

The Compagnons de France, the first official youth movement to spring up in France after the defeat, had a special relationship with Uriage. The idea for the Compagnons came from a grouping of youth movements, called the comité jeunesse de France, which a young "Sciences Po" graduate and Inspecteur des Finances, Henri

Dhavernas, had set up in Paris immediately after the armistice. Dhavernas had been acting chief commissioner for the (Catholic) Scouts de France and he had quickly acquired the backing of old scout Paul Baudouin, of his fellow Catholic scouts Pierre Goutet and Father Forestier, of the head of the Protestant Scouts, Jean Gastambide, and of Fraisse from the JOC, for his new organization. Already registered as an association in July 1940, having secured financial support from Vichy and promises of *cadres* from extant youth groups, Dhavernas's Compagnons organized their first camp from 1 to 4 August 1940 in the Randan forest, near Vichy. Forty-five representatives of France's youth movements, twenty-five from secular, and twenty from confessional, met and agreed to a "Charter of Randan," which asked government support for all of the existing youth organizations but also for the creation of the independent "Compagnons de France" to "develop the personality of youth while respecting and deepening the convictions of each one."[41]

The Compagnons de France, like Uriage, was both a pragmatic way to unify French young people and a reflection of the romantic, anti-liberal, anti-modern mentality of many pre-war Catholic intellectuals. The name "Compagnons" had been chosen to signify the "compagnonnage" of the medieval journeyman. The organization resurrected medieval phraseology: under the "Maître Compagnon" there were "Provinces," "Pays," "Triades," and "Compagnies," each of which had a leader. "Compagnies" with more than fifty "Compagnons" were divided into "Équipes" of ten boys, each commanded by a young "chef d'équipe" who was to be "an example and guide for each Compagnon."[42] The same insistence on authority, obedience, rank, and leadership as would appear later at Uriage included "colours ceremonies" with a solemn salute, sometimes given kneeling. The military-style dark blue uniform consisted of a beret, blue shirt (emblazoned with the movement's emblem, the "coq gaulois"), shorts, or ski trousers. There was also an official Compagnons' salutation (which was not dissimilar to the Nazi greeting).

In the rural Compagnies the young unemployed were put to farm work, and in the urban Compagnies all social classes were determinedly mixed. Compagnies of some fifty men were placed at the disposal of public water, forestry, bridge, and highway services, and worked at projects like reclaiming land, harvesting grapes, constructing athletic fields or aiding refugees. The strict (and rather anti-intellectual) daily routine was composed of 0630 Reveille, 0715 breakfast, 0730 "Hébertisme" warm-up (as at Uriage), 0800 inspection, 0815 "colours" ceremony and short inspirational talk, 0830 to noon work, 1215 lunch, 1330–1630 work, 1645 snack, clean-up, laundry, make-and-mend, 1730 sport or vocational training, 1815 talk by the leader (an expansion of the topic introduced at the morning ceremony), 1830 educational classes, 1915 dinner, 2000 entertainment.[43] Director Guillaume de Tournemire, who had served under Marshal Lyautey in Morocco, would tell the Compagnons: "Our world-view places the community above the interests of private individuals ... [and encourages] community-oriented habits in the new generation."[44] The Compagnons, Marshal Pétain told them, were to be "the National Revolution's vanguard."[45]

The Compagnons movement was much smaller than the Catholic youth or scout organizations but, as one of the two movements that was officially sanctioned and directly controlled by the new government, it was closely observed. Rival organizations with leanings toward collaboration with the Germans such as the Francistes, the Jeunesses Populaires Françaises, and the Jeunes de l'Europe Nouvelle, tended to deride or envy the Compagnons. Many Catholics tended to be unsympathetic to Dhavernas's movement because they feared that its zeal for "communitarian habits" might foster a totalitarian state operation. Thus Pierre Limagne of La Croix, when recording in his diary Pétain's 15 August 1940 visit to the main Compagnons camp, saw a new importance given to "a new youth movement of a fairly disturbing, official kind."[46] Mounier complained about the "inflation" of the number of Catholic youth leaders associated with the Compagnons and confided his fear to Msgr Guerry that it was indeed the precursor of a totalitarian youth organization (a misgiving that the secretary of the Catholic hierarchy shared). But not long afterwards, in October 1940, Mounier noted that he found the Compagnons to be about the best thing at Vichy, having "healthy intentions," et cetera.[47]

Not only did Dhavernas, as founder and first leader of the Compagnons, enjoy Baudouin's backing, but he was also the son of one of Vichy Education Minister Jacques Chevalier's best friends. Having been told to expect up to 500,000 unemployed youths in the movement, Dhavernas began prudently by setting up facilities for half that number. This proved wise because the expected clientele for the movement never materialized: unemployment never reached the scale expected, young refugees were able to return home, and the Chantiers de la Jeunesse drained off potential Compagnons who were of military age. Thus the numbers in the Compagnons were much less than expected; nevertheless, the movement received the enormous sum of 19 million francs in subsidies, in addition to an initial sum of 6.1 million francs handed over personally to Dhavernas by Baudouin, between October 1940 and January 1941.[48]

Beginning in the summer of 1940, the Compagnons camp-school at Randan held twelve successive *stages*. Although we have no record of the relationship between the Randan school and Dunoyer de Segonzac's fledgling institution at la Faulconnière,[49] the "Positions Compagnons," a summary of the movement doctrine as set out by the founders, seemed to embrace the same personalism as that of *Esprit* or Uriage, calling for the respect of the person at the service of the community, over against the two errors of individualism and collectivism.[50] In fact, besides Scout André Cruziat, several personalists were shaping the ideology of the Compagnons: Louis-Émile Galey, a volatile co-founder of *Esprit* who had moved from Mounier's review and its "Third Force" street-fighting auxiliary to work with Gaston Bergery's Parti Frontiste and paper *La Flèche*, was "chef de provinces" while Jean Maze, who had also passed from the "Third Force" to work with the Parti Frontiste and *La Flèche*, ran the *Compagnons* weekly, for which he immediately elicited contributions from Emmanuel Mounier.[51]

The personalist ideas in the Compagnons camp, and the high profile of this vocabulary at Uriage, shows how the personalism that had permeated Catholic elites in the 1930s quickly worked its way into National Revolution youth programs. A whole network of dedicated people was to lead the young into a movement for revitalized, united national community free of permissiveness and individualism, and suffused with a respect for the human person. The call was for "spirituality," for leadership, obedience, and authority, with strong beliefs in invisible realities, and a reverence for Marshal Pétain.

In both the Compagnons and the Uriage communities a spirit of juvenile rebellion, of the gay camaraderie of a "gang," accompanied, somewhat paradoxically, an emphasis on rank, external conformity, and discipline. To these the Compagnons added the anti-capitalism and socialist impetus of former self-styled Third Force "revolutionaries" merged with the anti-parliamentarianism and anti-liberalism of former disciples of Maurras. Catholics were suspended, as it were, between the conservative or reactionary influences in the National Revolution and the radical aspiration for a personalist community. Thus impulses heretofore thought to be in conflict were brought together by a common hope in the potential of the new regime, with its promise of unprecedented opportunities for youth.

Each youth movement was introduced by one of its directors in a book with a synthesizing perspective published at Uriage in the fall of 1941. The chapter on the Compagnons de France demonstrated its affinity with Uriage. Under the rubric "Position du mouvement" there were not only the expected texts on youth, work, and family but also discussions of current issues such as domestic politics, foreign policy, "Gaullism," "collaboration," and communism.

The Compagnons were described as civic and not political ("not part of the state but they are for the Marshal's state because, having freely adhered to the Marshal's positions, they want them put into practice") but hostile to Gaullism as advocating service to a foreign army and encouraging civil war. Deferring to the political decisions of the Marshal, they were "conscious of conforming to his thinking when they made the point that economic and political collaboration ... could in no way be taken as a spiritual ascendancy ... They taught the French conception of the person to their members ... believed in a 'European new order' in which France could affirm her spiritual values." They were "revolutionary" insofar as they rejected "the world of money" but they were also resolutely hostile to communism, "red totalitarianism sold out to foreigners." They liked to have people from different spiritual groups (religious or philosophical) at the heart of their movement, but insisted on maintaining a total independence from these groups.[52]

For the Compagnons, therefore, as for Uriage, "personalism" was a key word in the crucial task of articulating France's role of collaborating in the New Order while remaining "herself." For this group, too, Emmanuel Mounier and Jean Lacroix's language suggested the Third Way for France.

The influence of Uriage on the Compagnons was particularly noticeable in its periodical for *cadres*, *Le Chef Compagnon*, which sometimes quoted *Jeunesse ... France!* directly. Beginning with the "Bayard" cohort (November 1940), the chefs or assistants of the Compagnons were taught in training courses at Uriage. But there may have been some perplexity regarding the new Compagnons movement, even at Uriage: was not its goal of enroling the mass of young people, and setting out a doctrine for adolescents, at least quasi-totalitarian?[53] During the winter months of 1940–41, Mounier worried over certain of its directors showing signs of extreme authoritarianism.[54] And then there was the uncontrolled spending of the Compagnons' vast subsidies in money and material. Minister Jacques Chevalier was shocked by that, coming on top of the movement's ambition of creating its own doctrine. In fact the Compagnons only escaped dissolution when Dhavernas resigned and a kind of provisional trusteeship was established over the organization.[55] But it was soon clear that the troubles of the Compagnons, like those of Uriage, had to be seen in the context of a power struggle in some of the institutions of the

National Revolution, involving challenges to the roles of certain high-profile Catholics or personalists.

THE RISE OF THE
TOTALITARIANS

That Dhavernas had been the innocent victim of a power struggle became apparent in the events that followed his dismissal. In the struggle for succession that followed until May 1941, an attempt was made to bring the Compagnons closer to the German camp.[56] The establishment of the Darlan government in February had opened the way for certain alumni of Doriot's Parti populaire français and members of the "Worms group" to work openly for a single authoritarian French youth organization. Among those interested in the potential of the Compagnons for this was Paul Marion, secrétaire-adjoint to the vice-president of the Council for Information, who had created a propaganda office in April. Soon Marion was trying to advance his allies who were in the movement, such as Jean Maze and the young handicapped war veteran and intellectual Armand Petitjean. But the provisional directorate of the Compagnons, supported by Garrone and his men at the scj, and enlisting the help of Uriage, fought Marion's move.[57] After the first meeting of the directors of the youth movements at Uriage in March, which the Compagnons' Cruziat attended, the Compagnons' journal took a position in the quarrel on pluralism, drawing from articles of Mounier as well as from the reports published on the meetings of the youth leaders, notably by *Jeunesse ... France!*.[58] Subsequently the Uriage school organized a short special session for the *Chefs Compagnons* from 7 to 14 May; of the forty-two trainees present, more than half were living in the camp-schools of the movement, and many at the national centre in Lyon. Among them were many of the intellectuals involved in the movement's doctrinal work: Michel Deltombe, Jean-Marie Despinette, Guy Horlin, Charles Maignial, and the brilliant young writer Maurice Clavel, who was assigned to write the "charter" of the movement.[59] (After the war Clavel would become a prominent columnist at *Le Nouvel Observateur* and one of France's best-known left-wing Catholic intellectuals.)

Just after the special Compagnons session at Uriage there was a general meeting of the directors of the Compagnons on 18 May at Vichy, where Dhavernas's replacement was to be elected. Dhavernas proposed as his successor Armand Petitjean, a militant war veteran (and, apparently, close collaborator of the young veterans' activist François Mitterrand)[60] and ex-*normalien*. A talented and passionate man, Petitjean was disgusted by the defeat, French decadence, and the treason of her elites, and called for a "virile socialism" to mobilize the energies of youth.[61] Petitjean was Paul Marion's candidate as well as the favourite of others in the movement.[62] But Louis Garrone's preference, Guillaume de Tournemire, was supported by Dupouey, de Knyff, and André Cruziat, who brought in Uriage support for Tournemire in the form of testimonials from major Uriage figures such as Father Maydieu and Jean Lacroix. De Knyff then gave equally favourable reports he had gathered at the Uriage session of the *Chefs Compagnons*.[63] After Tournemire's victory, Georges Rebattet was chosen as assistant *Chef Compagnon*; he, too, was a friend of Uriage, where he became a regular visitor. Thus the new heads of the Compagnons, who began reorganizing the movement in August, felt very close to the Uriage team that had contributed to their election.[64] But the unsuccessful effort of Paul Marion and the "totalitarians" to take over the Compagnons from the Catholic personalists and their allies was only a first round in a protracted battle, as we shall see.

Marion and his ally Pierre Pucheu did not take this defeat lying down, but fired off a barrage of criticism of Compagnons' ineffectiveness. Petitjean resigned from the movement, as did his friend Maze, who then became a vociferous critic of the Compagnons, dismissing the sgj as "the last place where the Révolution Nationale was going to be made" and declaring that he wanted to be part of "a really revolutionary body": "The sentence 'The Compagnons movement is against nobody' is unacceptable. 'Une fleur au chapeau, à la bouche une chanson' [a popular Compagnons song] is all very nice but not enough. [Perhaps one needs] a knife in one's belt, if necessary, to fight [... the enemies of the National Revolution, not the Germans]." Maze joined Marion at the ministry of information and began to lobby insistently for a "jeunesse unique."[65] In October 1941, as an official of the secrétariat général à l'Information, Maze held a meeting at Vichy with the heads of the quasi-fascist Jeunesse Française d'Outre-Mer and disgruntled Compagnons who had broken with the new direction of the movement. There were attacks on the sgj, and notably on Garrone, Segonzac, and Tournemire. Maze and his friends envisaged the constitution of a new state youth movement, officially sanctioned, at least (if it could not have all French youth to itself), which promised, rather ominously, that it would not shrink from "revolutionary violence."[66]

Despite the fact that *Chef Compagnon* Tournemire had these powerful right-wing critics, and may have owed his position to Uriage, he soon had his own doubts about Segonzac. When Segonzac's creation of the Équipe nationale d'Uriage in fall 1941 provoked serious tensions with Garrone, *Chef Compagnon* Tournemire "spelled out his doubts about Uriage clearly. The ENC did not convey an impression of equilibrium, of order, sufficient for inspiring confidence ... on top of that he reproached Uriage for wanting to construct its activities on the basis of personal attachment [to Segonzac]."[67]

In fact this was the beginning of a divergence that would separate Segonzac more and more from his fellow officers, like Tournemire, for whom loyalty toward the Marshal demanded strict discipline. The incident also reveals a first hint of what would be growing "political" problems concerning the cult of personality in the Uriage community, or Segonzac's prickly independence (which the alumni later preferred to remember as his proto-Resistance leanings).

While the École Nationale des Cadres exerted tangential influence on the Compagnons de France, it was directly involved in the rebirth of the French Youth Hostel movement (Auberges de Jeunesse) in the free zone in spring 1941. The "laïc" youth hostel movement bothered the Vichy regime in so far as it proved to be a nursery of French nazis, contemptuous of Pétainism.[68] The leadership of the new Camarades de la Route which were born from Uriage's efforts to refurbish the hostel movement was given to Pierre Ollier de Marichard (nicknamed "POM") who remained an instructor at Uriage while he ran the organization. The energetic Marichard also contributed to *Jeunesse ... France!* and helped found the magazine *Marche de la jeunesse* which Uriage published in co-operation with other movements.[69] Under Marichard the new Camarades de la Route sought a "style of life" where the *ajiste* (youth hostel movement) rebellion against the world of the machine and bourgeois individualism would translate itself into the affirmation of a communitarian humanism.[70] The public locutions of the Camarades de la Route (like those of Uriage), with their few references to the National Revolution or the Marshal, recalled those of the École Nationale des Cadres or the review *Esprit*. The Camarades' revolution against the bourgeois spirit would "recreate communitarian reflexes," while respecting the diverse spiritual families, and developing "a living and humane culture, forming the total man, solidly tied to his *métier*, his profession, and his country."[71] In sum, the Camarades de la Route were another example of the singular influence of Uriage's ideas on the first institutions of the National Revolution.

Jeunesse et Montagne was another movement in Uriage's orbit, and not dissimilar in mentality and goals to Uriage's Uzos school. But Jeunesse et Montagne created, in autumn 1940, its own École de

Cadres to train its own chefs d'équipe. The founder and director of the school, Henry Ripert, an artillery captain, teacher, and mountaineer, was a friend of the Abbé de Naurois. He soon had a working relationship with Uriage, to which he sometimes sent trainees.[72] But the Jeunesse et Montagne centres soon seemed a mixed bag, with some being described by their members as brutal, or having "crazy methods,"[73] but even this movement was a way for Uriage to influence the new generation in France.

The establishment of the Équipe nationale d'Uriage in fall 1941 was a sign of the loyalty of its alumni, and the dynamism of the Uriage community's *mystique*. Uriage's influence on leaders of the Catholic scouts, the Compagnons, the youth hostel movement and other organizations in the National Revolution suggested that the school could inspire at least some young people more than the older Catholic youth organizations or the partisans of an openly Fascist or nazified France. As the Uriage community became always more independent and distinct, it sought to clarify its notion of a personalist and communitarian revolution by planning an intensified six-month training program geared to creating an elite among the elite. But, as the war began to turn against the Germans, Uriage began to run into new rivals and critics on all sides of the political spectrum.

The Struggle for Youth

JULY-DECEMBER 1941: SIGNS OF DIVISION

By the second half of 1941, the Vichy government was beginning to split over the direction its "youth revolution" should take, as the tensions that followed Uriage's upgrading into an institution began to come into the open. The École Nationale des Cadres d'Uriage was dominated by devout and idealistic Catholics whom the "realists" around Admiral Darlan considered naive (patronizingly referring to them as "sacristy fleas"), while the hard-line proto-fascists at Vichy like Gaston Bergery or Pierre Pucheu made more and more disparaging remarks about "scoutish and churchy (*calotin*)" youth leaders. But no one could ignore the fact that these Catholics had been able to construct some viable youth institutions in difficult circumstances; for the time being this rendered them irreplaceable and brought them a degree of respect. Although Georges Lamirand at the SGJ always backed Uriage he was, in fact, a sort of boyish itinerant national cheerleader for the National Revolution and the Marshal. He was in a vulnerable position because he could be bullied into compromises by tough "authoritarians" such as his propaganda director in Paris, Georges Pelorson, or the crypto-Nazi staff of the École des Cadres at La Chapelle-en-Serval.[1] In fact there was a more general danger that altruistic, generous, but somewhat fuzzy-minded, "social Catholic" enthusiasm for the National Revolution could be co-opted by hard-headed Nazifiers, and drawn into Nazism itself. The disquieting evolution of Belgian Catholic youth leaders was a pertinent example.[2]

Jérome Carcopino, holder of the Chair of Roman History at the Sorbonne, director of the École de Rome and of the École Normale

Supérieure, succeeded the Bergsonian mystic Jacques Chevalier as minister of education in February 1941 with the determination to head off both German interference and extremism at Vichy[3] (Chevalier had heavy-handedly instituted the observance of "duties toward God" in the French school system during his tenure as minister).[4] But Carcopino, in his effort to rationalize the school situation, soon felt himself the object of hostile manoeuvres on the part of a whole clerical clan led by Chevalier. While Carcopino got on well with youth officials such as La Porte du Theil and Borotra, the distinguished academic's relationship with Lamirand, whom he had problems controlling, soon proved more difficult. As for Louis Garrone's Péguyist rhetoric (his clichés about the importance of "incarnating the spiritual in the carnal," etc.), it simply got on his nerves. Before long Carcopino realized that while he might be the head of national education, and could talk about reforming it, he had little real control over youth, which often remained "clerical" and personalist turf. Soon there was an open power struggle between Carcopino, who, as minister of national education, was trying to reduce Lamirand's power, and the latter who, staunchly defended by Marshal Pétain,[5] clung to his SGJ.[6]

The issue of "the clericals" also figured importantly in Uriage's relationship with Vichy. In his talk at Uriage on 2 June 1941, Darlan had suggested that tough-minded people realized that the Nazis were going to win the war and that young Frenchmen should adjust their perspectives accordingly. The admiral had made pretentious remarks about "his" fleet, "his" policy, et cetera, and had made anti-clerical allusions, all of which found their way back to Pétain via a report written by a Jesuit of Fourvière, who transcribed what an auditor told him of Darlan's talk.

Darlan was furious at this breach of confidence. But from Segonzac's point of view, the negative side of Darlan could be summed up in "a single phrase," as he told Emmanuel Mounier: "He lacks the sense of the spiritual." But Mounier, who heard a range of opinions one month later at Uriage, concluded that there had been a mutual attraction: in spite of his disclaimers, the Vieux Chef had been impressed by Darlan. In Mounier's words, "Darlan certainly swayed people for a while. He was aristocratic and charming, and at first won people over." In the wake of Darlan's visit, the Uriage school received important signs of favour in high places (notably generous food and financial allocations) as it began preparing to train the elite of young governmental functionaries in an obligatory *stage*. This new role for the school represented, at least in Mounier's view, "the very negation of the inspiration" for an institution that had been drawing young men hand-picked for the special qualities of spiritual life and character valued by the personalist network.[7]

During the second half of July, a new course (the "Richelieu" cohort) began with 100 trainees, including 40 prospective officials from the Foreign Affairs, the Colonial, and the Interior ministries who had been obliged by the government to enrol. What did the ministries want from Uriage training? According to a note composed in the Foreign Affairs administration, three "advantages" were expected: a treatment for individual vices ("excessive individualism, an insufficient spirit of discipline, scorn for material tasks"); a reinforcement of the sense of national solidarity (through a community life experience for young people of various social backgrounds), and a lucid vision of "the present situation of France, the common duties that situation created for French people ... and the personal obligations that became incumbent on future servants of the country from this situation."[8]

Some young men of the Richelieu cohort soon made it clear that Uriage was not for everyone by approaching each day's activities with a listless, bitter, or ironical attitude to the point where the morale of the course was soon seriously affected.[9] Even earlier, there had been a hostile reaction from at least one member of the "Mermoz" cohort of May 1941 who complained anonymously to Vichy about Uriage's idiosyncrasies. The official who was concerned with the matter concluded his analysis of "l'esprit d'Uriage" by remarking that the school seemed, at least to him, to be a sort of "clerico-laïc Pontigny"[10] which seemed much influenced by the mentality of the former Dominican review *Sept*.[11]

By the summer of 1941, then, the Uriage school had its critics on all sides of the religious and political spectrum. Nor was it universally admired in the more progressive circles of the Catholic intelligentsia. In his memoirs describing the climate favourable to Vichy that reigned in France at the beginning of 1941, at the very moment where he himself was joining the Mouvement de Libération nationale, embryo of the future movement Combat, Claude Bourdet recalled the situation of his close friends as particularly ambiguous and tragic:

the Catholic intellectuals ... [were] honest, [but] taken in by the "Péguyiste" gibberish in vogue in the most patriotic circles of the regime: I am thinking in particular of the men of Uriage, like Dunoyer de Segonzac, and of certain directors of the Légion des combattants, like François Valentin. People in whom political illiteracy and a certain mysticism were closely linked were tempted to regress to the "Sacred France" concept, to imagine, in the shadow of the Marshal, a sort of social fraternity, simultaneously rejecting both the French Revolution and capitalism, according to their dream of a revised, idealized, mythical Middle Ages. All this might well lead certain people to fascism and, alas, did. Others, like the men of Uriage and Valentin, pulled back in time.[12]

A somewhat similar perspective was given by an old friend of the Esprit group, the Catholic poet Max-Pol Fouchet, who came from Algiers to join fellow writers and artists in a meeting organized by Jeune France at Lourmarin in September 1941:

There was in that period, I think, a kind of spiritual searching, to which was often joined patriotic and political resistance soon giving the latter the character of a crusade, a vague chivalric aspect. Not without some confusion, moreover, because the "spirit" of the École des Cadres d'Uriage, that of certain Chantiers de la Jeunesse, the texts of the "Christique" poets, the sermons on the return to the land and on the artisan, the homilies on work and family, were mixed in a conglomeration in which Péguy himself, invoked by this side and that with an equal enthusiasm, claimed as patron by everyone, would hardly have been able to recognize his own descendants.[13]

But while Uriage may have seemed a bit confused or muddle-minded to some of its instructors' friends, it seemed to be displaying far more disquieting qualities to certain members of the Action Française. In July Mounier was the object of a wave of criticism over the role of his personalism at Uriage. L'Action Française asked:

Could the magnificent work of training an elite of leaders for our youth camps, as accomplished at Uriage and elsewhere, be underhandedly eroded and destroyed by muddled minds, amateurish champions of cloudy ideas? We believe there is a real danger here: the National Revolution is vital, above all, in the clarity of its principles ... in its spirit. If these principles should become obscured, and this spirit corrupted, if one replaced it with the bankrupt stupidities of Mounierist personalism, everything could be ruined.[14]

In fact, this warning was published on the very eve of an order from the Vichy government forbidding Segonzac to employ Mounier as a lecturer at Uriage.

Even more vociferous critics of Uriage surfaced among the French spokesmen for closer collaboration with the Germans. Marc Augier, former director of the Auberges de Jeunesse, was a fervent admirer of the Nazi Ordensburgen; he was disappointed with the lack of racism at Uriage, and with what he saw as excessive tolerance for the democratic spirit.[15] On 24 July Augier, by then a notorious Hitlerite, published a strong critique in one of France's highest-profiled pro-Nazi organs, Alphonse de Chateaubriant's *La Gerbe*. Augier attacked the "individualism" of Uriage's ideas, arguing that the school's personalism effectively worked toward "saving the old liberal values and blocking the route to the communitarian new order" because:

historical groups ought to be fused in a common faith and the individual ought to surrender his liberty for the good of the group. The Christian Middle Ages is a striking example. "Personalism" is a nefarious doctrine which, in the name of the dawning new order, I adamantly reject. It is a philosophical conception of man that belongs to those "lies that have done us so much harm" [Pétain].[16]

Thus Uriage, and particularly the personalism at Uriage, had its critics; this was soon evidenced by an ideological purge at the newly upgraded school. The first victim was one of the architects of the school, the chaplain René de Naurois. De Naurois later recalled that he had indulged in irreverent remarks and gestures during Darlan's visit.[17] Very soon after that he left the school, not only because of ostensible pressures from Vichy to purge him, but also, it seems, because Segonzac found him "too much to the Left." Beuve-Méry found him too "*excité*", "too much the warrior," and told him, "*you* are not the chaplain that we need."[18] Subsequently Emmanuel Mounier was ordered eliminated as a lecturer, too, as a result of what Uriage's friends perceived to have been a campaign orchestrated by Henri Massis against his old antagonist.[19]

If Mounier's voice was silenced at Uriage, his personalist friends such as Beuve-Méry, Lacroix, and d'Astorg, and their ideas, remained firmly in place there. The editor of *Esprit* was replaced for the prestigious July course by two nationally known intellectuals from Pétain's personal entourage. René Gillouin lectured on "the doctrine of the new French state" to the "Richelieu" cohort in July, and returned to Vichy to describe his visit to the Marshal, eliciting the latter's "profound satisfaction."[20] Pétain's quasi-official biographer René Benjamin led a *veillée* at the Uriage chateau on 26 July 1941 during the course of which, a Uriage stalwart noted, he verbally painted "an extremely living and picturesque portrait of the Marshal." The hall seemed "to drink in his words and warmly applauded."[21] Benjamin, in turn, published a lyrical evocation of his stay at what he called the "Château de l'Âme" where young people were being taught to prefer the style of Péguy and Marshal Pétain to the de-virilizing influences of a Proust, Gide, or Valéry.[22] Neither Gillouin nor Benjamin seem to have made any critical references to Mounier or to his personalism in their talks to the school and, in fact, Pétain speech-writer Gillouin, who had already intervened with censors on Mounier's behalf, expressed his sympathy and indignation at the silencing of the review *Esprit* in September, which Mounier judged as "astonishingly courageous" in the circumstances.[23] Gillouin, who had been present at the birth of "personalism," and shared Uriage's spiritual bent, appeared faithful to his personalist ideas.[24] In sum, the offensive against de Naurois, Mounier, and *Esprit* seemed directed more against personalities than against the basic orientation of the school.

For the Catholics, at least, Uriage – with or without Mounier (and many of its more conservative friends were probably happy to see him leave) – continued to symbolize the hope for *their* kind of trans-formation of the country. The school's celebration of the major Cath-olic feast of the Assumption on 15 August vividly demonstrated one aspect of their kind of Catholicism. Segonzac revelled in ceremonial occasions and was able to combine this one with the eve of Uriage's first birthday. On 14 August not only alumni but also young people from the various youth movements began arriving at Uriage. The next day an elaborate high mass of celebration was said by the bishop who came up from Grenoble for the occasion: trumpets sounded the raising of the colours at the moment of the elevation of the host, and taps for the dead when the burial of Christ was invoked. The festiv-ities continued in the afternoon with a spectacle of the *Tréteau Volant* and the Comédiens Routiers which included a memorable scene of a France cut in two, symbolized by soldiers holding a cord across the stage.[25] The Assumption Day activities showed the Uriage school to be a proud, confident, and national institution – albeit with a dis-tinctly Catholic-Christian flavour – enjoying a core of loyal supporters among the young.

This Catholic or "clerical" bias of the Uriage community did not go unnoticed, and was not universally appreciated, among the par-tisans of the National Revolution. For example, Uriage had a stormy relationship with the very different, even frankly pagan, École des Cadres in the occupied zone. The École Nationale des Cadres received new legal status with the law and decree of 11 August 1941. This revision of the statute of 7 December 1940, which was being elaborated since May, was meant to improve and normalize the situ-ation of the school's personnel, but it also made a place for a new, potentially rival, school in the northern zone.[26] There seemed to be a plan to integrate Uriage with this new institution, despite Segonzac's strong reservations about it.

SGJ official Louis Garrone shared many of the ideals, and used much the same language, as the *Péguyistes* and personalists at Uriage. But, apparently under considerable pressure, he intervened and eliminated the free-wheeling chaplain de Naurois, as well as the participation of Emmanuel Mounier, in July.[27] Criticism of Uriage came from both anti-clericals and right-wing Catholics. In the fall, Garrone complained that Uriage was being attacked from opposite sides, by non-Christians for its clericalism, and by Christians for holding up "notions as equivocal as 'honour' or 'virility' as the basic educational values."[28] So out of deference to the fears of certain bishops about the ultimate ambitions of Uriage, Garrone told Segonzac and his team that it was not for them to educate (that was for the schools) or to lead individuals to personal character reform (that was for "natural and spiritual families").[29] As for Segonzac's notion of civic education, the youth official underlined obedience: "I do not wish to condemn an interest in doctrine, but it is for you to understand the National Revolution, not to invent it. Reforming France is not a matter of your ideological preferences, but a fact of authority. We must simplify our obedience."[30] Garrone attributed Uriage's straying from Pétain's authority to Mounier's influence and so also had him ousted from Jeune France, and then from the Psychological and Pedagogical Institute of Lyon. Mounier, Garrone told Pierre Schaeffer, had "already been responsible for all the misfortunes of Uriage."[31] After having isolated the problems with the Uriage project, Garrone said that he "very sincerely desired a precise agreement that would unite all the interested responsible persons" to save "the common work that was now very much in danger." He declared that the doctrine of the school was henceforth to be fixed, and that he had personally set it out with the help of several individuals, notably Messieurs Bégué and François Perroux.[32] Garrone assigned one of his counsellors to sketch out Uriage's ideological orientation, with special attention to the four "Maîtres" of the National Revolution: Proudhon, La Tour du Pin, Péguy, and Maurras.[33]

On the first anniversary of the school in September *Jeunesse ... France!* proudly announced that about 1,600 young men had passed through either the longer or the shorter sessions of the school.[34] Most of them had been trained in groups of 15 to 20 which, as much as possible, had been made up of a mixture of social categories (as an appended complete list breaking down the different occupational backgrounds of the past trainees illustrated).[35] Segonzac proudly reaffirmed Uriage's basic commitments:

Uriage represents an act of faith in the National Revolution, and its fate is bound up with the success or failure of that vast enterprise of renewal ... This team has marched full tilt behind the new master of France, linking its destiny to his, hoping to exemplify his basic thinking with the most sincere faith ...

A leader is first of all ... a sort of superior person in his manly qualities, with all that entails ... great moral stature, a body devoid of weakness, the ability to take charge, a feeling for the human as well as a large and profound intelligence. To choose leaders for a single quality is an error, as absurd as confiding an important command post to a big-muscled brute or to the most eminent, but myopic and timorous, of scholars.

With that in mind the National Leadership School had important plans:

Uriage's ultimate and ambitious goal is to create a veritable leadership school ... During [a first six-month course] we will try to provide future leaders with the most precise knowledge of diverse national psychologies: those of the schoolteacher, the worker, the peasant, the engineer, the officer; we will teach them economics, give them philosophical, political, and religious training, and, above all, strive to instill in them character and a true sense of teamwork by making use of the generous possibilities provided by well-conceived athletic activities.

Uriage, according to the Vieux Chef, had no intention of displacing the *grandes écoles* and other specialized training schools but was simply selecting those of their graduates with the gift for leadership and "accentuating that gift in a decisive way." Despite the concern that sometimes arose over "the Uriage doctrine" Segonzac's school endorsed nothing apart from that contained in the speeches of the Marshal, and the school was "trying with immense faith and immense fidelity to live its principles, insisting upon those that seemed the most important: primacy of the spiritual, a demanding sense of honour, reverence for the *Patrie*."[36] This *credo* may have been largely directed against the school's critics, but it did reflect Segonzac's notion of Uriage as the best expression of the *Marshal's* thinking (if not that of his government). The Chef believed that this could be demonstrated through the creation of the elite of the National Revolution's elite in a six-month training session. Uriage promised that "the *jeunes chefs* who would benefit from it would constitute the best justification of the new educational methods" that were the pride of the school.[37]

By the end of September it was clear that Pierre Pucheu and Paul Marion, newly powerful at Vichy, were challenging Uriage from another direction. The tough new Pucheu-Marion group, and the placing of Youth rather than under War under the Ministry of the Interior, undermined the relative autonomy that Georges Lamirand, playing on the personal support of the Marshal, had enjoyed at the SGJ. The new situation also eroded the authority of Louis Garrone, who had become known as the interlocutor of the episcopacy. Both men were henceforth subject to pressures and growing threats.[38] Thus the silencing of Mounier, and therefore, eventually, of Uriage, took place during a struggle between competing forces and interests. When Vichy was an "extraordinary" regime, with a distinctive orientation set out by Pétainist ideologues like Lamirand and Garonne, Uriage did well. But when pro-German forces ascended at Vichy and brutal, anti-clerical elements became involved in youth policy, the "sacristy fleas" at Vichy and Uriage came under attack.

It was not only the men of Uriage who, in the fall of 1941, were beginning to be pressured in the France of the "New Order." Cardinal Gerlier confided to Uriage's Chombart de Lauwe that he was being pressured by Pucheu's cabinet in the Interior Ministry to show some flexibility toward the idea of bringing all French young people together into a "jeunesse unique."[39] Segonzac himself was called to Vichy for what promised to be a dramatic interview with Pucheu at the end of September 1941, but he returned relatively reassured. Pucheu had "explained his plan and his formula: France needs a totalitarian regime integrating Christian humanism" but, as Mounier noted, "The Vieux Chef came back saying in a serene tone of voice, 'I sized up the situation – careerists, the impotent, and pederasts. Not at all dangerous.'" Mounier would soon be told that a coalition of adversaries had brought an end to Pucheu's plans by the beginning of October. The bishops had reiterated their opposition to a single youth organization, Lamirand and Garrone had been able to raise support, and the Marshal had become more and more irritated, to the point where Admiral Darlan and his circle began to back off from their strong support for the Pucheu-Marion group.[40]

In October, however, a new École Nationale des Cadres was created by Marion's secrétariat général à l'Information et à la Propagande (SGIP) which answered directly to Darlan, vice-president of the Conseil. The "École Nationale des Cadres civiques" was opened that month at Mayet-de-Montagne, near Vichy. Mayet seemed directly inspired by Uriage: intellectual work (divided into courses, lectures, and study circles) alternated with practical exercises (apprenticeship to modern propaganda techniques), sports activities, and group leadership (veillées, etc.). But the spirit of the school, despite the variety of the lecturers, seemed closer to the crypto-Nazism of Doriot's PPF than to Pétainism.[41] Still, while most of the lecturers at Mayet were men from Marion's circle such as Gravier, Gaucher, Chasseigne, and Gaït, there were also, in 1941, talks by friends of Mounier and Segonzac like François Perroux, Pierre Dominique, and Du Moulin de Labarthète. There was also, in March 1942, a visit from Jew-baiter Xavier Vallat.[42] On the one hand, the Mayet school flattered Uriage by imitating it, but on the other it threatened Uriage's role as the mother-school or "spiritual university" of the National Revolution.

Part of Uriage's reaction to these challenges was to consolidate its ties with its faithful in the Équipe nationale d'Uriage alumni organization – a development that was by no means universally welcomed. The reticence of Garrone before the creation of the ENU was shared by diverse administrators of youth organizations, above all by the self-styled "apolitical" Catholics devoted to the Marshal. At the beginning of November 1941 Louis Lallement met Chombart de Lauwe, then on a round of visits, at Vichy. The young ethnologist gave Lallement a report for Segonzac on the contacts he had made at Lyon with Cardinal Gerlier, with "Chef Compagnon" Tournemire, and with Dary, head of the Scouts de France. All three of the Catholic youth leaders had expressed worries about the new initiative of Segonzac: was the ENU an official organization or a secret society? Was it a new educative movement in competition with the others or a political organization? Did Segonzac intend to constitute a "parallel hierarchy," or a super movement, with men coming from diverse milieux and united by a devotion to his person?[43] Just what was Segonzac up to? The Catholic leaders, particularly, worried about his innovative "ecumenism" and the way Uriage seemed more and more centred on *him*, not Pétain.

Louis Garrone, who had often defended Uriage in the past, confessed his own reservations: "It is unacceptable that the Uriage School comport itself like a private institution," he complained. "Is Segonzac the chief of a band, or a director of a school?" In an apparent effort to reassert the SGJ's authority over the regional schools, three study days for their directors and *directrices* were organized at Vichy from 20 to 22 November 1941. They were announced as a *stage d'information civique*; included lectures on the *Patrie* (Achille Mestre), Work (François Perroux), and Family (Pierre Reynaud); and were "intended to allow the cadres of the schools to complete their training and receive indispensable instructions."[44] Garrone spelled out his worries over the ever present dangers of liberal democracy in an article on the situation of Youth in 1940, notably denouncing "the venture of the democratic state – an enterprise underhandedly totalitarian – which, under the banner of a discerning education, uproots [youth], detaches them from natural communities and particularly from the nation, severs them from their traditions, and models them on an abstract type purported to be the new man."[45]

Following his hero Péguy's thinking, Garrone could not understand why his fellow Péguyistes at Uriage had such a need for innovation. He could see no need for the more distinctive, innovative, and exploratory side of the École Nationale des Cadres, for, as he explained not long before his own resignation, there was much to be said for the old (Catholic) traditionalist idea that true liberty consists in deferring to just and wise authority: "It is precisely because the National Revolution is a political fact of that sort that the soul ought to adhere and can do so without compromising itself ... It can do so because, far from alienating its liberty, it discovers its only possible fulfillment."[46]

Garrone, then, in his capacity as Directeur de la Formation des jeunes, did his best to try to keep Uriage in line but, despite his disapprobation, Uriage persevered and it was Garrone who was effectively purged from the SGJ at the end of 1941. The anti-clericals at Vichy had condemned his lack of firmness in the face of the demands of the episcopacy. But the firing of Garrone did not seem to imply a sudden new insecurity for the school. On the contrary, in February the ENU acquired an official existence. And also the much anticipated training *stage* of six months finally began (on 8 February) thus giving a relative guarantee for the immediate future.[47]

1942: THE SIX-MONTH TRAINING SESSION

The six-month training session – which ran from February to July 1942 – was the culmination of a considerable effort on the part of the Uriage community. This intellectual labour was reflected by the fact that at the end of the six-month session the Uriage library had more than 1,500 volumes, of which about 300 were devoted to literature and reports, about 300 to history and geography, 100 to philosophy, and 100 to religion. The recent works of Jacques Maritain, Romano Guardini, and the theologians Congar, Daniélou, de Lubac, and Valensin figured alongside classics and popularized works aimed at young people. The Uriage library also had a place of honour for the classic texts of the personalist revolutionaries and "planists" of the 1930s: the works of Robert Aron, Arnaud Dandieu, Denis de Rougemont, and Henri Daniel-Rops of the Ordre Nouveau movement; the writings of rail-road technocrat Dautry. It also had the works of the members of the Esprit group such as Henri-Irénée

Marrou, Lacroix, Mounier, Perroux, P.H. Simon, as well as of one of their most admired thinkers, the Belgian neo-socialist Henri de Man, and his French disciple, the Christian socialist André Philip. There were also books by Hyacinthe Dubreuil and Verger. The basic readings for a "social Catholic" like Segonzac, interested in syndicalist and corporatist theories as well as Maurrasian doctrine, were to be found there. These readings included the works of Le Play, La Tour du Pin, Romanet and Henri Guitton, periodicals such as the Jesuits' *l'Action Populaire*, the "social Catholics'" *Semaines sociales*, the *Cahiers de la Nouvelle Journée* and the publications of the Dominicans' Éditions du Cerf. These were complemented by the writings of Dolléans, Jouhaux, Lefranc, the publications of the *Centre de culture ouvrière*, and the works of Jacques Bainville, Charles Maurras, and Louis Salleron.[48]

The Uriage reading list suggested that there could be a harmonious relationship between the progressive "social Catholics," personalist revolutionaries and "non-conformists" of the 1930s, and the major ideologues of the Action Française and the extreme Right. From the late 1930s to the outbreak of the war certain avant-garde intellectuals such as Emmanuel Mounier at *Esprit*, and Alexandre Marc and Robert Aron of *Ordre Nouveau*, had worked to create an organizational framework for just such a transcending of old antagonisms as that which the Uriage mix accomplished. The pre-war personalist effort to create a network of contacts committed to transcending the "old" Right and Left in the name of a national revolution celebrating the primacy of the spiritual, and a "communitarian personalism," had helped create a future support network for Uriage.[49]

The Uriage study group also did a good deal of bibliographical work: Uriage published a whole series of guides on different themes. Pedagogy remained a specialty, however, with Jean Lacroix's sophisticated critical bibliography which stressed the importance of the *Théorie de l'éducation* of the progressive theologian Lucien Laberthonnière.[50]

The documentation service of Uriage also printed a "Bibliographie sommaire de Culture générale" of 100 titles, referring readers to diverse suggested collections. Intended to help the directors of the regional Écoles des Cadres and the youth organizations create a library, the choices were mostly recent publications – "three or four good-quality books in the principal branches of culture" – and reflected the tastes in the school library. The Bibliography, presenting the books in alphabetical order according to authors, cited, as the first ten, Alain, Robert Aron, Jacques Bainville, Karl Barth, Roger

Bastide, Louis Baudin, Nicholas Berdiaeff, Henri Bergson, Georges
Bernanos, Jules Blache (*L'homme et la montagne*); in the middle of the
list figured Légaut, Edouard Le Roy, Maxime Leroy, Henri de Lubac,
Lucius, Henri de Man, Jacques Maritain, Dom Marmion, H. Masse
(*L'Islam*) and Thierry Maulnier. The ten final names were P.-H.
Simon, Sombart, Pierre Termier, Thibon, G. Urbain (*La science*),
Valéry, Vialatoux, G.Viance (*Force et misère du socialisme*), Weygand, et
Wilbois.[51] Again, it was a mixture of old Right traditionalism, per-
sonalism, and progressive religious thinking.

The attitude with which one should approach these readings was
set out in Eric d'Alançon's exhortation to the six-month *grand stage*
instructors:

The great objective of this six-month *stage* ought to be to ARM the students
against enemies, interior or exterior, who threaten the values of the spirit
(primacy of the spiritual, sense of the universal, role of the intelligence) ...
to resist the snobbish scepticism of the university, as well as the collective
hysteria or excitation resulting from clever propaganda (Radio, Ordensburg
pedagogy, perhaps Mayet de Montagne, etc.). Beyond that immediate end
... it is nothing less than establishing, on the ruins of traditional forms of
teaching, the bases of a new humanism. Developing complete men involves:

a) Rediscovering spiritual values (essentially the primacy of the spiritual
and the true meaning of strength).

b) Uniting efficiency and culture, a culture fuelled by inspiration and not
by pressure.

A truth ought to be up front for everyone, at each moment: the six-month
session marks a decisive battle the outcome of which will be the life or death
of the school.[52]

For this special training session Segonzac insisted, for whatever
reasons, on having only married men as chefs d'équipe, and so two
of those chosen, Hoepffner and Cazenavette, moved up their marriage dates to accommodate him.[53] Then the future chefs d'équipe
underwent, from 1 to 15 December 1941, a session of psycho-
pedagogical advanced training at l'Institut de recherches et d'applications psychologiques et pédagogiques of Lyon. Louis Garrone, who
had created this institute, had organized this session for the directors
and *directrices* of the Écoles des Cadres of the SGJ whom he wanted
to bring back under his control. The importance of the six-month
course was underlined by the range of speakers who addressed its
future instructors in Lyon. There was important input from several
doctors,[54] psychologists,[55] and well-known philosophers such as Lacroix, Gabriel Madinier, and Gabriel Marcel. Another lecturer was the

peasant-philosopher of the National Revolution Gustave Thibon,[56] who had hosted, on his beet farm, the social activist mystic Simone Weil in the early period of the war. In what may have been inspired by her exploratory pre-war work experiences,[57] the preparation of the instructors for the six-month session then concluded with a *stage*, from 1 to 15 January, in a mine in the coal basin of Saint-Étienne. That work in the depths, involving total sharing of the life of the miners, was a physical and moral endurance test that prepared the instructors to lead their trainees through similar experiences.

From 16 to 22 January the directors of the school and the Study Bureau got together with the instructors to plan what was now described as the school's major project of the year, the six-month *stage* which was to be a synthesis of all of the school's previous training.[58] The instructors were told that the central focus was to be the global and personal development of each trainee: each *stagiaire* was to evaluate his own aptitudes and develop his personality while simultaneously participating in a community and striving for efficiency in all of his activities.[59] As Gilles Ferry said of the six-month session: It "mobilized the whole school ... There was a very close tie between the work of the Study Bureau and the pedagogical activities of the team leaders. This was not the case for the short-term *stages*."[60]

The best men for this six-month session were sought through appeals sent out to the SGJ network and the youth movements, to certain administrations and businesses, to the Équipes nationales d'Uriage, and to friends of the school. This resulted in 105 applications, all from volunteers, for the sixty available places. Beginning on 1 February there was a week of examinations based on a triple medical, psycho-technical, and general selection procedure – the third test consisting of repeated interviews held by the instructors of the school. Candidates were judged on things like "emotivity," "intelligence," and "will." Sixty-three trainees were finally chosen, among whom some were already candidates for, or entitled to, positions in the Youth administration, while others were established civil servants who were granted a professional leave for the program. In this would-be elite of the National Revolution there were eighteen responsible for the training of youth (twelve from the SGJ and six from movements), eleven schoolteachers, eight officers, seven students, six workers, three engineers, two in agricultural work, and eight in diverse other professions. Of the seventy-two whose age is known, more than two thirds were between twenty and twenty-five (fifteen had been born in nineteen-twenty), three were eighteen or twenty, and three were over thirty.[61]

Joffre Dumazedier, in a series of articles in *Jeunesse ... France!*, described how the course would begin by stressing obedience and the primacy of collective life, then would go on to emphasize the spirit of initiative and the autonomy of the trainees, while seeking an equilibrium between authority and liberty, exterior order and the unblocking of individuals, community life and personal vocation. The rhythms of the week and of the day systematized regular school practices: absence of free time, counter-balancing activities and hours. The four days dominated by intellectual work (Tuesday and Wednesday, Friday and Saturday), were separated by two others that would give a larger place to sport and outdoor activities (Thursday and Sunday). Monday was the day for free excursions for trainees. The work week, opened by a *veillée* on Monday evening and the introductory study circle of Tuesday morning, finished with a synthesis study circle on Saturday in which the whole class reunited for a cultural presentation, and heard the Vieux Chef draw conclusions from the cycle.

Each day, between the double morning assemblies (one for calisthenics, the other for the raising of the colours) and the evening *veillée*, was divided into one-and-one-half-hour sequences. That was the length of the lectures (including the questions and the responses that followed), the study circles in teams, the sessions of physical education, the manual work, and the time allotted for personal study (at the end of the afternoon each day). The outdoors and personal work each occupied three hours on the days when there were no lectures. It was thought thereby to obtain better concentration without tension and to avoid monotony, fatigue, and distraction.

The pedagogical method adopted was intended to offset what were claimed to be the more obvious faults of university training: individualism, the splitting up of subjects and disciplines, the tendency to verbalization or theoretical systematization without relating it to life experience, the degeneration of the faculties of decision and action. Therefore it was not only to facilitate the assimilation by the students of the material put before them that new methods were sought. Culture and the progress of learning were to be put in their true place: at the service of the development of the person and his capacity for commitment and action in "the real world." The experiencing and observation of facts were placed at the basis of an intellectual enterprise that was then to result in reasons for acting and instruments for action.

Here are some of the highlights of the Study Plan of the "Stage de Formation, 1942":

1st cycle: "French Decadence and the Mission of Youth." In the third of three lectures on French decadence (economic and social, political, intellectual and moral), Father Des Alleux spoke on "Religious Decadence."

2nd cycle: "The Effort of Youth." Father Dillard spoke on American youth, followed by Chombart de Lauwe on the Hitler Youth, and then Dumazedier and Segonzac on the work of the SGJ and the effort of youth ...

5th cycle: "Character" included Lochard on "The Education of Virility" and d'Astorg on "The Call of the Hero and the Saint."

6th cycle: "Self-Identity" with Reuter on "The Dangers that Threaten the Personality" (press, cinema, radio).

7th cycle: "Education." Dumas spoke on "The Comparative Teaching of Adults and Adolescents."

8th cycle: "The Leader." Abbé Courtois {director of *Coeurs Vaillants*} on "The Personal Qualities of the Leader."

9th cycle: "The Community." Reuter on "France, Community of Communities"; Chombart de Lauwe on "The Soil and Human Types."

10th cycle: "The Community of Blood." Mme Brunet on "Marriage and Self-Identity" and Van de Velde on "The Politics of the Family" ...

12th cycle: Beuve-Méry on "The Capitalist Enterprise."

13th cycle: "Social Peace." Me Deschizeaux (an early member of Ordre Nouveau become Deputy) on "The Professional Orders" ...

15th cycle: "The State." Final lecture: Abbé B. on "Parish and Community"...

18th cycle: "The masters of French Political Thought." [4 lectures] Paul Reuter on "The Masters of French Political Thought." Father Henri de Lubac on "Proudhon, French Socialist," Paul Reuter on "Maurras, French Nationalist," Beuve-Méry on "Péguy, Socialist, Patriot, and Christian" ...

20th [concluding] cycle. "The Essential Values." Chevallier on "The Virile Order and Efficacy in Action," d'Astorg on "Morality and Honour," Gadoffre on the "Crisis of Man and Humanism."[62]

If the six-month *stage* was the harbinger of a totally new French educational system, it would be one with a non-Marxist socialist component, personalist philosophizing, and an emphasis on virility, decentralized communities, and religious training. The strong representation of priests was particularly noticeable but, as a result of the concern of men such as Chevallier or the Compagnons' leaders with making Christian spirituality efficacious, there was a striking absence of references to evangelical virtues. The focus of these cycles was on spirituality, folk community, tradition, knightly honour – the qualities valued by Proudhon, Maurras, and Péguy, particularly the latter. The inventiveness of the program shows that the Uriage school was no mere holding operation in a perilous situation, but rather an ambitious enterprise that inspired serious contributions from a host of social thinkers. The six-month session demonstrated, again, how Uriage combined the ideas of "personalist revolutionaries" with Maurras and the legacy of the Action Française, and thus reconciled the "old" Right and the new Catholic Left in a new synthesis. Emmanuel Mounier had, at first, been important to that effort, but after his expulsion other intellectuals brought their contributions. Several did not share Mounier's views on the issues of the day and found his thinking abstract and complex. Among the more important influences were great figures from before the first World War like Péguy, Henri Bergson, and Marx, as well as contemporary writers such as François Perroux, Guéhenno, and Henri de Man. Medieval culture and values, the art of the cathedral builders, the influence of monastic orders, the honour of knights also nourished imaginations at the "Château de l'Âme," and the school's uplifting (if typically romantic) motto became *Plus est en nous.*[63]

AN ANTI-INTELLECTUAL INTELLIGENTSIA

If the Uriage study program seems imposing, we must also recall that the school had a very ambiguous attitude toward book-learning. Dunoyer de Segonzac had articulated the school's attitudes toward intellectuals early in the life of school: "Our universities were full of young students, future prize-winners for intelligence, but ... [also] winners for overlong, excessively greasy hair and thin, pimply untidiness. Their teachers were not giving them the best example." As for abstraction-producing intellectuals in general: "The intellectual that we knew (and perhaps even loved) was too refined, pale, and delicate. He suffered from a psychological and physiological impotence by which we have been, and still are, deeply afflicted."[64]

During the six-month session the visiting lecturers reiterated similar themes. A succession of medical doctors insisted on the importance of salubrious thinking. In his talk on "The Physical Decadence of French Youth, Its Causes and Remedies," for example, Étienne Berthet affirmed that "the National Revolution demands profound reforms in all areas; in the area of health, as in the others, it is crucial to propagate healthy ideas, to struggle against those lies, as Marshal Pétain has said, that have done us so much harm."[65]

An important, and not universally appreciated, part of the Uriage experience for the six-month trainees remained sweating under high-profile physical educationist Roger Vuillemin. According to

Vuillemin, Uriage training, besides insisting on the centrality of sports, also required "the cultivating of the intelligence" because:

The school holds that those French elites recruited in examinations and educated in the *grandes écoles* were too often false elites. While excellent in manipulating concepts, and at technical virtuosity, they too easily lost the sense of the real. Our new elites must be convinced that the richest culture, the only worthy of that name, is the one that integrates the largest reality the most solidly. Abstraction is only a sterile or dangerous game if it is not a means of attaining the highest realities. Alongside of it, manual work takes all of its value as a culture, as does all effort that runs up against the resistance of things.[66]

Gilles Ferry, something of an intellectual himself, employed Nietzschean imagery and somewhat obscure prose in his own anti-intellectual rhetoric:

Today we resent you, you colourless thinkers who hide in the cavern of concepts, your feet tied up in the gigantic spider webs of your reasoning. *Sorbonnard* speechifiers, reasoners, sociologists, and pedagogues of all stripes, you, deaf and blind as you are, have disfigured our mother tongue ... On the pretext of thinking more clearly, or more highly, you have scorned language, clung to that heresy of a distinction between form and foundation. But language has taken its revenge in falsifying the instrument; you have deformed what you wanted to achieve. Your disincarnated thought floats miserably in the fog.[67]

Ferry went on to denounce the "culpable off-handedness of the philosopher who does not try to be human and accessible, and immediately leads us into the cavern of concepts," who is always striving for "a facile superiority over mere mortals who are not familiar with abstract monsters," and for whom "the least symptom of life is considered suspect." He trumpeted that there was "one more revolution" for him to accomplish: "flee the cavern of concepts."[68]

It was ironic that an educated man such as Ferry should eschew clear thinking in spring 1942, just when insightful people were beginning to suspect that the war was turning against the axis powers, and the notion of Pétain's independence from German control was more and more difficult to sustain. Taken individually, these moralistic polemics are understandable, but when they are placed in the context of Uriage's deference for Dunoyer de Segonzac, and Segonzac's unshakeable deference for Pétain, one gets a glimpse of the most questionable characteristic of Uriage. It was a form of education that blatantly ridiculed clear, critical thinking. Uriage was, to a considerable extent, a sophisticated and well-thought-out, but anti-intellectual, alternative to the republican educational system represented by pre-war elite institutions like the École Normale Supérieure. From the high battlements of the Château the men of Uriage cast their gaze all the way back to the Middle Ages, making it perilously easy to overlook the dirty business of war at their very feet.

Even at Uriage, the anti-intellectualism of certain instructors was not appreciated. Joffre Dumazedier, as we have seen, wondered about Vuillemin's approach to physical education: "[Coubertin was] another world. Vuillemin had doubts about all that." Vuillemin's whole philosophy was "'sweat,' 'suffer,' to 'be a man.'"[69]

An unabashed admirer of Uriage, who interviewed a host of its instructors and alumni, admitted that "at Uriage one found, in certain people, a primal and unhealthy anti-intellectualism that the Marshal and the luminaries of the regime would certainly not disavow. [Also] a religiosity, a candour, a boy-scoutism that might appear laughable and old-fashioned today."

And behind that, he concluded, there were underlying factors, such as the basic world view of the school, its attitude toward the immediate Republican past: "Disgust, sickness, nausea best describe the common opinion and general feeling. No one at all at Uriage would have anything to do with parliamentary democracy, liberalism, individualism, or pre-war life in general. That period, yesterday's world, which caused the defeat, was henceforth dead."[70] Alumnus Paul Grillet characterized his own mentality at the time as reflecting that of the school in general; he spoke of "totally rejecting parliamentary democracy," of "radical questioning of the society," of the priority of living "in another society."[71]

These sorts of remarks characterized Uriage publications up to the time of the launching of the six-month session, and seem to reflect the general thinking at the school.[72] Meanwhile, the school's leaders sincerely thought they were being apolitical: years later, Dunoyer de Segonzac ingenuously talked about Uriage "not taking a position on the political level" – but he admitted to never having heard a single favourable world about the Third Republic on the premises.[73]

The anti-intellectualism of Uriage grew out of anti-modernism, traditional Catholicism, military tradition, and various philosophical

158 The Knight-Monks of Vichy France

currents that had surfaced in the nationalist and Catholic revival of
the late nineteenth century. The six-month session was pretty much
a home-grown phenomenon as neither SGJ officials, nor any high-
profile advocates of the official doctrine spoke to the trainees.
(Although René Gillouin was to have presented the major texts of
the Marshal at the end of June, he cancelled his lecture after Laval,
on his dramatic return to the government, had demanded that Gillouin quit the Marshal's entourage and leave Vichy.) Uriage also
seems to have kept some distance between itself and the Action
Française. Paul Reuter, lecturing on Maurras, warned that Maurras's
disciples had to interpret his thought in the light of Christian values,
and reintroduce into politics the primacy of the moral imperatives
that Maurras denied; he even warned of the danger of being led by
positivism, via racial theories or biological conceptions of the nation,
to "theoretical and practical national socialism."[74]

Uriage seemed determined to offer a Péguyiste-Christian-socialist
alternative to Nazism. Beuve-Méry's talk on "Péguy, French Revolutionary" was presented in polished form to the last training courses
of the school in November and December 1942, and then mimeographed and circulated in the Uriage network (twenty-three pages
of text followed by twenty-six pages of extracts and a bibliography).
Uriage's director of studies saw a global confrontation of three major
currents of thought (overblown nationalism become fascism,
socialism become soviet communism, weakened and insipid Christianity), and set out the Uriage response with treatises on Péguy and
socialism, Péguy and the nation, Péguy and religion, and a reflection
on France's mission.[75] We should note that liberal democracy was not
even worth mentioning, while Uriage's *péguyisme* was assumed to be
a bold new synthesis with the wind in its sails.

The second part of the six-month training session was less tightly
crammed with activities, divided as it was by two weeks of work in a
factory and on a farm.[76] The governing idea of the training session
was the total reconstruction of the national and international communities. The principles were taken less from the mainstream doctrinal texts of Pétain than from Uriage's version of the National
Revolution, particularly the notions of person and community in
Péguy or the personalist thinkers.[77]

The written evaluations composed by the team leaders at the end
of the course – more elaborate than those for the ordinary sessions
– described the general image, aptitudes, and work habits of the
trainee, his character, his comportment, and recommendations for
his future employment. (Collated and reviewed, they allowed the
head of the school to determine the assignment of the individual

trainee). About half of them would return to their careers as students, teachers, officers, or, most often, administrators in the youth movements. The others would be assigned to the various posts offered by the SGJ and the Commissariat au Travail des Jeunes. A dozen were to be placed in regional or departmental offices and twenty in regional schools.[78] Eight other six-month graduates would be placed at the head of centres for young workers or of Maison de Jeunes, while the Compagnons, the French scouts, and the Christian trade unions for young people were to take back the leaders they had sent for Uriage training. Several trainees would be set up in the occupied zone, others in Algeria, notably at the école d'El-Riath. Two proved to be outstanding and were retained as instructors at Uriage.[79]

All in all, the six-month *stage* demonstrated how the Uriage experience had formed a distinctive method to train new leaders for a range of tasks for a new kind of France. It showed that it could play a practical, efficacious, long-term pedagogical role in a National Revolution conforming to its ideals.

JULY-AUGUST 1942: THE "GRANDE FÊTE"

The high point in the life of the École Nationale des Cadres d'Uriage may have been the extravagant festival that took place at the Château Bayard during the summer of 1942 to celebrate the graduation of the first six-month class, the "Verdun" cohort. In fact, the community-school of Uriage was, like several other youth institutions under the Vichy regime, always rather festive. Segonzac had, for example, helped organize at the chateau several merry and colourful marriages of *stagiaires* or instructors that had involved the Uriage professional theatre company.[80] But on Saturday, 31 July 1942 at 2 P.M., a particularly large festival began, organized to highlight the "christening" of the class that had just finished its six-month *stage*, as Segonzac suggested that a vast gathering of the Uriage family should mark the occasion. It served also to boost alumni morale and provide them with a common goal. "Remember," Segonzac admonished his former students, "that *we are an elite*[81] and we will prove it in these days of the Grand Rassemblement of the Équipe d'Uriage."[82]

Two days of festivities were planned and instructor Henri Lavorel, who had worked in film before the war,[83] had been made the master of ceremonies for what was intended to be a triumphant meeting, demonstrating the national *rayonnement* of the Uriage school.[84] On that afternoon the delegations of eight regional schools (including the young men from El Riath who made the trip from North Africa), each to be composed of fifty members, began gathering at the school as the culmination of a journey that, more and more, "took on the air of a pilgrimage." The final section was covered on foot or by bicycle (the Christian spartans from the legendary Uzos school cycled 800 kilometres to get there). The regrouping of the regional delegations between Grenoble and Glières, supplemented by young people from a host of other youth organizations, preceded a mass ascension to the chateau, in echelons, of between 1,000 and 1,500 young people.[85] All of the Grenoble region's leading celebrities, political leaders, professors, religious leaders, sportsmen, and directors of various organizations, particularly those involving youth, were also invited.[86] Also present, of course, were the heads of the regional Écoles des Cadres and dozens of former stagiares of Uriage delegated by their different regions.[87] Youth secretary Georges Lamirand could not come, but he sent a telegram in which, in his usual effusive style, he spoke of Uriage alumni who "have focused profound and grateful affection on the Vieux Chef, and you know with what sincerity I share it! That, too, I would have been happy to say before them. Let me convey the assurance of my faithful attachment to everyone, and with all my strength, with the faith that love of the *patrie* inspires in us, we will continue the mission that the Marshal has given to us, more closely united than ever before."[88]

Saturday afternoon was spent in rehearsals and followed, that evening at 9 o'clock, by a theatrical pageant written by Bertrand d'Astorg, "*Le jeu du glaive et du château, Mystère pour célébrer la communauté des chefs de l'École Nationale des Cadres et de ceux qui sont venus recevoir leur enseignement.*"[89] It was played by the members of the Équipe d'Uriage and the Comédiens Routiers and consisted of an allegory with Le Chef, the voices of Jeanne, Bayard, St. Louis, the White Lady, the Black Lady, et cetera, in a debate on the destiny of France. There was a theme of common destiny, and the need to galvanize for action. The play went over well with most of the young auditors, and a few actors' voices even seem to have trembled with emotion. Observers found the handsomest part to be the closing ceremony: the men of the regional schools, at the call of the master of ceremonies, arrived running to the podium, followed by Uriage (the students and the *chefs*). The Vieux Chef climbed onto the plateau and said a few words. Commands cracked in the air, and then there was a lowering of the flag, followed by singing of the Marseillaise in a mood evoking a sacred love of the fatherland. At the instant when the Vieux Chef shouted "Jeunesse!" and all responded "France!" the echo picked up the cry, which resounded throughout the valley, giving the impression of a magnificent response.[90] Leni Reifensthal could doubtless have made an immortal film of it.

The next morning's activities began at nine A.M. at la Châtaigneraie when, as for the first birthday of the school the preceding summer, the tanned and fit young men joined in a solemn Catholic liturgy. Chaplain Father des Alleux celebrated the mass assisted by the prominent youth activist Father Doncoeur; Father Maydieu gave the sermon. There followed a general assembly in the stadium with a parade and colours ceremony serenaded by the regimental band from Grenoble. The mass demonstrations were minutely orchestrated; the directors of the school had called for "impeccable discipline, virile attitude, faultless appearance" in what was to be a manifestation of "faith and will."[91] This was followed by sports competitions (jumping and 100-, 800-, and 8,000-metre races), and an elaborate demonstration of Hébertisme. There followed the Vieux Chef's "christening" of the Verdun cohort during an "extremely sober ceremony" in which, according to a sympathetic observer, "all was in proportion, up to the standard of the men and of the country." The morning ended with the assembly singing the inspiring *canon* of Uriage:

De nos ruines, de nos fautes,
nous partons la rage au coeur.
Préparons nos combats
Sans trêve et sans peur.
Que remontent à nos lèvres
Le mot fier, la chanson pure.
Retrouvons entre nous
La vie simple et dure,
Tous ensemble, dressons-nous.
Dans nos âmes, dans nos corps,
Nous voulons des Français décidés et forts.

The afternoon was less formal, with military music and then a succession of stage performances by groups such as the Compagnons de la musique, the Équipe Lyautey, and Basque dancers. The formal activities ended with the lowering of the colours;[92] but for those of the instructors, or Comédiens Routiers, who wanted to hear the famous bearded, sandal-shod mystical poet Lanza del Vasto sing and read, the evening continued "chez d'Astorg." Del Vasto, who was about to publish his *Pélerinage aux sources* (1943) at the time, was much admired in the Catholic milieu; according to one of the instructors present,

That extraordinary man, who is a vagabond troubadour, and has visited Tibet, India, Palestine, is truly of a special race. Wisdom, silence, poetry, nobility. *He attracts people to himself. He is a prince.* His singing reminds one of *Gregorian Chant*[93] and Arab melodies, and his guitar accompaniments are very sensitive and reinforce the sonority and expression of words. He promises us a Noël written for the radio."[94]

That a wandering holy man and poet like Lanza del Vasto, who lived outside of the century, weaving his own clothes and tending sheep, should fit in so naturally to the great Uriage christening rite was symptomatic of the mentality of a school for elites which was also the "Château de l'Âme." It was a curious mixture of militarism and romantic Christianity, the cult of leadership and good taste, medievalism and spirituality, elitism and the scout spirit.

Not all of the Grande Fête pleased everyone: some of the *chefs* found the allegorical play rather heavy-handed,[95] and not all of the instructors had participated in the preparations with Segonzac's kind of enthusiasm.[96] The Vieux Chef, however, seemed to experience the ceremony through a mystical prism as representing Uriage's remarkable ability to unify, and its spiritual power to bring young Frenchmen together in a truly moving and spectacular way. "In that completely new stadium, around the pavilion," he wrote not long after the Grande Fête, "there was not only the best of the French provinces; alongside them thronged the young people of the Chantiers de Jeunesse et Montagne, *the diverse youth movements, we believe, all assembled in the same place for the first time.*"[97] Segonzac was beginning to believe that perhaps only Uriage and himself could bring together all of the National Revolution youth movements. "No doubt people will later marvel," he mused, "that one could achieve on 1 August 1942, in the circumstances one knows, the spirit, the tone, of those 1,500 boys assembled, melded at Uriage, into one body, one single soul."[98] The head of Uriage seemed to fuse his Catholic belief that virtuous people constituted the Mystical Body of Christ with his soldierly fidelity to the Marshal into a transcendental vision of what the National Revolution could become.

Uriage under Attack (March 1942– January 1943)

SIGNS OF TROUBLE: TESTIMONY BEFORE THE CONSEIL NATIONAL

The grandiose triumphalism of the Grande Fête at Uriage in the summer of 1942 masked the fact that the school, by that time, had serious difficulties with the government, fuelled by powerful rivals and critics. One sign of trouble had been the successful pressure exerted on the school the previous summer, apparently by Henri Massis, to do without the Abbé de Naurois and Emmanuel Mounier; another was the fact that Mounier was abruptly incarcerated in early 1942 on suspicion of Resistance activities. The government's concern over the youth movements led to a summons to Vichy of their leaders, including Segonzac, to explain themselves.

The youth leaders were to appear before the prestigious Conseil National of the National Revolution, some of the most important conservative Catholics and loyal Pétainists concerned with the youth in the country (several of whom we have met before). The twenty-one active members included Msgr Beaussart, auxiliary bishop of Paris; Gaston Bergery, former neo-radical politician become adviser to Pétain and ambassador; pastor Boegner, president of the Fédération protestante de France; Professor Marcel Blanchard, rector of the University of Grenoble; Abel Bonnard, (collaborationist) conseiller municipal of Paris; Henri Dorgères, the peasant organizer; Robert Garric, Commissaire Général du Secours national; General Lafont of the Scouts; General de La Porte du Theil of the Chantiers; François Valentin, formerly director of Catholic Action become head of the Légion des combattants; ambassador André François-Poncet; Henri Massis, *chargé de mission* at the SGJ become promoter of a "doctrine civique" for the young; and Louis Dunoyer, professor at the Faculté des Sciences in Paris (and paternal uncle of the director of Uriage). Pierre Dunoyer de Segonzac's defence of Uriage before them provides a revealing insight into the nature and character of the so-called National Revolution in March 1942.

Pétain's opening talk, which set the tone of the meeting, had been composed by the Maurrassian intellectual (and Uriage's friend) René Gillouin, and articulated Massis's concern that there be solid logic and clarity in the youth program of the National Revolution.[1] Segonzac was soon embarrassed to find that his Uncle Louis figured, with Bergery and Bonnard, among the strongest advocates of a strong and coherent "national doctrine" for youth,[2] and that he used this argument to urge a mandatory program for all the Écoles des Cadres.

Segonzac did not attack this unwelcome suggestion head on but, adopting a deferential attitude, was modest in his portrayal of the Uriage school's ideological orientation and ambitions. Then Professor Blanchard, breaking his habitual silence, spoke of his admiration for Uriage, and when he concluded that Uriage was "on the intellectual plane, a pinnacle," received warm applause.[3] In two subsequent instances, according to the official minutes, the members of the commission also applauded eulogies of Segonzac. The Vieux Chef felt himself "absolved" after his appearance and attributed much of the sympathy for Uriage at the meeting to a "brilliant" defence of the school by Gaston Bergery.[4]

The youth leaders whose interrogations by the Conseil National followed Segonzac's did not have as pleasant an experience. Jacques Bousquet, director of the national leadership school in the occupied zone, when asked to reassure the Conseil that the two national schools were homogeneous, responded: "that there was similarity in teaching in the schools of Uriage and of La Chapelle-en-Serval, and only minor pedagogical differences ... The programs are identical ... the speeches and messages of the Marshal are studied and explained in a parallel way at Uriage and in the occupied zone."[5] But Bousquet's comportment had "'shocked' the commissioners (on entering he gave them a fascist salute) and he had not hidden 'his sympathy for the totalitarian spirit.'"[6] Bousquet's movement had become formally dedicated to fighting "Gaullist propaganda" and while this provoked the reservations of the moderate president of the Conseil National, Gilbert Gidel,[7] it was heartily approved by hard-line anti-Gaullists such as Bonnard, Bergery, and Dunoyer.

During the appearance of Chef Compagnon Guillaume de Tournemire before the commission, Bergery denounced various signs of

"Gaullism" in the Compagnons. Tournemire, put on the defensive in spite of the support of President Gidel and Valentin, did not elicit the same warm reaction that Segonzac had inspired. Bonnard even said he was surprised that the Compagnons had not yet been dissolved. In his more general comments, Bergery called for a strong governmental control over youth so as to form them in "an egalitarian, but not class, socialism, born from the German revolution, blended and humanized in the French crucible."[8] He seemed to think that a revamped Ecole Nationale des Cadres d'Uriage could guide this blending and humanizing.

Henri Massis took the opportunity afforded by the discussions of the Conseil National to vigorously denounce the influence of Mounier and of the *"progressistes"* Catholics on Uriage. On 10 March 1942, at the time of the examination of the general report, Massis, who had long prepared for the meeting, called for the creation of a "Conseil Supérieur de la Jeunesse" charged with elaborating a "doctrinal manual." It was to prevent the revival of the intellectual "disorders" that had surfaced before the war in certain Catholic milieux and then subsequently at Uriage. He read "extracts of articles appearing in 1934, 1935, and 1938 in the publications of M. Emmanuel Mounier" and said the same group "was anti-Munichois in 1938 and is now Gaullist. It was the very group that inspired the doctrine taught at Uriage. It was a scandal that could no longer be tolerated." He saw the best solution in assigning the elaboration of youth doctrine to a "Conseil Supérieur de la Jeunesse."[9] Massis's attack on Mounier's ideas was immediately seconded by Segonzac's Uncle Louis, who "deplored that a *chef* as distinguished as that of the Uriage school had had the weakness to allow the influence of Mounier and his henchmen at his place."[10] His previous applause notwithstanding, Uriage's chief could see the pincers closing.

The final report to the Marshal's Cabinet recommended the reforming of the École des Cadres in a way that would advance the "Third Way" youth revolution that the Pétain entourage advocated. It noted the differences between the schools of the free zone, where Dunoyer de Segonzac's Uriage was providing an "apolitical education" debased, however, by excessive "individualism" and "a democratic spirit contrary to the principles of community," and the situation in the occupied zone where Bousquet's school at La Chapelle-en-Serval was engaging in simple "political propaganda" that tended to ignore its educative role and exude a "totalitarian influence."[11]

On 20 March 1942 an ominous note was sent to the *Cabinet civil* by the hard-line "unitaires" complaining of Lamirand's having allowed "intellectual disorder" at a Uriage "still contaminated by the doctrine of a man presently in prison for conspiracy" and "having allowed the *administration de la jeunesse* to become infiltrated by a "Christian democrat" tendency decried as much by [Catholic] laymen as by the highest French ecclesiastic authorities." The report suggested an almost total change of the directors of the SGJ "completely impregnated with the spirit of M. Garonne" and provided a list of replacements (among them Jean Maze, Georges Pelorson, Robert Loustau) as well as directors for the new movement "Jeunesse de France."[12] By March 1942 even the very *pétainiste* Conseil National had individuals impatient with the general drift of the National Revolution, and particularly the insufficiently authoritarian Christian style of places like Uriage.

JOCKEYING FOR POSITION (MARCH–SEPTEMBER 1942)

Laval's return to power on 18 April 1942 was a bad sign for the Uriage people, for Pétain, bowing to German pressure, had recalled Laval to the government just seventeen months after expelling him. From this time, Laval became, in fact if not in title, the true head of state. By the *Acte constitutionnel* No. XI the Marshal delegated him with "the effective direction of the interior and exterior politics of France." From this time Pétain seemed more and more a prisoner of the Germans and of Laval. The Darlan era at Vichy had definitely ended, and most of the personal associates of the Marshal – including friends and backers of Uriage such as René Gillouin – were obliged to leave Vichy.[13]

This appears, in retrospect, as a crucial date not only for Uriage but for a certain "Vichy that might have been." The men of Uriage would have been surprised by the insistence of subsequent historians[14] on a persistent basic collaborationist orientation in the regime and Pétain's complicity in the policies of Laval. In fact, at this time Uriage began displaying a spirit of "Resistance" to Laval out of fidelity to Pétain.[15] Segonzac and a number of other faithful Pétainists, stunned by the events of March–April 1942, began adopting "Resistance" attitudes because they thought their hero, Pétain, had been effectively removed from power. Soon their enemies in the regime were actually moving against them. The Uriage people began to assume that Pétain was really a "prisoner of the Germans," if not of Laval, and only gradually, as we shall see, did Segonzac's unqualified faith in Pétain become shaken. Segonzac did not suspect that secret complicity of Pétain with collaborationist policies that has been claimed by recent scholarship.[16]

It was no accident that the former directeur de la Jeunesse, Garonne, who had tried in vain to exert some control over Uriage, was replaced by the very symbol of the movement for a single youth movement, Georges Pelorson. Named on 9 June 1942, not long after Laval's return to power, Pelorson "had as his mission to make [Lamirand] march in a straight line, threatening him with secession" if his young associates did not conform.[17]

Then, on 22 June, the whole dining hall of the school heard Laval declare on the radio that "he desired the victory of Germany because, without it, tomorrow Bolshevism will be installed everywhere." Laval urged French workers to leave voluntarily for the other side of the Rhine that prisoners might return in their stead. In the castle dining hall, "everyone got up from the table," Father des Alleux later recalled, "and I observed a revolution in everyone's heart. Everything changed from that moment on."[18]

On 2 August, just after the Grande Fête, Segonzac travelled to Paris to participate in a meeting of over two hundred delegates representing the regional commissions du travail des jeunes, as well as the associations of young people from all of France.[19] At least one youth leader refused to participate in that meeting because he feared the government was trying to politicize the youth movements, to push them into doing things they had not done before.[20]

With the obvious intention of bringing to heel *chefs* of the regional schools who were too dependant on Uriage, Pelorson organized for them, from 16 to 27 August, a meeting at the École Nationale des Cadres of Mayet-de-Montagne, a school that had now become totally devoted to the Vichy government and officially designated to compete with Uriage.[21] The heads of the regional schools were told to cancel their training sessions and close their schools in order to attend. Jean Stouff, member of the équipe des Anciens d'Uriage, was delegated by his comrades, at Segonzac's request, to "express their thinking." It was he who privately kept the Vieux Chef, who had come secretly to Mayet de Montagne to give directions, informed.[22] In response to Pelorson, who reproached him for maintaining such a reticent attitude at the meeting, particularly toward the new stress on anti-semitism by the new Vichy authorities, Stouff replied: "I have always respected authority, but for two years we have been working with Uriage ... we live a profound discipline in regard to it. We have an official *chef* whom we know, the Vieux Chef. We follow the Marshal; he has not asked [that we take] anti-semitic positions."

The Uriage people grew particularly touchy about the issue of authority when, during the discussions, Jean Gravier, a humble *chargé de mission* at the sGj, spoke as if he had authority over the mother school. The Uriage delegation made it plain that they considered themselves to be under Segonzac's orders and would give their reactions to outside ideas only later.

It soon became clear that this was no mere debate over niceties but that the question of the orientation of the youth movements interested the highest government authorities. At 6:00 P.M., the visit of the head of the government was announced, and Pierre Laval himself came in, pretending not to know who the people were at the meeting and asking if they had a *chef*. When Stouff spoke for the group, presenting a summary of the work of Uriage, the wily Laval responded that he had just been told how Uriage ignored his policies. That same night, after another altercation, *chef* Alain Desforges, another Uriage alumnus, was ordered to leave; the other *chefs* quickly returned to their own rooms and packed their bags, lined them up at the entrance, and insisted they were leaving with him.

Such was the hold of Segonzac over his alumni that Gravier and his colleagues seem to have decided they had no choice but to invite the Vieux Chef himself to the meeting to calm everyone down, and this was done. Segonzac's precipitous arrival allowed the session to finally end in an "ambience of complete relaxation" but, the Uriage network gloated, Gravier and his colleagues left with a sense of a "total failure."[23] For the time being, at least, Segonzac and his disciples, despite their growing difficulties with the Vichy government, could continue steering their self-styled *pétainiste* course.

GERMAN MEDDLING

A factor of growing importance in the evolution of the Uriage school by the fall of 1942 was evidence that the war was turning against the Germans, resulting in German high-handedness and increasing strictures on France. The fact that anti-semitism was an issue at the meeting described above was a reflection of a larger situation in France in which what Uriage took to be a dishonourable and German-imposed racism was being displayed by the Vichy government. Already on 7 December 1941 the Prefect of the department in which Uriage was located (Isère) had sent a letter to mayors asking them for a list of known, and reputed, Jews.[24] During the middle of the following summer, on 12 July 1942, the Germans ordered the arrest of all French Jews in the occupied zone. On July 16 there was the raid of the Vel' d'hiv' in Paris took place, and on August 26, forty-two Jews were arrested in Haute-Savoie.[25]

At Uriage, Paul de la Taille, who was charged with aiding Jews, was put into contact with Father Pierre Chaillet at Lyon by

Segonzac.[26] (Founder of *Témoignage Chrétien* and member of Combat, Chaillet was one of the leaders in the actions taken on behalf of Jews in Lyon). Segonzac and Uriage were not above suspicions about the Jews themselves, as we shall see, but they seemed to have been contemptuous of the brutal anti-semitism of Laval and the Germans.

Of far more pressing concern to most French young people then anti-semitism, however, was the prospect of being forced to work in Germany. From early 1942, the Germans began hunting for volunteer workers in France to help prop up the faltering German war effort. The former Gauleiter of Thuringia, F. Sauckel, was named ministre plénipotentiare de la Main d'oeuvre in the occupied territories on 21 March 1942, and from June 1942 to June 1944 he would demand a significant number of workers from the French government on four occasions.[27] On 4 September, under pressure from Sauckel, who had asked for 240,000 volunteers, the French government passed a law requiring men from eighteen to fifty, and celibate women from twenty-one to thirty-five, to do "everything the government might judge useful in the highest interest of the nation."[28] The law rendered hundreds of thousands of French people liable to forced labour in Germany – and ignited massive opposition to the occupation forces and the government.

Negative remarks about the Germans surprised some of the Uriage trainees; they were particularly surprised that such opinions could be ventilated in an "official" school. For example, a complaint was lodged with the minister by a shocked informer, a Lycée official who charged that Uriage was "clearly anti-governmental" and "anti-German"; it was dismissing the current actions of the government to its trainees as being carried out under German pressure, and arguing that nothing constructive could be done until after the end of the occupation. At Uriage, French papers were held to be in the pay of Germany, and only Swiss ones credible. Militantly collaborationist publications such as *Gringoire*, *La Gerbe*, or *Je suis partout* were treated as traitorous, the work of madmen. Seditious things had been said, particularly by Reuter and by Jeanneney, son of the former president of the Senate.[29]

In early September Segonzac was again visited by his old school friend Henri Frenay, who had vigorously denounced *La Relève*, describing Pierre Laval as a "slave merchant" in the Resistance paper *Combat*.[30] On the eve of his departure for London, Frenay wrote: "I spoke with Segonzac at length at the veillée. He is sad and morally tortured. He is tempted to resign and join us, but is that in accord with his duty? I said to him: 'Old friend, I am leaving for London. On my return I shall come to see you. When I return I will tell you what I have seen and heard over there. You will have thought things over; things will have happened. One day you will join us.'"[31]

During the period March 1942 to September 1942 Uriage changed from being a faithfully Pétainist to a militantly anti-German, hence anti-Laval and anti-collaborationist, institution. Yet as they moved toward resisting the Germans, neither Segonzac nor Frenay attacked the Marshal himself, or those ideals of the National Revolution that the Marshal was thought to personally represent. It was a spiritual tightrope act that could not go on forever.

Thus Uriage was becoming known as a Pétainist "Resistance" institution, and this began to cause difficulties. Shortly after his conversation with Frenay, Segonzac was told that he was "in danger of being fired if not arrested"; he rushed to Vichy to see Bonnard, minister of national education, and expressed his views "very freely and openly" to him. Segonzac then judged it "useful" to pay a tactical visit to the Marshal, who sent him on to Laval, with whom he conversed for three hours – becoming convinced that Laval was patriotic and sincere.[32] Back at the school, on 16 September Segonzac urged his Conseil des chefs, on this second anniversary of the school, to hold to their morning rituals and to sign a motion of confidence in the Marshal. But d'Astorg, Lavorel, Dumazedier, and others complained, particularly about the increasing brutality being shown toward Jews by the Vichy government.[33] In the end a toned-down confidence motion was accepted. "The game is worth playing," Segonzac told his men; "if not I wouldn't be here."[34] It was, however, a game he could not win.

Segonzac, with Beuve-Méry, decided that the school's days might well be numbered and its priority should be to influence the *stagiaires*, to reinforce the alumni network, and to set out strategic options until it might be necessary to go into hiding. In the interim, on Saturday 19 September, the Vieux Chef and his knight-monk instructors left for a retreat at the austere hermitage-monastery of the Grande-Chartreuse.[35]

Segonzac and his men returned from the Carthusians with a determination to arm themselves with more than spiritual weapons. At the end of September, Segonzac summoned the carpenter (who since the beginning of the month had been a permanent functionary of the school) and told him that he was to work at night preparing hiding places for arms. "Night after night," Cacérès recalled, "I sawed the boards of the old chateau in secret places, to conceal ... between long, broad beams, all sorts of objects: grenades, revolvers, plastic explosives, Bickford fuses, etc."[36]

In the meantime there continued to be pressure on Georges Lamirand from such partisans of the New Order as Pelorson to bring Uriage and the youth movements to heel. Lamirand and Pelorson held another meeting on 3 October, at Ecully, where Pierre Ollier de Marichard represented the Uriage team. The meeting, however, almost dispersed in the uproar over inflammatory racist language employed by some of the participants.[37] On 20–21 October 1942, twenty-eight of the leaders of the ENU met at Uriage to hear major talks by Segonzac, Beuve-Méry, and Dumazedier on the new direction the school planned to take in the circumstances, and a position paper decrying the "aborting" of the National Revolution, and calling for a new twentieth-century humanism, was circulated.[38] It asserted: "We believe that there is a fundamental equality among men prohibiting all definitive privilege of race, that spiritual values predominate over all others, thus requiring the general respect for liberty, indispensable for the development of the spirit ... That a new man will flourish only in community life ... That ... man finally only lives spiritual values ... in giving himself, in generous communication with the other, in community life."[39]

Thus, at a time when the Resistance movement was beginning to call for liberty in France, Uriage was still insisting on the need to eliminate "individualism" in a post-liberal Europe. In many respects, the new philosophy of "personalism" came to fruition in this Uriage context, much more than in the philosophical treatises and erudite reviews of the 1930s. That ideology was made to mould groups of people into newer, richer, communities, in a world that would follow upon the collapse of liberal democracy. Symptomatically, the school also remained much concerned with the idea of an "Order," as the text shows. At the end of the year, Segonzac evoked it clearly for the first time in a public text, in tracing the result of the community experiences conducted at Uriage. The internal dynamism of the search for a "style of life," combined with the theoretical insights of social thinkers such as François Perroux, would certainly culminate, he wrote, in the constitution of something original:

In a very remarkable little book, M. François Perroux analyzed and defined the "community" with more precision and profundity than anyone before, at least in France. "The community," he says, "is an organic and spontaneous whole, a work of history; it organizes complementary functions into a hierarchy which fosters and expresses the fusion of activities and consciences around common elements and in the light of common objects. It eventually manifests an organization corresponding to its content and its structure.

At Uriage, the small group of young men coalesced in its dedication to the formation of "chefs" has experienced and is still living in a way that corresponds to that definition of community.

The Vieux Chef also suggested that there was a mysterious dimension in all of this:

But, inexorably, by the very experience of community life, and *also doubtlessly by the feeling, more precise each day, of having a mission to express the real France's political conscience, the relatively instinctive community of the early days tends to open onto the suprarational. We are not completely masters of the consequences.* [my emphasis][40]

A document for private circulation described the evolution of the Équipes nationales d'Uriage as along similar lines: the only men qualified for the urgent task of social reconstruction would be those moulded in the new orders developed in the orbit of a mother-community. They would be imbued with a contagious "communitarian spirit," forming small communities at the heart of various professions that would serve as social prototypes as well as vehicles for testing new projects.[41]

THE CLOSING OF THE SCHOOL (DECEMBER 1942)

All of this made Uriage sound more and more independent within the National Revolution, and its *chefs* more and more autonomous. On 3 November 1942 Beuve-Méry told the instructors that "the Revolution of 1940" was "an aborted Revolution," and that the "the socialist revolution realized by Hitler in Germany, promised by Doriot in France," had in fact become perverted by "an inhuman ideology which masks the most monstrous imposture."[42] Clearly the École Nationale des Cadres de la Jeunesse was becoming more and more contentious and non-conformist.

On 9 November Uriage's old friend and patron, the beleaguered Georges Lamirand, came to sound out the situation at the Château Bayard for himself.[43] Then he addressed a "confidential note" to his superior, Bonnard, in an effort to answer criticism of the school:

despite the limited means at his disposal, Dunoyer de Segonzac has succeeded in giving more than 2,000 people a sense of the National Revolution, in awakening in them notions of honour, sacrifice, and community life purged of all egotism. Certainly some of his staff have made mistakes ...

out of a poorly perceived patriotism, but, on the one hand, these people are no longer on the present team of instructors, and on the other, Dunoyer de Segonzac has perfectly understood what we want of that school. [Segonzac's] loyalty toward the chef de l'État is total: I have had some personal demonstrations of it during these last days; the Uriage team showed itself to be faithful at its post, and resolved to execute the orders of the Marshal.

Was Lamirand being naive or disingenuous? In fact, the oath that Segonzac had asked of his men some weeks before made this assessment seem quite plausible, at least as far as Segonzac's loyalty to Pétain was concerned. And in his report, the youth secretary called attention to other, practical considerations:

Moreover, Dunoyer de Segonzac enjoys immense prestige, not only with the young people he has trained, but with all who have met him: industrialists, *cadres*, workers, civil and religious authorities. Now as the fatherland is going through dark days, I think the departure of Dunoyer de Segonzac would constitute a grave injury to the government and to the chef d'État himself. It would be hard to understand why we would dispense with such a pure force, one with no other object than of serving the country in perfect fidelity to the chef d'État, and obeying the strict directives given him.

Lamirand even associated his own fate with that of Uriage school: "The problem seems so important to me that I pledge myself ... to assure personally the control of the École Nationale des Cadres d'Uriage, serving as a personal guarantee to you of the teaching and the education provided there."[44]

For Georges Lamirand, at least, the École Nationale des Cadres d'Uriage seemed one of the most important achievements of the National Revolution, right to the bitter end. He leaned over backwards to see Segonzac's side of things and defend him. But it was to no avail: reports hostile to Uriage continued to be sent to the government (and forwarded on to the school).[45]

Great tensions arose between youth institutions and the government, and at Uriage itself, on the issue of obligatory labour service. Prominent Church leaders urged young people to go to work in Germany rather than go into hiding. In late 1942, for example, Father Forestier buttressed his plea for Chantiers de la Jeunesse fidelity to the Marshal with his own arguments from moral theology and those of his colleague Father Doncoeur, which he annexed to his text. Recalling that St. Thomas taught that "one can never do what is evil, even to bring a greater good out of it," the general chaplain of the Chantiers argued that to disobey the government would be to opt for "free examination, the individual who makes himself the rule of life, the man who makes himself God" – thus giving in to anarchy. And then there were the supernatural attributes of Pétain: "The Leader, when he is loyal and of good will, has the right to illuminations from on high. Through ours, God will direct our destinies toward the shore of salvation. The Marshal remains the precondition for unity. He is the very symbol of our liberty."[46]

In the January official publication of the Scouts de France, commissaire général Eugène Dary drew upon this teaching of Forestier to urge obedience and discipline on the Scouts. This was frankly based on the hope of a New Order which the Marshal had promised and whose "messages express what we have dreamed of for twenty years, what we have tried to exemplify in our lives and what the older men among us fought to establish ... that France might live."[47]

This high-minded moralizing translated into an effort to dissuade young people from trying to leave France via Spain, or from adhering to the Resistance, but rather, eventually, to encourage their submitting to the sinister requisition to join the obligatory labour service in the Reich.[48]

Here the traditional Catholic stress on obedience tended to encourage working for a regime given to tyranny and brutality. Could these *curés* have kept silent rather than exhorting work in Nazi Germany in the name of Christian duty? At Uriage, in any case, the priests' attitude was openly criticized – above all after the end of November when it was learned that Hitler had ordered the occupation of Toulon and the disarming of the French army.[49]

The occupation of the free zone by the Germans meant a crisis at Uriage. On 1 December the "Conseil des chefs" met at the school, under the Vieux Chef who had just returned from Paris. But those hoping for dramatic action were disappointed: he spoke of starting up a new six-month training session and reproached those who wished to discuss other things. A participant noted "disappointment ... on all the faces."[50] Segonzac was determined to steer the school away from precipitous action, and his attitude toward the Resistance was still by no means clear.

On Thursday, 3 December, all normal school business was suspended for a day of meditation under the direction of Father Maydieu on the theme of "Les devoirs du chrétien d'Uriage." The *veillée* included readings from the prophets and the Apocalypse, music, and nocturnal adoration of the sacrament.[51] Two weeks later, on 17 December 1942, Roger Stéphane, sent by Resistance leaders (and

Catholics) Georges Bidault and Menthon, and accompanied by Paul Reuter, returned to Uriage to sound out Segonzac's intentions.[52] At 9:00 A.M. Stéphane was ushered into the office of Segonzac where he found the Vieux Chef somewhat incoherent on the question of the Resistance:

> We did not sit down. I explained to him the purpose of my visit, specifying that I was only mandated to negotiate. His reception was infinitely more favourable than Reuter had led me to think it might be. Priority question for him: unity in dissent. Then he specified his political position: he was violently anti-mason, from whence came his hatred for Darlan (suspected by some of being a freemason) ... he did not concede the French having the capacity of governing themselves by themselves. He denied being an advocate of tyranny, which is, for him, the opposite of authority. There is, he said, tyranny when the authority is arbitrary and anonymous. Local tyrannies undermine the central authority. [He went into a] long tirade on that subject.

As to the question of Uriage's relationship with the Resistance, Stéphane concluded that: "Dunoyer de Segonzac is nevertheless disposed, and even desirous, of collaborating if a tactical-ideological agreement is reached. He would put his cadres at our disposition, [men] capable of becoming from one day to the next the managers of France, from mayor to minister." A bit taken aback by the elitist presumption in that affirmation, Stéphane nevertheless decided that secondary disagreements should not block an effort to negotiate at the highest level. He arranged meetings for the Vieux Chef with fellow Combat members Teitgen, Menthon, and Frenay.[53] (Once again, Combat was trying to help a number of prominent Catholic Pétainists to get involved with the Resistance, before it was too late.)

On 19 December there was another religiously oriented general *veillée* in the Château – this one led by Father Dominique Dubarle.[54] This event took place in the context of a series of ideologically oriented lectures for which Hubert Beuve-Méry had set the tone with his call for a modern and popular "mystique communautaire," and his outline of the material, moral, and political conditions for its absorption by the French proletariat. The authors most often cited in this series were François Perroux, the Proudhonians, Berdyaev, Father Chenu, Henri de Man, Thierry Maulnier, Dubreuil, and Romanet, all of whose texts were circulated.[55]

Uriage interests at this end of 1942 were certainly high-minded and, as this list of thinkers suggests, particularly focused on the most creative and innovative social thinking, specifically that oriented toward "getting beyond" Marxism. There was a notable interest in the ideas of the personalist economist and Pétain counsellor François Perroux: Beuve-Méry, from his earliest lectures at the school (after demonstrating that class struggle was a given, and that it was vain to denounce it if its causes were not attacked) made regular references to Perroux's work on the transformation of businesses into "communautés de travail." Joffre Dumazedier, another of the Uriage school's leading social thinkers, argued that: "The Marxist revolution could only be defeated by a revolution that hoped to surpass it: if the bourgeois elite wants to take its just part in that communitarian revolution, it will pay attention to history, or history will be made ... against it."[56]

Dumazedier conceived the project of the three-day seminar on economic and social doctrines that was finally held on 22–24 December.[57] He believed that the diversity of the spiritual families represented at Uriage, with men nourished by Marxist, nationalist, or Christian thought, would enable the team to transcend sterile ideological confrontations. The convergence that appeared, associating an affirmation of spiritual values with hope in a social revolution, would be extended "to the point of achieving the harmony of tendencies essential to a fresh Revolution." Yet, for Uriage's critics, all this was taking place, much as it had five hundred years earlier among the Byzantine theologians, with the barbarians at the gates.

The instructors who participated in that collective enterprise, directed by Gilbert Gadoffre, were to work "each in the line of his spiritual family, in the search for that transcending."[58] After the general exposés of Gadoffre (Method), of Ferry (doctrines and propaganda), and of Cacérès (workers' revolutions in the twentieth century), the major currents of thought were presented by Dumazedier (from Marx to de Man), by Poix (from Maurras to Thierry Maulnier), by Ollier de Marichard (from reformist biblicism to André Philip), by Father Maydieu (from Social Catholicism to Berdyaev), by Poli (the work community of Perroux) and by Reuter (the plan of the CGT), and, in the end, collective conclusions were established.[59]

In their special concern for the spiritual dimension of revolution, Uriage theorists often cited the pamphlet of an original young Dominican theologian Marie-Dominique Chenu, *Pour être heureux, travaillons ensemble*. Chenu thought workers ought to participate in the common culture and bring their own experiences to it. Dumazedier found several of the Dominican's ideas about spiritualizing work and the community directly relevant to the concerns of Uriage, as when he suggested how human value could be incorporated into the most demanding work:

It is that incorporation [Dumazedier cited Chenu as writing] that must be considered when discerning how the economic realm not only will respect moral values coming from the outside but will incarnate moral values in itself. In short, it is not the body that is too large, it is the soul that is too small. Or again, as Bergson said, "The enlarged body is awaiting its supplement of soul." The essence of the drama is there.

Chenu, according to the Uriage instructor, had the perspicacity to realize that the "grandeur or, to put it better, the truth" of worker aspirations in the whole nineteenth century lay in the new sense of the human dignity of the worker, for, as Chenu put it:

Because it is a discovery of man, at the scale of those that would successively give humanity the Roman citizen, the feudal knight, the bourgeois of the medieval communes, the humanist of the Renaissance, Cartesian man. Who does not see that in the course of the last one hundred years misses the coming of a true human grandeur, and will henceforth find himself outside of the march of history, like a blind man who has wandered outside of a procession'."

And Father Chenu also grasped the new sense of the human person that had been articulated in the Château Bayard as indicated when he wrote that communitarian work tended to develop something special:

the sense of his creative responsibility and the sense of communion in the person (Maritain) ...

It is the person to whom is assigned the vocation, it is he who carries the message; it is only by him and for him that the nations and classes have a vocation to accomplish, and a witness to bear ... *Fraternité, liberté*, a vocation to accomplish and a testimony to bear.[60]

Uriage interest in Chenu demonstrates that the school was perceptive about what was new in social theorizing in France in 1942, and on the lookout to put it to use. It was no accident that Father Chenu left the ideal of *égalité* out of the vocation and witness of the personalist community cited above: like the theorists at the Uriage school Chenu was, and would remain, interested in the role of charismatic spiritual elites (e.g., the worker-priests, a special interest of his) in creating personalist communities. The old militant egalitarianism of the Revolution of 1789 (or that of important left-wing elements in the Resistance) did not fit so neatly into this perspective.

Beuve-Méry, for his part, cited Péguy while juxtaposing the extremes of an idealist and inefficacious spiritualism over against a cult of efficiency through strength which led to oppression. The lecture of Beuve-Méry, constantly reiterated in diverse forms during the 1942 sessions, made Péguy the prophet of the new revolution. Beuve-Méry foresaw three names emerging from the tragic crisis that gripped Europe: Marx, Nietzsche, and Péguy; France had to respond to the challenge of Marx and Nietzsche by undertaking "the revolution that remains to be accomplished" in the steps of Péguy.[61]

An important contribution to the distinctive sense of the spiritual at Uriage was at least partially shaped by another young theologian, this one a Jesuit – Henri de Lubac. De Lubac had contributed to the school's Péguyist notion of spirituality with his exposition on *Ordre viril, ordre chrétien* which he had presented to the special session for chaplains on 25 June. An expert on the thought of the anti-clerical anarchist Proudhon, de Lubac argued that it was necessary to find a Christianity "more adapted, more incarnated, more efficacious, stronger." Christian virility did not consist in "seeking out strength while ceding to a sort of vertigo in the presence of contemporary enterprises" but rather in "practising with strength ... the values and virtues of Christianity, which are summed up in Charity."[62]

Out of all these heady speculations came an idea, which became extremely important to Uriage, of a kind of "super-revolution," a "Revolution of the twentieth century." School documents confidently asserted that "nothing can stop it" – it was "unlimited, affecting all peoples; touching all domains." This revolution was seen as transcending Vichy France and even Europe: it was part of a larger vision, which seemed inspired by the thinking of de Lubac's close friend, the daring speculative evolutionist theologian in exile in China, Father Pierre Teilhard de Chardin. Hubert Beuve-Méry, a great admirer of Father Teilhard, promised that this revolution of the twentieth century was "the grandest transformation to which humanity ever submitted ... It is perhaps the bloody birth of a true "collective being of men," of a humanity of which the bolshevik or national socialist masses are only a monstrous prefiguration, an aborted attempt."[63] Perhaps only an evolutionist view could encourage one to be so up-beat in decidedly down-beat times in France.

Hubert Beuve-Méry was central in bringing this grandiose theological perspective into the day-to-day teachings of the school, as he cited both the research of François Perroux on the communitarian economy and various Christians who were trying to restore the sense of the collective characteristic of original Christianity.[64] And since individualism and unbridled capitalism seemed condemned by history, the "new" spirit of Christianity had to be pursued within the context of the new, post-liberal, European New Order. In Beuve-Méry's words, "the communitarian consciousness must be revived, the most primitive and profound sources of the Christian mystique rediscovered."[65]

This was hardly your typical democrat's ringing call for resistance against racism, authoritarianism, and the rule of the fist. Once again, the school's study director seemed to be on a totally different plane from everyone else – thinking in terms of Uriage's furnishing land-clearing monks to a Europe overrun by barbarians. Earlier that year, in an even more romantic vein, he had asked:

Cannot those people now so appalled at the spectacle of the collective gestation of the collective being of man see the opportunity (doubtless unique) for the divinization of the world and of man that is implied by a Christianity forced back ever more profoundly to its vocation? The necessity and possibility, thanks to the incarnation, of substituting a community of love, where a man only loses himself to better realize and personalize himself, for those inhuman communities in which the being is dissolved?[66]

Uriage's study group's ethnologist, Paul-Henri Chombart de Lauwe, struck a Barrèsian note as he waxed eloquent over the peasant communities of rural France, rooted as they were in the soil and the earth:

Par la terre et par le sang la communauté s'incarne dans la matière. Sur cette terre qui modèle l'homme et que l'homme travaille, le groupe humain plonge ses racines. Ses ancêtres y dorment et son sang y est mêlé. Le cimetière du village est le lieu de ce mystère d'union.

Chaque famille a sa tombe et chague village son cimetière. Chaque patrie élève des monuments à ses héros. "La Mère Patrie," dit Jean Lacroix, "est la terre infiniment fécondée par les tombeaux qui donnent sans cesse naissance aux berceaux, dans une sorte de rythme sacré." Terre et sang sont nécessaires pour que vive la communauté.[67]

This exalted romanticism combined with apocalyptic mysticism, charged with optimism despite France's utter destitution, was central to the mentality of Beuve-Méry and of the whole Uriage school. Rooted in the deepest of religious and philosophical beliefs, the Uriage world view was a stunning contrast to the basic attitudes of many anti-fascists who appealed to them to join the Resistance. Though rooted equally in the French tradition and facing a common enemy, the two camps hardly spoke the same language.

On New Year's Eve there was a poetry *veillée* at the Château directed by Gilbert Gadoffre. "People were hugging one another to welcome the new year. Then the Vieux Chef came in. He was striking, stick in hand, in his *canadienne*. He announced that the school would close the next day, 1 January."[68] The decree deciding the dissolution and closing of the school had been signed by Laval and Bonnard on 27 December,[69] but Segonzac only got denials from Lamirand, from whom he formally demanded the motives for this measure. The suppression of the school had been neither decided by the chef d'État nor explicitly demanded by the Occupation authorities. The secrétaire général à la Jeunesse, who said he himself had not been consulted, declared he regretted the disappearance of an establishment that he had appreciated and supported until the last day.[70] Back at the school there was a large nocturnal ceremony of farewell, "very moving and dramatic." Later the team divided up the Uriage flag in the hopes of being able to put it back together later, each member keeping a piece in his wallet.[71] It was a fittingly romantic gesture, the stuff of dreams, but Uriage itself was more than a dream: we shall see later that the elite school's alumni went away with more than a patch of cloth.

In retrospect, the fate of Uriage seems to have been hostage to the status of Georges Lamirand and of idealistic Catholics of Lamirand's stripe in the institutions and organizations of the National Revolution. The knight-monks of Uriage, like Lamirand, had been criticized for a constraining attachment to their own culture and their fellow Catholics, and hence an inability to reach the country at large, particularly young people of working-class background. The unsuitability of the life at the "Château de l'Âme" at Uriage for young peasants and workers had something to do with its undoing. Perceptive men such as Emmanuel Mounier had worried about the inability of the clergy, and of old-fashioned Catholics like Segonzac, to "reach" the working classes since the beginnings of the National Revolution. Their shortcoming in this regard was a common weakness of many of the Catholics who worked for the Vichy regime with their own version of a National Revolution in mind, their "Vichy that might have been."

Fascist-oriented, or frankly Nazi, rivals coveted the role Uriage claimed to play in the National Revolution, as we shall see. But as the war turned ever more against the Reich, and Vichy's show of independence from an occupant now brutally exploiting the entire country faded, the dream of a credible National Revolution faded too. The men of Uriage, however, pursued their own, stubbornly consistent, sometimes paradoxical, course from 1943 to the liberation. Rather than merely marching to a different drummer, the personalists, like Joan of Arc, set off to save the country on their own.

CHAPTER EIGHT

Exile from the Castle, the Order, and the Flying Squads

The closing of the École Nationale des Cadres d'Uriage at the end of 1942 marked the end of the golden age of a community that had brought together some of the best and the brightest people to create a new kind of France. It was succeeded by a period that many of the alumni, in retrospect, saw as the best, the most heroic, even the most important, period in their lives. The activities of the Uriage group during the disintegration of the Vichy regime and the liberation of France are interesting and instructive, if not the most important from our point of view.

THE FALLEN ANGEL

When Uriage was closed down, two meetings were held, in early January 1943, to discuss the fate of the regional schools. In the first gathering, the heads of ten regional schools got together in secret in Lyon. They were debating what to do when Segonzac came and persuaded everyone to disband out of solidarity with Uriage. In the meeting later that day at Vichy between Lamirand and the regional directors, one of the latter (speaking for the others) had a heated exchange with Lamirand. He then gave Lamirand his resignation – precipitating the mass resignation of the rest.[1] The director of the women's school at Ecully announced that she, too, was resigning. Lamirand was sufficiently innocent that he could profess astonishment at this blow-up. In fact he had not expected it and, to his bitter disappointment, the sinking of the flagship Uriage brought down his SGJ's entire network of schools in the southern zone.[2]

Leaders of the sister youth organizations were shocked but not displeased. The Bureau d'études of the Chantiers de la Jeunesse had already huffily disapproved of Uriage people as "superficial" or "syndicalists,"[3] and now General de La Porte du Theil, referring to the events surrounding Segonzac's dismissal, told Lamirand, "if you had any guts, you would have arrested him at the exit door of your hotel!"[4] De la Porte du Theil had taken Segonzac publicly to task for his earlier arrogance in going to demand explanations from the Head of State, and he was now further angered by this provoking of the collective indiscipline and resignation of the chefs of the regional schools: the Vieux Chef had thereby demonstrated "precisely the sort of pride as that shown by the defiance of the first fallen angel, dragging thousands of others along in his ruin."[5]

Segonzac responded privately to La Porte du Theil by citing his need to defend loyal Uriage and the National Revolution against the sabotage of its enemies:

The decision of the *chefs* of the regional schools was spontaneous. However, I encouraged it, for the following reasons: Monsieur Lamirand, when consulted on the reasons for the closing of the Uriage school, admitted that it was not a decision of the chef de l'Etat, nor explicitly desired by the Germans, nor dictated by a serious motive, that he himself had not been consulted and in fact regretted the closing of an establishment he had encouraged and supported to the last. So it seems that Uriage's demise resulted from a rather obscure conspiracy oblivious to the interests of the state and of the country.

Beyond that, Segonzac recalled that he had never received the smallest hint that he was thought to be wavering in his fidelity to the "true" spirit of the National Revolution: "You reproach me for being diabolically set in my errors. What errors? In thirty months, I didn't receive one directive, program, or reproach concerning the teaching given at Uriage. On several occasions and until the end of 1942, my superiors – Monsieur Pelorson in front of the chefs of the schools, Monsieur Lamirand at Uriage itself – warmly expressed sympathy and approbation."[6]

In sum, Segonzac sincerely seemed to think he had had only the full backing and encouragement of Vichy authorities, but had been done in by jealous rivals. This was the picture of the internal politics of the National Revolution that Beuve-Méry began presenting to the Uriage network. Neither Segonzac nor Beuve-Méry questioned the whole purpose of the National Revolution, as the former charged that Uriage had been undermined by small-minded critics and competitors, and the latter that Vichy had been corrupted by traitors and immoral characters who were ruining everything. There was no fundamental questioning of the collective enthusiasm for "anti-individualist" communities, the abandonment of liberal institutions, the fanatical fear of communism, or the anti-semitism, all of which had served the sinister purposes of the Pétain government.

Uriage's troubles with Vichy and La Porte du Theil led Beuve-Méry to air his views before various youth organizations. On 25 January he lectured on "Nazism and youth" to the cadres of the Chantiers, reunited for a meeting at Chatelard, near Clermont-Ferrand. There he lunched with their chaplain Father Forestier, and, he later recalled, tried to discourage their officers from sending Chantiers youth to Germany.[7] That Uriage's director of studies could talk on that theme to that audience at that time may mean that it was not so much Uriage's *ideas* or ideology that were under attack, as Dunoyer de Segonzac's headstrong leadership.

Général de La Porte du Theil's concern about Uriage's influence proved well founded when prominent leaders of the Chantiers, such as commandant Xavier de Virieu,[8] director of the École régionale des chefs des Chantiers de la Jeunesse of Collonges-au-Mont-d'Or (and old friend and comrade-in-arms of Segonzac), began to show Uriage-like doubts about their government-approved activities. But in January 1943 as Virieu resigned, several youth leaders – Tournemire, head of the Compagnons de France, de La Porte du Theil for the Chantiers, and General Lafont for the French scouts – offered to provide Lamirand with new elite instructors to start Uriage up again, without Segonzac and his men.[9] Beuve-Méry, who took over the leadership of a group that was still maintaining *une vague étiquette extérieure*, gave another lecture on Portugal. And then on Saturday, 30 January, there was a nostalgic goodbye dinner for the faithful remnant at the school ("pork in all its forms"), followed by a final *veillée* in the *grand carré*.[10]

What attitude did hard-line anti-religious French Nazifiers have toward the Uriage school by this time? At the end of January the new magazine for National Socialist French Youth, Philippe Merlin's[11] semi-monthly *Jeune Force de France*, was patronizing, sarcastic, and Nietzschean:

There was formerly, at Uriage, a school for the training of youth leaders, which little by little extended its influence ... [to] all of those on whom the National Revolution's well-being depended. It would be infantile to believe that the teaching of Uriage consisted in Gaullist propaganda. From the altitude of the Château one saw much further and larger. Thanks to contacts with the universal Protestant federation, with the Dominicans, the Jesuits, and other large religious or philosophical organisms, of which a long list may be found in the registers of the SDN (League of Nations), it was a question of continuing to instill salutary fear and a sense of life's incertitude in men's hearts.

In the circumstances, this was inadmissible:

But Uriage spread its doctrine ... [and] the danger for the French state was: Byzantium was discussing the sex of angels at the very moment it was taken by assault.
The closing of that theatre of metaphysics and unreality is a good sign. The multiple provincial branches called the École régionales des cadres are also breaking up ...
Nothing will remain of that ridiculous farce that would have had people believing in "the respect of the human person," "the union possible in diversity," and other nonsense perhaps worth discussing in 1900, but rather arcane today.
With a whole world at war ... one acts.[12]

Thus militant collaborationists derided Uriage as a tender-minded and impractical enterprise at the very heart of the *pétainiste* National Revolution. All of the faults of that so-called National Revolution from the proto-Nazi point of view had ornamented Uriage: Christian moralism, crabbed clericalism, effete intellectualism, timidities over the Nietzschean life-style. For its nazifying critics Uriage *was* the National Revolution, and displayed all of its worst infirmities.

Most collaborationists did not fault Uriage for crypto-Gaullism, individualism, subversion, duplicity, liberalism, democratic sympathies, pro-Republicanism, or anything of that sort. Rather, for them, the Uriage community represented a certain tender-minded model or vision of the National Revolution, which faded, fortunately, during the course of the war.

CATHOLIC BROWN SHIRTS IN THE CASTLE: THE *MILICE* AT URIAGE

New men – mystical fascists committed to a bizarre, Catholic-Nazi vision of the National Revolution – took over the Château Bayard at Uriage after the departure of Segonzac and his entourage in early 1943. Life at the chateau became what some thought it should have been under Dunoyer de Segonzac, and therefore something of a caricature of the original Uriage experience – and a striking example of the degeneration of Vichy institutions as the war turned against Germany.[13]

On 11 February the Uriage instructors learned that they would be replaced by men from the new and already notorious Milice, an organization created at the end of January at the direct request of Hitler, who invited Laval to form an auxiliary police to maintain internal order. The *fascisant* war hero Joseph Darnand,[14] named as its secretary-general and effective administrator, came from a strong Catholic background[15] and, in Bertram Gordon's words, "although the Catholicism of the Milice was but one component in an amalgam that included Nietzschean romanticism and German and French racialism, it stands out as an element taken very seriously in the organization."[16] It was decided that the new Milice would establish its new École des Cadres, something of a successor to that which the SOL (Service d'Ordre Légionnaire) had maintained at Saint-Cyr-au-Mont-d'Or, in the facilities left vacant by the École Nationale des Cadres at Uriage.

Impatient younger members of the extreme Right were now given the chance to make their mark through the SOL and the Milice. Both organizations adopted an elaborate ceremonial combining scouting, Catholic, and fascist ritual, reflecting the increasingly youthful composition of the two organizations.[17] Thus, by April, the Château d'Uriage became "the great centre for the training of the Milice leadership for all of France."[18] Thus while retaining only a few members of Uriage's service personnel and a skeleton presence of mostly service personnel from the old Uriage school,[19] the Château Bayard became something of a Wagnerian dream-castle of the devoutly Catholic, and fiercely anti-Communist, extreme Right. It also became "effectively and symbolically a pinnacle of armed collaboration and terrorist repression" until the liberation.[20]

The Milice school was commanded first (and however improbably) by a French Canadian – Professor de la Noüe du Vair, a proud Doctor of literature and Thomist philosophy, Maurrassian, and mystical Catholic: "At Saint-Martin-d'Uriage was the heart-beat of the well-born and well-raised Milice – Catholic and monarchist. There were not, there would not be, tortures, assassinations, extortion of funds. Here one was among gentlemen. They were *chouans* [members of the vast counter-revolutionary peasant movement against the Revolution of 1789], but with elegance. They wore white gloves."

At the side of Du Vair was Lieutenant Carus, who had been on the English coast at the beginning of July 1940, resolved to go down with his ship, the *Mistral*. Unlike Segonzac, who had lived in a villa nearby, Du Vair lived as ruler of the Château Bayard, like a great feudal lord, in the castle itself, with his wife and a flock of children. Everyone attended mass each morning. Commanding officer's pennants with the Du Vair coat of arms waved in the breeze over Uriage (as well as a good number of tricoloured banners, although certain members of the staff – such as du Vair's lieutenant Count Jacques Dugé de Bernonville – wanted them replaced by the white and gold fleur de lys of the monarchy).[21]

At first glance the school made a good impression on observers. At a time when Vichy France no longer had an army, and Saint-Cyr was closed, the *stagiaires* and *aspirants* were drawn by the military character of the school, by the fine figure cut by their *chefs*, most of whom were young. Courses were attended by "scions of the *haute bourgeoisie* organized into platoons of thirty young men between eighteen and twenty-five recruited directly from the *lycée* or the university.[22] There were few agnostics or Protestants, but some aspiring military officers who would have liked to have gone to Saint-Cyr. There were also a few *syndicalistes* and intellectuals with Communist backgrounds (honoured as experts on the mysteries of the Kremlin and from whom one expected to learn useful things) in the new community.

The trainees would get off the train at Grenoble and (like the bands from the regional schools who came for Segonzac's Grande Fête some months earlier) walk up to the school in groups, via mountain roads, singing. They were met by Du Vair who spoke of rebuilding France, of discipline, saying that the Milice and Uriage were precisely what had been lacking to the decadent fatherland of the past. And then there were the long hikes in the forest, the bivouacs, the campfires, the *veillées*, and the raising of the colours each morning, in impeccable uniforms, against the background of ramparts and pine trees, as in the previous regime of Uriage.

Du Vair's personality dominated the new Uriage community, much as Dunoyer de Segonzac's had before him. Like Segonzac, the Acadian intellectual was an ardently mystical Catholic monarchist devoted to France. Although a North American of only distant French ancestry, Du Vair's family had shown a remarkable fidelity to the land of their ancestors: his grandfather had returned to the old continent to fight in the French army in 1870, his father had done the same in the war of 1914, and Du Vair himself returned to France in 1939 by the first boat after the declaration of war. The miliciens of Uriage adored him, as their predecessors had Segonzac. He had all sorts of eccentric political ideas (one of his favourite homiletic subjects was that Canada would inevitably return to French control since French Canadians were having more children than their English compatriots).

The medieval panoply of Du Vair's Uriage might have seemed romantic, but the whole operation was oriented toward providing political education for elites, producing propagandists, and providing the military training needed to fight a civil war. A school document explained how it trained two categories of students, much as the old Uriage had, and used some of the same political theorists:

The *stagiaires, cadres* or future *cadres* of the *Fédérations régionales* and *Unions départementales*, would spend a two- or three-week period, and take courses in education, proficiency, or information, which were as much political as military.

The *aspirants*, chosen from the ranks of the *Franc-Garde*, future *cadres* of the permanent units, would receive a few months of solid political instruction and a state-of-the-art technical training, which would prepare them for their role as *chefs*.

Political training:
– a profound study of the doctrinarians of the nineteenth century who helped shape our political line: Proudhon, Renan, de Maistre, de Bonald, Gobineau, Maurras, etc.

But there were also ominous new subjects for study not found in Beuve-Méry's program at the old Uriage, such as:

– the study of communist methods, a critical analysis of concrete cases concerning various regions
Military training:
– focused simultaneously on guerilla war and on street combat. An exhaustive study of the fighting that, in Germany, preceded the advent of national socialism.[23]

The military training given the Milice cadets at Uriage, or later in the training camps of the Franc-Garde, did not involve learning how to fight tanks or regular infantry units. Like the SOL before them, the Milice and the Franc-Garde were trained as an army for civil war, for the defence of challenged authority. And, in effect, the Milice would become a little *versaillaise* army: like the Versailles army of 1871 it would fight not the Germans who were occupying France but "subversives" – the opponents of legal (and German occupation) authority.

Among the Milice there were misfits and eccentrics but also a good number of generous and idealistic people who, as an informer said, were "burdened by false ideas, and who didn't see things very clearly." If one told the young men who came to Uriage in the spring of 1943 that within eighteen months very many of them would be in Germany, in German uniforms, they would never have believed it. Nor would they have imagined that they would eventually be accused of treason for being at a school directed by a distinguished patriot such as Dr. de la Noüe du Vair.

Besides being a mystic and philosopher, the supreme *chef* de la Noüe du Vair was an inveterate plotter and, already by the summer of 1943, was paying for it. Since he was neither Niçois like so many of Darnand's old friends, nor an alumnus of the *Cagoule*, nor a former member of the *corps franc* of the 24th BCA, Du Vair was not accepted as part of the Milice inner circle and was a suspect character at their headquarters in the Hôtel Moderne at Vichy. Du Vair became the object of the same kind of jealousy that had been Segonzac's undoing: he was considered pretentious and too popular among the traditionalists and royalists of the middle-level *cadres*. Also like Segonzac, he was reproached for his impassioned monarchism and fervent Catholicism. High-level Miliciens began to urge Darnand to fire him.

At the same time, back in Uriage, Lieutenant Carus noticed that Du Vair was corresponding with the Comte de Paris, heir to the throne of France. Carus informed the other *chefs* and was called onto the carpet where he told du Vair that he wanted to have no part in the ambitious plotting going on at the school.

Du Vair, knowing that people at the Hôtel Moderne were out to thwart him, began planning dramatic action: to march on Vichy, oust Laval from power, and remove "the camouflaged republicans" from Darnand's entourage (if not Darnand himself) to prepare the way for the restoration of the King. He confided his projects to his closest lieutenants and then to a meeting of the departmental heads of the Milice at Avignon: he told them that they should not shrink from a coup d'État, that Laval was sabotaging the National Revolution, and that their own Vichy headquarters had to be purged. Most of the *chefs* seemed rather hesitant, and one of them informed Darnand.

Having failed either to raise an army at Avignon or to raise enough troops on his own to march on Vichy, Du Vair returned to Uriage in ill humour, suspecting treason, and began a purge. He had his own lieutenant, Carus, arrested and confined to quarters by his special guard, sub-machine guns in hand. Du Vair, counting on the support of the majority of *aspirants* or *stagiaires* (about sixty-eighty young men), as well as the thirty men of the special guard, began preparing for trouble.[24] Then, on 22 or 23 July, after two weeks of rumours at St. Martin that he was going to be fired, Du Vair – who seemed to believe, like Dunoyer de Segonzac, that he enjoyed the special favour of Pétain – went to Vichy to appeal directly for the Marshal's support. Apparently Pétain encouraged Du Vair to resist his rivals and advised him to withdraw his staff from the school if he was not successful in consolidating his control.[25]

On Saturday 24 July, the tough and brutal Darnand arrived, having been preceded by a substantial bodyguard devoted to him, to find the Château Bayard's gates closed and the whole community in a state of alert. What was he to do about this rebellious vassal? Mount ladders to the castle battlements, prepare Greek fire and bombards, move a battering ram against the postern? He declared in front of the whole community that Du Vair was a "traitor" (even, according to what some heard, a "shit") and ordered his expulsion within twenty-four hours, emphasizing that any attempt at rebellion would be broken.

Apparently Du Vair was then betrayed by the special guard, who opened the doors to Darnand's miliciens; they, revolvers in hand, chased *chef* Du Vair back into his apartments. While Du Vair's maid, on her knees, was imploring the attackers to show mercy, a Capuchin priest (the former chaplain of the Foreign Legion in Syria who had been living in the chateau for a few days) intervened and told Darnand that if anyone were harmed he would cite him as personally responsible in his report to the Marshal. Darnand recalled his men, and Du Vair was allowed to withdraw, provisionally, to the Villa Marie in the village of Saint-Martin below.

Members of Du Vair's team were also attacked, and there was yet another brawl in front of the St. Martin Church on Sunday morning,[26] but in the end, although Du Vair's men had been seen jumping from the windows during the height of the attack, no one was killed or seriously injured during Darnand's storming of the Uriage castle. But a scandal was narrowly avoided, for during the uproar in the castle a voice had been heard shouting, "Burn the crucifix! Burn the crucifix!" At the Capuchin's insistence, Darnand made an investigation as to who was responsible for those shouts, and finally had to attribute them to his own chauffeur. Concerned to avoid a religious incident, he gave the Capuchin a short, signed declaration in his own handwriting, certifying that nothing would be changed in the religious status of the school. Nevertheless, the affair was brought before the Bishop of Grenoble who withdrew permission to have the Sacred Host and daily mass at the school.

Darnand finally assumed personal direction of the school and named, on the spot, another Maurrassian of Canadian origin – Giaume, a leader of the JFOM – as his representative.[27] The two main formal complaints against Du Vair were (1) his efforts to take control of the Milice by acquiring the allegiance of the young men who enrolled in the training sessions in his chateau, and (2) the strong pressure he put on them to attend mass and go to communion. The justice of this last complaint was verified many times. But the first accusation, by far the most important to Darnand, seems to have been equally well founded. Like Segonzac, Du Vair later haughtily defended his reputation by charging that he and his loyalists had been fired for being insufficiently Nazi.[28] Similar complaints could probably have been, and probably were, lodged against Dunoyer de Segonzac's administration of the old École Nationale des Cadres. Perhaps something about the dramatic mountain setting of the Château Bayard encouraged ardent Catholicism, royalism, oaths of fealty, and grandiose schemes for transforming France. It was not an atmosphere conducive to humility, or to obedience to anyone other than the Chef.

THE MILICE AND THE EMERGENCE OF FRENCH CATHOLIC FASCISM

By the fall of 1943 the Milice had 29,000 members of both sexes, including a few hundred of the elite *Francs-Gardes*, and of these about 10,000 were actively participating in semi-military or policing activities.[29] By 1944, Darnand had built the Milice into what American intelligence saw as the most formidable pro-fascist political organization in Vichy France,[30] an organization that did not abandon the strong religious tone set by Catholic monarchists like Du Vair.

On the surface the doctrine of the Milice differed little from the ideas expounded by the northern zone collaborationist movements, as in the "Twenty-One Points" taken over from the SOL, which endorsed corporatism, the primacy of labour over money, and national and racial "purity," while explicitly condemning Gaullism, communism, freemasonry, and Judaism. But point twenty-one supported "Christian civilization" and this gave the Milice a crucial difference in tone from the northern zone collaborationist parties.

It is true, however, that all collaborationist movements eventually came to at least pay lip service to the ideal of Catholic France: Jacques Doriot, despite his Communist past, gave a vibrant oration at the Catholic pilgrimage site of Lourdes and had meetings with French church leaders in attempts to secure their support, while Marcel Déat was especially careful to point out that his attacks on clerical influence in politics were not to be construed as anti-Catholic. The

Catholicism of the Milice, however, was more deeply rooted in the movement than was the spiritualist rhetoric of Doriot's collaborationist PPF or Déat's Rassemblement National Populaire (RNP). Although not as pronounced as in the imagery of the Rumanian Legion of the Archangel Michael, the ideal of the Christian crusader was as much a part of the Milice's intellectual baggage as it had been central to the imagery of Dunoyer de Segonzac's Uriage. Despite its reputation for brutality, the Milice retained a boy-scout kind of innocence and naïveté, less influenced by the sophistication of Paris than were other collaborationist organizations. In its simplicity, the Milice resembled the Franciste movement more than either the PPF or the RNP, and Darnand was temperamentally closer to the Franciste leader, Catholic war hero Marcel Bucard,[31] than to either Doriot or Déat.

The most eloquent spokesman for the Milicien crusading knight ideal, indeed for the axis cause in France, was the Catholic poet and journalist Philippe Henriot, who had come to the Milice with a deep-seated conviction that Christian civilization was engaged in a life and death struggle against Bolshevism.[32] The Milice of Darnand and Henriot emerged in 1943 as a representation of provincial fascism – more traditionalist, simpler, perhaps more naïve, rougher than the more self-conscious intellectualized fascisms of writers such as Pierre Drieu la Rochelle and Robert Brasillach, or even of the leadership corps of the PPF, and Déat's RNP. In December 1943 German pressure pushed Darnand and Henriot into the government. Henriot became Secretary of State for Information and Darnand was named Secretary-General for the Maintenance of Order, a new position grouping all French forces responsible for the maintenance of order under his control. Just as the Milice's Uriage school was built upon the resources created by Dunoyer de Segonzac and his men, so the organization confiscated other materials from the other Vichy youth institutions, such as the Chantiers de la Jeunesse, which began to collapse in the axis débacle.[33]

Although the Milice began, particularly in their Uriage school, as nice Catholic boys from "good families," their spirit began to resemble, more and more, that of the German freebooters of the early 1920s described by Ernst von Salomon in his book *Die Geächteten* (The Outlaws).[34] And the appointment of Darnand, Henriot, and later Déat to the government completed the transformation of the Vichy regime into a thoroughgoing fascist state.[35] In 1944 Henriot embraced a Christian fascism with the overriding ideal of an armed and militant church. In the words of a contemporary:

Henriot is listened to by everyone, enemies or supporters. Families shift their meal times so as not to miss him. There is no one left in the street at the

time he speaks. This popularity indicates to what degree the French love
oratorical contests, venomous attacks, and talent. If Henriot had had the
microphone starting in August 1940, de Gaulle in his London studio would
not have played his game so easily. Many things, without doubt, would have
happened differently.[36]

Henriot's remarkable success was yet another example of the rise
to power and influence of high-profile Catholics under Vichy, for the
notion of a French Catholic fascist in the government service mes-
merizing French radio audiences would have been improbable before
the war. And when Henriot was assassinated by the Resistance in
June 1944 his importance was such that Cardinal Suhard felt obliged
to preside over the funeral service in the Cathedral of Notre Dame.[37]

The Catholic fervour of many militant collaborationists came to be
translated into virulent anti-communism – both on the eastern front
and at home. Henriot, Darnand, and many of their Milicien followers
from the smaller towns of the southern zone represented a Christian
fascism, different in tone from the more secular spirit of Doriot's PPF
and Déat's RNP. That a largely Catholic France had many Catholics
in the collaborationist movements is not surprising, but the unusually
large number of collaborationists with strongly Catholic educational
backgrounds is. Darnand and Bucard are examples from among the
leaders, as we have seen. It is also true that fascism seemed particularly attractive to renegade Catholics searching for a total world
view and ritual, a sense of community, which they could substitute
for that of the Church.

The Milice was particularly oriented toward Catholic ritual and
tradition, and even pronounced anti-clericals such as Doriot and Déat
made their peace with the Church. (Déat died in hiding in an Italian
monastery, in the bosom of the Church, ten years after the war
ended.) Then, too, the knight-monk was central to the Milice, whose
ceremonies, and oaths taken on one's knees, recalled those of the
church. One result of the naive and unbalanced idealism of Du Vair's
Uriage community was that it was not long before the Milicien Christian crusader was fighting beside the neo-pagan Nietzschean warrior
in the Waffen-ss. The French "ultra"-collaborators reflected the whole
ambivalence of fascism with respect to the Christian tradition.[38]

This Catholic fascism was a significant, if disturbing, result of a
period in which Catholics were far more influential and powerful
than they had been in the pre-war Republic. After the war many of
them, preferring to remember fledgling Resistance efforts such as
that of the *Témoignage Chrétien* group (marginal at the time), misrep-
resented the more general, immediately influential role of militant

Catholicism in the period, furnishing many of the key men among the French collaborationist elites.

Bertram Gordon, a specialist on the collaborationists, put it this way: "The significance of the collaborationists lay not in their strength but in the fact of their existence, demonstrating the presence of fascism, even if in a weakened form, in France."

It is estimated that during the occupation some one or two hundred thousand French actively identified their own interests and those of France with Hitler's New Order, forming a radical Right.[39] But how many more – particularly among the Catholics – identified their own interests, those of their church, and those of France, with the cause of world fascism?[40]

Back in the Uriage castle, in any case, there was a genuine diehard, mystical commitment to the fascist cause in the person of the new *chef*, Jean de Vaugelas. Dismissed from the French Army for racialism before the war, he had gone on from the Chantiers de la Jeunesse to succeed Du Vair as head of the school. A devout Catholic monarchist like his Acadian predecessor, de Vaugelas took charge of the unit formed in February 1944 to destroy the *maquis* of the Resistance at Glières. Du Vair, after having been arrested and forced to resign from the Milice, was killed in obscure circumstances in Germany in 1944. Both of these men vividly illustrate the forces that led patriotic and traditionalist officers to identify with the cause of Nazi Germany.[41] On 5 July 1944, less than one year after Du Vair's deposition, the Château Bayard was attacked again, this time by the Resistance, and the miliciens there obliged "to quickly evacuate the chateau." At least six Uriage miliciens would eventually be condemned to death by a court martial and executed.[42] In the meantime members of the old Uriage community had emerged as heroes of the Resistance, as we shall see.

THE URIAGE ORDER

While the white-gloved Milice at *Chef* de la Noüe du Vair's Uriage prepared for French civil war, Pierre Dunoyer de Segonzac's men tried to discern what the future, immediate and long-term, might hold for them. The idea of creating an Order of the knight-monks of Uriage had been in the air for some time and now the *chefs* said to themselves, as one of them put it, "we ought to find a way to conserve the bond between us, and as there has always been something rather monastic about the very essence of the team, why not formalize it?"[43] While Eric d'Alençon favoured an explicitly religious order and refused to join anything less, and others wanted something much stronger, a few dozen men and some women formally promised to live, under the orders of Segonzac, in an Order conforming to "the spirit of Uriage." Its provisional constitution stressed authority and allegiance:[44] "The commitment in the Order ought to take the form of a simple but serious ceremony with a particularly solemn character. The *chef* reads the formula of commitment ... insisting on absolute discipline in the Order's hierarchy and the total discretion that it entails, allows the postulant to reflect for a few moments, and invites him to commit himself, while the audience stands for the ceremony."

This insistence on the value of obedience at a time when many French people, particularly many Catholics, had been ill-served by this "virtue" was another instance of the Uriage community's apparent refusal to question the roots of the Pétainist experience, or to realize the risks in Segonzac's unquestioning loyalty to his superiors.[45]

Rather than fighting for liberal or democratic values in an oppressive situation, the men of Segonzac's circle were preoccupied with promoting spiritual values in tightly disciplined, hierarchical communities such as their Order. From early 1943 Segonzac kept a very low profile, staying for the most part in the Château de Montmaur, near Gap, where Antoine Mauduit sheltered and armed escaped prisoners, dissidents, and others on the run. Segonzac could feel quite at home there: the community of like-minded people that this mystical Catholic founded, "la Chaîne," was inspired by, and used the rites of, an order of knighthood.[46] Meanwhile, in early 1943, the remnants of the Study Bureau, now called the "Thébaïde" community and working under the direction of Gilbert Gadoffre, moved into the third castle to lodge Segonzac's community: the Château de Murinais, near Saint-Marcellin, above the Isère valley. This secret think-tank was eventually composed of twelve members, and included recent additions to the Uriage team (such as the Lyon Catholic student leader and future *Esprit* editor Jean-Marie Domenach, and Simon Nora). The Murinais group apparently had the long-term aim of elaborating "the Summa" – a distillation of Uriage reflections on "the crisis of the twentieth century," and a list of ways to initiate a new order of civilization by developing new elites.[47] This was in line with the school's first mission of regenerating France via an educational program conceived by and for elites (*cadres*). Events had not dissuaded them from their ideas.

Everyone in the Uriage orbit favoured giving their Order a spiritual foundation, one recognizing the existence of spiritual realities, their primacy in the moral life, and their absolute value. For the somewhat ingrown, fervent community coming out of the castle-school who had experienced a unique "style of life," a few key words such as "honour," "friendship," "fidelity," "devotion to the common mission," "efficiency," and "communitarian personalism" expressed a whole collective experience. Was this a language likely to find nation-wide resonance?

There was a revealing exchange in the debate over the "spiritual foundation" of the Order when Dumazedier proposed to renounce it in favour of a "revolutionary humanism." Father Maydieu re-sponded to the difficulty of an order's accepting men of different spiritualities, particularly non-believers, that the difficult was "per-haps not insurmountable, since in the conjugal community itself the Church does not absolutely impose unity of belief."[48] Thus Maydieu, matter-of-factly comparing the bonds in this Order to those in a marriage, set out the notion of a "first degree spirituality" common to believers, agnostics, and atheists as the bond of the Order – a notion accepted, at least provisionally, by the group.[49] Thus, as France entered a period of resistance struggle against the occupier, Segon-zac's friends worried over the cohesion of their Uriage community, one of the salient features of which had been to make men of diverse, even opposed, metaphysical convictions co-operate, with a sense of complete spiritual solidarity.

In spite of great external obstacles, the Order met regularly during 1943 to discuss issues concerning its form and its future. Supported by local communities who relied upon it, it became, after the *Équipe* became clandestine, the new communitarian support of Uriage. The Council of the Order, composed of Beuve-Méry, Ferry, and Duma-zedier, helped Segonzac administrate and represent it.[50]

Thus, in contrast to the Resistance movements that were formed to fight the occupier and were not yet preoccupied with what would follow the liberation, the Order's highest priority was responding to what it called "a crisis of civilization," for it saw the liberation struggle as just a stage in the reconstruction process.

The first directives given to the nascent communities of the Order, therefore, counselled realizing the "style of life" that ought to char-acterize the new man, while preparing to intervene in the revolu-tionary phase that was approaching. Members of the Order were advised to "familiarize themselves with the functioning of the dif-ferent gearwheels of the country, until the time when they would themselves be in place to assure their functioning." Those with offi-cial posts were told to keep them as long as, in conscience, it was possible for them to do so, in the name of a "politics of presence."

But any hostile action toward the occupier was forbidden until further notice.

Representatives of the Resistance sounding out the intentions of Segonzac were struck by his serene assumption that he and his men (without elections, of course) should be running the country, and eventually would be. As far as interacting with the Resistance ("dissidence") was concerned, Uriage people were told to deal with its leaders, "avoiding masonic and foreign influences," and to make others understand that there was no question of returning to the pre-war Republic but that rather the problem of a new France should be treated "in a frankly revolutionary spirit."[51] Thus Segonzac, still forbidding criticism of Pétain and acts of hostility against the Germans, was calmly planning for "his" people to run the country after the war – along post-Liberal, post-Republican lines. In this strange manner, this Catholic "Resistance" Order began to lay the groundwork for a firmly anti-Communist, anti-masonic, and anti-individualist national community committed to spiritual values.

Despite its high-minded humanistic rhetoric, the Order had some authoritarian, sexist, intolerant, and racialist ideas, and not just anyone could enter into that tightly disciplined, secret society. Its earliest guidelines reflected special attitudes toward Jews, freemasons, communists, women, and priests. While clergymen (pastors or priests) could belong to the Order, it was decided to limit their number "so as to avoid giving a clerical flavour to our activities." Women were "admissible" but "one had to watch out for their habitual lack of discretion." But the Order had to be "rigorously protected" against free-masons, while "for the time being, avoiding a hostile attitude toward them. At least one must be sure that absolutely not a single one enters into the Order."[52] As far as Jews were concerned, there was some sympathy for their plight, but, nevertheless, a rigorous interdiction:

Israelites are not admitted as members of the Order, or as novices. If we are resolutely hostile to anti-semitism, particularly as practised since the armistice, we ought not to underestimate the danger of a Jewish revenge [movement] nor ignore the existence of a Jewish international whose interests are opposed to those of France. [Even if] Our present attitude remains in the framework of an aid to oppressed Israelites.[53]

These Order guidelines reveal how the Uriage group, as late as 1943, had failed to question the roots of prejudices and racial hatreds that had generated some of the Vichy government's worst abuses.

Segonzac and his men seemed determined to remain Pétainist despite the persecution of the Jews and other minorities and the growing evidence of Pétain's personal hypocrisy and his abasement. If the Order was itself determined to exclude Jews *on strictly racial lines*, how could they formulate a fundamental critique of the Vichy racialist policies that, we now know, sent tens of thousands to their deaths? The exclusionist clauses in the Uriage guidelines were discreetly hidden, and even when a few French Jews became integral parts of the Uriage community,[54] were apparently never regretted or repudiated.

The Uriage Order was determined to manipulate France's educational institutions, and "cultural, corporative, regionalist, or social organisms" as well. Like Du Vair's Milice back in the Château Bayard, Segonzac's Order studied the rival groups competing for power in France and the conditions required for preserving legal authority and national unity in the circumstances, and thus gave a high priority to understanding power groups such as "the French national socialists publishing the review *Idées*, the free-masons, the synarchy movement, the Communist party, the AF, the PSF, the Radical Party, the SFIO, etc." It was suggested that members of the Order be specially charged with "observing, even temporarily joining, these groups in a way so as to get to know them ... the doctrines, methods, means and principles of their members." But this kind of infiltration had to be undertaken "progressively, with much care, ... particularly in regard to the communists who are seen as threatening a *coup de force.*"[55] Segonzac's Order began studying ways to counter a Communist attempt to seize power during an anarchical phase of the liberation of the country.[56] This was a period in which there were some Resistance groups (i.e., groups resisting the German occupation of their country) who were still loyal to Pétain and seemed more interested in hunting down Communists than Germans. Many people in the Uriage network were ultra-nationalists but hardly instinctive liberals or democrats, hence their peculiar, special "Resistance" orientation: they wanted the Germans and the collaborators out, but they didn't particularly want the Republicans, and certainly not the Communists, back in. It was a juggling act with a lot of pins in the air.

Uriage people were not alone in fearing the Resistance Communists. Back in the Uriage castle the Milice were scrutinizing Communist tactics in order to combat them as efficaciously as possible. The head of the Resistance movement Combat, Henri Frenay, told his old friend Segonzac, when he met with him in Algiers at the beginning of 1944, that while the communists were "courageous" Resistance fighters, they seemed to him, more and more, to be "preparing to take power."[57] And, in fact, there was a general phenomenon of non-Communist resistance movements being appropriated by Communists.[58] The Uriage group perceived enemies both at Vichy and among the collaborators, and even potential enemies in the Resistance. Typically, they turned in upon themselves, sought discipline and coherence, and followed their own strategy and goals.

In 1943 the Uriage community was organized on a national scale. The central core was formed by the general staff, Segonzac's co-workers, who were responsible for a sector or a region. The primary circle was that of the full members of "the Order" – racially pure, enrolled in secret, and organized in a rigorously hierarchical and compartmentalized way – around whom gravitated a larger circle of sympathizers or "novices." Although not yet initiated into the secrets of the order, they would later be involved in certain of its activities in the framework of an umbrella movement called the "Équipe de France," which was in turn organized in local communities directed by members of the Order. Women were admitted to the Order (albeit grudgingly). A provisional council, named under Segonzac as the "head of the Order," included Hubert Beuve-Méry, Gilles Ferry, and Joffre Dumazedier. Monthly "decisions" would transmit the details of organization and action to members of the local communities and at each one of its levels, authority was exercised by a directory of three members (command, doctrine, action), named and revocable by the head of the Order, and charged with taking initiatives and responsibilities.[59]

Regarding the Germans, the Order decreed abstaining, for the present, from all hostile acts: "Every act of violence that is not undertaken on the orders of the responsible chef or not approved by one," wrote Beuve-Méry, "should be made the object of an exemplary punishment." As far as the Vichy government was concerned, the Order could not approve its failings: a general attitude of defiance was required, but it was not the time for members to leave official posts as long as they were "not required to take political positions contrary to their conscience"; they should, however, "prepare themselves for the future".[60]

By the middle of 1943, Segonzac's network had to recognize that the fighting in Europe had turned completely against the Germans: the 6th German Army surrendered in front of Stalingrad; the allied troops, under Eisenhower, landed in Sicily and, during the month of August, succeeded in liberating it. In September, Italy surrendered and Corsica was liberated. An allied landing in France seemed possible, even impending. On all fronts the summer of 1943 constituted a turning point of the war. This was also the case for the French army which was, from this time, reunited under the commander-in-chief, General Giraud, while in the political domain the figure of General de Gaulle loomed ever larger.[61] By the fall of 1943, as the German military situation deteriorated, the Vichy government was subject to even more onerous demands by the occupation authorities and thus had less and less room to manoeuvre.

At a meeting of the Order in early October 1943, Dunoyer de Segonzac, clarifying his personal attitude toward the Marshal and his government, came as close as he ever would to admitting Pétain's personal failings and errors in judgment. But he insisted that the original Uriage community not abandon the best in the National Revolution: "I would like to stress what was healthy in the NR, even if only on the level of principle or of ideas that will never get beyond the dreaming stage. Don't forget that soon we will see a strong reaction against the NR, all the more excessive for the fact that its leaders will, alas, certainly be mediocrities capable of mindless dismantling but incapable of construction."

As for Pétain:

It is better to draw a discreet veil over the Marshal rather than attack him. We served under his orders, and it is useless to deny it or even to regret it. His cabinet's intercessions saved us on several occasions.

Personally, I believed, beyond reason, that he was still master of the game and that he was capable of redeeming actions. He was not a great man, we are now certain of that, but he was not a traitor either. At the most he was a weak and vain old man.

Finally, any attack against soldiers bothers me. I retain the esprit de corps and I have contempt for people who befoul their profession.[62]

It had taken a long time, but Dunoyer de Segonzac finally admitted to being misled in believing Marshal Pétain had been heroically struggling against Laval and the villains. He was no longer encouraging his men to defend the Marshal (and in fact few, if any, of them would), but neither was he encouraging any real soul-searching over the origins of the Vichy regime and that "ease and naturalness" (Zeev Sternhell) with which a pro-fascist regime had been installed in France. A few weeks later Segonzac would leave to seek a meeting with de Gaulle to try to throw his lot and that of his men in with the Free French. It would hardly be surprising if he were not welcomed with open arms.

While the Vieux Chef prepared to meet de Gaulle, Beuve-Méry took over the Order project and set it on the high road of spiritual renewal. Uriage's director of studies saw "the essential task of the Order and the Équipes d'Uriage" as "bringing together valuable men, ennobling them ... beyond the materialism of money, blood, or productivity. To restore a soul, to rediscover the truly spiritual. The essential, in one's self ... is the spiritual ... We want to incarnate that project of Bergson."[63] In the short run the members of the Order wanted "a rousing of French will to rebuild the country."[64]

It was soon clear that the leaders of the Order were already concerned over the Third Republic–like, "conservative" influence that the United States could have on postwar France.[65] Before leaving Segonzac decided to do something more practical to give efficacy to the Order's ideas and founded, "rather hastily," the NERF (Nouvelles Équipes de la Renaissance Française), a movement intended to be more open, popularizing, and militant than the Order (which had been reserved, as we have seen, to a minority of the chosen).[66]

A Jewish member of the Uriage network later summed up the significance of the whole Order effort: "The Order was both utopian and very moving. It rather resembled an Order of Knights ... I don't think one can understand anything about Uriage without grasping that idea ... Even if, already at the time, a few were smirking and even if, in retrospect, Segonzac himself kept a certain distance from the project."[67] In truth, the Order did capture something of the essence of the Uriage experience and it did reveal something basic, original, enduring – and disturbing – about the Uriage mentality. It had all the advantages and all the perils of a self-confident and exclusive elite with a mutual, mystical attachment to the sense of community.

THE *ÉQUIPES VOLANTES*

In March 1943 what was left of the old Uriage team (notably the Study Bureau) moved into the Château de Murinais overlooking the village of that name, nine kilometres above Saint-Marcellin, between Grenoble and Valence. Here was yet another dramatic medieval backdrop for the Uriage network's next efforts to affect France's political evolution. Small groups of Uriage people, usually consisting of three men and calling themselves *équipes volantes* ("flying squads") – the expression, according to member Jean-Marie Domenach, was taken from the vocabulary of the Russian revolution – went out to share Uriage ideas with the fugitives, dissidents, and resisters hiding in the surrounding countryside.[68] Many of those they went to see were merely boys fleeing obligatory labour service in Germany, and, like the vast majority in that situation, they were not particularly interested in fighting in the Resistance.[69]

At the Château de Murinais there was a conscious effort to recreate the inspiring atmosphere, and to adapt the ideas, of Segonzac's Uriage to a rapidly evolving political and military situation. This involved a constant coming and going of former instructors, message bearers, and friends of old Uriage, which could not have escaped the attention of the residents of Murinais (including the potential informers among them).[70] Uriage faithful Cacérès described the special atmosphere created by Segonzac's lieutenant, English professor and veteran Uriage instructor Gilbert Gadoffre:

Gilbert, the master of la Thébaïde, directed our work. He was somewhat rigid in his comportment and his asceticism, but also, with an unfailing openness, he represented the order we would dream about at times. He had taught French literature in a great English university and had a particular love for everything in the seventeenth century. He retained a very British refinement in his position, displaying reserve and extreme courtesy. Short, lively, upright, bright-eyed, attentive to all observations, Gilbert managed things elegantly.

And there was an additional important presence:

Another conspirator, Beuve, who we sometimes called William the Silent, was always in a morose mood with his eyes half-hidden by heavy lids, his high-placed brows, his tight mouth. That didn't prevent his having a great sense of humour and an uncompromising frankness; he listened, like a sleepy cat, to our discussions, then, at the end, as if involuntarily, after a few last draws on a pipe he seemed tired of smoking, he would develop irrefutable argumentation exactly opposed to that which had just been presented.

And, in the evenings, there was the romantic ambience of old Uriage:

The afternoon passed rapidly; night fell quickly. I would return to the Thébaïde, intoxicated by the mountain air, eyes full of enchanting scenes. In the great hall, seated in a circle on the ground around a fireplace burning heavy oak logs, we went over the morning's work. After the evening snack, we would go for a time to the music room. I had not been hallucinating the day of my arrival. Gilbert, master of the Thébaïde, was playing the harpsichord ... In the half-light, all sat and listened. Afterwards we went back up to our cells and often worked on through the night.[71]

Simon Nora (one of France's most prominent economic planners after the war, then one of the younger newcomers to the Uriage group) described how he came to share the Murinais community's experience:

I was of the pacifist Left: auberges de la jeunesse, *Giono*, etc. In this context, the war had meant for me the discovery of a French people who in fact I had not known; and of the fatherland ... I was living in the heart of a community with whom I was in profound solidarity ... I met Dumazedier through one of the heroes of the Grenoble Resistance, Germaine, ... [and] became integrated into Gadoffre's team.

The role of the *équipes volantes*, Nora recalled, was to constitute a self-conscious elite transmitting the Uriage community's ideas to the raw youth, the untutored, in the Resistance camps:

Our presentation [to the resisters] was wrapped in a syncretism centred on the human person. That philosophy of the person, close to Mounier's, permitted a triple recuperation: of patriotism by the men of the Left, of populism by the Catholic and patriotic tradition, and of the human body by intellectuals. All of this came from a feeling that may not have been very healthy but was strongly felt: that a minority, accepting of its responsibilities and with a sense of duty, had the role of catalyst to play. We didn't live that intense complicity of the Resistance in a conspiratorial way, but we did share the hope that in basing [our activities] on a tightly knit network and fraternity we could be the yeast in the dough.

The itinerant, lyrical, flying squads "sang the poets – Hugo, Aragon – and cited excerpts from Teilhard de Chardin."[72] But Nora also admitted that the *équipes volantes* were sometimes considered as "the privileged, the *intellos*, coming to give lessons to the peasants."[73]

Jean-Marie Domenach, who had been in the last class before old Uriage had closed, had less critical, probably more typical, memories:

I spent ... the happiest days of my life there [in the *équipes volantes*]. First, because we were totally free ... At bottom, we had everything going for us. We had, first of all, a sense of being exceptional sorts of men. With our weapons, our false identity papers, our mentality of being aristocratic defenders of democracy, we were above the swamp. At the time, Gadoffre had me read the book of Jünger, *Sur les falaises de marbre*.

And, yes, one felt oneself among the "happy few":

We simply felt ourselves to be more courageous than the others. In fact, we were already free. We regarded those who slept down on the plain with a certain superior air while we were in the forest, on the heights. And all the time we were fighting for justice, liberty, democracy, fraternity. We hung about with the *maquisards*. We sang with them. We recited the poems of Hugo, Péguy, or Aragon to them.[74]

For Cacérès the carpenter, too, it was a romantic time, as he remembered arriving with the two other men of his *équipe* at the intensely spiritual Boimondau community on their plateau hide-out in the mountains, thirty kilometres from Valence:

When we would arrive with the *équipes volantes*, in the night, by sure paths, a feeling of great joy would come over us once we came in sight of the plateau. Once past the look-outs, we would enter into a world of liberty. We would sit down in a large kitchen, open around the clock. Soup would be waiting. A rule like that in the Gospels made hospitality the first virtue even when that was difficult. Resupplying was a sort of miracle. On that plateau, on a barren soil, everything that could possibly grow was being cultivated with meticulous care. No one ever complained, whatever the privations.[75]

Père Maydieu later put the nostalgia for the lost community experience in a more theological perspective, recalling how:

All those who took part in the Resistance retain a nostalgia for that time where we found ourselves in a total fraternity ... the joy I found when I was able to leave Paris and spend a few hours in that Thébaïde ... where former Uriage instructors were preparing for their new task as instructors of the *maquis* ... Those young men believed all sorts of different things but bore striking witness ... to the birth of French concord; they related their joy ... at seeing ... despite all sorts of difficulties, a consensus as strong as their own in all the sections they visited.[76]

A big part of Uriage people's consensus was a refusal to return to the pre-war regime. Murinais instructor Gilbert Gadoffre remarked that (as far as the *équipes volantes* and the guerillas of the Resistance they contacted were concerned): "If one had told them that once the war was over, the *train-train* [daily grind] of the Third Republic would begin again, they would all have mutinied, left immediately." For, as Simon Nora remembered: "What united us ... was disgust with the Third Republic. We had all experienced a profound feeling of impotence, of mediocrity, of national decline. We thought that there was nothing worth saving on that side."[77]

In retrospect, it must be said that the Thébaïde in the Château de Murinais fell well short of bringing together France's most notorious anti-fascists or defenders of the oppressed. Rather it served as a centre for preserving, and further advancing, an anti-liberal and anti-republican, an all-transforming, French personalist and spiritual community that had been sketched out under the gigantic portrait of the Marshal in the lecture hall of the Château Bayard. And, despite the obvious dangers involved in living in community in this isolated chateau when the occupation forces were hunting out pockets of fugitives or resisters, it was not, at first, pervaded with a sense of life-or-death struggle against the Germans. As one of the women there recalled: "One should not mythicize the secrecy. We were living in the country surrounded by farms where we went for food. We also went to get the mail at the post office of Saint-Marcellin. There was a constant coming and going of people unknown to the area. In those conditions how could one be clandestine?"[78]

Despite its celebration by Uriage alumni as the greatest, most heroic age of the school, there remains something ambiguous about the Resistance period of Uriage – despite the tragic, even heroic, deaths of several members of the *équipe*. Dunoyer de Segonzac's network does not fit neatly into the ideas most of us have of the French anti-fascist movement because they had several things on their agenda besides fighting fascism. Would it have been possible for the members of the school to live in such high-profile settings if they were not receiving at least some quiet protection "from above" (among friends of the school who were still at Vichy)? The Thébaïde seemed to fear the unexpected from the Germans but not from the Vichy authorities. And, given Segonzac's track record and basic political opinions, what should the *Pétainist* element at Vichy have against him save, perhaps, a lack of discipline, and contacts with dubious elements? Until fairly late in the game Segonzac could have been considered "one of theirs," despite the criticism of Vichy that would be levelled by Uriage people, particularly by Beuve-Méry.[79]

In July 1943 groups from the *équipes volantes* began operating in the Vercors, a rugged region noted for its active *maquis*. At the same time there appeared a clandestine *Radio-Journal*, created by Segonzac's old officer friend Xavier de Virieu at the Château Virieu, in another effort to reach out to the *maquis*.[80] But the *équipes volantes* soon found they had a Marshalist reputation or were even associated with the Milice now installed at Uriage, and so sometimes met "a strong mistrust" among the Resistance groups.[81] The civilian *chef* of the Vercors, Eugène Chavant, for one, distrusted the *équipes volantes* because he saw them as representing a *Uriage pétainiste*. The heads of the *maquisard* camps, too, were very mistrustful, and it was always necessary to cajole them into hosting the "flying squads." They were afraid of being infiltrated, overrun by the army, Uriage, et cetera. [82] Fernand Rude, a *maquis* officer, recalled how a resister, who would be killed a few months later, had reproached his leader, in 1943, for having brought a Uriage flying squad to their camp:

The men ... were completely disgusted to see the arrival of ... a brainwashing *équipe volante* from the dissolved centre for the training of *cadres* at Uriage escorted by my superior officer ... All was not to be rejected out of hand in what that team had to say, but there was a bit too much of trying to save a tiny little bit of the Révolution Nationale; my men very coldly received these people who had come to pity them, anaesthetize them, and lavish beautiful words about their future social role upon them. Sweaters or pants would have been infinitely preferable. My superior should have recognized that an institution such as Uriage, which carried the Vichy trademark, could hardly be popular in the *maquis*.[83]

The reticence toward the *équipes volantes* in the Vercors camps changed when Captain Alain Le Ray, who had taken a training session at Uriage in October 1942 and subsequently saw himself as part of the Uriage team, was made the military commander of those *maquis* and got on well with his civilian partner Chavant.[84] Uriage group legitimization was highlighted by a large meeting in the Arbounouze clearing in the Vercors, on 10 August 1943, where the Murinais community's *chefs* and troops, with Beuve-Méry, Dumazedier and Cacérès, were in attendance. Given the *maquisard* mistrust, the fact that so many people finally got together at Arbounouze, was, as a Uriage team veteran recalled, "no small matter."[85] According to Le Ray: "In the very heart of the Vercors, for two days, in a series of talks, discussions, we explained to all of our comrades what constituted the heart of our doctrine for the liberation of the country. *And Uriage provided us with the essential element.*"[86] In retrospect he thought: "That meeting was destined to give us a soul, to create fraternity ... All the *chefs* of the Vercors were there for that ... and many friends came to join us."[87] The Uriage community had become firmly engaged in the Resistance – but on its own terms, and with its own agenda, focused less on the expulsion of the Milice and the Germans from France, and the dismantling of Vichy, than on shaping the orientation of a postwar regime that would succeed the allied victory. That long-term vision, however, would soon be blurred by events.

During the night of 12–13 December 1943, at half past midnight, a company of the Wehrmacht, from one hundred to two hundred men (perhaps an element of the 157th Reserve Infantry Division stationed at Grenoble), apparently accompanied by a few *Miliciens*, surrounded the Château de Murinais and dynamited the entry portal.[88] The Thébaïde community had been warned and escaped in time, but the enemy forces carried away a few innocent bystanders, who never returned. It was a chilling event for a team that had been so basically happy despite the tragedy and suffering of war. Cacérès recalled how "it was still snowing, the night was beginning to fall when the news came: the Germans have taken la Thébaïde ... still today I feel, in writing that phrase, the feeling that overcame me at the news: they had taken away my happiness forever."[89]

Most of the Uriage team went to Paris. Among the most prominent were Raymond Dupouy, the administrative support for the team, who lived in Combs la Ville in a south-eastern suburb, and Gilles Chaine and Jean-Marie Domenach, who lived in the XVIe arrondissement in the home of the sister of the avant-garde theologian Père Dubarle. Here, until the month of April, they reconstructed the famous *Somme*, which had been destroyed by the fire at Murinais.[90] Dupouy gave everyone the funds necessary for his mission, a part of which was furnished by M. de Peyrecave, director of Renault, on a monthly basis, in support of Uriage's efforts to thwart the purposes of the French Communist Party.[91]

Eventually a book resulted from the collected effort of the Murinais group: a general evaluation of the Uriage experience, *Vers le style du XXe siècle*, by the Équipe d'Uriage under the direction of Gilbert Gadoffre (Paris, 1945). It presented, in somewhat laundered language, the favourite themes of the Uriage school about the need to go beyond both capitalism and Marxism, create anti-individualist communities, nurture spiritually oriented elites, et cetera. In Daniel Lindenberg's words, there were "relatively nuanced remarks about national socialism, more a reflection of the state of mind of 1942 than that of 1945."[92] This reiteration of the basic ideas of the Uriage community since the early days of the National Revolution demonstrated that those people "had learned nothing, and forgotten nothing." The men of la Thébaïde, after the war, would not be given to public critical self-analysis, or disillusionment. They stopped short of attacks upon the weaknesses or treason of certain personalities at Vichy. For the time being they had to come to terms, not with the ambiguities in their past, but with the ever more powerful Charles de Gaulle.

CHAPTER NINE

De Gaulle, the Network, and the Liberation

THE VIEUX CHEF SEES DE GAULLE

While the Free French in London knew very little about Pierre Dunoyer de Segonzac, the Uriage community, or the Order,[1] their informers in France sent strong warnings about the youth organizations that promoted the fascistic regimentation of French young people. An anonymous young intellectual of the Gaullist resistance, describing the state of the leading legal youth organizations in spring 1942, saw the French Scouts as "the conscious or unconscious, admitted or unacknowledged inspiration for everything that the RN did in the area of youth." He noted that Father Doncoeur's *Péguy, la révolution et le sacré* had preached "a delirious and totalitarian mysticism, total sacrifice, the abandonment of liberty, thought and life, to the *chef*," and the scouts were under his sway, manifesting

a blind, obstinate obedience, a determination to save a project once undertaken at the price of any compromise at all, a refusal of all free examination, of any possible recalcitrance. A scout, by definition, does not engage in dissidence ... No propaganda can have any effect; they are irreducibles. Only the removal of their leader (Father Forestier, a close friend of General de La Porte du Theil, whose attitudes are similar) could change something.

In contrast, Dunoyer de Segonzac's École Nationale des Cadres d'Uriage, leaning toward some Resistance positions, "displayed a certain independence of judgment and courageous attitude from the first days of its existence, which quickly made it the bête noire of all the French nazis, from [Pierre] Pucheu to Father Forestier." But the document concluded that Uriage did not have a sufficiently resistant position to attract those deeply involved in loyalist institutions into the Resistance, it lacked political intelligence, and its school had "no insertion into the reality of the nation."[2]

By 1943 there were some mixed, but fairly positive, reports on the use that could be made of the Uriage network to London, but there were also elements fiercely hostile to Uriage there. For example, at the meeting of Free France's "Conseil de la Jeunesse" in London under Maurice Grammont there was a sharp attack by the representative of the Jeunesses socialistes on the presence of Uriage's old chaplain the Abbé de Naurois, then chaplain of the Naval Forces of Fighting France, who had to deny the charge of being an agent of the Uriage group on the Conseil and defend the orientations of the school. De Naurois's critic saw no good at all in Uriage's record: "All those who collaborated or organized something worthwhile under Vichy brought water to Vichy's mill. We must retain nothing of Vichy's creations. Moreover, if Vichy kept Uriage until the end of 1942, it was because Uriage served the *equivocation of Vichy*."[3]

All in all, the Vieux Chef should not have expected to have been accepted with open arms when he went off to meet the Free French leaders, who were preparing an attack on the mainland from liberated North Africa, in early 1944, especially when he had spent much energy warning about the need to circumvent the Communists in the French Resistance.

Segonzac made his way down to Gibraltar where he took an American DC3 for Algiers in the first weeks of 1944.[4] There he spent three months seeing people he knew to explain "the real situation of France," and he later tried to arrange the parachuting of some officers onto the mainland to help take the *maquisards* in hand.[5] He told his friend Frenay:

I am now in direct rapport with General Revers, head of the ORA, with your comrades of *Combat*, and have also met men of the Front National. There is no unity, only rivalry, among them all, to say the least. It is very disappointing. So I came here to see Giraud, de Gaulle, and you to try to understand things for myself. The Resistance must be pulled out of that bedlam. You can help me ... Could you get me an interview with General de Gaulle?[6]

While Segonzac was preoccupied with the Communist threat within the Resistance, the general, as Segonzac would learn, was primarily concerned with expelling the Germans from France. Frenay went to see de Gaulle and explained to him who his friend Segonzac was: "his role at Uriage, his human qualities, his influence on thousands of valuable cadres, his clandestine activities and, finally, the purpose of his trip." But the general only stuck on one fact: Segonzac had been, for more than two years, at the head of a school dependent on the Vichy government. De Gaulle concluded: "No, Frenay, I will not see your Vichyites."

The founder of *Combat* tried to get him to reconsider:

"But General, this man is coming from the battle and returning to it. Perhaps tomorrow he will lose his life there. Is that a Vichyite?"

"Yes, because he was not a mere functionary, but a manager, a leader. His attitude, whatever his intentions, contributed to the terrible confusion in public opinion."

"General, if it is true that Uriage depended on Vichy, the school nonetheless trained men who were profoundly anti-Nazi who had strong reservations about the so-called Révolution Nationale. This wasn't missed by the Gestapo and that's why they tried to arrest Segonzac, and why Uriage was closed. Now it is the école des cadres of the Milice.

And then, General, can one forget that in the first years the Resistance was made up of only a very small number of individuals? Trying to reconstruct France with only them would be to isolate oneself from the country rather than leading it. To reject a person like Segonzac would be an error, in my judgment, and, I believe, an injustice."

"Frenay, I gave you my opinion and I am asking you not to insist."[7]

Segonzac finally got an interview, nevertheless, but the general received him rather coldly: "My last contact with General de Gaulle," Segonzac remembered, "dated from 1940. I had been struck by his calm, although our defeat had almost been consummated, and by the courtesy, even affability, he had showed toward me. But this time I found him glacial, making no allowances for the particularities of my situation, very unequivocal. Without even allowing me to finish setting out my point of view, he said a few words that did not allow for a reply."

Thus Dunoyer de Segonzac failed to convince de Gaulle and the Gaullists to try rallying "patriotic" Vichy people still held back by loyalty to the Marshal. Nor did he obtain the massive aid that he requested for the training and arming of the interior Resistance. His reception was particularly bad from the officers in Gaullist units, whether latecomers to the Free French cause or not, who tended to display "a frowning intransigence toward others": General Leclerc, whom Segonzac had known well, even refused to see him. Segonzac was granted a private interview by General Giraud but Segonzac found him "distraught" (Giraud had just learned of the condemnation to death by the Free French of collaborator Pierre Pucheu, whose effort to change caps by coming to North Africa Giraud had allowed and encouraged).

Admittedly a "bit nonplussed" by his reception from de Gaulle and the others, Segonzac received some comfort from General Jean de Lattre de Tassigny, *"homme fin et sensible"* (and former participant in Robert Garric's communitarian social Catholicism projects), who invited him to dinner with a group including Pleven and Menthon. De Lattre was trying, in this way, to maintain contacts between civilians and military people and to keep informed about the thinking of the occupied French, whether avowedly of the Resistance or not. Apparently de Lattre did not intend to freeze out people like Segonzac (who would later fight under his command during the liberation of France); he seemed to have allowed the Vieux Chef to make a tour of the regiments stationed in Algeria and Morocco (in which Segonzac saw some of his old friends) in what he recalled to have been a not very successful effort to persuade some officers to be parachuted onto the mainland to help take charge of the *maquis*.

On returning to Algiers, Segonzac later recalled, he was offered, "as a kind of honourable out," he thought, the command of a regiment with a rank of colonel. The offer was professionally attractive, but he claimed to have declined because he didn't feel at ease among the people in North Africa, and above all because he didn't want to abandon his Uriage friends and their projects.[8]

At the beginning of April 1944, with the allied landings more imminent and Segonzac still in North Africa, a worried Beuve-Méry organized a meeting of the Uriage people in Paris, at the Catholic faculty. Resistance military leader Le Ray, who presided, said that the time had come to prepare large-scale operations in concert with the Armée secrète (AS). An insurrection in the large cities was envisaged from the time when the allies, having landed, would approach.

It was judged important to be there. That France not passively sit by and let herself be liberated was important for the future politically. So again, the Uriage focus was on "participating" in the Resistance so as to be able to influence the liberation and postwar political situations. But Beuve-Méry did not appreciate Le Ray's push for military action – even at this late hour. One evening when they were dining together, he complained to Le Ray: "You are doing something unfortunate. You are involving all our people in direct action that will deplete a *precious capital* [my emphasis] that we will need later."

Le Ray later commented: "That incident marked a profound difference in our conception of our role … Our skirmishes, our ambushes, all that seemed like *a circus* to him. He thought it wasn't worth the lives of the young men of the future that had been confided to him."[9] It seemed that for Beuve-Méry the postwar political struggle against a return to pre-war decadence was the highest priority; he thought it folly to have his elites killed to rid the country of the Germans when the Americans could do it. He needed the best and the brightest to transform France in accordance with Uriage ideals – to neutralize the threatened postwar American influence. His lieutenants, such as Jean-Marie Domenach, soon began to reflect that special Uriage perspective in their writings. As if to reinforce commitment to the distinctive Uriage line, fifteen members of the Uriage network, three women among them, took the formal Order oath to Segonzac on the day of the meeting in Paris. They included Chaine, Domenach, Paul Delouvrier, and Alain Le Ray himself.[10]

After three months' absence, Segonzac made his way back to Paris where he rejoined a good part of his team. He had reached the Spanish coast by submarine and made a clandestine crossing into France. He explained that despite Frenay's support he had been coldly received by the head of the CFLN, but had met most of the members of the committee, numerous officers, and political representatives of the consultative assembly. He concluded that, beyond the disappointments,

General de Gaulle has a very strong personality ... extraordinary ... its sense of grandeur, spirit of independence carried to the extreme, intelligence, energy, taste for command and nobility of style are its principal characteristics.

A certain pride, a lack of warmth in human relationships, to say the least, a difficulty in forgetting wounds to his pride form the reverse side of a medal cast in bronze.

What is certain is that on the level of foreign relations, General de Gaulle has maintained the French point of view without a moment of weakness. On the domestic scene he imposed himself as leader without the slightest demagoguery.

In these two roles, he established himself, without rival, as the only viable candidate for the post of the head of tomorrow's government.

We of the Order and of the Movement ought to support him; he is our best chance."

Segonzac wanted a strong and nationalistic leader out of concern over the role that the United States might play in liberated France, for the Americans might block the realization of the best in the old National Revolution:

The Americans constitute a genuine danger for France. It is a very different danger from that which Germany represents and from what the Russians might eventually pose for us. It is in the economic and moral sphere. The Americans could prevent us from carrying out the obligatory revolution and their materialism does not even have the tragic grandeur of the materialism of the totalitarians. While they [the Americans] make a veritable cult of the idea of liberty, they do not for a minute feel any need to liberate themselves from a capitalism more dominant among them than anywhere else. It seems that overindulgence in well-being has diminished the vital force among them in a disquieting way.

Thus, on the very eve of the Normandy landings, as Americans were taking a front place in the decisive fight to liberate Europe, Pierre Dunoyer de Segonzac worried over the results of their lack of "tragic grandeur" and "vital force" in a liberated France. He set an attitude toward the United States for the Uriage network after the war.[11] He also correctly sensed de Gaulle's reservations about the Americans (and sympathy for some of the ideals of the old National Revolution) and that was another important reason to back him.

Segonzac concluded that it was de Gaulle who could save France: "General de Gaulle ought to be the head of tomorrow's France. He merits it by the almost heroic way in which he has defended the interests of his country, because he has shown the true qualities of the proven Statesman, matured by four years of a very difficult political experience."[12]

Following his poor reception from the head of the Free French, Segonzac must have realized that time was running out; he therefore stopped hesitating and commanded the Order and the Movement to support de Gaulle. His reflections on his encounter with the general, accompanied by notes of Beuve-Méry analyzing the total political and military situation, were widely circulated in the Uriage network.[13]

Segonzac began trying to establish some discipline in his NERF, and in the Order, particularly concerning the Communists. He warned against consorting with them: "engaging in politics does not mean to finesse, trick, lie during the normal work week, but rather to remain firm on the essential ... The Communists are masters in political matters. In this area they will outdo the men of the movement for a long time. This is why one must not join the Front National (directed by the Communists), to preclude even the possibility of a common political movement."

Despite all the ecumenical Resistance rhetoric, then, Segonzac remained a militant anti-Communist who advised his Order to follow: "simple and irreproachable goals: defence of General de Gaulle and the Algiers Committee, the installation of their qualified representatives at the moment of the liberation of the territory, to the exclusion of all other purposes."[14]

In fact this tardy rallying of the Uriage Order to the Algiers Committee discredited it in the eyes of certain Resisters, as did the "Vichyite" reputation that was attached to everything connected to Uriage.[15] And then there was the refusal to take up arms: Segonzac admitted, on 1 June, that the Order had been sometimes "considered as a peaceful refuge" for "action without risks." There was also a project to join the National Committee of the Resistance (CNR) which "could not come to fruition."[16]

On the eve of the Normandy landings, Segonzac had been personally rebuffed by de Gaulle, and the Uriage group was kept at arm's length, if not entirely rejected, in the Resistance movement. Within a few months, however, with the liberation of national territory, people from the Uriage network would take the forefront in Grenoble, Paris, and other cities as among the most prominent voices of liberated France. From June to December 1944 Uriage people "came from nowhere" to assume high-profile roles as representatives of the Resistance. One might observe that this could be no surprise to Segonzac – they had, after all, been trained to lead.

THE ALLIED LANDINGS, THE *CORPS FRANC BAYARD*, TRAINING *CADRES* FOR THE "REVOLUTION OF THE TWENTIETH CENTURY"

While others gathered arms, or prepared their getaways, in anticipation of the allied landings in France, the Uriage group focused on acting quickly to fill the political void that would follow the departure of Italian or German occupation forces. While Segonzac's people had been placed under the command of de Gaulle and the liberation army, they also prepared to move into several areas of France, particularly in the cities of Grenoble and Paris, with ambitious plans to provide the *cadres* for the "Revolution of the twentieth century". This would entail working with de Gaulle and his men but heading off the Communists, Americans, old-fashioned Republican politicians, and others who might spoil this new opportunity for young elites to precipitate a form of National Revolution.

Before leaving for North Africa, Segonzac had founded, "a bit hastily" and over the objections of Beuve-Méry, the NERF (Nouvelles Équipes de la Renaissance Française), a movement that claimed to be more open, mobilizing, and militant than the Order (which had been reserved, as we have seen, for a minority of the chosen).[17] By the end of 1943, the whole "Uriage Movement" was referring to itself as the NERF.[18] In December 1943, Alain Le Ray resigned from his military responsibilities in the Vercors, and was named head of the NERF, but Beuve-Méry, as the head of the Order, still took on the major responsibility for ensuring that the Uriage group undertook activities that were "in the guidelines of our thinking."[19]

But it was proving difficult to keep the group coherent: on 3 February the members of the *équipes volantes* from Murinais who had taken refuge in the windswept mountain monastery of Esperron were attacked by the Germans. Since, according to Cacérès, the *équipes volantes* had no arms, "to try to flee in case of attack was our sole chance for safety."[20] They only got away, under a hail of bullets, due to a prodigious slide down a sharp cliff cushioned with pine needles.[21] Although the Uriage group's "resistance" was largely non-violent, and their ends "political" rather than military, their furtiveness made them subject to suspicion and considerable danger.

Not everyone agreed on the tactics or ideas of the Order. One of the Uriage inner circle's few non-Catholics, Joffre Dumazedier, confessed that he was developing more and more sympathy for the extreme Left. He wrote to Beuve-Méry (code name "Berthier") on 21 March 1944 that some of the group at la Thébaïde had become tired of Beuve-Méry's "total pessimism" and "blasé statesman" posture, which led the journalist to "putting in the same sack the three great political movements that are fighting over the world. Dumazedier concluded that he and his friends, "while not sharing the point of view of democrats, nor of orthodox Communists, cannot share yours either." (In fact, while Beuve-Méry was considering fascism and democrats "as in the same sack," Dumazedier, no democrat either, was becoming more and more involved with the French Communist Party.) Dumazedier recognized that Beuve wanted something that was "very Christian," though not "completely a neo-theocracy, nor medieval," but that boiled down to contemporary Catholicism trying to adapt to new problems. Dumazedier granted the existence of "spiritual realities": that it was still "essential to affirm, over against the ignorance of a certain materialism and a certain modern sociology, that they exist, have appeared in all epochs, and alone furnish an irreducible basis for the liberty of the human person and his power of loving." But Beuve-Méry's problem, Dumazedier told him, was that his "personal tendency has always been thwarted by free-thinkers like myself and by Churchmen like Father Maydieu. In fact you want ... "the Christian *kolkhoz*."[22] Thus Dumazedier touched on the Christian-communist impulse behind Uriage, the strong vein of puritanism and asceticism that put many off. He pushed for a more proletarian focus in the coming revolution.

In spring the NERF published a manifesto, written by Dumazedier, which suggested that liberated France would "rediscover in the travail of the worst of battles the direction of its revolutionary path," and that the liberation might well promise many of the goals of the true National Revolution as envisaged by Uriage. The "struggle against Hitlerite Germany" had not been joined simply to return to the pre-war situation after the victory: "*we have taken the oath to be done with that decadence* ... we want a bold and living republic, inspired by a great spirit of rebuilding and basing its strength on an empire in full expansion, on a country overflowing with children ... a republic rediscovering its true mission in an economic and social revolution: leading the masses toward dignity and happiness." A true "national community" would succeed the abolition of "the capitalist privileges" that were smothering the country, and allow the proletariat to be reintegrated into the nation, and thus create a community that "would be able to breath and live."

And with all of the characteristic virile and elitist language of Uriage, the manifesto also called for a national community with power for the "best," not only the brightest:

It ... must be organized into ... a hierarchy no longer ruled automatically by those with the most diplomas, or the richest, but by the best. At all levels the recruiting and progressing of elites, and new institutions, must be advanced; *écoles des cadres, maisons du peuple, instituts collégiaux* must add to their radiance ... to accelerate and crown that ascent, new men will appear, attached to honour more than to their own lives ... veritable missionaries of a virile fraternity.

Thus there was still more evidence that at least some Uriage veterans had "learned nothing and forgotten nothing" since the school was founded with such optimism a few years earlier. Such a frank and unashamed reaffirmation of elitism – however much Europe had suffered from enemies of democracy, liberalism, and egalitarianism – was typical. But the key people in the Uriage movement, including the heavy representation of old family aristocrats among the leaders, remained absolutely convinced of their own elite status, of the importance of elites in general, and of their own special ability to summon forth and train those elites (including the odd "prolétaire," such as Cacérès, from the masses).

The NERF manifesto concluded, on a lyrical note, that they wanted to make a special appeal to all those who had broken with capitalism, asserting that "other things exist besides financiers and politicians"; one could now take heart "in the coalition of tough and fraternal men."[23]

A striking feature of the Uriage *mentalité* revealed by such documents is its relative insensitivity to those irrational and authoritarian impulses of the 1930s that poisoned Pétainism – the cruelty toward minorities, the blind allegiance to authority. As D-Day approached the Uriage people were still describing the regrettable legacy of the Third Republic – and not Pétainism – as the "decadence" threatening the French. The Pétain regime represented, Beuve-Méry argued, serious disappointment and unforgivable treason. But it did not require soul-searching as to its psychological or cultural bases, or those forces that brought it to power so easily and naturally.

As the allied landings approached, the Vieux Chef considered trying, with the help of Resistance leaders such as Frenay, having the Uriage movement admitted into the heart of that Conseil National de la Résistance (CNR) that already constituted "the embryo of ... national representation."[24] But he was less interested in the Uriage group's role in the armed struggle than in their influencing the new leadership in France. He proclaimed the Order's basic goal to be "the formation of an elite of educators" who were "to create original experiences, and find methods and new techniques in the domain of education."[25] And in the dramatic months that followed Uriage people launched a host of programs, as we shall see.

URIAGE TO ARMS!

The landing on 6 June 1944 and the order for the mobilization of the Forces françaises de l'intérieur (FFI) that accompanied it brought the signal for a general transition to military activity in the Uriage movement.[26] From the beginning of June, Segonzac was in the Tarn region, as he had the agreement of Marquis Charles d'Aragon, the political head of the zone (whom he had met on his return from Algiers at Msgr Bruno de Solages's) that, in principle, he take command of the FFI of that region. But on arrival he found that the Tarn command had been given to a classmate, who, in turn, offered him the command of its southern section (the Vabre and Montagne noire area).[27] Thus Segonzac obtained *in extremis* a military command in the FFI – thanks both to the Marquis d'Aragon and to a former Uriage trainee active in the Vabre *maquis*, industrialist Guy de Rouville.[28] His foot was now firmly in the door of the Resistance.

Characteristically, and despite the security risks, Dunoyer de Segonzac set up his first headquarters in another castle – the Château

de Bonnery (which he soon had to abandon for a modest farm).²⁹
By 10 June Segonzac had a *maquis* of two hundred men which he
christened the "corps franc Bayard" in honour of the Uriage chateau.
It was made up of three different groups of equal number around
Vabre which were directed and organized by old royalist Segonzac
(as if it were the seventeenth century) along religious lines: Catholic,
Protestant, and Jewish.³⁰ By early July Segonzac had summoned
veteran Uriage instructors Beuve-Méry, Gadoffre, Ferry, Domenach,
Cacérès, Hoepffner, and Rouchié to help him train his troops. With
the agreement of the bishop's office, he installed his men in the Prat
Long seminary where they organized pedagogical and propaganda
projects.³¹ One of them recalled the scene:

We lived for three weeks there. The seminary lodged vacation colonies, and
accepted some relatives of seminarians *en pension*. They all took us for a
study group. The Superior who knew a bit more about our real nature, while
always appearing charming, trembled night and day. As to the nuns, they
were worried about boys and girls living together in the same section of their
peaceful residence. One day the Superior asked Beuve-Méry to give a talk
on the international situation to the seminarians. We were stupefied. This
happened in a clearing in the moonlight, and the young priests kept thanking
us and asking questions.³²

Although the Uriage movement naturally seemed to gravitate
toward Catholic milieux, Segonzac's friends kept trying to spread the
Uriage message among the *maquis*. A Jewish resistant, member of
the Hagenau group, recalled how they were visited by a reincarnated
équipe volante: "One afternoon, dressed in a large loden cape, Beuve-
Méry came to talk to us of the past: a tragic evoking of errors and
betrayals by someone who had seen them from close up. For his part,
[Gadoffre] spoke of the future and particularly of university
reform."³³

So despite Segonzac's call to arms, the Uriage group had turned
primarily to "training" people ... even after the Normandy landings
... and not only in the area where Segonzac had his FFI command,
but across the entire country. Jean Le Veugle, for example, was
ordered by Segonzac to go to Rennes and seek out members of the
Uriage network, take part in the liberation of Brittany, and then try
to create an *école des cadres* along Uriage lines. The first course at
Rennes began on 28 June 1944 and, among other things, was concerned with the question of what sort of France one should try to
achieve at the liberation.

This Rennes École des Cadres proposed a doctrine to the trainees
made up simultaneously of the communitarian personalism of

Mounier, the spiritualist evolutionism of Teilhard de Chardin, and the "socialism coloured by Christian humanism" of Hubert Beuve-Méry. Over and above that, Le Veugle's school [was] "strongly inspired by chivalry, and a bit *vieille France* in the spirit of the Vieux Chef." They spoke about the liberated French renouncing the splintering of the old political parties, and uniting in the reconstruction of the country on new foundations.

Chef Le Veugle explained in his memoirs that because there were many trainees from the local *petite noblesse* and from relatively narrow intellectual and political backgrounds at his school, much of the Uriage vocabulary, ideas about "the French proletariat," "marxism," and "the revolution of the twentieth century" were new for them. But he saw them quite stimulated by the call for a "transcending" of marxism that would incorporate its economic analyses and social demands, but not its materialist philosophy. It was not a question of wanting to "beat" the communists, such as the FTP (Francs Tireurs et Partisans) who had played such an important Resistance role. Le Veugle's men claimed to be "realists" above all, recognizing that one had to be strong and supported by a solid faith to deal with them [the Communists]. They had to show that they understood all of the Communists' aspirations, and then, after granting the justice of these, "one had to lead them beyond the narrowness of dialectical materialism and nudge their doctrine and activities toward ... a more totally human revolution, one that no longer neglected man's spiritual dimension."[34]

This lofty and optimistic world-historical perspective retired Pétainism and fascism to a reassuring perspective, because, in the words of theologian Teilhard de Chardin (after Bergson), "everything which rises must converge," all great collective enthusiasms were inspired by spiritual forces that would inevitably lead to a greater spiritualization of mankind. Thus the cause of the Resistance was not "the struggle for liberty and democracy against authoritarianism" but rather an inspiring, if imprecise, will to create a "personalist" community between the values of East and West.

In this volatile political context such language justified heading off the Communists and reasserting the hegemony of the old noble Catholic families. All in all, the Uriage movement was setting out the perspective of a spiritual and moral elect who could see farther, and more clearly, than the superstitious and money-minded masses.

One should note that the position of Uriage in regard to the Communists, like that of the Resistance in general, evolved during 1944. The extreme initial mistrust, even hostility, was transformed, during that fateful year, to an appeal for union. That being said, a certain vigilance doubtless persisted because of the "hidden" agenda of the Communist Party. This guarded attitude was revealed in an internal *équipe* communication: "The Communists have too often been in the first line of the battle against the Nazi occupier for it to be just, or possible, to hold them aside. Every effort to rebuild the French community without them, or against them, must be contested. (But) a loyal effort to reach a common ground with the Communists does not mean submitting, in a servile way, to all their pretensions."[35]

Segonzac knew by this time that some of his men were strongly attracted by the Communist Party – particularly Dumazedier, Cacérès, and Ollier de Marichard (all of whom would enter the party after the war). Another member of the *équipe*, Roger Bonamy, an important figure at the liberation of Grenoble, had had a dual membership since spring 1944.[36]

Segonzac and his group felt secure enough to have a celebration on 14 July 1944 in a woods on a road a few kilometres above the seminary. A huge flag pole had been set into the bank the day before and four machine guns were placed to protect the four approaches. L.M. Ardain recalled the scene:

Beuve-Méry had put on his École d'Uriage instructor's uniform ... All that had a little whiff of liberty that went right to the head. Many *abbés* came, too, and brought children from the summer camps along with them! Standing on the hillside I saw six or seven *maquis* from the sector arrive ... Some were in the uniform of the French Army, others in linen shirts and *espadrilles*. Some were well armed, but others had practically nothing. Commander Dunoyer de Segonzac had them pass in review, and said a few phrases which, although were simple, were spoken in a tone of conviction that had everyone listening attentively and emotionally and it did everyone good. Then he gave the command "Garde à vous: Attention pour les couleurs; envoyez," and it seemed that I had heard it just the day before, the intonation was so familiar. Yet it was 31 December 1942 that he had given it a last time on the playing field of the disbanded school ... The bugle call echoed strangely in a forest from which the Boche might storm out a minute later, and the flag, finally our flag, rose slowly and unfolded in a clear sky. Many people were silently crying as they went back to their cars. I felt intoxicated, intoxicated with hope.[37]

But the hope soon became tinged with sadness as, in July, the fight to liberate French territory brought news of the deaths of Uriage men. Segonzac thought of bringing their bodies back for burial under the flag near the Château Bayard.[38] Also that month, Raymond Dupouy had a former secretary of the école d'Uriage arrested and executed (several members of the équipe later said that she was gotten drunk and tortured before being shot) by the Isère Resistance. She was alleged to have worked for the enemy for six months, slept with Italian and German officers, and betrayed twenty-seven persons to the Gestapo – among whom, perhaps, were several members of the team itself.[39]

In August Segonzac became involved in his first major Resistance military engagement and, over his colleague Beuve-Mery's objection, carried it off with typical aristocratic panache and antique chivalry. On 19 August Segonzac went to see the German commander of Mazamet, who was planning to retreat by a special forty-wagon armoured train to rejoin the large German detachment at Castres, and said:

"I am in charge of all of the *maquis* of the area. You will not leave Mazamet alive, and your men will be uselessly massacred. Surrender with all your material, and we will guarantee the lives of all your men." "The meeting of the Field of the Cloth of Gold," grunted Beuve-Méry. The German Commander, a fat man with a round face and shaven skull, answered: "I have orders to return [to Castres]; I'm going through." Segonzac responded with equal dignity saying, "Until this evening, then."[40]

Segonzac organized an ambush on the train tracks seven kilometres out of Mazamet. Beuve-Méry blurted "*Quelle connerie!*" to whom Segonzac's idea of warning the adversary of his intentions seemed silly, to say the least.[41] But thanks to an American commando bomb squad, who blew up the locomotive, the train was stopped; it took fire, and after a night's resistance the German soldiers raised the white flag. Segonzac still took pride in his victory years later: "I was delighted to remark [to the German commander] the justice of my predictions and immediately sent his men and material into the mountains, the officers being allowed to keep their arms. Rigorous orders were given, and obeyed, that prisoners be treated according to the Hague convention."[42]

Segonzac went on to direct the surrender of Castres and, once his zone was liberated, regrouped his unit of Corps franc Bayard volunteers. On 20 October 1944, as they were advancing along the front, commanded by Segonzac, the Corps franc Bayard became the third regiment of Dragoons (later renamed the twelfth). The Vieux Chef led them to link up with the army of de Lattre in Burgundy.

Not long afterward, Segonzac became involved in a curious confrontation with General de Lattre, the same man who had broken Gaullist ranks to show kindness to him in North Africa. Summoned at midnight, Segonzac was required to travel several hours in the rain to appear at General de Lattre's command post of the 1st army installed at Besançon. Segonzac had apparently forgotten that the "3rd Dragoons" of the armistice army had bridled at General de Lattre's refusal to obey the surrender order when the Germans had invaded the free zone. That title "therefore dishonoured ... merited definitive obliteration." Segonzac's resurrection of it was taken amiss by Lattre who, after sharply berating him, ordered that the regiment be called the 12th dragoons instead, in honour of the regiment in which the general had served in 1914, among whom he had suffered a lance wound in the face. Thus, integrated into the 1st army, Segonzac's 12th dragoons compiled an excellent record in the fighting in Haute-Saône, in the Vosges, and in Alsace.[43]

THE ROAD TO POWER!
GRENOBLE, PARIS, *ESPRIT*, *LE MONDE*

On 25 August General von Choltitz signed the surrender of Paris. In the Isère Valley, the members of the team thought that the war would be over quickly and the Vieux Chef told them to prepare an inspirational and educative program for that area, even to make a "model city" of Grenoble.[44] In fact, the Uriage group was very strong in that regional capital down on the river plain below the Château Bayard: from the morrow of the liberation the Comité départemental de Libération de l'Isère (CDL), assigned to reorganizing important sectors in civic life, would be set up at Grenoble under Roger Bonamy, the Uriage Order's "Communist" and a faithful member of the team. Even Grenoble's mayor, Lafleur, was a former *stagiaire* and a friend of Uriage. The city was therefore a logical choice for Uriage projects, given the network of relationships that the movement had created there. In that mountain city the Uriage group intended to form the cadres that France would need, and to constitute "exemplary prototypes" of the "communities of revolutionary educators" – strongly rooted in the local population and ready to spread their influence throughout the area. Grenoble would be the privileged setting for experiments engendering the new sort of society foreseen in the *Somme* (Summa).[45] Beuve-Méry even envisaged Grenoble as the avant-garde capital of the France of the future.[46]

As early as 4 September the Isère Comité départemental de Libération created an Education Commission, with Joffre Dumazedier as secretary, which proceeded to create an organization with a national audience, *Peuple et Culture*, with Uriage men such as Nora, Cacérès, Ferry, Le Veugle, Bonamy, Le Ray, etc.[47] Dumazedier wanted to use the departmental education commission to create a national popular education movement, independent of unions and parties, and suited to training "men capable of creating and animating the new social structures that were to be created."[48]

Meanwhile, in the mountains above the city, the Château Bayard was cleansed of the last vestiges of the Milice, and Xavier de Virieu set up a military school created by the directors of the military resistance and those responsible for the new integrated army. De Virieu, at the school's opening ceremony, explained why the assembly was gathered on the field around the flag:

It is first of all an expiation. Too often in the pure sky of Uriage, impure hands have raised our three colours ... those who would dare to play the Marseillaise after having wanted a German victory.

We think that the time for fusion has come, that the spirit of sacrifice which is the lesson of our dead will be the ferment for it. As in the great days of its history, the French Army has come forth in a defensive reaction from the authentic people of France, whose soul it should be. That is why the school was born; it is in that hope, in that certitude that our eyes will now contemplate this flag.[49]

The new Uriage military school had been established by Segonzac's friend Colonel-Marquis Xavier de Virieu, apparently under the patronage of Segonzac's superior, General de Lattre. The general was trying to amalgamate the *maquisards* with the First French Army newly landed in France and thought an *école des cadres* could forge combined forces to join in the campaign to liberate Belfort.[50] The revived Uriage simultaneously taught the military, personal, and social subjects because it wanted to produce "complete men of action," meaning men "who knew how to think out their actions."[51] Among the Uriage alumni who hastened to the revived school were veteran instructors Gilles Ferry, Jean Le Veugle, Gilbert Gadoffre, Louis Poli, Paul Grillet, and Pierre Cazenavette, as well as Louise-Marie Ardain, and Yvonne Jacquot who would be Virieu's secretary.[52] Its graduates went off to join in the final struggle against the German army, and before the school was closed at the Armistice, several among them had lost their lives at the front. Segonzac, years later, lauded that "collège d'humanisme militaire," but regretted "that such an ennobling experience had not been encouraged at all by the army high command.[53]

At the liberation of Annecy on 19 August, members of the Uriage-Annecy team were holding key posts in the Comité départemental de Libération, and on 1 October the Commissaire de la République at Lyon established, on the initiative of Uriage-Annecy, "Marquisats" – a centre of studies and information geared toward the training of *cadres*, trade unions, and a whole range of youth and sports movements.[54] The local team, in concert with Beuve-Méry and Dunoyer de Segonzac (who was returning to professional military occupations), named Gilles Ferry as director of the centre on 1 December.[55]

While Grenoble quickly became the prototype of the Uriage movement, Uriage also had noteworthy connections in Paris, as became evident when, having created new *écoles des cadres* and social and cultural movements in the liberated provinces, it began to move into Parisian publishing and journalism.

In the last months of 1941, Emmanuel Mounier, who had been in retrospect the most important philosophical influence on the school, had been forced into silence by enemies in the Vichy government. After having been imprisoned (with Henri Frenay's secretary) in early 1942 for alleged contacts with the Combat movement and then exonerated after a hunger strike protesting his innocence, Mounier had retired to reading and research in the village of Dieulefit in the Drôme area with a few friends, including the noted Catholic poet Pierre Emmanuel. At Dieulefit in September 1943, and again in 1944 just before the liberation, Mounier had held two secret "Esprit" meetings attended by a good representation of Uriage people – notably Jean Lacroix, Gilbert Dru (a comrade of Domenach in the last Uriage class who would die as a Resistance hero), and Beuve-Méry, as well as Uriage's old friend from the *Jeune France* movement, Paul Flamand. Mounier planned to revive the review *Esprit* as soon as possible and launch major "Esprit"-movement books via a new publishing house, which would be built up from the embryo of the pre-war Éditions du Seuil, Flamand's tiny utopian Catholic publishing house.[56]

Mounier returned to Paris in September, just after the liberation of the city, secured *Esprit* access to the very limited stocks of paper then available (Sartre and his comrades had to wait almost a year to publish *Temps modernes* – soon *Esprit*'s only major rival as the most prominent intellectual review of postwar France).[57] The directing committee of the new journal included Lacroix, Paul Flamand, and soon Lacroix's former student, Jean-Marie Domenach. "Les Murs blancs," an "Esprit" community at least partially inspired by the Uriage experience, was established on the grounds of a romantic old estate said to have belonged to Chateaubriand at Châtenay-Malabry near Paris. Besides the Mouniers and the Domenachs, it came to include the families of historians Henri-Irénée Marrou and Michel

Winock, Sorbonne psychology professor Paul Fraisse, and philosopher Paul Ricoeur, among others. *Esprit* jumped from a pre-war circulation of between 3,000 and 4,000 to four or five times that, and it would grow steadily throughout the nineteen-fifties and sixties.[58]

In launching the "new series" of his journal, Mounier deftly painted its colourful history, retouching its intellectual tradition, its Vichy and Uriage experiences, and its postwar prospects with a cautious eye on the new political climate. Abandoning the pre-war and Uriage "neither Right nor Left" emphasis, he described personalism as a leftist movement deriving from "the tradition of humanist socialism peculiar to France since 1930." Under Vichy, Mounier argued, "Esprit" people had chosen to fight in "open clandestinity" rather than flee the danger. "The stupidity of the Lyon censor" had enabled him to pursue this tactic. He described the *Esprit* of 1940–41, often diffusing the same Mounier lectures that had captivated the trainees at the Uriage school as a subtle series of Resistance documents in which "each phrase hid a dart, each synopsis an ambush." The youth programs supported by the personalists had become "a rallying point of the opposition," and when Vichy had finally discovered Mounier's true motives, *Esprit* had been summarily suppressed.[59]

Thus in his post-liberation issues Mounier sidestepped the early enthusiasm at Uriage for Vichy's national renovation projects, downplayed the rival forces that struggled for power in the National Revolution, and minimized the influence of Uriage and personalism on Vichy. Instead he depicted the personalist movement (and hence, by implication, the Vichy leadership schools where his personalism was taught) as the proud possessor of excellent Resistance credentials – as being of the socialist tradition, and so Resistant right from the beginning.

Mounier's bold and artful revision of the history of *Esprit* set the postwar tone toward the Vichy period in general, and the Uriage experience in particular.[60] Already in January 1945 Jean-Marie Domenach took a very hard line, defending the death sentences being meted out to collaborators of the defunct regime, and was seconded by Jean Lacroix and Mounier. *Esprit* was also unforgiving of Pétain during the old man's trial.[61] Thus a movement that had been held suspect by the Gaullists and Resistance groups as *Pétainiste* just a few months earlier began forging a *pur et dur* Resistance image by endorsing harsh punitive measures against those accused of treason.

But while hard on fascists at home, Mounier's journal was exemplary in showing compassion for defeated Germany: *Esprit* essays helped originate the movement for French rapprochement with the "new Germany"; the Comité d'échanges avec l'Allemagne nouvelle, which *Esprit* had inspired, was founded in Mounier's office.[62] Throughout the postwar period people whose world-historical views were influenced by *Esprit* would be pioneers in the effort to "think European" and bring Germany and France closer together.[63]

At the same time, from late 1944, Mounier's close friend Paul Flamand had gathered the resources to try to make Éditions du Seuil a competitor with the major Parisian publishing houses (many of which had been weakened by their compromises with the authorities during the occupation). "Esprit" collections or series (even including one publishing novels) were to be the core of the new house. The journal began publishing essays from the "Summa" which Gadoffre, Domenach, and the others had set out during the great days of the *équipes volantes* of the Château de Murinais. The whole document was then published under the title *Vers le style du XXe siècle* by Éditions du Seuil[64] as a daring new analysis of the crisis of the modern world and the revolutionary solutions that the new regime that issued from the Resistance should bring to them. Bertrand d'Astorg, who had been at Uriage and was now helping edit *Esprit*, was left to finesse the continuity between the earlier aspirations of Uriage and the postwar revolutionary positions of the journal.[65] In September 1945 Mounier moved his offices into the heart of the Latin Quarter, to the third floor of the building that had recently been taken over by the Éditions du Seuil on 27 rue Jacob, near Saint-Germain-des-Prés. Although *Esprit* would always remains administratively and financially independent of Seuil, there was a very close and complex working relationship between the two institutions run by young men who had cemented their friendship in the early days of the Révolution Nationale.[66]

The review *Esprit* and the Éditions du Seuil would rise together to leading positions in the intellectual, cultural, and political life of postwar France. This ascension from obscurity and marginality to prominence, power, and influence was due to the support of "the network" and to the power vacuum left by the purge of collaborators, as well as to the dedication and talent of the Uriage people and their friends.

BEUVE-MÉRY AND HIS *MONDE*

While the rise of *Esprit* and Éditions du Seuil from relative obscurity to central positions in French intellectual life was remarkable, Hubert Beuve-Méry's ascent was even more so. At the end of August 1944, he had come from Castres to Paris, having been charged by Dunoyer de Segonzac to plead with an unfriendly General Koenig, head of the FFI and military governor of Paris, for the integration of the Tarn irregulars into the regular army. Having accomplished his mission (with the aid of a Uriage alumnus in the general's cabinet), Beuve-Méry did not return to Segonzac's side at the front: he was the linchpin of the Uriage group's plans to help fill the political void left by the departure of the occupation authorities and the disintegration of the Vichy government. While Dunoyer de Segonzac was the symbol, Beuve-Méry was the brains of a dedicated nationwide organization with a strong sense of collective identity, an agenda, and extensive connections – particularly in administrative, religious, and military circles. He represented young Catholic intellectual elites who had been excluded during the Third Republic, had experienced a heady renaissance in the interwar period, and had been catapulted to central roles under Vichy. He and they were determined to preserve their new power and influence.

At first Beuve-Méry went to see the former Catholic youth leader Georges Bidault, Jean Moulin's successor as head of the National Council of the Resistance, and now at the Quai d'Orsay. Bidault offered him the ambassadorship to his old posting of Prague. Declining this offer, Beuve-Méry contacted old friends of the Dominican movement: Father Maydieu, Stanislas Fumet, and Ella Sauvageot, among others.[67] At the moment of the liberation of Paris, Madame Sauvageot organized the reappearance of the important progressive Catholic periodical *Temps présent*; in September she proposed that Beuve-Méry become the editor in chief and he accepted. But it would be only for a few months: several Uriage men had joined the de Gaulle administration's effort to expurgate French journalism of collaborationists (and block access to the Communists) and they soon had a far more important position to propose to their old study master.[68]

At this time, in General de Gaulle's inner circles, there were discussions about creating a major new national daily to replace *Le Temps*, France's most prestigious and important newspaper during the Third Republic. Founded in 1829, firmly rooted in the Enlightenment and liberal traditions, *Le Temps* had been justly celebrated for the competence of its journalists, the weightiness of its articles, and the quality of its information, particularly on foreign political matters. But (to the indignation of some) the paper was condemned at the liberation – not so much as "collaborationist" (which, relatively speaking, it had not been) as for having favoured the Munich agreements, and having been controlled by "special financial interests." The new government passed an exceptional law (which, as Beuve-

228 The Knight-Monks of Vichy France

Méry himself later admitted, was aimed directly at *Le Temps*) stipulating that newspapers that had continued to appear in the southern zone after 26 November 1942 would be confiscated. *Le Temps* had only closed down on 29 November 1942,[69] and although many of its journalists were in the Resistance, it came under the force of the law. The new daily was to take over the confiscated equipment, printing presses, and building of *Temps* on the rue des Italiens – as well as most of the personnel and editorial team (albeit purged of certain elements).

For Pierre-Henri Teitgen, de Gaulle's minister of information – and one of the founders, in November, of the Mouvement républicain populaire (MRP: Christian Democratic Party) – there was still the major problem of finding a director for the daily. He asked Paul Reuter, who was in his cabinet, to suggest a man to run "an 'unofficial' newspaper, a sort of replacement for *Temps*." Reuter returned with Paul Delouvrier (another former Uriage instructor) who was assisting François Bloch-Lainé, then in charge of the expurgation of the French press (granting or refusing authorizations to publish). The latter two men proposed Beuve-Méry.

In fact their old *chef* seemed the ideal candidate: a Catholic and a seasoned journalist who had disassociated himself from the *Temps* position on the Munich agreements. Although an administrator in a Vichy institution, the forty-two-year-old journalist had came to fight in the ranks of the Resistance, and had a reputation as something of a specialist on international affairs. Beuve-Méry was also authoritative, immensely competent, completely selfless and dedicated. Once again he proved charismatic, and after an interview with Teitgen and a warm endorsement from Minister of Foreign Affairs Georges Bidault his nomination was approved.[70]

Beuve-Méry hesitated to resign from *Temps présent* but toward the end of October, having been pressed by concerned ministers and former editors of *Le Temps*, and exhorted by Fathers Maydieu and Chenu, he accepted the post. With characteristic high-mindedness and asceticism he made it clear that the future associates of the new *Le Monde* were to consider themselves the executors of a state-confided mission, and so to exclude all possible financial profiteering. They were also to manifest, as clearly as possible, by legal statute, a firm commitment to create a new society. The new newspaper was to be freed of all political, economic, or financial influence,[71] and so an independent directing committee was established, with a strong liberal democratic (and Huguenot) presence in the person of René Courtin.[72]

As had been the case for *Esprit*, access to the precious stocks of paper were secured. This infuriated the frustrated Communists of *L'Humanité* who contrasted *Le Monde* to the papers that grew up in the Resistance, charging that it was still the organ of big financial interests, but now in collusion with high-level civil servants named by Vichy who were still at their posts.[73] One week later, on Monday, 18 December, the first *Le Monde* appeared. Renewing a *Le Temps* tradition, it was dated the following day and in other respects, apart from the title, the format seemed almost identical to the great liberal daily.

In fact, however, despite the similarity in appearance and the fact that most of the old *Le Temps* staff joined the new paper, Beuve-Méry's *Monde* was, from the outset, something different. Working there was not just a job, as would be made evident on the occasions when there were large rallies of support for Beuve-Méry involving Uriage alumni, during the two major crises threatening Beuve-Méry's direction. As one of the alumni recalled, "We would have done anything to save *Le Monde*."

Le Monde was, at the beginning, a bit Uriage. The journalists were poorly paid. There was a total selflessness and an extraordinary moral rigour. It was the values of Uriage incarnated in the press ... It seemed to us an exemplary paper and Beuve, for me, incarnated the perfection that we had dreamed of, hoped for, during the war. There were many of us who subscribed to *Le Monde* from the first issue, and that meant for life.[74]

In the words of a sympathetic historian, the teams of *Le Monde* and of the École Nationale des Cadres d'Uriage "resembled one another like two sisters" and there was "a very close proximity between the spirit of the school and the positions on day-to-day issues taken by the paper."[75] Old *Esprit* hand and personalist essayist Pierre-Henri Simon became the chief literary critic, while Jean Lacroix kept personalism in the mainstream of French intellectual life with his philosophical essays and reviews.

Beuve-Méry's newspaper was certainly the greatest postwar success of the French press. Created in December 1944, *Le Monde* reached 100,000 copies in 1945, 200,000 in 1958, and 550,000 in 1975. In 1987 its circulation was around 500,000. From the sociological point of view, it built its appeal by addressing a France of teachers and *cadres*, and its success was a reflection of the rise of the very same middle and upper-middle classes whose mentality and opinions it helped form.[76] And *Le Monde* came to have the particular virtues and vices of its founder, and of the Uriage school he had done so much to shape.

Beuve-Méry's former comrade René Courtin, soon to be his critic and rival in a power struggle at the paper, recalled how from the first days of *Le Monde* "Beuve" was a driven man,

arriving early in the morning, cutting short his meals, always the last one to stay at the office, reducing his absences to the minimum. He imposed on himself the scrupulous duty of rereading all the papers, directly and firmly orienting the editorials, watching over the administration and the accounts, negotiating with the workshop. Suspicious, Beuve-Méry sniffed out and combatted all those who came from outside to lay traps for him or his paper. Indulging in neither the spirit of comradeship or that of complacency, impervious to the flattery of the famous and the intoxication of power, he lent maximum class and dignity to the paper; personally indifferent to riches although without wealth, living modestly, he little by little acquired a tacit and unquestioned authority.

Beuve-Méry was not only an honest man but also a sensitive one.

But Courtin also saw the passionate blind-spots in his former colleague:

For him, the quality of the inspiration was much more important than the quality of the results. A Catholic liberated from all conformity, and so truly Christian, he sought above all the safeguarding and perfection of man. Civilization only had meaning in his eyes when it was at the service of the person. His ideal was the communitarian society, and the individualistic impulse seemed of satanic inspiration to him.

Thus, as Courtin seems to imply, Beuve-Méry had the virtues – and vices – one might expect to find in an elite religious order like those Dominicans who had nurtured him in his youth: he was ascetic, high-class, extremely moral, and lived for the joy of working within a tightly knit fraternal community toward achieving excellence and collective perfection. But he had a visceral dislike for individualism, self-indulgence, and luxury; he also had a strong prudish side, and feared the effects of "American culture" on old Europe. He also distrusted unbridled democracy, hated anarchy, and disdained the vulgar tastes of the masses – as would be evident in his abhorrence of the events of May 1968 in France. If France would have to choose between American "immorality" and Eastern bloc puritanism, which would he chose?

In Courtin's words, Beuve-Méry's "rare qualities" were "unhappily offset by terrible weaknesses":

Beuve-Méry came from an obscure background and had had a difficult youth. Such a rise to prominence as his, just because it was exceptional and meritorious, would constitute a difficult challenge for any man to surmount. Vulgar souls tend to draw an unpleasant vanity from their success and repudiate their origins which they then try to hide, by adopting the worst faults of the bourgeoisie. Beuve-Méry's complex attests to a quite different quality of soul but is no less redoubtable. He feels an immense contempt for all those who occupy an important place, who have succeeded – particularly "capitalists," and politicians even more, doubtless because they lack true values in his eyes. That contempt covers another, carefully hidden, complex, of which one cannot know whether it is a complex of inferiority or superiority, the two feelings remaining ambivalent. His sensitivity is all the more intense for his health being poor, and he mulls over his bitterness during an insomniac's long nights.[77]

Beuve-Méry suffered from those profound tensions that sometimes characterize clerical personalities: experiencing the distance of the gnostic who felt "different" – somehow superior, or is it inferior? – from the self-indulgent mass, and not feeling good about his body ... except when he was punishing it in alpinism. He lived for, drew his inspiration from, the company of ascetic men seeking perfection according to ancient spiritual traditions, together, in a communitarian spirit. And, like Mounier and the rest of the elite of progressive Catholics, he thought the whole of society should be taught to share his values. But since this was not likely, society should allow itself to be led by its best and brightest, the products of its elite schools.

Beuve-Méry's peculiarly puritanical attitude toward money was shared by other serious Catholics of his generation (François Mitterrand is one example) and his repugnance toward luxury and self-indulgence, according to Françoise Giroud, carried over to Le Monde:

He made a point of not being richer than his employees, he made his wife (a comrade from the same faculty) and four sons travel third class. When he broke his leg while mountaineering on some summit where his taciturn alpinist's fancy led him, he refused treatment other than that of the local hospital ... He never forgot that he began his life pulling a push-cart to pay for his studies.

And always the question of purity returned:

But it must be said that to have contempt for money, and what it brings, is relatively easy for a proud man who believes in his mission and who, beyond pleasures, pursues only one joy: the bitter joy of being alone, of being the only one lucid, the only one to stay pure.

Beuve-Méry has more than contempt for money: he is fearful of what it does to corrupt and weaken the best of men. And it's almost a weakness, a fear.[78]

In sum, Beuve-Méry had noble virtues, considerable abilities, and great qualities, but these were offset by Christian-puritan fears and obsessions that would have a decisive effect on his political perspective.

THE ATLANTIC ALLIANCE OR NEUTRALITY: THE CRISIS OF 1951

"It was perhaps in the European question," Bernard Comte concluded, "that the importance of the Uriage spirit for *Le Monde* was most clearly seen."[79] The first crisis that opposed René Courtin to Beuve-Méry was over the signature of the Atlantic Pact and the rivalry between the two superpowers: should *Le Monde* support neutrality or alignment with the United States? In opting for European neutrality in the cold war Beuve-Méry simply applied the old personalist theory of the necessity for a Third Way between communism and capitalism to international problems. As a result, in 1951, Beuve-Méry's directorship was seriously threatened, forcing him to organize a large rally of two or three hundred people. Many alumni of Uriage came who "would have done anything to save *Le Monde*," while his supporters spontaneously formed committees in many departments of France. A meeting organized by Maurice Duverger, Professor of Law (and right-wing journalist during the war) assembled 350 people on 11 December: among them 31 professors from the Sorbonne, the Collège de France, and the faculties, and 36 members of the Conseil d'État, the Cour des Comptes, and the Inspection des finances. They personally signed a motion in support of Beuve-Méry's position,

declaring that if, as a result of a modification in its present management, *Le Monde* stopped offering the guarantees of critical spirit and liberty that give it its value, they would have the right to demand an accounting of those who would bear the grave responsibility of having stripped a newspaper whose independence is indispensable to the international dissemination of French thought of its liberty.[80]

Certainly *Le Monde* had become a precious national asset and a great, independent, journalistic voice. One could also argue, however, that there was a characteristic pretentiousness and self- righteousness about this document: was Beuve-Méry, himself, totally independent of pre-rational ideological commitment? What was *Monde's* conception of "French thought"? Why could not one simply defend competent journalism or the preconditions for objective and lucid analysis? In fact the *Monde* milieu reflected the point of view that everyone had a self-serving ideology – except progressive Catholics, because *they* were committed to "advanced," pure, selfless positions (even when these positions led them to accommodate the Stalinists and weaken the Western alliance). In the *Monde* way of thinking, to be "independent" meant to be free of American "capitalist" influence. But it also meant a pre-rational conviction of the nefarious nature of that capitalism.

THE ÉCOLE NATIONALE D'ADMINISTRATION: NEW REPUBLICAN ELITES

Through Gilbert Gadoffre, and to a certain extent Simon Nora, the old Uriage-Thébaïde team participated in the postwar debates that led to the creation of the École Nationale d'Administration. But the specific project that Gadoffre defended then, the particular school of high civil servants sketched out in *La Somme* on the "Revolution of the twentieth century," does not, in the end, seem to be the one retained by the official in charge of the project, Michel Debré. Among the points *La Somme* made about creating a new national elite school was its insistence on the need to grasp the forces at work: "the unconscious, heredity, obscure instincts. It is impossible to understand the comportment of twentieth-century men in ignoring these things, impossible to understand the temptations to which so many foreign countries have given in, to employ the new knowledge from genetics, organized propaganda, the excitation of collective instincts and sublimations to act upon the masses."

It urged that discipline be maintained: "[Regarding] *Education and the sense of command.* Obedience will always remain the best school for *chefs*, and to accept an almost military rigour from 27 to 30 years of age, to be capable of profiting from it and to come out of it hardened, requires an uncommon strength of character and a profound sense of the value of leadership." It also suggested that an Uriage-like outdoor vigour be required: "Those who bear up poorly under this asceticism will be eliminated: their response to the rigour of the school will have the value of a test. Aerial and mountain sports will develop a taste for risk and initiative in the others, a vigour in reflexes, solidarity in the face of danger."[81]

And while these particular elements of Uriage thinking were not retained in the final project by de Gaulle's lieutenant, Debré, the whole notion of the need for a national managerial elite, and a national elite school to develop them, certainly owed much to the Uriage experience. And, according to an authority on Uriage, "to hear Simon Nora, former director of the ENA, speak of the present and future missions of the school today after forty years of *énarchie*, one can't help but note a bit of the old spirit."[82] At the very least, the École Nationale des Cadres d'Uriage encouraged the mentality that led France to create an École Nationale d'Administration and accept the leading societal roles of its elite graduates.

The creation and duration of the ENA was still another indication that the Uriage community and what it represented before, during, and just after the war is far from dead in contemporary France. There has been surprisingly little soul-searching about the extent or depth of the totalitarian temptation during that period. Indeed, as their survival from Pétainism to Gaullism suggests, Uriage ideas about the need for true community and elite leadership may speak to something very deep in the French, or French Catholic, character. One may attribute the Uriage community's resilience, on the one hand, to a protean ability to accommodate change, à la Talleyrand. Or one may regard it, on the other hand, as having the permanency innate to a group who discovered a "style" suited to the century, if not an eternal truth. There has never been a shortage of voices raised to defend both interpretations.

Epilogue

The École Nationale des Cadres d'Uriage may have been the solitary inspiration of a visionary young cavalry officer but it brought to common fruition a host of important "underground" movements of the 1930s. The euphoria of the great days at the Château Bayard represented the culmination of a period during which the hope of a communitarian spiritual revolution led by the young generated great enthusiasm and hope. The Uriage school brought together some of the best and the brightest young representatives of anti-democratic and anti-liberal thinking that the country had produced since the revolution – philosophers, ethnologists, doctors, economists, legal scholars, physical educationists, psychologists, and theologians. And with the support of the only openly counter-revolutionary French government since the great Revolution, these people saw themselves as having a mandate to invent new ways of educating leaders and new forms of community life, to rethink the country from top to bottom. They did this with enthusiasm, dedication, imagination, and, it must be said, curious results.

A communitarian impulse was essential to the Uriage enterprise: its key men had been nurtured on ancient hierarchical and collective beliefs and practices fused with the elated sense of political and spiritual revival peculiar to the 1930s. While a Catholic core accepted a few other young people sympathetic to "the spiritual" or to the special sense of community the school afforded, the non-believers, Jews, and Protestants remained the exception. Uriage, during its heyday, was fired by its sense of being the linchpin of a conservative revolution, a National Revolution "from above" that would restore spiritual vitality to France, announce a new golden age for the Church, and create a new kind of national community.

While military men and the scouts were important, Catholic churchmen directly or indirectly contributed important features to the Uriage style. While women did make up a part of the Uriage experience, it was essentially a matter of a community of men – hard on themselves as well as the young who were put in their charge, rejoicing in the collective, communal quest for perfection and the fraternal joy that it brought. The Uriage community became, as the chaplain remarked, bonded by a relationship comparable to marriage.

The peculiar conditions of war had united them, and peacetime saw a profound nostalgia for the experience. For many, as one of them put it, the end of the Uriage community was "the end of happiness." There was little sympathy for women's liberation at Uriage but a good deal of chagrin over the fact that, after the war, people married and got involved with their families and could no longer live as *moines-chevaliers*.

Again and again, the memoirs of the *chefs* of Uriage reveal a nostalgia – but not so much for living and dying for a great ideal, or for the liberation of their country, as for an experience of adventure, intellectual and spiritual communion, and virile fraternity. For many of them this need seemed to have been rooted in strong (by our standards, oppressive) Catholic backgrounds, and a form of mystical prayer life, which seemed powerful and on the rise fifty years ago but, apart from certain intense marginal groups, has all but disappeared from contemporary France.

In 1940 men of this cast of mind thought they enjoyed as much support for their views than at any time since the Enlightenment and the French Revolution. And the brightest people at Uriage even dreamed of rolling back both, of launching the movement for a New Middle Ages from their Alpine castle. For many writers and artists who perceived the Vichy regime, at least in the early period, as something special, distinct, original, even precious, Uriage was the high point. For there, young men lived out a very new (and very old) way of being French, a "Revolution of the twentieth century" that, while proudly independent and not subservient, allowed the French people to create communities partaking of the benefits of the post-liberal and post-individualistic European New Order.

Did Uriage articulate a "French Fascism" or "French National Socialism"? The men of Uriage would have found the terms much too crude and reductionist to adequately describe their aspirations. What they wanted was a civilized and spiritualized national community that could stand on its own in a new kind of Europe, after the "Revolution of the twentieth century" had finally put liberalism and parliamentary democracy, as well as capitalism and marxism, to rest. This was why, at the liberation, they could not share the national joy at the arrival of the Americans with their jeeps, chewing gum, dollars, and sanguine assumption that Old France would become "Just Like Them."

It must be said that for all of their resentment at the defeat, and their sufferings under the occupation, many Uriage people found something both repulsive and fascinating about the Germans. They certainly did not reject, out of hand, everything the German conservative revolution represented: they even saw world-historical themes that the Germans had missed – from a new approach to ethnology to a daring, new, spiritualized evolutionary theology that brought all modern collective enthusiasms together into a mystical convergence. The latter vision would effect the French Catholic mentality after the war, partly because the Uriage community had learned it first-hand from its most articulate representatives. For the time being, however, the "knight-monks" were content to take from the Germans whatever might prove of methodological use.

The Uriage people were remarkably bright, competent, dedicated, and ambitious. They were extraordinarily successful at eradicating their *pétainiste* image and establishing themselves at the very core of the Resistance. They were very fast on their feet during the liberation – particularly in Grenoble and Paris – and in setting themselves up as the mainstream of the new "Resistance" culture of postwar France. Through all of this, however, they retained that adamant anti-individualism and anti-liberalism rooted in the National Revolution that made one wonder what had happened to the Resistance after all.

Unfortunately, perhaps, these deep impulses led several of them to a rather naive communitarian "dialogue" with Stalinists and to dismissing much of the liberal and democratic heritage of their country as outdated and irrelevant. If Uriage alumni made some rather serious errors in judgment before, during, and after the war, they, like religious sectarians, tended to refuse to admit them. Yet the attraction and power of the "Uriage experience," of "communitarian personalism," was such that they could claim the fidelity of much of an intellectual generation.

This may help us to understand why and how *both* the directors of France's most important newspaper and her most important "humanist" intellectual publication, as well as her most important economist, saw their ideas as in the line of the Uriage experience. The similarities of France's most important interdisciplinary colloquia and France's new École Nationale d'Administration, were no accident. Similar experiences had had decisive effects on a host of young people who were resourceful enough to take advantage of the opportunities that came to them from "out of the blue." Then, too, these people forged bonds between one another in very difficult circumstances and shared a community experience that could be interpreted by hostile (and even objective, or sympathetic) observers as suspect. Thus they formed an Order community with a quasi-religious bond, and stuck together, for the gratification this afforded, as well as for mutual defence and mutual advancement.

An important part of the Uriage legacy was spiritual/religious insofar as several key figures in the movement constituted a sort of mafia in secularized, sceptical France. And although often "socialist" (like François Mitterrand) they were fiercely "anti-materialist" – hence anti-American – but equally anti-Communist, in hoping to "spiritualize" that community (as four years earlier they had sought to "spiritualize" the National Revolution).

The appeal of a tightly knit community of intellectuals in the modern world was certainly a great attraction for the Uriage network, as was the prospect of deferring to authoritative moral figures like Beuve or Mounier who could "lead" complex debates over difficult issues. But certain bottom-line Uriage network positions – for example, Beuve's or Mounier's leadership, sexual liberation, the Vichy experience, distrust of the United States, a "progressive" attitude toward Stalinists – were not subject to much divisive discussion. The men of Uriage could proclaim their love for liberty with great eloquence, yet sometimes find freedom uncomfortable when it came too close to home.

One striking thing about the Uriage group, in retrospect, was the absence of analysis about the factors that led to the rise of an extreme Right in France in the 1930s. Their "Somme" simply avoided situating their own experiences in the context of the rise of fascism. This was the same kind of tunnel vision that made Segonzac so insensitive that he sought to name a "liberation" army corps after one that had earlier refused to join the Resistance. Something deep within these people did not, and does not, want to see mainstream liberal democracy, much less "Americanism," in France: they have a consensus about another kind of Europe – more "spiritual," more communitarian, more "personal." And there remain a number of influential Europeans, and not only the leader of the European Community and the Pope, who were touched – at times directly, often indirectly – by the Uriage experience, or the ideas in vogue there. These figures, born and educated to be leaders, continue fighting, for good or ill, for the community of their dreams.

Notes

INTRODUCTION

1 A considerable controversy was generated by Bernard-Henri Lévy's
L'idéologie française (Paris, 1981) which claimed that there had been a
distinctive French fascist intellectual tradition, and that the Uriage
school was its peak. His book was widely denounced as a careless
polemic, but then the important studies by Zeev Sternhell, *Ni droite ni
gauche. L'idéologie française* (Paris: Seuil, 1983), *Neither Right nor Left,
Fascist Ideology in France*, revised ed. (Berkeley: University of California
Press, 1986), and *Naissance de l'idéologie fasciste* (Paris: Fayard, 1989),
and Philippe Burrin's *La dérive fasciste. Doriot, Déat, Bergery, 1933–
1945* (Paris: Seuil, 1986) made the debate serious among authorities
on the period. See also Michèle Cointet-Labrousse, *Vichy et le fascisme*
(Paris: Brussels, 1987); Pierre Milza, *Fascisme français* (Paris: Flammarion, 1987); Robert Soucy, *French Fascism: The First Wave, 1924–1933*
(New Haven: Yale University Press, 1986).

2 Robert Paxton, author of *La France de Vichy, 1940–1945* (Paris: Seuil,
1973), is, like the leading authority on the Action Française, Eugen
Weber, and the pioneer of the notion of a French Fascism, Robert
Soucy, an American. W.D. Halls, whose *The Youth of Vichy France*
(Oxford: Clarendon Press, 1981) is the best study of the subject, is
English. Philippe Burrin teaches in Geneva and Zeev Sternhell at the
Hebrew University of Jerusalem. Antonio Costa Pinto, who has
written the most balanced assessment of the entire debate to date,
teaches in Lisbon.

3 The most important extant general study is Jacques Duquesne, *Les
Catholiques Français sous l'Occupation*, (slightly) revised edition (Paris:
Grasset, 1986). See also René Bédarida, *Les Armes de l'Esprit, Témoi-
gnage chrétien (1941–1944)* (Paris: Éditions ouvrières, 1977) and *Pierre*

Chaillet. Témoin de la résistance spirituelle (Paris: Fayard, 1988); Gérard Cholvy and Yves-Marie Hilaire, *Histoire religieuse de la France contemporaine*, 3 (1930–1938) (Toulouse: Privat, 1988); Jean-Louis Clément, "Monseigneur Saliège archevêque de Toulouse, 1926–1956" (Ph.D. thesis, Université de Paris, 4, 1990); Adrien Dansette, *Destin du catholicisme français, 1926–1956* (Paris: Flammarion, 1957); Henri de Lubac, *Résistance chrétienne à l'antisémitisme. Souvenirs 1940–1944* (Paris: Fayard, 1988); the research papers in *Églises et chrétiens dans la Deuxième Guerre mondiale. La région Rhône-Alpes*, ed. Xavier de Montclos (Lyon: Presses universitaires de Lyon, 1978) and *Églises et chrétiens dans la Deuxième Guerre mondiale. La France*. (Lyon: Presses universitaires de Lyon, 1982); Msgr Émile Guerry, *L'Église catholique en France sous l'Occupation* (Paris: Flammarion, 1947); André Latreille and René Rémond, *Histoire du catholicisme en France*, 3 (Paris: Spes, 1962); Alain-René Michel, *La JEC. Jeunesse étudiante chrétienne face au nazisme et à Vichy (1938–1944)* (Lille: Presses Universitaires de Lille, 1988); Xavier de Montclos, ed., *Les chrétiens face au nazisme et au stalinisme. L'épreuve totalitaire, 1939–1945* (Paris: Plon, 1983); Émile Poulat, *Naissance des prêtres ouvriers* (Paris: Casterman, 1965); *Spiritualité, théologie et résistance. Yves de Moncheuil, théologien au maquis de Vercors*, Colloque de Biviers (1984), ed. Pierre Bolle and Jean Godel (Grenoble: Presses de l'Université de Grenoble, 1987).

Étienne Fouilloux's article "Instruments, relais, et cadres du régime: Clergé catholique et régime de Vichy," presented to the colloquium "Le régime de Vichy et les Français" of the *Institut d'Histoire du Temps Présent* (CNRS) (Paris, 11–13 June 1990), gives an idea of Professor Fouilloux's important research on the Catholic clergy and the Vichy regime. Paul Christophe's *Les Catholiques devant la guerre, 1939–1940* (Paris: Éditions ouvrières, 1989) provides a new and more lucid perspective, based upon previously unstudied archives, on French Catholics in the period just prior to the establishment of the Vichy regime. A similar viewpoint is reflected in Yves R. Simon's 1941 book *The Road to Vichy, 1918–1938*, revised edition, with a new introduction by John Hellman (Lanham, Maryland: University Press of America, 1988).

4 The citation is from Sternhell, *Neither Right nor Left*, 299. The study of the JEC by Alain-René Michel (*La JEC*), though at times uncritically favourable to his subject, is a well-researched and welcome addition to the literature.

5 W.D. Halls, "Catholicism under Vichy," in *Vichy France and the Resistance. Culture and Ideology*, edited by Roderick Kedward and Roger Austin (Totowa, New Jersey: Barnes and Noble, 1985), 144. This collective volume also contains three essays (of nineteen) much

241 Notes to pages 5–11

concerned with the Uriage school and/or Emmanuel Mounier. One of these is a spirited attack by the long-time representative of the *Esprit* group in Great Britain on certain historians, such as the author, who are reproached for denigrating the reputation of the school (Brian Darling, "Uriage: the Assault on a Reputation," *ibid.*, 147–58). The other two essays (Derek Robbins, "Uriage: the Influence of Context on Content," 159–70, and John Wright, "Emmanuel Mounier, *Esprit*, and Vichy, 1940–1944: Ideology and Anti-ideology," 171–88) are useful and more even-handed. The volume has been unjustly ignored by French scholars.

6 Roderick Kedward, "Introduction," Kedward and Austin, *Vichy France*, 3.

7 Charles de Gaulle, in the mid-1930s, was one of the first members of the "Amis de *Temps Présent*," joining a section near the garrison where he was stationed (Maurice Schumann, Alexandre Marc, interviews with the author).

8 ["Je rejetais totalement la forme de démocratie parlementaire que nous avions vécue, avec toute cette comédie de gouvernements qui accomplissaient un record de longévité quand ils avaient duré quinze jours! C'était à vomir. Et je n'ai pas été étonné du tout de la défaite. Au contraire je m'y étais préparé. Et Uriage, pour moi, c'était le désir de participer à un mouvement de remise en cause de la société sur le plan de réformes fondamentales de ses structures. Je voulais qu'il s'opère un 'Octobre 1917' ... Le problème, c'était de mettre en place une société autre que celle qu'on avait connue. C'est tout. C'était la société des hommes qu'il fallait changer. C'était ça la priorité: vivre dans une société autre."] Paul Grillet, cited in Pierre Bitoun, *Les homes d'Uriage* (Paris: La Découverte, 1988), 73.

9 Pierre Dunoyer de Segonzac, in *Le Vieux Chef. Mémoires et pages choisies* (Paris: Seuil, 1971).

10 Among the most prominent cases are the newspaper *Le Monde*, founded by the former director of studies of the École Nationale des Cadres d'Uriage, Hubert Beuve-Méry, with several former instructors or graduates of that elite institution, and *Éditions du Seuil*, which was created by Paul Flamand, a key figure in the Vichy cultural association "Jeune France." For "Jeune France," see the excellent study by Christian Faure, *Le projet culturel de Vichy. Folklore et révolution nationale, 1940–1944* (Lyon: Presses Universitaires de Lyon, 1989).

For a recent pained reflection on the ability of the "Uriage mafia" to punish the school's critics, see Bernard-Henri Lévy, "Et puis il y a Uriage," in *Les aventures de la liberté* (Paris: Grasset, 1991), 159.

M. Lévy comments that "my taking that fascinating episode [of Uriage] as an example of the tenacious obscurity in which much of

242 Notes to pages 12–14

our contemporary history remains shrouded made me the object of a campaign of misinformation and calumny; some day I shall reveal its events and hidden side."

11 See John Hellman, "Personnalisme et fascisme" (with responses from Denis de Rougemont, Paulette Mounier, Jean-Marie Domenach) in *Le Personnalisme d'Emmanuel Mounier, hier et demain. Pour un cinquantenaire* (Paris: Seuil, 1985), 116–42.

12 The work of a scholar who, for several years, had regularly defended the reputations of the Uriage school and Emmanuel Mounier as bastions of the Resistance, Professor Comte's 1,246-page thesis, "L'École Nationale des Cadres d'Uriage. Une communauté éducative non-conformiste à l'époque de la révolution nationale (1940–1942)" (Lyon, 1987), his life's work, is a significant scholarly achievement and has brought to light a great deal of material. An abridged version, with some modifications, was published as *Une utopie combattante. L'école des Cadres d'Uriage, 1940–1942* (Paris: Fayard, 1991).

13 "Préface," in Comte, *Une utopie*, 9, 12.

14 Professor Comte commented: "I preferred the risk of seeming too close to the men I studied and too understanding of what one could call their naiveté or prejudices, rather than remaining alien to their mentality and their motivations. Moreover, in abundantly citing texts and evoking critical interpretations, I have given my readers the possibility to look at things in a different light and form their own conclusions based on the facts, and not on approximations and the simplifications of superficial information." We must be grateful to him for that. Comte, *Une utopie*, 18.

15 Ibid., 549.

16 Pierre Bitoun's *Les hommes d'Uriage*, based primarily on interviews, celebrates "the men of Uriage," and clarifies the influence of the school at the time of the liberation and in the postwar period. Sociologist Antoine Delestre's *Uriage, une communauté et une école dans la tourmente, 1940–1945* (Nancy: Presses Universitaires de Nancy, 1989) employed some valuable new primary source material, much of it supplied by his uncle Paul de la Taille, former secretary to the head of the school, and brought the story of the Uriage movement beyond 1942, to the end of the war. Professor Delestre also clarified the fascism issue by demonstrating that Uriage was *pétainiste* in the eyes of important elements of the Resistance, and of General de Gaulle.

17 Pierre Giolitto, *Histoire de la jeunesse sous Vichy* (Paris: Perrin, 1991), 649.

18 Daniel Lindenberg, *Les années souterraines, 1937–1947* (Paris: La Découverte, 1990), 95–6, 101, 105–6, 112, 132, 135–6, 182, 201–2, 207–9, 214–46, 265–67.

19 In 1974, M. Hubert Beuve-Méry encouraged the author to consult
his extensive archives on the Uriage school which were then the exclusive purview of Professor Comte, who had already been doing
research on the school for a number of years as his doctoral project.
But M. Beuve-Méry was subsequently, and to his regret, dissuaded
from this course by the historian directing Comte's work. One month
before his death in 1989, Beuve-Méry, along with Pierre Dunoyer de
Segonzac's former secretary, Paul de la Taille, painstakingly oversaw
the transfer of a truckload of Uriage materials to the Archives départementales de l'Isère in Grenoble where they are presently being
classified for access by the general public. The author is grateful to
M. Yves Soulingeas, Directeur des Services d'Archives de l'Isère, for
his permission to study these one hundred and sixty dossiers before
the classification process was complete. His assistant, M. Jacques Mau-
rier, and other members of the archival staff, were also very courteous
and helpful. M. Beuve-Méry's amused encouragement and proud
fidelity to the Uriage experience were also important.

A number of the archival references given in this book were temporary and may be different in the final Archives départementales de
l'Isère classification system. All subsequent archival references are to
this material or Uriage material previously deposited in the Grenoble
archives unless otherwise noted.

CHAPTER ONE

1 Eugen Weber, *Action Française* (Stanford: Stanford University Press,
1962), 444.
2 Bernard Comte, "L'École Nationale des Cadres d'Uriage. Une communauté éducative non-conformiste à l'époque de la révolution nationale (1940–1942)" Ph.D. thesis, Université de Lyon 2, 1987, 23, 25,
29. Hereafter cited as "Uriage."
3 There is a vivid portrait of him in Simone de Beauvoir's memoirs of
the period of her Catholic schooling, *Mémoires d'une jeune fille rangée*
(Paris: Gallimard, 1958), 251. Garric was also a founder of the *Cité
Universitaire* of Paris.
4 Robert Garric, *Le message de Lyautey* (Paris: Spes, 1935).
5 Paul Doncoeur, *Cadets* (Paris: Art Catholique, 1924).
6 Comte, "Uriage," 62–3.
7 Weber, *Action Française*, 444–5.
8 Massis's attachment to the legacy of his old friend Péguy was behind a
persistent personal animosity toward the young Catholic editor of the
review *Esprit*, Emmanuel Mounier. Mounier's first book – a contribution to a collective work on Péguy published in the late 1920s – Massis

Notes to pages 17–20

had found misguided, falsely "Péguyist" and pretentious (Paul Mazgaj (authority on Massis), letter to the author, 30 November 1989).

9 Gillouin had been a telling critic of the Action Française before turning Maurrassian, and then openly pro-fascist, himself. Cf. Weber, *Action française*, 195.

10 Cf. Comte, "Uriage," 63. Vichy's leadership schools were created at a time when the regime was interested not simply in revitalizing the youth of the country but also in furnishing "new men" to replace the "decadent" "old elites".

11 On Alibert see W.D. Halls, "Catholicism under Vichy: A Study in Diversity and Ambiguity", in *Vichy France and the Resistance. Culture and Ideology*, ed. Roderick Kedward and Roger Austin (Totowa, New Jersey: Barnes and Noble, 1985), 134–5.

12 Comte, "Uriage," 23, 108.

13 This rather utopian and apocalyptic group had close ties to other young visionaries such as those of the Esprit and Ordre Nouveau groups.

14 Most of my information on this society comes from my interviews with Alexandre Marc and the Marc correspondence. See also Comte, "Uriage," 53.

15 Comte, "Uriage," 1119, 1121–2.

16 Segonzac himself came from a very large family by today's standards. On 16 September 1937, he had married, at Saint-Félix-Laurageias (Haute Garonne), Mlle Marie-Antoinette de Roquette-Buisson, daughter of a cavalry officer. In spite of the privations of the war years, they would have ten children. Antoine Delestre, *Uriage, une communauté et une école dans la tourmente, 1940–1945* (Nancy: Presses Universitaires de Nancy, 1989), 11.

Other officer-instructors at the school would also have very large families. Segonzac's early co-director at Uriage, Eric d'Alançon, even outdid him by having sixteen children.

17 This book reflected the ideas of the Ordre Nouveau and Esprit groups to which de Rougemont belonged. Cf. Comte, "Uriage," 78, 335.

18 For an account of this campaign, see Pierre Dunoyer de Segonzac, *Le Vieux Chef. Mémoires et pages choisies* (Paris: Seuil, 1971), 70–2. See also Delestre, *Uriage*, 11.

19 Along with Captains Xavier de Virieu and Huet. Xavier de Virieu was the scion of a noble family considered historical rivals to the Alleman family of Uriage. He may have had something to do with the confiscating of the Château Bayard as site for the school, and would certainly play a crucial role in Segonzac's career during the last two years of the occupation. In the final months of the war, he would

try to re-establish a leadership school "for the Resistance" in the Uriage château. The "cercles sociaux" seem to have had much the same mentality and objectives as Robert Garric's Équipes sociales and, like them, furnished dedicated personnel for Vichy efforts to break down class barriers among young people in the name of patriotism and spiritual values.

20 Pierre Goutet.

21 Cf. Delestre, *Uriage*, 10–13.

22 Cf. Dunoyer de Segonzac, *Le Vieux Chef*, 81.

23 The idea that Segonzac, a patriot bitter at the defeat, went alone to Vichy and persuaded the naive authorities there to set up a school to revitalize the country and prepare resistance to the occupant is central to the Uriage myth. But even Bernard Comte, despite his sympathies for Segonzac, felt obliged to point out that Segonzac's project was, from the outset, cautioned against by the highest governmental authorities and envisaged by them as playing a central role in the National Revolution. Cf. Comte, "Uriage," 85.

Comte often seems drawn to supporting his subject's interpretation and describing Uriage as very unimportant and marginal in the Vichy context; at other times Comte is drawn to admitting the importance of Segonzac's project to the highest French authorities. Clearly Segonzac and his closest associates, for whatever reason, later downplayed their high-level support, and importance within the early National Revolution.

24 This is an important contradiction to the drift of Segonzac's subsequent narrative: the founder of Uriage wanted it understood, after the war, that the school had been an eccentric personal, marginal, "Resistance" project to put young people back on their feet again. He wanted it thought that the enterprise had been cleverly carried on under Vichy's nose, as it were ... and that it had not been, as some had claimed, the establishment institution for developing the teachers of Vichy's "new men," the elites who were to work to change the country according to the ideals of the National Revolution.

25 Cf. Comte, "Uriage," 87, 89, 95.

26 Delestre, *Uriage*, 19–20, 22.

27 Daniel Lindenberg, *Les années souterraines, 1937–1947* (Paris: La Découverte, 1990), 200–1.

28 In the period before the war the "cercles sociaux" of officers, created in 1934, touched "around fifty garrisons in France" and "nearly a thousand officers" (according to Général de la Chapelle, cited by Robert Hervet in *Les Chantiers de la Jeunesse* (Paris: France Empire, 1952), 261–2). According to de La Chapelle, the members of these "cercles" circulated minutes of their individual meetings with the

representatives of youth movements (scouts and *jocistes* in particular) to one another.

These "cercles" made up a significant, if still largely unknown, part of the background to the National Revolution of Vichy as "particularly after the social and political events of 1936," they grouped together to discuss social issues. Among the future Vichy youth organization leaders were Dunoyer de Segonzac (Uriage), Tournemire (Compagnons de France), Gèze, Virieu, Courson, Nouvel, Montjamont, Goussault (Chantiers de la Jeunesse).

29 Cf. Pierre Bitoun, *Les hommes d'Uriage* (Paris: La Découverte, 1988) 41.

30 Raymond Hubert, a lawyer, like his friend Lamour.

31 Raymond Hubert had rented the farm and the agricultural *domaine dépendant* on the Château to two aspiring farmers. One was the lawyer Philippe Lamour, former youth leader in Georges Valois's *Faisceau* (France's first fascist movement), pioneer of Franco-German youth contacts, and editor of the avant-garde review *Plans* in which what would become Uriage ideas (such as communitarian personalism) were articulated in the early 1930s. By this time Lamour had become, he later recalled, a militant anti-fascist (Lamour interview with Christian Roy).

32 "Always Ready!" was the French Scout slogan.

33 Philippe Lamour's description of Dunoyer de Segonzac's visit to La Faulconnière is in his memoirs, *Le cadran solaire* (Paris: Robert Laffont, 1980), 199–200.

34 Most possessed the *baccalauréat* and seemed to have been practising Catholics.

35 Comte, "Uriage," 98; M. Chombart de Lauwe vociferously rejected the allegation of Eugen Weber, in his *Action Française* (445), that he had been a member of the Action Française.

36 This movement later fused with the maverick young radical leader Gaston Bergery's Parti Frontiste, in which Izard took an important post for a time. Bergery became an influential figure in Pétain's entourage in the early Vichy regime and eventually defended the Esprit group at Uriage against their critics in the meeting of the National Council of the National Revolution.

37 The trip is described by Jacques Madaule, *L'absent* (Paris: Gallimard, 1973), 115–16. The Abbé de Naurois was also a close friend of André Déléage, a co-founder of *Esprit*, whom Emmanuel Mounier had to keep at arm's length because of his volatile temperament and his excessive sympathy for what Mounier called "certain Hitlerite themes." Déléage's style troubled the prominent *Esprit* backer Jacques Maritain.

247 Notes to pages 23–6

Cf. John Hellman, *Emmanuel Mounier and the New Catholic Left, 1930–1950* (Toronto: University of Toronto Press, 1981), 44–8, 53, 77, 94.

38 According to de Naurois: "I had a friend called Henri Ripert, an alpinist, son of a colonel from Grenoble, with whom I became friends during the period when, doing my military service in Grenoble, I met his family and we did alpinism together ... I did not yet have a post in my diocese because the outbreak of war surprised me in Berlin where I was studying. So I was available ... Henri Ripert wrote to me that Dunoyer de Segonzac was looking for a chaplain for an 'école de chefs.' I went to see Segonzac at Vichy. We lunched together and at the end of the lunch he told me: 'You're hired.' My bishop [Msgr Salièe, his relative and a special friend of the personalist milieu] agreed to lend me to Segonzac, as chaplain of the school, I was thirty-four years old." Cited in Delestre, *Uriage*, 18.

39 Comte, "Uriage," 128. The subsequent expropriation of the Château d'Uriage was even more heavy-handed, and demonstrative of high-level support from an authoritarian government.

40 Delestre, *Uriage*, 19.

41 Comte, "Uriage," 107, 128.

42 "We had problems organizing our second session," one of the instructors, Jean Devictor, indicated, "because Général de La Porte du Theil, head of the Chantiers, did not want to hear anything about Uriage." "He didn't understand that duplication of the training of youth," Commander de la Chapelle confirmed. According to Inspector General Basdevant's recollections, the head of the Chantiers caused the rupture between the Chantiers and Segonzac's school because he himself had not created the latter. Cited by R. Josse, in "L'École des cadres d'Uriage, 1940–42," *Revue d'histoire de la Deuxième Guerre Mondiale* 61 (January 1966): 55, n.2.

43 Comte, "Uriage," 112–13, 126; Robert O. Paxton, *La France de Vichy, 1940–1944* (Paris: Seuil, 1973), 162–3.

44 Comte, "Uriage," 114, 116–17.

45 Delestre, *Uriage*, 24.

46 Prominent among them was Joffre Dumazedier, a member of the *ajiste* movement (auberges de la jeunesse), who came from outside of that Catholic, royalist, often professionally military, network that furnished so many of the school's instructors. Dumazedier would become an important representative of the non-Catholics in the school. Cf. Delestre, *Uriage*, 25.

47 Almost all of the postwar reconstructions of the history of the school, including Segonzac's (cf. *Le Vieux Chef*), took the line that what became the Uriage School was a personal initiative of Segonzac's, and

had been created, and continued, because of the ignorance or indifference of Vichy authorities.

48 Comte, "Uriage," 121, 123; W.D. Halls, *The Youth of Vichy France* (Oxford: Clarendon Press, 1981), 18.

49 And, as we shall see, there would be tensions between Segonzac and that school over its nazified style.

50 Bitoun, *Les hommes*, 38.

51 According to Uriage school legend, the neglected Château and a neighbouring property were simply taken over from a restaurant-keeper. Cf. Delestre, *Uriage*, 34. But according to the Templeton family, present owners of the Château, the circumstances were far more dramatic and brutal. The young countess who had inherited the Château from her childless uncle a few years before represented the same Alleman family that had owned the castle for one thousand years and maintained a private family museum (including a "Bayard room" which boasted original medieval furnishings associated with the great knight, and items given the family by the grateful archaeologist Champollion) and a substantial art collection.

  The countess was at her severely war-wounded aviator-husband's bedside in the American hospital of Paris when she was told that "the army had taken over the Uriage Château." She rushed down to Grenoble to find the property under seal but she entered, with the aid of family servants, during the night and was able to cut some of the family paintings from their frames and salvage them. As in similar cases at the time, the countess was given the choice of disputing the government's confiscatory action (in very difficult and unpromising circumstances) or accepting an inequitable cash settlement. She chose the latter and so ended the Alleman family's thousand-year proprietorship of the Château Bayard – but not the bitterness over the expropriation, both in the Alleman family and in the Uriage area. After the war the castle belonged to the French army, which neglected it, until it was bought by the Templetons.

52 The painting was reproduced on the front page of the 22 March 1941 issue of *Jeunesse ... France!* where it was described as "moving" and attributed to "Madame Malespina, wife of an artist-instructor" at the school.

53 With the kind guidance of the present proprietors, the author was able to visit the chateau, which has been closed to the public since 1945, in July 1990, as repairs and renovations were beginning. A few souvenirs of Segonzac's school and of the Milice remained: symbols chalked or painted on the walls and, according to the Templetons, a skeleton found in the well. There is a vivid description of a visit to

Segonzac at the chateau in Roger Stéphane, *Chaque homme est lié au monde* (Paris: Le Sagittaire, 1946), 166.

54 Comte, "Uriage," 134.

55 This figure was confirmed in relevant legislation on 11 August 1941, and varied according to the different states of the training, and needs for auxiliary personnel at the school, between 1941 and 1942, according to the school archives (102 J 12). Cf. Delestre, *Uriage*, 35.

56 *Journal Officiel*, 1 January 1941; Delestre, *Uriage*, 35. In January 1940 one u.s. dollar was worth almost thirty francs.

According to the Uriage archives (102 J 12) the key personnel received the following salaries: Dunoyer de Segonzac: Fr 4,167, Beuve-Méry: Fr 3,900, Chombart de Lauwe: Fr 3,000, Paul de la Taille: Fr 3,000.

According to Daniel Lindenberg, it took 3,500 francs a month to support the average family, and certain workers' salaries – which would remain frozen during the duration of the war – were Fr 4.5 francs an hour. In contrast, Georges Suarez made at least Fr 30,000 a month for his writings in the collaborationist paper *Paris allemand*, as did the director of a Parisian art gallery who worked with the same sorts of people. A chic restaurant in Paris could cost Fr 400 a head at this time. Lindenberg, *Années*, 134.

57 They were also supplied with a pair of half-boots with leather laces, a pair of wooden shoes, a pair of slippers [*chaussons*], two pairs of socks, a blue jersey, athletic pants, a canvas covering, and a canvas jacket. Cf. Delestre, *Uriage*, 39.

58 Delestre, *Uriage*, 55. Segonzac took it upon himself to exercise a de facto surveillance over the religious practices of Catholics, as we shall see illustrated in several instances.

59 Comte, "Uriage," 140–1. Could one imagine "consecrating" a graduating class in a republican leadership school, such as the postwar École Nationale d'Administration?

60 Cf. the lectures of M. Courrière, 17 October 1940, mimeographed text of 14 pages (school archives). Lectures given in October 1940 are in the Uriage archives (102 J 39). (This particular one is also cited in Delestre, *Uriage*, 22.)

61 This frail intellectual's experiences while working in factories in 1934–35 became notorious with the publication of her factory journals, *La condition ouvrière* (Paris: Gallimard, 1951). She was able to get her initial job at the Alsthom factory with the help of a company administrator, Auguste Detoeuf, a friend of hers who was interested in helping efforts of intellectuals and economic planners to make peace between the classes in France. Similar goals would inspire Vichy

legislation. See her essay "Expérience de la vie d'usine," *Économie et Humanisme*, Marseille, 2 (June-July 1942), 187–204.

62 Comte, "Uriage," 120, 141.

63 Cf. Ibid., 211.

64 Ibid., 209. Perhaps the most thoroughgoing criticism of Vichy's measures toward the French trade union movement was the impressive book *Traditionnalisme et syndicalisme* (New York: Éditions de la Maison Française, 1943) written in exile in the United States by the Catholic trade union leader and medieval historian Paul Vignaux.

65 Delestre, *Uriage*, 23.

66 Ibid., 56. For some reason, the seminal roles of Garric and his *équipes* are never given their due by the alumni of the school despite near unanimity among historians on their importance. Perhaps Garric and the *équipes* were, in retrospect, too embarrassingly "Catholic" for a school that became defensive about the charge of clericalism. It may also be related to the general tendency to minimize the role of Catholics in the ideological origins of the National Revolution.

67 Cited in Bitoun, *Les hommes*, 44.

68 De Naurois later claimed (interview cited in Bitoun, *Les hommes*, 48) to have attended the founding congress of *Esprit* at the resort village of Font-Romeu in the Pyrénées in the summer of 1932, but there is no mention of him in Mounier's detailed, unpublished diary account of the discussions among the fewer than twenty participants during that week. When Mounier met him in 1935, he described de Naurois in his diary as a "turbulent seminarian ... sympathetic to us" who, after a discussion on marxism with two socialists, took him to see Msgr Saliège, "the socialist bishop ... who told me that marxism is the most beautiful spiritualist movement of the nineteenth century." (Mounier, "Carnets 8", 9 March 1935) (unpublished).

De Naurois's friend André Déléage did, however, lead a delegation of six from Toulouse (including an experienced older man who had been a member of Georges Valois's French fascist movement, the Faisceau) to that Font-Romeu meeting and, in effect, unsuccessfully tried to take over the journal *Esprit* by making it the organ of a new international workers' organization. Mounier disapproved of what he called "the Hitlerite language" in Déléage's plans for the personalist movement. See John Hellman, "The Origins of *Esprit*: Ecumenism, Fascism, and the New Catholic Left," *Third Republic/Troisième République* 9 (spring 1980): 63–122.

69 André Déléage led a group of forty Third Force militants to participate in what were later perceived to be proto-fascist anti-government riots during the dramatic evening of 6 February 1934. See Hellman, *Mounier*, 77.

70 On Izard's role within Bergery's party see Philippe Burrin, *La dérive fasciste, Doriot, Déat, Bergery, 1933–1945* (Paris: Seuil, 1968).
Here are de Naurois's recollections of those years: "I was at the founding Congress of *Esprit* at Font-Romeu. That even led me farther. While remaining extremely tied by friendship and even affection for Mounier, I had much more faithfully followed, with an even more profound intellectual and spiritual complicity, a boy who died in 1944, killed in the war, André Déléage. He was librarian at the University of Toulouse at the time and often came to see me in the seminary. Through him [Déléage] I was in contact with Georges Izard, the founder of the Third Force – who had fused with Bergery's movement: one didn't know who Bergery was at the time; there was a latent irony to the period. I remember a Third Force Congress at Tours. Though I was a seminarian, who is cloistered like a monk, I obtained the authorization of the superior to go to that congress. On either side of the speaker's platform there were red flags. A communist saw me, a priest, an ecclesiastic in a soutane! He attacked Georges Izard, the president, saying: 'You are kidding, you are not serious, you have a priest with you.' But Izard took it lightly and made a joke of it, asking me to step forward and make a few remarks. I was capable of making virulent anti-capitalist declarations at the time. I was very sensitive about that. I did not see any possible accommodation with, or remedy for, the vices of capitalism" (Abbé de Naurois interview, recorded in Bitoun, *Les hommes*, 35).

71 For a description of a trip to Germany that de Naurois organized for the "amis d'*Esprit*," see Jacques Madaule's *L'Absent*, 111ff. See also, Bitoun, *Les hommes*, 35; Comte, "Uriage," 144.
André Déléage, a librarian at the University of Toulouse and student of Marc Bloch under whose direction he earned a doctorate in history, was a fervent admirer of what was going on among German youth before Hitler came to power, and had played a decisive role in the founding of *Esprit*. The swashbuckling Déléage was helped by Georges Izard in his effort to turn members of that journal's activist auxiliary, the "Third Force," into the street-fighters he led during the ominous anti-Republican riots that nearly toppled the government on the night of 6 February 1934. Emmanuel Mounier finally became disquieted by Déléage's rhetoric and, at Jacques Maritain's insistence, he worked to disassociate him from *Esprit*. On Déléage see Hellman, *Mounier*, 37–9, 41, 44–8, 51, 53, 77, 94, 104, 131.

72 Years later, this is what Chombart de Lauwe recalled: "I was much marked by my work with the Équipes sociales of Garric, particularly at the time of my military service ... Also, I wanted to do a doctoral thesis on youth. And I began with Germany and Italy. That made me

sense what Nazism was. And then I met de Naurois at Berlin where he already knew of the existence of the camps. ... [and he] spoke to me in Berlin of Dachau." Bitoun, *Les hommes*, 50.

In fact, an interest in German youth was a particular characteristic of the Uriage circle, as we shall see: Hubert Beuve-Méry, who would become director of the Study Bureau, published a notable book on Germany, *Vers la plus grande Allemagne*, in 1939, and had a particular interest in efforts to transform German (and Portuguese) youth, as did Emmanuel Mounier (who had ties with young Harro Schulze-Boysen and the Strasser-wing of the National Socialists). Mounier's close friend Jean Lacroix studied and wrote on adolescents thus exemplifying a persistent special concern at *Esprit* and Uriage, where changing the mentality of young people was seen as the key to changing society as a whole.

On the links between Franco-German youth contacts in the early 1930s and the Uriage school, see John Hellman and Christian Roy, "Contacts et convergences des non-conformistes de France et d'Allemagne autour de 'l'Ordre Nouveau' et de 'Gegner' (1930–1942)," papers presented to the International Colloquium *Les relations culturelles franco-allemandes dans les années 1930*, 1 (Paris: Deutscher akademischer Austauschdienst & Institut d'histoire du temps présent (CNRS), 1990), 35–46.

73 Cf. Comte, "Uriage," 207–8, 226.

74 Cited in Bitoun, *Les hommes*, 73–4, 82.

75 At one point, Bergery decisively defended it, as we shall see. Bergery's "Front Commun" and "Parti Frontiste" were built from members of *Esprit*'s "Third Force," notably André Déléage's best friend and *Esprit* co-founder Georges Izard, and Robert Aron, co-founder of *Ordre Nouveau* (and future historian of the Vichy regime). On this see Hellman, *Mounier*, and Philippe Burrin, *La dérive fasciste*.

76 "La Voie française et les exemples étrangers," *Jeunesse ... France!* 1 (December 1940). A complete collection of this periodical is in the Uriage archives (22 J 43).

77 Alexandre Marc and René Dupuis, *Jeune Europe* (Paris: Plon, 1933). In this book, the young German-speaking Russian exile Alexandre Marc (Lipiansky) drew a comparative portrait of European youth movements, which included a rich description of the situation in Germany, where Marc's charismatic friends were struggling against Hitler and his followers for control of the German youth movement.

In Germany, Paul Distelbarth, an influential intellectual, subsequently painted an optimistic portrait of the French youth movement, stressing the central role of the Catholics, in his *Neues werden in Frankreich* (Stuttgart: Ernst Klett, 1938), 180–3.

See Hellman and Roy, "Contacts et convergences."

78 See Pierre Ordioni, *Tout commence à Alger, 1940–1944* (Paris: Stock, 1972), 106–15, on the Catholic intellectual revival as central to the effort of the sgj to create a distinctively Catholic "order" in France.

79 Delestre, *Uriage*, 35n.7.

80 Comte, "Uriage," 135–6, 138.

81 Conclusion of Lamirand's speech to the youth festival in Toulouse on 29 December 1940. Reprinted in Georges Lamirand, *Messages à la jeunesse* (Clermont-Ferrand: Éditions Sorlot, 1941), 15–16.

82 The late Jean Lacroix told me that he went to Uriage at Mounier's urging. He seemed decidedly uncomfortable in discussing the school, not at all proud of the experience (despite the fact that he remained on the staff after Mounier was forbidden to lecture there) (interview with the author, 2 August 1973).

83 Delestre, *Uriage*, 61. When Mounier and Lacroix were invited to go to Uriage, they were also encouraged by another priest-friend, the Jesuit Lucien Fraisse, who knew several instructors at the school (testimony of Father Fraisse, cited in Delestre, *Uriage*, 61).

Fraisse's brother Paul, later professor of psychology at the Sorbonne, was a close associate of Mounier just before the war and after the liberation, when he would live with Mounier and several Uriage veterans in "Les Murs Blancs" community at Châtenay-Malabry, near Paris. "Les Murs Blancs" was originally intended to become a centre for the training of adolescents but became, instead, a sort of commune for key personalities of the journal *Esprit* and the personalist movement. After Mounier's death in 1950, Professor Fraisse, as president of the "Amis d'Emmanuel Mounier" for many years, espoused Mounier's intellectual legacy.

84 The events were later recalled as follows:
De Naurois: "I met Beuve-Méry at a dinner at the home of Lacroix. He had on riding breeches and *molletières* and didn't have a coat although it was very cold in Lyon. Returning to Uriage, I told Segonzac that we should have Beuve-Méry come to the school, stressing the fact that his family, his wife and four children, were in the occupied zone, that he had no work and that he really had to be in straits to be about in the streets of Lyon that way in the middle of a glacial, damp fog. Segonzac agreed to invite him for two lectures."
Beuve-Méry: "When in October or November 1940, I saw for the first time, at Emmanuel Mounier's, the Abbé René de Naurois, I certainly didn't suspect that our conversation on the disarray of French young people would have such important consequences for me." Cited in Bitoun, *Les hommes*, 46–7.

85 This is a passage omitted from Mounier's diaries as published in his collected *Oeuvres*, 4 (Paris: Seuil, 1963). (Some other unpublished passages are transcribed in Comte, "Uriage," 200, 202.)

254 Notes to pages 34–7

86 Mounier, unpublished diaries, cited in Comte, "Uriage," 219. Apparently, however, Doncoeur – who later seemed far less reticent about the ways of the occupation forces than Segonzac was – would have little to do with Uriage after this.
87 Comte, "Uriage," 225–6.
88 Mounier, "Entretiens 11," 14 January 1941, in Mounier, *Oeuvres*, 4, 688.
89 Cf. Delestre, *Uriage*, 61.
90 Halls, *Youth*, 271.
91 Mounier, *Oeuvres*, 4, 688–9. On Guerry's reticence about the youth movements, see also Halls, *Youth*, 271.

   After the war, Guerry would become the most prominent apologist for the French Catholic Church's actions and attitudes during the occupation, particularly in his book *L'Église catholique en France sous l'Occupation* (Paris: Flammarion, 1947). The forthcoming studies by W.D. Halls, and Étienne Fouilloux, on the church in the period should be of considerable interest.
92 Mounier, *Oeuvres*, 4, 689.
93 Comte, "Uriage," 230. After the war, the men of Uriage would almost all recall that what had been uppermost in their minds at the time was the creation of a tiny island of health and integrity in a "suspect" Vichy regime.
94 Besides Georges Lamirand, whose support for Segonzac would prove unflagging, there was the well-known tennis champion Jean Borotra, and the head of Pétain's Civil Cabinet, Dumoulin de Labarthète, who was the brother of a close friend of Segonzac killed in 1940. Cf. Comte, "Uriage," 267.

   Professor Comte disagrees with P.-H. Chombart de Lauwe's later insistence that Uriage was, from the outset, reticent about Pétain and the National Revolution, and very different from other groups subsidized by the sGJ. The documents show that Uriage was initially devoted to the Marshall, and had close friends at the sGJ. Cf. Comte, "Uriage," 272–3.
95 Mounier, "Entretiens 4" (20 December 1940), *Oeuvres*, 4, 682.
96 Comte, "Uriage," 193.
97 Mounier's lecture was later published, in modified form, as "Pour une charte de l'unité française," *Esprit* 103 (August 1941), 689–711.
98 Comte, "Uriage," 197.
99 But, in any case, Mounier's presence in this Study Bureau was secretly vetoed by higher authorities at Vichy. Mounier, "Entretiens 11" (13 April 1941), *Oeuvres*, 4, 705.
100 Mounier, "Entretiens 11" (28 January 1941), *Oeuvres*, 4, 691.

   Mounier and his friends also feared for the future of the Compagnons movement because of Henri Dhavernas's ambitions there. Cf. Comte, "Uriage," 232.

101 It was later claimed by the alumni of Uriage that the important architect of Vichy youth policy, Henri Massis, had some tense moments with Segonzac when the former visited Uriage in late 1940. But there is some evidence to the contrary (for example, Massis published an essay in *Jeunesse ... France!* after his visit). In any case, while Massis was publicly friendly to Mounier, he had strong reservations about the man and his 1931 book on Péguy as well as about Mounier and *Esprit*'s subsequent growing influence on the younger French intelligentsia (many of whom were Catholics who had previously been involved with the Action Française). Massis seemed to have decided that Mounier's emotive and imprecise thinking would be dangerous at Uriage.

    While Professor Comte describes, in great detail, the history in the scout movement, and the Équipes sociales of certain figures in the background to Uriage (Commandant de la Chapelle, etc.), he does not say much about *Esprit* except to suggest that it was a progressive Catholic journal that had favoured the Popular Front, had been against Franco, etc. This is to ignore the Esprit group's interest, throughout the 1930s, in "revolutionary" pedagogical techniques, German youth movements, radical philosophizing, elite and Order communities, etc. Cf. Comte, "Uriage," 221.

102 Here are Beuve-Méry's later recollections: "After giving a lecture in a room at the Hôtel de l'Europe [in the village near the school] on "Europe of Today and Tomorrow" I was invited to return and even to stay. This was accomplished with the amiable complicity of the lady who would later become Madame Georges Bidault [Suzy Borel, later wife of the head of the National Council of the Resistance, after serving as an important Uriage contact at Vichy] who then consented to convert to a temporary assignment the teaching mission with which I had been charged in Portugal." Reprinted in Bitoun, *Les hommes*, 47.

103 Laurent Greilshamer, *Hubert Beuve-Méry* (Paris: Fayard, 1990), 19.

104 Ibid., 25–6, 32.

105 Riots occurred in the Latin Quarter in the Spring of 1925 when the Cartel des Gauches government named a militant pacifist, Georges Scelle, over a Catholic candidate for a position of professor of international law. The young law students marched with the Camelots du Roi – three abreast, with section leaders and in disciplined formation – to fight over this issue with pro-republican students and police in the Latin Quarter. After days of rioting, Beuve-Méry and his friends succeeded in closing down the faculty and forcing Scelle's resignation. Cf. Ibid., 34.

106 Beuve-Méry remembered Nizan as a "dilettante" sort as a student, tempted by fascism and by the religious life. Nizan would subsequently become a close friend of Sartre and Simone de Beauvoir, a

Marxist, and would be remembered as one of the greatest French
Communist writers of the twentieth century. Ibid., 36.

107 It would be interesting to see the membership roles, and follow the
political trajectory, of this group. The fear on the part of men like
Henri Massis of a sort of Dominican mafia at Vichy would later have
much to do with the undoing of the Uriage school. If there was such
a Dominican mafia, Beuve-Méry was very much a part of it, and from
the time that he was quite young.

108 Ibid., 37.

109 When he returned to Paris, Beuve-Méry was given an office in the
editorial quarters of the *Nouvelles religieuses* in the courtyard of the
convent of the rue du Faubourg Saint-Honoré.

Like a few other students in law and economics of the faculty, he
also joined a study group with Léo Lagrange, Alexandre Parodi,
André Philip, and Philippe Lamour (future tenant of the Château de
la Faulconnière) around Professor Achille Mestre, who was a prestigious figure at the time. Ibid., 38, 40–1.

110 After the war, Gilson would become an editorialist at Beuve-Méry's *Le
Monde*. Ibid., 41.

111 He asked for the hand of a fellow student in the faculty, Geneviève
Deloye, and she accepted, but (as was not so uncommon in their class
and generation) it was some time before they stopped using the "vous"
form with one another. They were married on 27 September 1928, in
the fashionable parish of Sainte-Clotilde in the seventh *arrondissement*
with Fathers Marie-Dominique Chauvin and Janvier officiating. After
a family banquet at the house of Geneviève's uncle on the Boulevard
Raspail, the young couple went for a 48-hour honeymoon ... to the
shrine of the Virgin Mary at Lourdes. Ibid., 41.

112 His friend Alfred Michelin was on the editorial committee, and several of his future colleagues and friends were involved with it: e.g.,
Jean Lacroix, then a young agrégé in philosophy, Pierre-Henri Simon,
normalien, moralist, and, like Lacroix, early member of the *Esprit*
group; Georges Hourdin, militant Christian Democrat and Catholic
journalist. There were also several men who would be ministers of
General de Gaulle fifteen years later, notably François de Menthon,
René Capitant, and Georges Bidault.

113 Ibid., 51.

114 Ibid., 54–5. Like others in this Dominican milieu, Beuve-Méry did
not have much confidence in "the people" but tended to have much
faith in elites who promoted ideologies.

115 "Endiguera-t-on le flot hitlérien?" *Politique* (July 1933), cited in Greilshamer, *Beuve-Méry*, 74.

116 Article in *Politique* (July 1933), cited in Greilshamer, *Beuve-Méry*, 76.

117 "Hitler à Vienne," *Politique* (March 1938), cited in Greilshamer, *Beuve-Méry*, 124.

118 Greilshamer, *Beuve-Méry*, 126.

119 Ibid., 135. De Montherlant would, like others of his mindset such as Pierre Drieu la Rochelle, evolve from contempt for the Munich agreements to sympathy for collaborationist efforts to "virilize" the French during the Nazi occupation.

120 Suzy Borel, functionary at the Quai d'Orsay and future key Uriage contact at Vichy (see note 101, above) gave Beuve-Méry behind-the-scenes information about Giraudoux's efforts. Ibid., 136.

121 Beuve-Méry later recalled his experience as one of being surrounded by four hundred aimless civil servants. Ibid., 137.

122 Jean Giraudoux had an old affinity for German culture. The former head of the artistic and literary section of the Quai d'Orsay, he was a talented *licencié* in German and had been a tutor in French to the family of the Prince of Saxe-Meiningen. From 1918, Giraudoux had been a consistent defender of French-German peace at any price. The rise of Hitler did not seem to profoundly alter his attitude and, as late as 1939, he had remarked that "You don't know the young Nazis, you don't know how handsome they are, how heroic, how they have the sense of sacrifice." One observer even noted that Giraudoux as French propagandist faced with Josef Goebbels was like having a flute opposite a trombone (according to Greilshamer, *Beuve-Méry*, 137).

123 Bernard-Henri Lévy, *Les aventures de la liberté. Une histoire subjective des intellectuels* (Paris: Grasset, 1991), 160.

124 Beuve-Méry later downplayed the importance of his work, saying he was assigned to drawing up a report on the prostitutes of Lorraine, and he only got into intelligence work because he happened to run into a friend who proposed this post. But the fact remains that this professor-journalist with special views of France's place in the European New Order had the sort of connections that enabled him to go fairly directly from Giraudoux's propaganda office, to army intelligence, to directing the Study Bureau of the Ecole Nationale des Cadres. Greilshamer, *Beuve-Méry*, 140.

125 Ibid., 143–4.

126 "Révolutions nationales, Révolutions humaines," *Esprit* 98 (March 1941): 283–4, reprinted in Beuve-Méry, *Réflexions politiques, 1932–1952* (Paris: Seuil, 1951), 131–2.

In his *Beuve-Méry* (151), Laurent Greilshamer cites this very passage up to the word "isolated" but considers it unfair that, in 1951, the royalist weekly *Aspects de la France* exhumed this article in which it discerned (as did Professor Zeev Sternhell more recently) adhesion to a German-dominated Europe. But it seems fair to say, when one studies the entire article, that Beuve-Méry foresaw a more authoritarian and Germanized Europe in which a France reconstructed along the lines of Salazar's Portugal would find its place.

127 Beuve-Méry lectured in freezing conditions at the Hôtel de l'Europe because the castle's heating system had not yet been refurbished. (The hotel was down below in the village of St. Martin d'Uriage and run by M. and Mme Thibault, friends of *Esprit*. It was used for lectures when the castle's heating system was not working properly.) See note 101 (above) and Beuve-Méry cited in Bitoun, *Les hommes*, 46–7.

128 Beuve-Méry never seemed to have the kinds of enemies or critics at Vichy that Mounier suffered. On Beuve-Méry's return, he published a favourable report on the Salazar government's youth movement, as he seemed to see Portugal's response to the European New Order as suggestive for France.

Quai d'Orsay archives cited by Laurent Greilshamer have Beuve-Méry requesting the transfer to Uriage during the Portuguese visit. Beuve-Méry, as previously noted, attributed his return to the intervention of Suzy Borel. He later referred to her as Uriage's best friend at Vichy (interview with the author).

129 Hubert Beuve-Méry, *Vers la plus grande Allemagne* (Paris: P. Hartmann, 1939), (Conclusion) 100–1.

130 "Révolutions nationales, Révolutions humaines," *Esprit* 98: 283–4.

131 Hubert Beuve-Méry, "Avec les chefs de futurs chefs, dans un château qu'habita Bayard," *Le Figaro* (25 January 1941).

132 The second *chef* was apparently a unique, and unusual, reference to Eric d'Alançon. As the school evolved, and d'Alançon left, Dunoyer de Segonzac's personal authority became increasingly pronounced, with Beuve-Méry as his second in command. For Catholics of that generation familiar with religious life and the military, this type of obedience might not seem unusual were it not for the fact that it here entailed *total* submission to three people!! (Shirley Baum, conversation with the author)

133 Several copies of the rules are contained in the Uriage archives (102 J 144).

134 A persistent problem for the Uriage leadership would be the question of how much Pétain knew, and approved, of what they were doing. Dunoyer de Segonzac, as we shall see, became convinced that the school had Pétain's personal support and owed a special loyalty to him for that because the old Marshall was doing his best in struggling for Uriage, and for France, against the collaborationists and unsavoury elements at Vichy. Thus, like his friend Henri Frenay, founder of the Resistance movement *Combat*, Segonzac could endorse the main

principles of the National Revolution, have a firm admiration for and faith in Pétain, and yet very soon adopt "resistance-leaning" positions of hostility toward Pierre Laval, certain collaborationists, and the German occupying forces.

135 Cf. Halls, *Youth*, 135.

CHAPTER TWO

1 Cited in Bernard Comte, "L'École Nationale des Cadres d'Uriage. Une communauté éducative non-conformiste à l'époque de la révolution nationale (1940–1942)", Ph.D. thesis, Université de Lyon 2, 1987, 343. Off-hand references to "the doctrine contained in the speeches of the Marshal" (whatever that was) were fairly frequent in early school documents.

2 See, for example, the "compte-rendu de stage de M.J. (ouvrier)," a mimeographed text by the school, 2 pages, 19 August 1942 (archives of the school), cited in Antoine Delestre, *Uriage, une communauté et une école dans la tourmente, 1940–1945* (Nancy: Presses Universitaires de Nancy, 1989), 25.

3 *Maréchal Pétain, messages au Français*, classement analytique by Charles Henry Amar (Grenoble: École Nationale des Cadres d'Uriage, 9 October 1942).

4 On this matter see Jean Lacouture, *De Gaulle, 1. Le rebelle* (Paris: Seuil, 1984).

5 "Radio-Jeunesse vous parle ... Un message du Chef de l'école d'Uriage," *Jeunesse ... France!* 13 (22 May 1941), 11.

6 Especially, he recalled, from Doctor Ménétrel, General Laure, and Henri du Moulin de Labarthète "whose brother, my best friend, a professional officer, had been killed in 1940 in Saint-Cyrien style, wearing white gloves." Pierre Dunoyer de Segonzac, *Le Vieux Chef, Mémoires et pages choisies* (Paris: Seuil, 1972), 102.

7 Delestre, *Uriage*, 27.

8 Emmanuel Mounier's thoughtful "Letter from France" to the American magazine *The Commonweal*, in which he described history having turned the page on liberal and democratic ways in this period, reflected what seemed to have been a common view at Uriage at the time. Cf. *The Commonweal* 33, no. 1 (25 October 1940): 11.

9 Much documentation on the Uriage alumni network may be found in the Uriage archives in the section "École nationale des cadres: Équipe nationale d'Uriage (ENU)" (102 J 117–41).

10 The talk may be found in the Uriage archives in the collection *Le Chef et ses jeunes*, no. 16 (22 J 33).

11 Cf. Joffre Dumazedier, "Renouveau de l'éducation populaire à la Libération: les antécédents (1941–1944) de la création de Peuple et Culture," *Éducation permanente* 62–63 (March 1982): 127–37.

12 Dumazedier, who had been named Joffre in commemoration of the victor on the Marne, had lost his father in the First World War, and had been raised by his mother and grandmother. Cf. Pierre Bitoun, *Les hommes d'Uriage* (Paris: La Découverte, 1988), 51, 60.

13 After the war he would become, with Cacérès, a leader of the well-known "Peuple et Culture" movement in France. His views on physical education were also influential: in the immediate postwar years he played a significant role in the debate that eventually led France away from the *Hébertisme* that had been the orthodoxy at Uriage – and then had been imposed on physical education instruction in all of France – toward a more pluralistic approach (Alain Lemée, interview with the author).

14 Emmanuel Mounier's role at Uriage at the time may have created some problems for Beuve-Méry in this effort, for Mounier was eventually prevented from serving on this organism by higher Vichy authorities (according to Mounier's diary; see below, note 15).

15 Cf. Mounier, "Entretiens 12" (28 July 1941), *Oeuvres* 4 (Paris: Seuil, 1963), 711–12.

16 "L'École nationale des cadres d'Uriage," *Esprit* 99 (April 1941): 429–31.

17 This lecture was reprinted as "Fin de l'homme bourgeois," *Esprit* 102 (July 1941): 609–17.

18 "Force et faiblesse du marxisme," Uriage, 17 July 1941 (mimeographed). Copies of Lacroix's lectures to Uriage may be found in the Uriage archives (102 J 14–22).

19 Cf. Daniel Lindenberg, *Les années souterraines, 1937–1947* (Paris: La Découverte, 1990), 242–4.

20 See Reuter, *Les trusts* (in the collection Le Chef et ses jeunes, no. 14) (Grenoble: École Nationale des Cadres d'Uriage, 1942) (22 J 31) and Comte, "Uriage," 327–8, 333–4, 346.

21 Jean-Jacques Chevallier, *L'ordre viril* (Grenoble: École Nationale des Cadres d'Uriage, 1943), 1, 9–11; see also Comte, "Uriage," 469–70.

22 Reich has many interesting things to say about this, and Catholic spirituality, in his book *The Mass Psychology of Fascism (1933)* (Harmondsworth, Middlesex: Penguin Books, 1970).

23 Comte, "Uriage," 359–60.

24 This was also another illustration of the fact that while some of the men of Uriage may have been trying to constitute "a little island of the Resistance" (as they often claimed in their post-war recollections),

others were contending for influence at the highest possible levels of government.

25 Among the typed Teilhard texts that remain in the Uriage archives are "Textes choisis: Comment je crois; Le christianisme dans le monde; Christologie et évolution" (22 J 51).

After a period of being held in suspicion by the Vatican after the war, Father de Lubac would be dramatically vindicated when he became a leading figure in the second Vatican Council and was subsequently named a cardinal by the personalist philosopher-pope Karol Wojtyla (see note 28 below).

26 *Esprit* 98 (March 1941): 281–4.

27 His Uriage lecture "L'explication chrétienne de notre temps" was reprinted as *Vocation de la France* (Le Puy: X. Mappus, 1941), 30 pp.

28 Comte, "Uriage," 354. This is a central idea in Father de Lubac's letters to his close friend Father Pierre Teilhard de Chardin at this time.

Bordeaux personalist Bernard Charbonneau has reproached Father Teilhard for such indifference to real people as opposed to "humanity" and attacked him as a pseudo-personalist crypto-totalitarian in *Teilhard de Chardin, prophète d'un âge totalitaire* (Paris: Denoël, 1963).

29 He would soon be involved with Father Chaillet in creating the famous Resistance journal *Témoignage chrétien*. Cf. Renée Bedarida, *Pierre Chaillet, témoin de la résistance spirituelle* (Paris: Fayard, 1988).

30 This vivid firsthand reminiscence is that of SGJ functionary Pierre Ordioni in his book *Tout commence à Alger, 1940–1944* (Paris: Stock, 1972), 110.

31 Comte, "Uriage," 260.

32 Ibid., 351.

33 "Le Chef de la jeunesse à l'école d'Uriage," *Jeunesse … France!* 9 (22 March 1941): 12.

34 There was a front-page account, complete with a photo, in *Le petit Dauphinois* (3 June 1941). A few months later that paper would laud the school plan to have young men destined to be prefects pass through Uriage to purify them of the political spirit. Cf. "Des hommes, des chefs et des cadres. L'émancipation des préfets," *Le petit Dauphinois* (19 September 1941) (22 J 13).

35 The Uriage alumni argued, after the war, that Darlan was wary of the school but grasped its importance, and so decided to take it over for his own purposes. This point of view seems to have been first put forward by Mounier in his diary, after a discussion with Segonzac in late July, when he reflected that: "Darlan certainly touched people's hearts for a time. He did it in high style … played

seductive, and at first it partially worked. But during his visit he grasped the importance of the school and the effects of that would soon be felt. Not that he was disposed to snuff it out, but rather to annex it. The advantages were immediate: attribution of strength rations that had been requested in vain for months, promise of a million for the weekly, etc. The school had 15 million in debts and they were liquidated overnight." Mounier, "Entretiens 12" (28 July 1941) in *Oeuvres* 4 (Paris: Seuil, 1963), 711.

36 Ibid. On the popular publication *Marche* see below, chapter 4.

In fact only a small percentage (less than 5 per cent) of the last three *promotions* of the year were sent to the SGJ because of this new dimension of the school's duties (Comte, "Uriage," 422).

What was the reaction of the men of Uriage to Darlan's intervention in the life of the school? In interviews or memoirs, years later (recorded in Bitoun, *Les hommes*, 89–91), they recalled some hostile feelings: former instructor Charles Müller remembered a visit of Darlan to Uriage in which the school manifested an overt hostility to him (a Resistance-leaning perspective that directly contradicts Bernard Comte's account). This is still another example from these years of a retrospective reconstruction of an event differing from the documentary and factual evidence, and from other retrospective elaborations of the same event that seem more persuasive. The memoirs of the leader of the future (originally quasi-Pétainist) resistance movement *Combat*, Henri Frenay, include a scornful account of the visit of that *méprisable personnage* Darlan to Uriage. (This contradicts Comte's evidence that Frenay's great comrade Segonzac and the others were much taken with Darlan and his enthusiasm for the school, and grateful for his practical aid.) The Abbé de Naurois recalled the visit as one during which Darlan said dishonourable things. And "after his departure there were arguments because he had impressed some of the men, who said that he was correct, one had to be reasonable, have one's feet on the ground, et cetera. I became indignant because there were already many anti-semitic incidents, et cetera. Anti-racist intransigence won out. Being of a rather impulsive nature, I made some violent remarks in the very courtyard of the château where everyone heard them. Of course that was reported to Vichy." For whatever reasons, Father de Naurois would be expelled from the school soon afterwards.

37 De Naurois recalled having the well-known postwar radical Catholic writer Maurice Clavel in his group. Several famous postwar radical Catholics also graduated from Vichy elite schools.

38 Beuve-Méry thought that the Abbé de Naurois was a peculiar and special sort of curé who looked more comfortable with grenades in his belt than in a soutane (interview with the author).

39 Cited in Delestre, *Uriage*, 108.

40 Bitoun, *Les hommes*, 91.

41 In the fall of 1942 the embittered de Naurois went to join de Gaulle in London, where he became chaplain of the Free French naval forces and defended the reputation of Uriage. He befriended, or tried to minister to, that strange Free French intellectual Simone Weil (and was present at her tragic death).

42 Mounier, *Oeuvres* 4: 711. As a result he published his text "Pour un humanisme français" (his December 1940 talk to the school) in his journal *Esprit* under another title, rather than as a Uriage *fascicule*.

43 Comte, "Uriage," 347.

44 Mounier, *Oeuvres* 4: 712.

45 Ibid., 712. Father de Naurois in Bitoun, *Les hommes*.

46 If Beuve-Méry had reservations about P. de Naurois, he also had some, though apparently less serious, about Mounier, whom he found at times too abstract, something of a word-spinner (interview with the author).

47 D'Astorg's wife had been a childhood friend of Segonzac. There is an informative interview with d'Astorg in Delestre, *Uriage*, 84, and a memoir by d'Astorg in *Le personnalisme d'Emmanuel Mounier* (Paris: Seuil, 1985).

48 He also attested that he learned what he characterized as important political lessons in the *Front universitaire antifasciste*.

49 Which, under Flamand's direction, would become one of France's most prominent publishing houses after the war.

50 The author is indebted to Alexandre Marc, and his unpublished correspondence, for information on this remarkable community.

51 Michel Winock, *Histoire politique de la revue "Esprit", 1930–1950* (Paris: Seuil, 1975), 151. For d'Astorg's mentality see his *La morale de notre honneur*, with a preface by Gabriel Marcel (Lyon: École Nationale des Cadres d'Uriage, 1942). See also Bitoun, *Les hommes*, 49.

52 Maydieu was seconded by the less well known and less imposing Father des Alleux (R.P. Vandevoorde, O.P.).

53 Charles de Gaulle was one of the earliest members of this organization (interviews with Maurice Schumann, Alexandre Marc).

54 For more information on Maydieu see Delestre, *Uriage*, 131.

55 Pierre Dunoyer de Segonzac, "Uriage," *La Vie Intellectuelle* August-September 1956. Part of this romantic recollection is reprinted in *Le Vieux Chef* (Paris: Seuil, 1971), 86.

56 Comte, "Uriage," 329, 355.

57 W.D. Halls, *The Youth of Vichy France* (Oxford: Clarendon, 1981), 322. It is interesting, at this point, to recall Du Moulin de Laberthète's subsequent remark that Henri Massis was a loyal supporter of the

Marshall, who had a special gift for perceiving Dominican intrigue and thirst for power.

58 Segonzac, *Le Vieux Chef*, 86.

This happened in bygone days, in times more poverty-stricken than ours, but richer in hope.

As we were much younger, even truly young, we chose to remake the world, between ourselves, in a sort of monastery which had harboured authentic knights in the Middle Ages, and then equivocal tourists in the twentieth century, and which hid our distress at being betrayed children ...

So it was necessary to rediscover reasons for living ...

The starting point was good; we brought together clients of all the parishes, all of them full of various preconceptions which had not yet crystallized into mutual animosity.

And from the outset the exhilarating feeling of a sort of spiritual unity that might well develop among us, in spite of our marked differences, took hold of us.

59 See chapter 9, below.

60 Perroux, a devout Catholic, had outlined his ideas in *Esprit* before the war, and remained in touch with Mounier and Lacroix. He had ties with the SGJ, but, aside from defending his friends in higher government circles, seemed not to have directly participated in the Uriage experience. He also became a close, life-long friend of Beuve-Méry. (He happened to make one of his regular calls to *Le Monde*'s founder, decades later, during my interview with the latter about Uriage. Perroux became one of France's most distinguished economists after the war but had a serious hearing difficulty and this was an explanation given by his friends for his refusal to grant any interviews touching upon his activities during the Vichy period.)

61 Cf. Comte, "Uriage," 368–70. Comte suggests that Beuve-Méry meant "race" in the relatively innocent "Péguyist" sense of that word.

62 Mounier, "Entretiens 12" (5 October 1941) (unpublished section).

63 A similar historical fatalism appeared among them in the face of Stalinism after the war, as *Le Monde* and *Esprit* would demonstrate.

Alexandre Marc, a founder of Personalism, recalled a meeting of progressive Catholics in the southern zone in which Marrou put forward this point of view with great eloquence and erudition, and his view carried great weight with his auditors (interview with the author). Marrou became one of France's most distinguished historians after the war and lived the rest of his life with the Mouniers and the rest of the personalist community in "Les Murs Blancs" at Châtenay-Malabry. Marrou did, however, have reservations about the hagiographical direction of Mounier studies after the war and encouraged a lucid and documented study of the personalist experience (interview with the author).

64 Comte, "Uriage," 372–3. This Resistance-leaning position seemed to leave open the question of what might happen if a more enlightened and civilized group of Nazis did become sincerely co-operative with the French, or even if the Abetz school (those who, like the German Ambassador in Paris, Otto Abetz, believed that a collaborationist France could effect her own kind of revolution within the framework of the New Order) won out over the colonialists.

65 *Gazette de l'inspection* (October 1941); cf. Comte, "Uriage," 377.

66 On 15 August 1941. This journal was to replace the important Catholic journal *Temps Présent* and was directed at this time by Stanislas Fumet – a friend of Resistance figures such as Jacques Maritain and Charles de Gaulle.

67 This kind of argument was often found in *Esprit* after the war, to defend itself against the charge of lacking doctrinal cohesion. John Hellman, *Emmanuel Mounier and the New Catholic Left, 1930–1950* (Toronto: University of Toronto Press, 1981), chapters 9–12. See also Comte, "Uriage," 378.

68 Several copies of this text exist in the Uriage archives (22 J 2 and 102 J 14).

69 Comte, "Uriage," 380.

70 Cf. "L'esprit d'Uriage." A book on "the sense of honour" is the object of an official but late (1942) exchange of letters between d'Astorg and Gabriel Marcel, to be found in the latter's newly deposited papers in the Bibliothèque Nationale. Marcel was apparently called on to theorize on the subject for Uriage while d'Astorg submitted to him a book on honour drawing upon the chivalric tradition, which he seemed to envisage as a doctrinal cornerstone in pursuing Uriage's work of reshaping France (hence the importance of the Marcel input) (Christian Roy).

71 Recall that 10 per cent of an initial session's trainees seem to have been seminarians.

72 There was this "solidarity," of course, unless you "wanted out," in which case you were expelled and possibly jeopardized your future in the authoritarian New Order in France.

73 Several passages from these "La Mission ... d'Uriage" texts are reproduced in Comte, "Uriage," 382–3. All of this might look rather totalitarian, but, according to Bernard Comte, the school had demonstrated its independence in this document for in not including a Lallement text on "Loyalty toward the Marshall," Uriage, he thought, demonstrated quite a difference from an organization such as the Chantiers de la Jeunesse, which institutionalized an "Act of Faith" in

the Marshall. The Chantiers claimed to be apolitical but fostered a "quasi-religious confidence devoid of critical spirit," which their chaplain, Father Forestier, made into a kind of political theology.

74 Cited in Comte, "Uriage," 384, 386. This text seems to be absent from the Uriage archives.

75 Cited in Comte, "Uriage," 387.

76 Instructor Joffre Dumazedier later described himself as having been in a very small minority as a *laic* with socialist leanings at Uriage. See Joffre Dumazedier, "Témoignage de Joffre Dumazedier," *Les Cahiers de l'animation* (INEP) 49–50 (1985): 158–63; Comte, "Uriage," 399.

77 Cf. Comte, "Uriage," 394–5.

78 Cf. Bénigno Cacérès, "Témoignage de B. Cacérès," *Les Cahiers de l'animation* (INEP) 49–50 (1985) 164–6. He says all of the *chefs* were agreed that education was the first and most important way to change man and to change society.

79 Dunoyer de Segonzac, "A la recherche des Chefs," *Jeunesse ... France!* 21 (22 September 1941): 5.

80 Ibid.

81 The incident is recorded in Comte, "Uriage," 395.

82 A (privately communicated) text of a Uriage instructor passed over to London described Beuve-Méry for the special forces of Free France in the summer of 1941 as: "A rather pessimistic temperament. Not many human contacts. Rather cold, behaviour of an energetic man who has much suffered, and not very leadership-oriented. [Due to his] handsome intelligence [he] is able to spread the influence of his thought, but because of his harshness and lack of charisma, not of his example." Cited in Laurent Greilshamer, *Hubert Beuve-Méry* (Paris: Fayard, 1990), 198.

83 Comte, "Uriage," 397.

84 In 1941, Étienne Borne tried to show the similarities and differences between "heroic" morality and Christian morality: "D'un héroïsme chrétien" in *Jeunesse et communauté nationale* (Lyon: L'Abeille, "Rencontres" no. 3, 1941); in 1942, Père de Lubac analyzed the notion of the "virile order."

85 One of the most influential books to come out of this kind of reflection was Henri de Lubac's *Le drame de l'humanisme athée* (Paris, 1944). See note 25 above.

86 Bernard Comte found it already associated with Beuve-Méry's predecessor at the Research Department, Lallement. Comte, "Uriage," 400.

87 In the immediate background to the Uriage Order were institutions such as the Société de St. Louis, which involved Jeune France activist Paul Flamand.

88 Cf. Comte, "Uriage," 400–1.

89 In *Ordre Nouveau* 8 (January 1933): 28.

90 See Hellman, *Mounier*, 87–95.

91 According to the testimony of one of the concerned, Paul Thisse, later a member of the clandestine Uriage network, an object of this order was to bar the route to Nazism [!] (testimony of Thisse). Recorded in Comte, "Uriage," 406. Thisse's lecture "Péguy: incarnation d'une nouvelle unité française" (25 January 1941) may be found in the classification "École Nationale des Cadres: doctrine. Tests fondamentaux" in the Uriage archives (102 J 15).

In fact, de Becker seems to have been the first to invite Nazis to Brussels in the interwar period to "dialogue" with young Belgian revolutionaries. Some such contacts are recorded in Mounier's unpublished diaries in that period. Thus de Becker's account of his activities is in marked contrast to that given by Dunoyer de Segonzac in *Le Vieux Chef*. See Raymond de Becker, *Le livre des vivants et des morts* (Brussels: Toison d'Or, 1942).

92 "Pour une technique des moyens spirituels," *Esprit* (February 1935), reprinted in *Oeuvres* 1 (Paris, 1963): 360.

93 Cf. *Ordre des compagnons de Péguy, textes et travaux* (Marseille, 1941). This was another Uriage-style community aspiration insofar as it was a lay order inspired by Christianity. It was made up of many of the Catholic intelligentsia who had shared hopes for a Catholic renaissance in the 1930s (interview with Alexandre Marc).

94 Comte, "Uriage," 402.

95 Jean Guitton, *Écrire comme on se souvient* (Paris: Fayard, 1974), 205–6.

96 A Lacroix lecture on "La pensée de Charles Péguy" may be found in the same dossier as that of Paul Thisse dated March 1941 (102 J 15) and another, without a date, in (22 J 39). Comte, "Uriage," 409.

97 See his disturbing "Letter from France" in *Commonweal* 33, no. 1 (25 October 1940): 11 in which he foresaw the long-term disappearance of liberty in Europe as well.

98 Mounier's "Entretiens 12" (5 October 1941).

99 The subsequently famous ecumenical monastic community of Taizé was not a "laic order," however, as it was run by clergy. Comte, "Uriage," 407.

100 J.P. Filliette, "Recherche d'un plan d'action," *Jeunesse ... France!* 11 (22 April 1941): 3.

101 The anonymous editor of *Jeunesse ... France!*, summarizing the conversation of Lamirand with the directors of the school. "Le Chef de la jeunesse à l'Ecole d'Uriage," 22 March 1941, 12.

102 Comte, "Uriage," 419.

103 Which the lively and ambitious, but often impoverished and marginal, pre-war intellectual teams such as Esprit and Ordre Nouveau, whose ideas flourished at the school, had not enjoyed.

104 A dossier including the plans of the properties confiscated remains in the Uriage archives (102 J 12). See also Comte, "Uriage," 308, 310, 312, 316. Only "Richelieu," title of the "higher civil servants" class of July 1941, was left out of the names for the cabins.

105 Bénigno Cacérès, the Toulouse carpenter become something of the professional proletarian at Uriage, remarked how impressed he was to find that in France of 1940 one could eat regularly and well. This must have had at least something to do with the popularity of the school.

106 Comte, "Uriage," 320.

107 The director of this well-known institution, which was run along the lines of an English public school, was Garrone's father-in-law, Georges Bertier. Comte, "Uriage," 291.

108 Halls, *Youth*, 134.

109 Comte, "Uriage," 292, 293, 295–6. Records of the special session held for the directors of the regional schools at Uriage from 7 to 13 July 1941 may be found in the school archives (102 J 70).

110 *Bulletin de presse du SGJ* (21 April 1941). Cited in Comte, "Uriage," 297.

111 Hourdin thought the idea, in its contemporary form, to be Alexis Carrel's.

112 "Des *Cahiers de la Quinzaine* à *Rencontres*," in *Foyers de notre culture*, Collection Rencontres no. 9, Éditions du Cerf (Summer 1942). Cited in Comte, "Uriage," 407–8.

113 Comte, "Uriage," 402.

114 *Journal de France, 1939–1944* (Paris: Imprimerie JEP, 1942), 189. Fabre-Luce was perceptive on this point for, as we shall see, the Order of Uriage – at least informally – did survive the France of Pétain.

115 *Vingt-cinq années de liberté*, vol. 2 of *L'épreuve (1939–1946)* (Paris: Julliard, 1963), 95.

116 In January 1941, Pétain had invited Bonnard, chancellor of the French Academy in 1940, to become a *Conseiller National*, a member of the prestigious group charged with developing a new constitution for France. He finally became Minister of Education on Pierre Laval's return to power with strong German backing in April 1942. Privately the Marshall nicknamed him "Gestapette" (from "Gestapo" and "tapette" – homosexual). Cf. Halls, *Youth*, 35. Bonnard's pederasty fuelled Segonzac's contempt.

In Jean Jardin's office, when the Germans occupied the Free Zone, Bonnard could not hide his joy at seeing these firm, virile, jack-

booted men marching into Vichy at last ("Assez de pantoufles!") for
he relished such displays of manly power. (Alexandre Marc, interview
with Christian Roy).

117 Comte, "Uriage," 289.
118 Halls, *Youth*, 136–7.
119 G. Pelorson, "Jeunesse 1941!" in *France 1941. La Révolution Nationale
constructive* (Paris: Alsatia, 1941), 215–31.

CHAPTER THREE

1 Dossiers on the special sessions for the École Polytechnique (102 J 71),
for *étudiants coloniaux* (102 J 72), or the École de l'Air (102 J 73) may
be found in the Uriage archives.
2 Bitoun, *Les hommes d'Uriage* (Paris: La Découverte, 1988), 65.
3 According to a non-dated inventory in the school archives that was
composed in spring 1942 and so remains incomplete (and only considers the most important training sessions of the school), the occupational breakdown among the trainees at Uriage included 26.2%
students (279), 7.7% workers (82). Most numerous of the occupations
represented among the trainees, over 30%, were the personnel of
industry and this showed the importance the school attributed to that
sector. Cited in Delestre, *Uriage, une communauté et une école dans la
tourmente* (Nancy: Presses Universitaires de Nancy, 1989), 59. This
occupational breakdown coincides with one published some months
earlier in *Jeunesse ... France!*
 The more complete mimeographed report by Hubert Beuve-Méry
in the Uriage archives in Grenoble (dated in pencil as "sans doute"
August 1942) breaks the *stagiaires* who passed through Uriage into
three categories: "stages d'information générale" (nine three-week and
six eight-day sessions) – 1,453 stagiaires, "stages spécialisés" (twenty) –
1,160 stagiaires, "stages de formation de six mois" – 67 stagiaires.
 Among the 1,453 in the general sessions he noted the three largest
categories as students (285), military officers (192), and teachers
(134). There were fewer workers (78) and relatively few representatives
of agriculture (25). Among the 1,160 in the specialized sessions a
majority was involved with directing the youth movements or regional
schools (332), a good number of students (307, if one included the
"colonials"), and leaders of "comités sociaux" (169). No worker or
peasant groups were noted.
 The elite of sixty-seven in the six-month sessions had its largest
single representation from the leadership of the youth movements or
the SGJ (twenty-two). There were ten teachers, nine students, nine officers, two workers, two artisans, and two representatives of agriculture.

Since the general sessions trained about 106 youth leaders, the specialized sessions about 332 and the six-month session about 22, this was the second largest category of young men trained at Uriage, after those in the student category. Cf. Hubert Beuve-Méry, "L'École Nationale des Cadres" (c. August 1942), pp. 5–6 (102 J 13).

4 According to the non-dated inventory in the school, (n. 3). Cf. Delestre, Uriage, 59 and the Beuve-Méry report of August 1942 (n. 3).

5 That less than 1 per cent of the Uriage trainees came from "agriculture" may seem surprising given the romantic attitude toward peasants fostered by the speeches of Marshall Pétain and by the writers in vogue at Uriage, like Péguy and others in the Catholic revival. But could peasants be expected to gather under young aristocrats in a confiscated chateau to celebrate the "glories" of their collective past under feudalism?

6 Thus wrote Jean Le Veugle, a Protestant and former stagiaire at Uriage, member of the Équipe in 1943, in "notes" that remain in the archives of the school (102 J 153).

7 Testimony of Madame Colette Souriau of the Uriage school, cited in Delestre, Uriage, 59. According to the Templetons, present owners of the chateau, the Alleman family had been well liked in the area and there was a great deal of resentment over the harsh and arrogant way in which the Château Bayard had been confiscated from its rightful heirs.

8 Louise-Marie Lozach'Meur recalled that: "There was much talk about Uriage in Grenoble and I quickly accepted [the offer of a secretarial position]. My mother was more reticent because there were positive and less than positive things being said. They called the instructors the 'monk-knights,' but often with a little smirk." Testimony cited in Bitoun, Les hommes, 56.

9 In discussing this issue Bernard Comte admits that there was something off-puttingly elitist about Uriage for working people. Bernard Comte, "L'École Nationale des Cadres d'Uriage. Une communauté éducative non-conformiste à l'époque de la révolution nationale (1940–1942)" Ph.D. thesis, Université de Lyon 2, 1987, 433.

10 As had been the case with many of the Catholic rejuvenation projects of the 1930s.

11 Comte, "Uriage," 435. Of 1,064 stagiaires (cf. Gilles Ferry, Une expérience de formation des chefs (Paris: Seuil, 1945), 91) who had participated in the longest training sessions and who were interrogated in spring 1942, the age distribution was as follows: stagiaires younger than twenty-one – 11.5% (97); between twenty-one and thirty – 55.3% (588); thirty-one to forty – 24.2% (258); over forty – 9% (96). (If

trainees under thirty were the more numerous, it is worth noting that there were a good number over forty.)

These figures are from a non-dated inventory that is thought to have been composed in the spring of 1942 and so is probably incomplete. Besides, it only considers the most important training sessions at the school. Cf. Delestre, *Uriage*, 59.

(The bourgeois social background of so many of the trainees was an aspect of the school that was largely ignored in retrospective remarks by Uriage alumni. This sheds interesting light on the real social role of the school that, despite the rhetoric, and even conscious motivations of the school's directors favouring a National Revolution, in fact tended to reinforce, if not advance, the hegemony of certain segments among France's pre-war directing classes, particularly certain Catholic groups, and other anti-Republicans of various backgrounds.)

12 On their backgrounds see Bitoun, *Les hommes*, 45.

13 Bitoun, *Les hommes*, 59.

14 This was told by Segonzac to Comte in a 1967 interview recorded in Comte, "Uriage," 549. The archives contain a letter from P. Legros, le Directeur General, Centre Artistique et Technique des jeunes du cinema, based in the Domaine Castelaras near Mouans-Sartoux, dated 7 August 1941, informing Segonzac that they intended to start shooting the film called "Chefs de demain" at Uriage in the middle of the month (102 J 19).

15 "Le problème social," *Jeunesse … France!* 33 (July 1942): 1.

16 Comte, "Uriage," 481.

17 "L'efficacité dans l'action" (lecture at Uriage) in "L'ordre civil et l'efficacité dans l'action," Le Chef et ses jeunes, no. 7 (22 J 29).

18 The recollections are cited in Bitoun, *Les hommes*, 66–7; details on the Uriage day are found in Hubert Beuve-Méry, "L'École des Cadres d'Uriage" (mimeographed), 2 (102 J 14).

19 Georges Hébert, "Avant-propos," *L'éducation physique, virile et morale par la méthode naturelle* 1 (Paris: Vuibert, 1942): viii, xii–xiii. (Interview with Alain Lemée.)

20 Cf. "Les pédagogies collectives extra-scolaires" in *Jeunesse et communauté nationale* (Lyon: Éditions de l'Abeille, No. 3, 1941); Comte, "Uriage," 484.

21 "Discipline" (editorial) in *Jeunesse … France!* 10 (8 April 1941): 1.

22 Article 2, "Règle des chefs" of the Uriage rules. Several copies of these remain in the Uriage archives. Cf. "La mission, l'esprit et la règle d'Uriage" (no date) (22 J 2) and "Règle de Communauté de chefs" (marked H.B.M., no date). This latter text includes the authoritarian provisions that "l'équipe sous les ordres des deux 'vieux chefs'

est dominée par l'idée d'un loyalisme absolu envers la personne du Maréchal Pétain, Chef de l'État Français ... L'obéissance aux ordres des "vieux chefs" est également totale." The school hymn is appended.

Handwritten Beuve-Méry notes in the same file suggest that it was thought inappropriate for the trainees to hide their thoughts on important issues from the *vieux chefs*.

23 "Uriage, École nationale des chefs – choses vues," by M.J. Torris, *Candide* (30 July 1941). A note on a copy of this article in the Uriage archives remarks that Torris was thirty-eight years old, embassy secretary in the ministry of foreign affairs at Vichy, and had been a *stagiaire* in the May–July "Mermoz" class.

A pencilled comment (by Beuve-Méry?) notes that this article was "trés élogieux et modéré, quoique pétainiste et darlaniste" (102 J 13).

24 Recollection of Ollier de Marchand (interview with Bernard Comte, 1967); Comte, "Uriage," 487.

25 President François Mitterrand was also raised in a relatively well off, but strictly Catholic, provincial family with much the same attitude toward money. It seems to have become an important component of his moral and political outlook. See Catherine Nay, *Le noir et le rouge ou l'histoire d'une ambition* (Paris: Grasset, 1984).

26 Comte, "Uriage," 487.

27 Cited in Bitoun, *Les hommes*, 62.

28 Bitoun, *Les hommes*, 73.

29 Years later, Paul Delouvrier said of Uriage: "For very many young people educated in the Catholic way, where one always said one didn't discuss politics, it was not so easy to determine to what republic one was going to adhere. There were many of us in 1942, and even in 1943, who thought that with de Gaulle, there was a risk of a restoration of the Third." Cited in Bitoun, *Les hommes*, 73. (Here we see the origins of the Pétainist Resistance-leaning position at Uriage, which would be of considerable importance later in the war.)

30 Cf. Comte, "Uriage," 488–90.

31 See Michael Marrus and Robert Paxton, *Vichy et les Juifs* (Paris: Calmann-Lévy, 1981), 192–3; Comte, "Uriage," 433.

32 *J'étais l'ami du Maréchal Pétain* (Paris: Plon, 1966), 181.

33 Mounier, "Entretiens 12," 29 August 1941 and 2 October 1941 (unpublished sections).

34 A personalist philosophy and language was central to Gillouin's subsequent book *Problèmes français, problèmes humains* (Geneva: Éditions du Milieu du Monde, 1944) in which, having been pressured out of the Vichy government, he articulated what he thought remained viable in the philosophy of the Révolution Nationale.

35 Marc Ferro has correctly pointed out the remarkable similarity in literary style between Pétain and Benjamin, who was one of the

Marshall's favourite authors. Cf. Marc Ferro, *Pétain* (Paris: Fayard, 1987), 256.

36 Alumni of Uriage said, later, that Benjamin was considered a spy for Pétain and so had been given the cold shoulder, and in general been poorly received, at the school. This is certainly not reflected in the subject's account of his visit, although Mounier, in his diary, did mention an element of mistrust.

37 René Benjamin, "La France retrouve son âme," [headline article] *Candide* 913 (17 September 1941).

38 W.D. Halls, *The Youth of Vichy France* (Oxford: Clarendon, 1981), 144–5; Comte, "Uriage," 454.

39 For a discussion of this publication, see the concluding section of this chapter.

40 "Notre Empire," *Jeunesse … France!* 16 (8 July 1941): 1.

41 P. Heidsieck, "Le chef d'après Lyautey," ibid., 6.

42 Comte, "Uriage," 477.

43 Nguyen Van Thoai, science student, on colonial youth; Mohammed Salah Belgued, student for the agrégation in Arab, on Islam; Van Thoai and Tran Thanh Xuan (École des Mines), on Buddhism and Confucianism.

44 Cf. Comte, "Uriage," 478.

45 Cited in Comte, "Uriage," 479.

46 Among the situations in which the most explicit use of personalist language was important one could cite the regimes of Diem in Vietnam, or Lebanon under Bechir Gemayel. Although the "leftist" French Esprit group later disclaimed responsibility for Diem's claims on their philosophy, a representative of the Lebanese phalange was an honoured guest at the journal *Esprit*'s fiftieth anniversary celebration. The French personalists, when they became sympathetic to Quebec nationalism, tried to disassociate themselves from Canadian Prime Minister Pierre Elliot Trudeau, who was a co-founder of a review, *Cité Libre*, meant to carry on the work of *Esprit* in North America.

47 Roger Stéphane, *Chaque homme est lié au monde* (Paris: Le Sagittaire, 1946), 166. Stéphane, as a representative of the Resistance, went to see Segonzac and found him hesitating as to what course of action to take.

48 Delestre, *Uriage*, 42.

49 Bénigno Cacérès, *L'espoir du coeur* (Paris: Seuil, 1967), 51–52.

50 Cited in Delestre, *Uriage*, 43.

51 Jean Le Veugle (future *stagiaire* and member of the Order of Uriage), "Journal d'un résistant" (unpublished), 40. Cited in Delestre, *Uriage*, 44.

52 Cited in Bitoun, *Les hommes*, 42.

53 Cited in Bitoun, *Les hommes*, 41.

54 "Notes sur le chef," *Revue des Jeunes* (January 1941): 17–18.

55 "Discipline," *Jeunesse ... France!* 10 (8 April 1941): 1.

56 "Intellectuels," *Jeunesse ... France!* 8 (8 March 1941): 1.

57 "L'armée et le pays," *Jeunesse ... France!* 25 (1 December 1941): 2.

58 "Radio-Jeunesse vous parle ... Un message du Chef de l'école d'Uriage," *Jeunesse ... France!* 13 (22 May 1941): 1.

59 Particularly by Hubert Beuve-Méry.

60 From *L'argent* in Péguy's *Oeuvres en prose* 2 (Paris: Gallimard, 1959), 1106–7.

61 Published as Jean-Jacques Chevallier, "Efficacité," in *Jeunesse ... France!* 8 (8 March 1941): 1, 3.

62 See also Comte, "Uriage," 471.

63 The Comte thesis reproduces a photo of historian Hours lecturing before the massive Pétain portrait (438).

64 Dossiers on the Richelieu session are in the Uriage archives (102 J 54–56); see also Comte, "Uriage," 438, 440.

65 But there were exceptions. A number of pre-war "personalists" disapproved of the whole enterprise as too close to the regime and refused to have anything to do with it. An example was Alexandre Marc, founder of the Ordre Nouveau movement and then one of the founders of *Esprit*. Several of Emmanuel Mounier's other friends voiced their disapproval of Mounier's involvement at Uriage to Mounier at the time. See my *Emmanuel Mounier and the New Catholic Left, 1930–1950* (Toronto: University of Toronto Press, 1981), 178.

66 This was presented in the same series as René Gillouin's talk on "the doctrine of the new French state" and another talk by Beuve-Méry's old mentor Achille Mestre. This militantly anti-republican professor of law (in whose study group Beuve-Méry had participated, with Philippe Lamour and others, as a Law student) had become a counsellor to the SGJ. See chapter 1, n. 108.

    One older trainee [Jacques Thérond, in retrospect, in an interview with Bernard Comte], who had been an Esprit group head in Pau before the war, retained "a very unfavourable impression" of Mestre's denunciation of the pre-war Third Republic. Comte, "Uriage," 433.

67 Comte, "Uriage," 442.

68 See Pierre Dunoyer de Segonzac, *Le Vieux Chef. Mémoires et pages choisies* (Paris: Seuil, 1971), 94; Comte, "Uriage," 443, 450.

69 In fact, Doncoeur, aside from his participation in the 1940 colloquium, visited the school at least a second time in February 1941, but his participation seems to have been limited to a reading from Péguy, during a *veillée*. According to Comte, who tends to stress the tensions between Uriage and notorious "collaborators," he was from that time held to be an alien, if not an adversary (Comte, "Uriage," 450).

70 Alfred Fabre-Luce, *Journal de France* (June 1941) (Paris: Imprimerie
    JEP, 1942), 189. Historians of Vichy France must be alert to what is
    left in and out of succeeding editions of works touching on that
    period.

71 Jean Lacroix, "Force et faiblesse du marxisme," two lectures of 17 July
    1941 (mimeographed document, 23 pages), cited in Comte, "Uriage,"
    445. According to Lacroix, Berdyaev was "one of the greatest contem-
    porary philosophers."
        A dense "personalist" lecture by Lacroix, "Primauté de la personne"
    (n.d.), 11 pp., citing Marcel, Blondel, Bergson, Renouvier, Mounier,
    and setting forth what must have been becoming Uriage doctrine, is
    also in the Uriage archives (102 J 148).

72 This was Segonzac speaking in "a typical session" in 1941, cited in
    Comte, "Uriage," 450.

73 Cited in Comte, "Uriage," 450.

74 Cf. Comte, "Uriage," 453; Hours taught in this period, exerting a
    decisive influence on the prominent historian of mentalities Maurice
    Agulhon. Although the *histoire des mentalités* is seen to be a recent dis-
    covery, the term "mentality" was in fairly common use among intelli-
    gentsia in the Vichy period. Philippe Ariès, who later did so much to
    shape this field, described the decisive role that exposure to a leader-
    ship school had on his notion of *mentalité*. The father of the historian
    of peasant mentalities Emmanuel Le Roy, Ladurie was a high official
    for rural affairs in the Vichy regime. Since the essence of the National
    Revolution was to be education, the goal of that education was not to
    be "mere book-learning," and certainly not critical thinking (which
    even the Uriage team, despite their own proudly independent judg-
    ments on political events, tended to denounce, from time to time, as a
    corrosive force), but rather a change in *mentalité* among young French
    people. Therefore it is not surprising that the term was in the air and
    that people were sensitive to the concept.

75 Course notes of André Lecoanet (September 1941), cited in Comte,
    "Uriage," 456.

76 "La jeunesse française," lecture of Garrone to the Richelieu cohort
    (July, 1941), according to the notes of trainee Jean Le Veugle. (102 J
    151)

77 Course notes of André Lecoanet (September 1941), cited in Comte,
    "Uriage," 466, 507.

78 Cf. *L'Illustration* (21 March 1942).

79 Jean Lacroix, *L'adolescence scolaire*, in Collection Le Chef et ses jeunes,
    9 (Grenoble: École Nationale des Cadres, 1942), 8, 35.

80 "Ton foyer dans ta cité, ta profession au service de ton foyer," lecture
    of 30 September 1941 (mimeographed, 11 pages) (102 J 148).

81 Anne-Marie Hussenot, "La Mission de la femme française," *Jeunesse ... France!* 12 (8 May 1941): 3.
82 Comte, "Uriage," 468.
83 We have seen how this meat ration was obtained in June 1941 in the wake of the visit of Admiral Darlan.
84 Cited in Delestre, *Uriage*, 86–7.
85 Cited in Bitoun, *Les hommes*, 61.
86 Testimony cited in Delestre, *Uriage*, 88. In general, however, Madame Müller had good memories of her time at Uriage.
87 Testimony of Gaby Audibert, cited in Delestre, *Uriage*, 86.
88 Bitoun, *Les hommes*, 61–2.
89 Several of the instructors' wives interviewed by Bitoun mentioned the fact that their husbands were seldom home during the heyday of the school. Then, too, Madame Dunoyer de Segonzac and Madame d'Alençon were setting an example by having very large families.
90 This is an interesting fact because Bernanos had had strong intellectual affinities with the Action Française and the kind of Catholics who made up the Uriage staff. Cf. John Hellman, "From the Radical Right to Resistance: De Gaulle, Maritain, and Bernanos," *The Chesterton Review* (Georges Bernanos–Special Issue) 15, no. 4 (November 1989) and 16, no. 1 (February 1990): 513–27.
91 Cf. Comte, "Uriage," 472; Maritain, then in self-imposed exile in the United States, received a letter lauding Uriage from the poet Pierre Emmanuel, but we do not know what he thought of the usage of his ideas at the school. Given his attitude toward the naiveté of his countrymen who were seduced by the rhetoric of the National Revolution, he would probably not have been pleased. Cf. J. Hellman, "Maritain, Simon, and Vichy's elite schools," in *Mortimer J. Adler, Jacques Maritain, and Yves R. Simon. Freedom in the Modern World* (Notre Dame: Notre Dame University Press, 1989), 165–80.
92 With the title *Entretiens pour de jeunes chefs.*
93 These were Segonzac's comments at the *veillée* of the September cohort; cf. "Les qualités à exiger du jeune Français" (mimeographed, no date) (22 J 15); Comte, "Uriage," 474, 540.

CHAPTER FOUR

1 Cf. *Réflexions pour les jeunes chefs* (Grenoble: Éditions ENCU, collection Le Chef et ses jeunes [July 1941]; second complete edition, October 1942) – a collection of the editorials of Segonzac that began each edition of *Jeunesse ... France!* The *Le Chef et ses jeunes* series published monographs by instructors outlining some of the basic doctrinal positions of Uriage.

For the role of the Vieux Chef's reflections see François Ducruy, "P. Dunoyer de Segonzac, chef de l'École des Cadres d'Uriage," "Notes sur le chef," *Revue des jeunes* (January 1941): 17–18 (a précis of Segonzac's notion of the *chef* as formulated by Ducruy); Wladimir d'Ormesson, "L'autorité du chef," *Figaro* (13 March 1941) and "Nécessité d'une mystique" (14 March 1941). (Extracts from the Ducruy text are cited in these two editorials.)

2 Constantly increasing during the first semester (from 22,000 copies on 24 December 1940 to 30,000 on 22 July 1941), the journal's circulation levelled off afterwards, fluctuating until December 1941 between 26,000 and 30,000 copies.

According to a document in the Uriage archives, the school intended to publish only 20,000 copies ("Projet de lancement d'un hebdomadaire de la jeunesse, présenté par l'ENC de la Jeunesse à Uriage") (Poli papers) (102 J 19). According to Bernard Comte the editors were disappointed that the circulation was not larger and that the publication never became self-supporting as they had hoped. Bernard Comte, "L'École Nationale des Cadres d'Uriage. Une communauté éducative non-conformiste à l'époque de la révolution nationale (1940–1942)," Ph.D. thesis, Université de Lyon 2, 1987, 498–9.

3 Comte, "Uriage," 500. *Esprit* would be happy to publish 10,000 copies, *La Vie Intellectuelle* 6,000, before the war. Manevy estimates the circulation of the *Action Française* as 40,000 in 1939.

Despite the fact that *Jeunesse … France!* was the publication of the government's "spiritual university," and one of the most prominent organs of French intellectual life in 1940–41, no copies exist in the Bibliothèque Nationale or, apparently, in any other library in Paris. They have been shunted to the unadorned annex of the Bibliothèque Nationale at Versailles, as seems to be the rule for papers of this period and/or those of a certain size. Most of the *Le Chef et ses jeunes* collection is in the Bibliothèque Nationale but may be consulted only with special permission "due to the poor condition of the bindings". Along with the issues of *Jeunesse … France!* (22 J 43), numbers 4–17 of the *Le Chef et ses jeunes* are now available in the Archives départementales de l'Isère (102 J 22).

4 See "Uriage's Regional Schools" below.

5 Psichari, who was killed in the First World War, was an intimate friend of Jacques Maritain, another one of those pre-war converts whose ideas were valued, and some of which seemed to come to fruition, at Uriage. A prototypical "knight-monk," he was cited by Jean-Jacques Chevallier as the progenitor of the special kind of "virile" literary style Uriage would foster. Cf. J.-J. Chevallier, *L'Ordre viril* (Grenoble: École Nationale des Cadres d'Uriage, 1943).

6 "Aspect de la Jeunesse italienne," *Jeunesse ... France!* 3 (24 December 1940): 10.
7 "La jeunesse hitlérienne," *Jeunesse ... France!* 5 (22 January 1941): 5.
8 "La jeunesse hitlérienne" (cont.), *Jeunesse ... France!* 6 (8 February 1941): 6–7, 9.
9 "Jeunesse Portugaise," *Jeunesse ... France!* 25 (1 December 1941): 6–7.
10 R. Raimondi, "Pro agricola," *Jeunesse ... France!* 21 (22 September 1941); Emmanuel Mounier, "Le seul mal de l'intelligence," *Esprit* 100 (May 1941): 506–9.
11 "Pour que l'esprit vive," in *Jeunesse ... France!* 22 (8 October 1941): 2. Père Carré became another link during this period between pre-war theologians, personalists, Catholic youth leaders, and Uriage. Like several other figures in this milieu, he would, decades later, be elected to the Académie française.
12 Cf. Zeev Sternhell, *Neither Right nor Left. Fascist Ideology in France* (Berkeley: University of California Press, 1986).
13 Thierry Maulnier, "Principes d'un ordre français," *Jeunesse ... France!* 26 (15 December 1941): 2–3.
14 According to the course notes of André Lecoanet, cited in Comte, "Uriage," 520.
15 Paul Nizan, "Sur un certain front unique," *Europe* (January 1933), reprinted in Susan Suleiman, ed., *Pour une nouvelle culture* (Paris: Grasset, 1971), 51, 53, 58–65.
16 "Le Maréchal refait la France," *Jeunesse ... France!* 6 (8 February 1941): 2.
17 Cf. Michel Dupouey, "L'aile marchande de la Révolution," *Jeunesse ... France!* 7 (22 February 1941): 1, 3.
18 According to historian François Bédarida, this is one of the strongest counter-arguments that could be made against the thesis that Uriage was a Resistance institution (interview with the author).
19 "En Syrie, dans le secteur de Palmyre," *Jeunesse ... France!* 19 (26 August 1941): 9.
20 Speech to alumni, meeting of 21 October 1941. A dossier containing notes from, and the speeches to, this important first meeting of the "Association amicale des Anciens de l'École Nationale des Cadres" may be found in the Uriage archives (102 J 117).
21 "Those treating more of social and personal questions than questions 'properly National Revolution,' so that the role of the school (is) essentially political." "Note sur le journal *Jeunesse ... France!* de l'École d'Uriage et sur l'utilité de nommer d'urgence un aumônier à cette École," Cabinet civil du Chef de l'État, sans date (November or December 1941). A.N. AG II 440 I. Cited in Comte, "Uriage," 530.

22 Comte, "Uriage," 531. Comte thinks that this was a sign of punishing the school for beginning a Resistance-leaning path. But he has very little to say about the more highly subsidized, largely circulated (and docilely Pétainist) paper *Marche, le magazine français* that Uriage published beginning 1 January 1941.

23 *Jeunesse ... France!* 23 (1 November 1941): 1ff.; Comte, "Uriage," 531.

24 Documents on these developments remain in the Uriage archives (102 J 19); see also Comte, "Uriage," 533.

25 In a letter from Roger Radisson to the Secrétariat Général de la Jeunesse (6 May 1941), and forwarded to Uriage by M. Pflimlin, "Le Chef de la Propagande, Secrétariat Général de la Jeunesse, Secrétariat d'État à l'Instruction Publique," envisaged publishing a sort of Catholic version of the periodical *Signal*. Radisson cited Stanislas Fumet as a reference (mentioning the fact that Radisson had worked with Fumet at *Temps Nouveau*), Father Desbuguois, director of *l'Action Populaire*, Father Barjon, editor of *Études*, etc. *Marche* resulted from this initiative. See also "Projet pour une revue française" (n.d.), 7 pages (signed R. Radisson) (102 J 19).

    Bernard Comte mentions that already in March the former *ajiste* Ollier de Marichard had proposed transforming *Jeunesse ... France!* into a more generously illustrated, large-circulation, 40-page monthly for young people. It was to be competitive with commercial publications. The habitual rubrics of the school would be conserved, but would be coloured by reporting; it would be a serial, and a review of current events. Comte, "Uriage," 534.

26 The initial subsidy requested was the handsome sum of F2,529,000. "Projet de lancement d'un hebdomadaire de la jeunesse, présenté par l'ENC de la Jeunesse à Uriage" (102 J 19) (Poli papers).

    This episode is one of those that contradict the recurring claim of Uriage alumni that their group had always maintained guarded views of the National Revolution in general and groups like the Compagnons in particular.

27 "A la recherche des Chefs," *Jeunesse ... France!* 21 (22 September 1941): 5.

28 Jacques Robert, "Le disciple de Monsieur Gide," *Marche*, 10 February 1942, 9.

29 Jacques Robert, "Le disciple de Monsieur de Montherlant," *Marche*, 17 February 1942, 18.

30 Jacques Robert, "Le disciple de Monsieur Gide," 9.

31 P.D. de Segonzac, "Les jeunes comparaissent ... ," *Marche*, 24 March 1942, 2.

32 "Bâtir la communauté nationale," *Marche*, 31 March 1942, 13. The flattering allusion to Cocteau was very odd in this context.

33 "L'Amérique dans la guerre," 7–8; "L'armée américaine," 9, in *Marche*, 17 February 1942.

34 "Veille d'offensives. L'Allemagne a achevé le cycle de la préparation totale. Cependant que les citoyens britanniques n'en sont encore qu'au stage d'entraînement militaire," *Marche*, 28 April 1942, 2–3.

35 "Trois routes percent le rempart du Caucase," *Marche*, 16 June 1942, 5.

36 According to Comte, "Uriage," 954.

37 G. Poincelet, "Dans le ciel de Syrie," *Marche* [special issue on *L'Aviation Française*] (c. September, 1942).

38 "La bataille de l'Atlantique continue," *Marche*, 2 December 1942, 9.

39 Bernard Comte's interpretation, based largely on interviews and postwar recollections, is that Segonzac and his inner circle moved secretly, but steadily and inexorably, into myriad Resistance activities throughout 1942. Despite the thoroughness of his documentation there are no references to *Marche* texts, even those by Segonzac, in his dissertation.
   Comte said of that review, citing his interview with Ollier de Marichard: "Ils [Segonzac and Philippe Gaussot of the Compagnons movement, who also worked on it] font travailler plusieurs journalistes lyonnais, liés au mouvement Compagnons ou à *Jeune France*, parmi lesquels dominent l'esprit et quelquefois les engagements de la Résistance." Comte, "Uriage," 953–4.

40 Cf. editorial *Marche*, 3 December 1942, 7.

41 "Ce qu'on lit dans les camps. Les prisonniers et le maréchal," *Marche*, 3 December 1942, 7.

42 See the dossiers "Écoles régionales des cadres" (102 J 142–146); Comte, "Uriage," 559, 565–7.

43 Comte, "Uriage," 567.

44 (A.N., F 44 2, SGJ, Cabinet) cited in Comte, "Uriage," 567.

45 Comte, "Uriage," 569.

46 According to Bernard Comte this was not true and the Scout leaders must have heard of an abortive project, or heard a baseless rumour (Comte, "Uriage," 569). But the Abbé de Naurois did organize a special training session for chaplains.

47 Circular, "Scouts de France" (16 January 1941), cited in Comte, "Uriage," 569.

48 Comte, "Uriage," 569–70.

49 The Coudon school. Lang's case was mentioned, in October 1941, as "*en suspens*" (in abeyance) (Comte, "Uriage," 592).

50 Circulaire du commissariat des Écoles des Éclaireurs Unionistes, 1, cited in Comte, "Uriage," 577.

51 Comte, "Uriage," 576–7. Professor Comte, basing his interpretation on what he was told by the Uriage alumni, described Mounier and

Uriage as constituting a counter-current within, and rival to, Vichy by this time. But instead of engaging in "Resistance activity" Uriage could be more accurately described as trying to create a broadly based "spiritualized revolutionism," if not a sort of "Christian fascism," over against the opportunistic and unimaginative functionaries in the Vichy government.

52 Letter from délégué adjoint Jean Crame to Alain Desforges, editor in chief of *Jeunesse ... France!* (then responsible for relations with the alumni of the national school), 19 June 1941. Cited in Comte, "Uriage," 571.

53 "L'équipe d'Uzos," *Jeunesse ... France. Cahiers d'Uriage*, 31 (May 1941), 44–5.

54 Cf. A. Desforges, "L'équipe d'Uzos," *Jeunesse ... France. Cahiers d'Uriage*, 31 (May 1942), 44–5; André Pierre, "Sortie de plein air à l'Ecole d'Uzos," *Jeunesse ... France. Cahiers d'Uriage*, 29 (March 1942), 53–5. See also Comte, "Uriage," 587–8.

55 Uzos School documents may be found in the Uriage archives (102 J 143); see also Comte, "Uriage," 588.

56 It was organized in December by Louis Marc (regional delegate from Montpellier).

57 Comte, "Uriage," 589.

58 For example, there was a report by *Renouveaux*, the review of the Jesuits' "L'Action Populaire" movement, on 1 November 1941. *Renouveaux* is a good source to use for following the Jesuits' attitude toward the Révolution Nationale in general, and toward Uriage activities such as the Mercuès school in particular.

59 Documents, including Uriage School-Bobigneux correspondence, remain (102 J 144); Comte, "Uriage," 601.

60 Le Veugle had accepted an invitation to join the staff of the École Régionale des Cadres at Chassiers after finishing the course there in spring 1941. Then, after being trained in the "Richelieu" course of Uriage in July, he became chef at Saint-Étienne.

61 Uriage archives (102 J 146); J. Le Veugle, "L'action 'jeune' à l'ENP de Saint-Étienne," *Jeunesse ... France! Cahiers d'Uriage* 31 (May 1942), 4 pp.; Comte, "Uriage," 596–7.

62 Comte, "Uriage," 594.

63 This is evident from the many files with material from former trainees in the Uriage archives, and their correspondence with the school.

64 "Fonctionnement de l'association: compte-rendu et conférences de la première assemblée générale (21 October 1941) (102 J 117); Comte, "Uriage," 599.

65 Ibid. (102 J 117); Comte, "Uriage," 602.

66 "Réunion générale du 20 Octobre 1941, Exposé du Vieux Chef,"
   3 pages, in the *Bulletin de l'Équipe Nationale d'Uriage* 1 (1 November
   1941) (mimeographed) (102 J 120).

67 Ibid.; Comte, "Uriage," 604.

68 See Uriage archives (102 J 153) on the El-Riath school; Comte,
   "Uriage," 572. During the Algerian struggle for independence after
   the Second World War, Segonzac would be sent by the French government to try to create a loyal, pro-French youth movement there.

69 Comte, "Uriage," 606.

70 The law of 7 December 1940.

71 Comte, "Uriage," 607.

72 The abbé Georges Guérin, national chaplain of the jocistes, persuaded Aubert, she said later, to enter into the SGJ to struggle against
   the danger of enrolling young women into a single movement with
   totalitarian tendencies. Interview with Mme. Picard-Aubert, 1979,
   cited in Comte, "Uriage," 608.

73 In the Payen residence, 25 chemin du Trouillat. Comte, "Uriage,"
   607–8.

74 See *Jeunesse ... France!* 20 (8 October 1941). But the Pau school would
   close at the end of the year. Comte, "*Uriage,*" 608.

75 Ravon, Georges, "Au centre d'Écully," *Le Figaro*, 14 January 1941.

76 Comte, "Uriage," 612–3. See Jean Jousselin, *Le rôle de la Jeunesse*
   (Lecture given 1 March 1941 at l'École libre des Sciences Politiques),
   Paris, 26 pages.

77 Coucou, "Des cadres pour les jeunes chômeurs en territoire occupé,"
   L'équipe, organe des routiers éclaireurs unionistes, 1941, 88–90.
   Comte, "Uriage," 614.

78 Jean Jousselin's ideas are reflected in a series of his publications during
   this period: *Le chef et son métier* (Paris: Éditions des Loisirs, 1942) (a
   book consecrated to his "Christian and humanist" conception of the
   leader); *École du civisme* (Paris: PUF, 1941) (a brochure in the "Bibliothèque du peuple" series of the Presses Universitaires de France, 64
   pp.); and *Les jeunes reconstruiront la France* (Paris: Presses Universitaires
   de France, 1942) (also in the "Bibliothèque du peuple" series, 64 pp.),
   another pamphlet explaining his pedagogical principles and methods.

79 Cf. François Sentein, *Minutes d'un libertin* (Paris: La Table Ronde,
   1977), 220, 238.

80 W.D. Halls, *The Youth of Vichy France* (Oxford: Clarendon Press, 1981),
   36.

81 German document cited in Halls, *Youth*, 142.

82 Halls, *Youth*, 309; Comte, "Uriage," 622.

83 Interview with Dunoyer de Segonzac in 1967, cited in Comte,
   "Uriage," 622.

84 Comte, "Uriage," 623.

85   Halls, *Youth*, 309–10.
86   Goutet was in the entourage of Paul Baudouin, who had helped found the Compagnons de France and had become the first director for youth in the ministry for family and youth set up in 1940. Cf. Halls, *Youth*, 133, 267.
87   H. Daniel-Rops, "Jeunesse féminine en zone occupée," *Revue des jeunes* 11 (15 September 1941), 8–10, 15. The attitudes toward women revealed in articles such as this are interesting from the point of view of the history of mentalities.
88   Cf. Comte, "Uriage," 625.

CHAPTER FIVE

1   J.-P. Filliette, "Recherche d'un plan d'action," *Jeunesse ... France!* 11 (22 April 1941).
2   See the dossier "Association amicale des Anciens de l'École Nationale des Cadres" (102 J 117); Correspondence with Pasteau and Théréne, who had become chefs in the Chantiers de la marine (June 1941). Cited in Bernard Comte, "L'École Nationale des Cadres d'Uriage. Une communauté éducative non-conformiste à l'époque de la révolution nationale (1940–1942)," Ph.D. thesis, Université de Lyon 2, 1987, 629.
3   Documentation on Uriage's central role in the organization of the Écoles régionales des cadres are in the Uriage archives (102 J 142).
4   Personal notes of Jean Le Veugle (at Bobigneux, 23 September 1941) cited in Comte, "Uriage," 631. Le Veugle's records of Uriage conferences are in the Uriage archives (102 J 151).
5   "Fonctionnement de l'association: compte-rendu et conférences de la première assemblée générale" (21 October 1941), 7–8, in Uriage archives (102 J 117).
6   Ibid., 8–9.
7   This is the conclusion of Professor Comte in "Uriage," 636.
8   According to Comte, "Uriage," 633.
9   "Équipe nationale d'Uriage" (Association des anciens élèves de l'école nationale des cadres), *Jeunesse ... France!* 24 (15 November 1941), 9.
10   Ibid., 9.
11   Ibid., 9.
12   Conclusion of the "Exposé du Vieux Chef," *Équipe Nationale d'Uriage* 1 (November 1941), 3. Copies of this review may be found in the Uriage archives (102 J 120).
13   See Uriage archives (102 J 117–22); Comte, "Uriage," 640.
14   Notes of Le Veugle on the days of 3, 7 December. Cited in Comte, "Uriage," 643; Le Veugle's papers are in the Uriage archives (102 J 149–153, temporary numbering).

15 Letter from Le directeur de la formation des jeunes (section d'Études) to M. le chef de l'ENC (21 February 1942), cited in Comte, "Uriage," 650.

16 Extract of the "Compte-rendu des contacts pris par le chef Chombart de Lauwe" (mimeographed, 2 pages), signed by L. Lallement and included in his "Liaison Vichy, 2, 6 November 1941" dossier. Cited in Comte, "Uriage," 651.

17 Cf. Comte, "Uriage," 641, 653.

18 Daniel Lindenberg, *Les années souterraines, 1937–1947* (Paris: La Découverte, 1990), 228. For more on *Économie et Humanisme* see ibid., 217–43, and the forthcoming thesis of Denis Pelletier which will demonstrate the importance of this group.

19 Comte, "Uriage," 662.

20 This exhortation was in "Principe du pluralisme des mouvements de jeunesse," a note published by *Jeunesse ... France!* 9 (22 March 1941), as well as in the reviews of the youth movements, at the request of the SGJ. Cf. Comte, "Uriage," 670.

21 Cf. Comte, "Uriage," 671.

22 (Lyon: Éditions de l'Abeille, September 1941). This book is cited in Comte, "Uriage," 671.

23 This is revealed in correspondence between Garrone and Msgr Chollet cited in Comte, "Uriage," 675.

24 Document cited in Comte, "Uriage," 677.

25 This is revealed in much material in the Uriage archives, (notably dossiers 102 J 1, 4, 6, 8, 11).

26 Comte, "Uriage," 689. This fact shows how it is an oversimplification to blame Henri Massis for the silencing and/or imprisonment of Emmanuel Mounier, and that it is not so easy to make Garrone into a patriotic hero in Vichy administration youth circles.

After the war, terrified of a Communist takeover, French Catholics tended to avoid blaming their fellow Catholics for their persecutions under Vichy.

27 W.D. Halls, *The Youth of Vichy France* (Oxford: Clarendon Press, 1981), 133.

28 In *Le Chef*, September 1940, cited in Comte, "Uriage," 690.

29 Philippe Laneyrie, *Les Scouts de France* (Paris: Cerf, 1985), 103–10, 134–8 (cited in Comte, "Uriage," 692).

30 Comte, "Uriage," 645, 693.

31 In an exposition made to the regional school heads' meeting of 20 October 1941. Cf. "Fonctionnement de l'association: compte-rendu et conférences de la première assemblée générale" (21 October 1941) in the Uriage archives (102 J 117). Documents relating to Uriage's relationship with the regional schools (102 J 142–146) as well as with other youth movements such as the scouts (102 J 6) are in the Uriage archives.

32 Document cited in Comte, "Uriage," 696–7.

33 Cf. René Wargnies, "Les Écoles des cadres du régime nouveau," *Cahiers de notre jeunesse* 2 (July-August 1941).

34 See Mounier's *Oeuvres*, 4 (Paris: Seuil, 1963), 693, recording Msgr Guerry's views on this problem. Also relevant are the remarks of André Villette, former national secretary of the JOC, speaking on "La Jeunesse Ouvrière Chrétienne pendant la guerre," during the meeting of the commission d'histoire de la vie religieuse, Comité d'histoire de la Deuxième Guerre mondiale, 13 June 1979, mimeographed, 46 pages, cited in Comte, "Uriage," 700.

35 Michel Riondet, SJ, federal secretary of the JEC Dauphinois.

36 Comte, "Uriage," 700 n.38.

37 A. Dumas, "Sessions d'étudiants de Pâques 1941," *Correspondance*, May 1941, 25–8, cited in Comte, "Uriage," 708.

38 Pierre François, commissaire national (éditorial), *Le Chef*, July 1941, cited in Comte, "Uriage," 674. In the same period there were some strong warnings about totalitarianism by French Protestant leaders. Cf. *Le Conseil Protestant de la Jeunesse*, Lyon, 1941, 16 pages.

Pastor Westphal explained in his preface how this tract was written "sous la contrainte de l'Esprit" in an effort to clarify Protestant reservations about racism, national totalitarianism, etc., while being committed "à la libération et au redressement du pays" (cited in Comte, "Uriage," 675).

39 Cf. Comte, "Uriage," 711–12.

40 On Scout impressions of Uriage see "Flamant" (Stephen Maret de Grenaud), "Impressions sur l'École supérieure des Cadres d'Uriage," *Le Routier* (February 1941).

As far as Jewish scouts are concerned, André Harris and Alain de Sedouy's *Juifs et Français* (Paris: Grasset, 1979), 79, contains an interview with Robert Munnich, former polytechnician and Chef Éclaireur Israélite de France who liked the camaraderie, the songs, explorations, and general ambience at Uriage but retained a "very deadly memory" of his experience because one had to take an oath of loyalty to Pétain at the end of the camp and he knew by that time that Pétain was *l'abandon, la trahison*.

Contrary to what Michael Marrus and Robert Paxton say in their otherwise careful book on Vichy and the Jews, Xavier Vallat did not present his doctrine on Jews at Uriage. The authors confuse the École Nationale des Cadres de la Jeunesse with the École Nationale des Cadres civiques.

41 Cited in Jacques Duquesne, *Les Catholiques français sous l'Occupation* (Paris: Grasset, 1966), 201.

42 *Un an de Révolution Nationale, juin 1940 – juillet 1941* (Lyon, 1941), 53.

43 A parallel but not very successful girls' movement – women had been represented at the first camp at Randan – the Compagnes de France, was started in 1942. There is material on the Groupements de Jeunesse féminine in the Uriage archives (102 J 11). For more detail on the Compagnons see Halls, *Youth*, 267–9.

44 Cited in Jacques Duquesne, *Les catholiques*, 203.

45 Cited in Robert Paxton, *La France de Vichy* (Paris: Seuil, 1973), 160.

46 Pierre Limagne, *Éphémérides de quatre années tragiques, 1940–1944*. 1. *De Bordeaux à Bir-Hakeim* (Lavilledieu: Éditions de Candide, 1987), diary note for 25 August 1940, 16.

47 Mounier, *Oeuvres* 4, 674.

48 Halls, *Youth*, 272.

49 Comte, "Uriage," 730.

50 A. Cruziat, "Positions Compagnons. Unité dans la diversité," *Le Chef Compagnon*, 15 December 1940. Emmanuel Mounier was then collaborating on the weekly publicity organ of the Community, *Compagnons*. A selection of early *Compagnons* documents may be found in Uriage archives (102 J 8).

51 From his position as a lieutenant of Bergery, Maze made a significant effort to bring together all of the different personalists on the eve of the war. His effort came to fruition in institutions like the Compagnons. For more on his role in these years see John Hellman, *Emmanuel Mounier and the New Catholic Left, 1930–1950* (Toronto: University of Toronto Press, 1981), 156, 167, 169, 172, 173.

52 Guy Horlin, "Compagnons de France," in *Mouvements de jeunesse*, Collection Le Chef et ses jeunes, 11 (Grenoble: École Nationale des Cadre d'Uriage, 1941), 87–91. The essays in that book included Pierre Dunoyer de Segonzac, "Mouvements de Jeunesse," 9; Pierre Cazanavette, "Le Scoutisme," 13; Albert Gortais, "Association Catholique de la Jeunesse Française," 42; Jacques Trouville, "La Jeunesse Ouvrière Chrétienne," 56; Guy Horlin, "Compagnons de France," 73; "Union Chrétienne des Jeunes Gens," 92; R. Casalis, "La Fédération Française des Associations Chrétiennes d'Étudiants," 99; Ollier de Marichard, "Les Auberges Françaises de Jeunesse," 104, "Les Camarades de la Route," 109; Charles Nicot, "Les jeunesses paysannes," 115; Henri Bartoli, "Les équipes sociales," 120; "Déclaration des Mouvements de Jeunesse," 133; "Plan de Cercles d'études sur les Mouvements de Jeunesse," 135. Bartoli's essay suggested that the Équipes sociales were now much more active than before the war.

The volume as a whole was a graphic illustration of Uriage's pretension to guide French youth under the Vichy regime.

53 Testimony of M. Hoepffner on the feeling of Segonzac regarding the Compagnons. Cited in Comte, "Uriage," 733. This retrospective

testimony about Segonzac's attitude seems plausible. But we must recall, on the other hand, that Uriage seems not to have hesitated at the prospect of working in partnership with the Compagnons to publish the periodical *Marche* in 1941. In general, Uriage alumni seem to have had a tendency to overemphasize the differences between the two movements.

54 Mounier, *Oeuvres* 4.
55 Comte, "Uriage," 734.
56 Halls, *Youth*, 273.
57 Comte, "Uriage," 734.
58 Marc Lelarge, "Vers un pluralisme actif," *Métier de Chef*, 1–4, May–September 1941.
59 See "Stage spécial des 7–14 mai 1941; Compagnons" (102 J 69); Comte, "Uriage," 735.
60 According to General de Gaulle's informants, François Mitterrand was part of the close entourage of this "very Action Française" man. Cited in Catherine Nay, *Le noir et le rouge ou l'histoire d'une ambition* (Paris: Grasset, 1984), 119. At this writing, M. Mitterrand has maintained silence about allegations of his having an extreme right-wing past.
61 Disappointed by Vichy, Petitjean would search out Drieu la Rochelle at the NRF in Paris, after having expressed his desperate rage in the book *Combats préliminaires* (Paris: Gallimard, 1941).
62 Halls, *Youth*, 274.
63 R. Hervet, *Les Compagnons de France* (Paris: France-Empire, 1965), 114.
64 Comte, "Uriage," 736.
65 Halls, *Youth*, 274–5.
66 Testimony cited by R. Hervet, *Les Compagnons*, 153–4.
67 "Laison Vichy, 2 to 6 November 1941, Report of Contacts Made by Chef Chombart de Lauwe," Uriage archives (102 J 12).
68 This is revealed by Bertram Gordon, *Collaboration in France during the Second World War* (Ithaca and London: Cornell University Press, 1980), and we will return to the anti-Pétainist collaborators in the youth movements in the first part of chapter 8.
69 The correspondence in the Uriage archives reveals Marichard and Segonzac trying hard to bring youth movements together in the *Marche* initiative (102 J 19).
70 Cf. documents of "Les Camarades de la Route" in the Uriage archives (102 J 11).
71 "Routes nouvelles," editorial of *Routes* (monthly bulletin of *ajiste* youth "Les Camarades de la Route"), no. 1, April 1942. Cited in Comte, "Uriage," 748.
72 Comte, "Uriage," 764.

288 Notes to pages 138-42

73 Cf. Lionel Terray, *Les conquérants de l'inutile* (Paris: Gallimard, 1961). In his description of "Jeunesse et Montagne," Terray alludes to the mixed quality of the different centres: some brutal, with "crazy methods."

1 The minister of education from February 1941, Jérôme Carcopino, later explained how he had reproached him for this, and had been obliged to disavow several of his projects.

Jêrome Carcopino, *Souvenirs de sept ans* (Paris: Flammarion, 1953), 517; Bernard Comte, "L'École Nationale des Cadres d'Uriage. Une communauté éducative non-conformiste à l'époque de la révolution nationale (1940–1942)," Ph.D. thesis, Université de Lyon 2, 1987, 780–1.

2 On the evolution toward Nazism of Belgian Catholic youth leaders such as Léon Degrelle and Raymond de Becker see John Hellman, *Emmanuel Mounier and the New Catholic Left, 1930–1950* (Toronto: University of Toronto Press, 1981), chapters 6–7.

3 He would hold this post until Pierre Laval's return to power in April 1942 – also a crucial date for Uriage, as we shall see.

4 W.D. Halls, *The Youth of Vichy France* (Oxford: Clarendon Press, 1981), 22–3.

5 On Pétain protecting Lamirand see Michèle Cointat-Labrousse, *Vichy et le fascisme* (Brussels: Ed. Complexe, 1987), 131.

6 See Comte, "Uriage," 781; Delestre, *Uriage, une communauté et une école dans la tourmente* (Nancy, Presses Universitaires de Nancy, 1989), 146.

7 Mounier, "Entretiens 12" (28 July 1941), *Oeuvres* 4 (Paris: Seuil, 1963), 710–12.

8 Documentation on this *stage* is in the Uriage archives (102 J 54–6). Document here is cited in Comte, "Uriage," 793, n. 33.

9 Comte, "Uriage," 793.

10 The Abbey of Pontigny was the setting for, among other things, the series of meetings of French "Planist" intellectuals that began in 1934. It was better known, beginning in the 1920s, for the annual "Décades de Pontigny," a series of high-powered symposia on general and contemporary themes to which hand-picked personalities were invited, and which were a fixture of pre-war intellectual life.

11 Copies of several letters to Vichy authorities questioning the loyalties of Uriage are in the Uriage archives (102 J 13). The document cited is in Comte, "Uriage," 795.

12 12 Claude Bourdet, *L'aventure incertaine. De la Résistance à la Restauration* (Paris: Stock, 1975), 43.

13 Max-Pol Fouchet, *Un jour je m'en souviens, mémoire parlée* (Paris: Mercure de France, 1968), 59.

14 Pierre Boutang, "M. Emmanuel Mounier contre Barrès," *L'Action Française*, 10 July 1941).

15 Comte, "Uriage," 796, n.28.

16 Marc Augier, "Marchons au pas, Camarades! une enquête sur la Jeunesse dans la Révolution Nationale," *La Gerbe*, 24 July 1941. The subtitles of this article are "Les Chevaliers sans armure" and "Ces messieurs les personnalistes."

17 Interview (previously cited) in Pierre Bitoun, *Les Hommes d'Uriage* (Paris: La Découverte, 1988), 90–1.

18 Interview with de Naurois cited in Delestre, *Uriage*, 108. This is confirmed by the tone of Beuve-Méry's remarks about the priest in his interview with the author.

19 "Entretiens 12," 28 July 1941, in Mounier, *Oeuvres* 4, 711. According to Bernard Comte, Segonzac, in a unique gesture, took up his own pen to respond to this challenge to his autonomy. He confided to Mounier that he was the author of the anonymous note in *Jeunesse ... France!* in which Massis, sickly "candidate for immortality" [i.e., the Académie française, to which, in fact, he was later elected] was ridiculed as the author of false rumours on Segonzac's health and on the health of his school. This acerbic allusion brought Segonzac a reprimand from the censor. Comte, "Uriage," 797.

20 Comte, "Uriage," 796.

21 According to the "Notes de stage" of J. Le Veugle. M. Le Veugle's documents are in the Uriage archives (102 J 149–153).

22 René Benjamin, "La France retrouve son âme," *Candide*, 17 September 1941. This celebration of Uriage is cited at length above and was reprinted in Benjamin's *Les sept étoiles de France* (Paris: Plon, 1942).

It is a significant text not only because it indicates that the foremost interpreter of the essence of "Pétainisme" thought he discovered it in its pure form at Uriage and eloquently put it in words but also because it shows that the school remained in high – perhaps unprecedented – favour during that summer of 1941 that brought about the purging of de Naurois and Mounier. (Bernard Comte suggests, citing a remark of Mounier's, that Benjamin had been unwelcome at Uriage, and that this was a period when there were already grave tensions between Pétain's entourage and a school already leaning toward the Resistance.)

23 Mounier, "Entretiens 12" (29 August, 2 October 1941) (unpublished section).

24 See Gillouin's subsequent book *Problèmes français, problèmes humains* (Geneva: Éditions du Milieu du Monde, 1944).

25 "15 Août à Uriage," *Jeunesse ... France!* 19 (26 August 1941) and notes of J. Le Veugle cited in Delestre, *Uriage*, 116.

26 Comte, "Uriage," 805, n.55.

27 Comte, "Uriage," 799.

28 Direction de la Formation des Jeunes, "Organisation et fonctionne-ment des Écoles des Cadres," Vichy (Archives of the school, c. Fall 1941, mimeographed text of 3 pages, not dated or signed), cited in Delestre, *Uriage*, 120.

29 Comte, "Uriage," 800, n.45.

30 Circular from the director of the Training of Youth (8 September 1941), cited in Comte, "Uriage," 801.

31 According to Mounier, "Entretiens 12" (25 August, 25 September, 7 October) (unpublished section).

32 Delestre, *Uriage*, 121.

33 Comte, "Uriage," 815.

34 About 1,000 in the normal sessions, and 600 in the special sessions. F. Ducruy, "Historique de l'École", *Jeunesse ... France!* 21 (22 September 1941), 8.

35 "La vie à l'École", *Jeunesse ... France!* 21 (22 September 1941), 6–7.

36 Pierre Dunoyer de Segonzac, "À la recherche des Chefs," *Jeunesse ... France!* 21 (22 September 1941), 5.

37 F. Ducruy, "Historique de l'École", 8.

38 Comte, "Uriage," 810.

39 Comte, "Uriage," 823.

40 Mounier letter to Xavier Schorderet (5 October 1941) in *Oeuvres* 4 (Paris, 1963), 717–18; "Entretiens 12" (5 October 1941) (unpublished section), cited in Comte, "Uriage," 812.

41 Comte, "Uriage," 812–13.

42 Correspondence Gravier-Du Moulin, A.N., A.G.II 440 CC III I. Cited in Comte, "Uriage," 813. For more on this school, see *Recueil des Con-férences de l'ENCC*, Edited by the SGIP (Bibliothèque Nationale, 80 R. 48168).

   Bernard Comte reproaches North American historians Eugene Weber, and Michael Marrus and Robert Paxton, for unfairly discred-iting Segonzac's school by confusing lectures given at the ENCC of Mayet with those given at the ENC of Uriage.

43 Comte, "Uriage," 818.

44 "Écoles des Cadres," *Cahiers d'Information* du S.G.., no. 1, cited in Comte, "Uriage," 821; for documentation on Garrone's project see Uriage archives 102 J 4.

45 L. Garrone, "Principes et plan d'action de la direction de la Formation des jeunes," *Cahiers d'information* 2: 1–4, cited in Comte, "Uriage," 803.

46 Louis Garrone, "L'objection de conscience," foreword article of the *Cahiers d'information* of the SGJ 3, no date, 1–2, cited in Comte, "Uriage," 803.

47 Comte, "Uriage," 823, 825; considerable documentation on the six-month stage is in the Uriage archives (102 J 98–105).

48 A general catalogue and analytical catalogues are contained in the Uriage archives (102 J 23).

49 See Hellman, *Mounier*, chapter 7.

50 Cf. Uriage archives "Service de documentation" (102 J 25).

51 "Bibliographie sommaire de Culture générale," Uriage, undated documentation, 4 pp. Cf. Uriage archives (102 J 23, 25) and Comte, "Uriage," 900–1.

52 "Notes pour les instructeurs sur le stage de six mois" by E. d'Alençon, 3 typed pages (document P. Hoepffner), cited in Comte, "Uriage," 905–6.

53 According to Hoepffner, only Pastor Lochard remained single among the instructors. Cited in Comte, "Uriage," 906.

54 Among them, Dr. René Biot, a distinguished member of the Conseil National de la Jeunesse, and sympathizer of Ordre Nouveau.

55 Bovet and Bourjade, among others.

56 J. Dumazedier, "Après la première Session de Lyon," *Jeunesse ... France!* 27 (1 January 1942), 8–9.

57 Simone Weil was much admired by the miners of St. Étienne after her work with them. Cf. John Hellman, *Simone Weil. An Introduction to Her Thought* (Philadelphia: Fortress Press, 1984), 33–6.
   The Ordre Nouveau group also organized *stages* of factory work before the war for its young intellectuals and technocrats.

58 See Uriage archives on the six-month session (102 J 98–105), and Delestre, *Uriage*, 135.

59 *Chefs* Hoepffner and Malespina published a testimonial on that experience: "La mine," *Jeunesse ... France!* 27 (1 January 1942).

60 Cited in Delestre, *Uriage*, 135.

61 Uriage archives on the six-month session (102 J 98–105); Delestre, *Uriage*, 137; Comte, "Uriage," 908.

62 Hubert Beuve-Méry, "Stage de Formation de Six Mois," in "L'École Nationale des Cadres" (mimeographed, c. August 1942) (102 J 14); Uriage archives, "Stage de formation des 8 février–24 août 1942) (102 J 98–105); Comte, "Uriage," 909–10, 912.

63 Cf. Bitoun, *Les hommes*, 75.

64 "Intellectuels," *Jeunesse ... France!* 8 (8 March 1941), 1.

65 Étienne Berthet, "La déchéance physique de la jeunesse française, ses causes, ses remèdes," *Jeunesse ... France!* 32 (June, 1942).

66 "La mission, l'esprit et la règle d'Uriage," "confidential" document, mimeographed (probably Spring 1941), Uriage archives (22 J 2).

67 Gilles Ferry, "Pour une pensée claire," *Jeunesse ... France!* 31 (May 1942), 19.
68 Ibid., 21–2.
69 Bitoun, *Les hommes*, 67. See above, chapter 3, "Daily Life."
70 Ibid., 72–3.
71 Ibid., 73. (This is cited at greater length in the introduction.)
72 This hopeful, apocalyptic mood was worlds away from the picture presented by the recollections of many of the alumni and ex-instructors about how what they had really wanted to do was to create a little island of resistance or "health" in a regime about which they were sceptical.
73 Dunoyer de Segonzac cited in Bitoun, *Les hommes*, 73.
74 Comte, "Uriage," 916.
75 Cf. "Charles Péguy et la révolution du XXe siècle" (1943?), in Uriage archives (22 J 15) and Hubert Beuve-Méry, "Péguy, révolutionnaire français" in "Charles Péguy" (directed by Jean Bastaire), *Cahiers de l'Herne* 32 (1977), 309–21. Cf. Comte, "Uriage," 917.
76 Material on the factory experience (from May 11–17, 1942) is in the Uriage archives (102 J 102). The trainees were each assigned to a farm in the Southwest; one of them was the property of M. Bonnet, a friend and regular lecturer at Uriage, at Savigny, near L'Arbresle (Rhône). Comte, "Uriage," 919.
77 Cf. "Organisation du stage" in Uriage archives (102 J 98) and the exposition of Reuter on the community, cycle 9, and note of the cahier of Jean Barthalais cited in Comte, "Uriage," 920.
78 L'école Sainte-Anne de Marseille, those of Saint-Bauzille at Montpellier, of Meyargues near Aix would receive the principal contingents, together with l'école d'Art-sur-Meurthe (near Nancy) in the occupied zone.
79 Jean Brivoizac and Louis de Poix. Affectation des stagiaires de la session de six mois, 4 pp., typed, undated, Uriage archives (102 J 99).
80 On the festivals of Vichy see the interesting monograph by Christian Faure, *Le projet culturel de Vichy. Folklore et Révolution Nationale* (Lyon: Presses Universitaires de Lyon, 1989).
81 Emphasis mine.
82 Cf. "Le mot du Vieux Chef" sent out to the Uriage alumni in Uriage archives (102 J 103).
83 Bitoun, *Les hommes*, 45.
84 Delestre, *Uriage*, 156.
85 See information on the meeting from various publications in Uriage archives (102 J 103), and Comte, "Uriage," 922.
86 Among those who came to the Fête were: M. Amande, a friend of the School, head of the cabinet of the Prefect of the Isère; Generals Tanant and Laffargue; Colonel Humbert, military commander of the

Department; MM. Merceron-Viat, conseiller national; and Perriaux, regional inspector, representing the director of general education and sports.

According to articles from *Le Petit Dauphinois, La République du Sud-Est*, and *La Dépêche Dauphinoise* of 3 August 1942 in the Uriage archives (102 J 103). The list of people to invite remains in the Uriage archives, ibid., and was essentially made up of Grenoble-area, rather than high-profile national, personalities.

87 According to the *Journal de bord des Comédiens Routiers*, cited in Delestre, *Uriage*, 156.

88 According to *Le Petit Dauphinois, La République du Sud-Est et La Dépêche Dauphinoise* of 3 August 1942 (Uriage archives, 102 J 103); also cited in Delestre, *Uriage*, 156–7.

89 "Le jeu du glaive et du château" ("The story of the castle and the two-edged sword. A mystery to celebrate the community of chefs of the École Nationale des Cadres and of those who have come to receive their teaching") by *chef* Bertrand d'Astorg, mimeographed, 38 pp., remains in the Uriage archives (102 J 103). It is cited at length in Delestre, *Uriage*, 157–60.

90 *Journal ... Routiers*, cited in Delestre, *Uriage*, 160.

91 Comte, "Uriage," 922.

92 *Journal ... Routiers*, and *Journal d'un résistant*, cited in Delestre, *Uriage*, 161.

93 Emphasis mine.

94 *Journal ... Routiers* and *Journal d'un résistant*, cited in Delestre, *Uriage*, 161.

95 Pastor Lochard and Ollier de Marchand found the text of the scenic play "dismaying" (in their *Journal ... Routiers*, cited in Delestre, *Uriage*, 156.)

96 Father des Alleux (R.P. Vandevoorde, O.P.) was suspect to Segonzac for having gone on an excursion into the mountains the preceding weekend with the others rather than preparing the Fête. Des Alleux recalled the event as "a manifestation of auto-satisfaction," a "bluff," "powder in the eyes," or, in short, "a psychological error." Cited in Delestre, *Uriage*, 156.

97 Emphasis mine.

98 Cf. "Le mot du Vieux Chef," *Équipe Nationale d'Uriage*, 4 (April 1942) in Uriage archives (102 J 120).

CHAPTER SEVEN

1 Gillouin later described how the Marshall asked him to write the opening speech for the Commission d'études des questions de Jeunesse (5 March 1942) and requested last-minute revisions. It was

composed from themes set out by Henri Massis, who wanted "the plan for a vast, solid, and durable edifice" in the area of the youth institutions. The Cabinet approved the tone of the Massis project, judging it however "very Maurrasian (intellectual, traditional) ... too long, too scholarly." Cited in Bernard Comte, "L'École Nationale des Cadres d'Uriage. Une communauté éducative non-conformiste à l'époque de la révolution nationale (1940–1942)," Ph.D. thesis, Université de Lyon 2, 1987, 843.

2 Pierre Dunoyer de Segonzac had often visited his paternal uncle when, at 17, he was preparing for Saint-Cyr at the Collège Sainte-Geneviève. That "man of science ... honest ... totally and passionately Maurrassian," introduced him into a "prestigious" Parisian intellectual milieu where he learned a great deal. Pierre Dunoyer de Segonzac, *Le Vieux Chef. Mémoires et pages choisies* (Paris: Seuil, 1971), 31–3, 104.

3 Comte, "Uriage," 852–3.

4 Segonzac, *Le Vieux Chef*, 104. It is unclear just what Bergery said in defence of Uriage. He was drifting in a more and more proto-fascist, even crypto-nazi, direction at the time and seemed a partisan of more regimentation, even of a "jeunesse unique," in France. It is unlikely that Bergery would have defended Uriage out of any liberal instincts. He did, however, have old ties with several personalists who were active at the school, as we have seen. Some old friends of *Esprit* such as L.-E. Galey and Jean Maze (whose effort to take over the Compagnons he backed) stayed close to him through most of the war.

On Bergery's drift toward a collaborationist position during these years see Philippe Burrin, *La Dérive Fasciste, Doriot, Déat, Bergery, 1933–1945* (Paris: Seuil, 1986), 360–84.

5 "C.R.A., no. 3, p. 16," cited in Comte, "Uriage," 854.

6 According to the informer of the cabinet of the chief of state (Note of 6 March), cited in Comte, "Uriage," 854.

7 Gidel was an ally of the relatively apolitical scholar who was minister of education at the time (Carcopino).

8 "C.R.A., no. 3–5," cited in Comte, "Uriage," 854–5.

9 "A.N./A.G.II 650," cited in Antoine Delestre, *Uriage, une communauté et une école dans la tourmente, 1940–1945* (Nancy: Presses Universitaires de Nancy, 1989), 149–50. Segonzac's response, putting down this idea of a manual, was "Les Écoles de Cadres," *Jeunesse ... France!* 30 (April 1942): 1–4.

10 "C.R.A., no. 7," cited in Comte, "Uriage," 859.

11 Anonymous note of the Civil Cabinet, Vichy, 13 March 1942, 4 pages (A.G.II, 440), cited in Comte, "Uriage," 861.

12 Jean Maze and Robert Loustau gravitated in Esprit/Ordre Nouveau circles before the war. This report seems to suggest how areligious

"personalists" jockeyed with Catholics for control of National Revolution institutions. Bernard Comte seems to exaggerate the tensions between these groups (e.g., by ignoring the fact that Bonnard wrote a hagiographical study of St. Francis, or that Maze helped personalists like Mounier when he could).

According to Comte, none of the men solidly favourable to Segonzac in the entourage of the Marshal (Doctor Ménétrel, General Laure, Du Moulin de Labarthète) or who expressed sympathy for him (Admiral Fernet, René Gillouin) had sympathy for the "personalist" orientations of Mounier, or the critical spirit of Beuve-Méry. But this is to ignore Gillouin's background, his concrete aid to Mounier, and his subsequent writings. Cf. Comte, "Uriage," 863–4.

13 Delestre, *Uriage*, 152–3.
14 The American historian Robert O. Paxton based his revisionist views largely on German archives (which may or may not be an accurate reflection of Pétain's position). The papers presented to the international colloquium on "Le régime de Vichy et les Français" organized by the *Institut d'Histoire du Temps Présent* (CNRS) in Paris, 11–13 June 1990, indicated that French scholars were intent on "taking back" the leadership in scholarship on the history of that period from foreigners, and that the French scholars' findings suggest that the general French population were less supportive of the Vichy regime than the foreigners have tended to assume.
15 As one example, Gillouin went on to publish "Pétainist" texts, very much in the line of the original National Revolution rhetoric, in Switzerland, as if it were no longer feasible in France – thus demonstrating that one could still believe in the National Revolution, but be strongly hostile to Laval and the "power" at Vichy. This seems to be the original cast of the Uriage "Resistance" activity.
16 This general view is supported by Delestre's sources from Uriage. They differ from Comte's, and seem more persuasive to me. Comte's most important living sources on the history of Uriage, basically from the postwar "Catholic Left," preferred to de-emphasize the fidelity of Segonzac and Uriage to Pétain. Delestre's sources, more centred on military officers and later Resistance efforts, tended to disdain this "Leftist" revision of the Uriage past and try to re-establish a balance on this point.
17 Pierre Limagne, *Éphémérides* (Lavilledieu: Éditions de Candide, 1987) (9 September 1942), 768.
18 Cited in Delestre, *Uriage*, 153.
19 Limagne, *Éphémérides* (2 August 1942), 688.
20 Pastor Charles Westphal, vice-president of the CPJ (and former member of an ecumenical circle parallel to the Moulin-Vert group in

1931) justified his refusal to participate in that Paris reunion by explaining that if the Protestants were "prepared to follow the work of the moral re-education of youth" in common with the Marshall they did not want to get involved with education and political action: "We do not want to become wedded to a political line, whatever it might be. It is a question of principle." Cf. his letter of 6 August 1942 (archives of the school) addressed to the secrétaire général de la Jeunesse. Cited in Delestre, *Uriage*, 163 n.114. Also on that meeting see Jacques Duquesne, *Les Catholiques français sous l'Occupation* (Paris: Grasset, 1966), 218.

21 "Compte-rendu de la réunion des chefs d'École au Mayet de Montagne" (18–27 August 1942) (confidential report), 6 pages (102 J 6); Delestre, *Uriage*, 164.

22 Jean Le Veugle, *Journal d'un résistant* (unpublished), cited in Delestre, *Uriage*, 164.

23 "Compte-rendu de la réunion des chefs."

24 For more detail on this see Madame S. Silvestre, "Les premiers pas de la résistance dans l'Isère," in *Revue d'histoire de la deuxième guerre mondiale*, July 1982; Delestre, *Uriage*, 169.

25 Delestre, *Uriage*, 169.

26 According to Delestre, *Uriage*, 70. In her recent study of Father Pierre Chaillet, Madame Renée Bédarida does not record such contacts but suggests that Father Chaillet was opposed to the participation of Catholics like Mounier in Vichy projects such as Uriage. Renée Bédarida, *Pierre Chaillet, témoin de la résistance spirituelle* (Paris: Fayard, 1988), 114. Paul de la Taille confirmed having been charged with contacts with Jews, and Resistance organizations concerned with Jews, by Segonzac (interview with the author, June 1990). See also Duquesne, *Les Catholiques*, 254.

27 Delestre, *Uriage*, 167.

28 Text cited in Henri Amouroux, *Les passions et les haines* (Paris: Robert Laffont, 1981), 128.

29 These charges are in the two-page letter addressed to the minister from the *proviseur* of the Lycée David d'Angers (Besson) explaining the experience of the Maître d'Éducation Générale at the lycée, M. Remordant, who had participated in an eight-day *stage d'information* at Uriage in September 1942 (probably the session of general information that took place from 20 to 27 September) (102 J 13).

30 Texts cited in Amouroux, *Les passions*, 110; Delestre, *Uriage*, 168.

31 Henri Frenay, *La nuit finira* (Paris: Robert Laffont, 1973), 221.

32 According to Roger Stéphane, in *Chaque homme est lié au monde. Carnets (août 1939–août 1944)* (Paris: Le Sagittaire, 1946), 176. Recalling the event years later, Segonzac cast the encounter with Laval in a

somewhat different light, recalling that "I must admit that when I was alone with Laval in his office, I was subjected to a magnificent piece of seductive eloquence. In contrast to Darlan, Laval knew how to talk to men with a remarkable intelligence, warmth, and simplicity. I was not convinced however, and said so to the president who listened to me without anger or apparent spite. But from that day I knew that I was condemned." Cf. Segonzac, *Le Vieux Chef*, 105.

33 The measures taken against Jews at this time are described elsewhere in this manuscript.

34 *Journal de bord des Comédiens Routiers* (unpublished), cited in Delestre, *Uriage*, 170.

35 *Journal ... Routiers*, cited in Delestre, *Uriage*, 170. According to Paul de la Taille it was a question of asking the Carthusian Father Abbot to find them some episcopal support.

36 According to Paul de la Taille, the first arms were obtained and furnished at Saint-Étienne by Octave Simon (who was part of the "Satirist" network in the Sarthe). (Cf. Henri Noguères, *Histoire de la Résistance en France* (Paris: Robert Laffont, 1972), 147. These arms were first of all hidden with a Savoyard peasant, a *jaciste*, who knew the chateau from having given his "témoignage" there to a *stage* in May 1942. "Témoignage de Bénigno Cacérès," *Les cahiers de l'animation* 49–50 (April 1985).

37 Particularly glib talk of a "French race." See summary of that meeting composed by M. Dupouey, 8 October 1942, 10 pages mimeographed (102 J 6).

38 "Directives générales de notre pensée et de notre action," 3 pages mimeographed (102 J 14).

39 Ibid., 1–2. Professor Comte considers this one of the essential Uriage texts and appended it to his thesis as Annexe V, 1143–45.

40 Segonzac, "Vie communautaire et style de vie," *Jeunesse ... France – Cahiers d'Uriage* 37 (December 1942), 1, 3.

41 "Comme nous nous situons," mimeographed (no date), 2 pages (102 J 117).

42 "Notes de l'exposé Révolutions manquées, Révolutions à faire par H. Beuve-Méry," Cahier dated 3 November 1942 and destined for the instructors. Beuve-Méry would give the same exposé to stagiaires in December. Cited in Delestre, *Uriage*, 171–2.

43 *Journal ... Routiers*, cited in Delestre, *Uriage*, 172.

44 "Note confidentielle" of Lamirand to Bonnard, Vichy, 18 November 1942, A.N./F.17. 13.367. Cited in Delestre, *Uriage*, 172–3.

45 A dossier entitled "Lettres de mise en cause de la loyauté des chefs d'Uriage vis-à-vis du gouvernement" (1942) is in the archives (102 J 13).

It includes, for example, the report of someone named "Boissin J.P.F.": "I continue to signal to you Dunoyer de Segonzac, director of the École des cadres d'Uriage, and Professor Paul Reuter of that same school (a presumed Israelite). On that later do an investigation." The unsigned uncompleted text of one page, dated Grenoble 26 November 1942, was noted "Copie d'un document trouvé sur le nommé Boissin J.P.F. le 22.11.42."

The school seemed well informed about hostile reports about it sent to Vichy officials.

46 "Notes de l'aumônier général," *Bulletin de l'Association des Anciens des Chantiers*, 21 November 1942. Cited in Comte, "Uriage," 1054.

47 E. Dary, "Travailler devant soi," *Le Chef*, January 1943, 365–8. Cited in Comte, "Uriage," 1055.

48 Cf. Comte, "Uriage," 1055.

49 Testimony of Georges Rebattet, who stayed at Uriage with Father Maydieu around 20 December. Cited in Comte, "Uriage," 1055.

50 *Journal ... Routiers*, cited in Delestre, *Uriage*, 178.

51 Ibid.

52 He arrived with Paul Reuter, having heard his lecture the previous evening. See his *Chaque homme*, 175.

53 Roger Stéphane, *Chaque homme*, 163–76; *Toutes choses ont leur saison* (Paris: Fayard, 1979), 169–71.

54 Dubarle, an escaped prisoner, seems to have spoken on the theme of "prisoners." Delestre, *Uriage*, 179.

55 Material on this project remains in the dossier "Journées d'études sociales: objectifs, programme, conférences" (December 1942) (102 J 17).

56 "Grande entreprise et paix sociale," synthesis note on the mixed *stage* of June 1942, mimeographed document, 4 pages, signed Dumazedier. Louis Poli papers (102 J 157).

57 Cf. The manuscript notes of Louis Poli on each of the lectures, and personal notes on the work community of Perroux (Louis Poli papers) (102 J 154–60).

58 Comte, "Uriage," 986.

59 J.D., "Journées d'études sociales: 22–24 December or 4–6 January," Uriage Documentation, typed, 4 pages, cited in Comte, "Uriage," 986–7.

60 Father Chenu's book appeared in the Bibliothèque du Peuple series. He would become one of France's most important Catholic thinkers after the war as a medievalist, social thinker, and theologian. See J. Dumazedier, "Civilisation du travail. Pour être heureux, travaillons ensemble." *Jeunesse ... France – Cahiers d'Uriage* 37 (December 1942), 39–41.

It is interesting to compare Father Chenu's ideas on work with those of Ernst Jünger in *Der Arbeiter* (1932). Chenu seems a central figure in accounting for the ease of the personalists' and Catholics' switch from Pétainist communitarianism to Stalinist collectivism (Christian Roy).

61 "Charles Péguy et la révolution du XXe siècle," mimeographed (undated) (102 J 15). This text, which was mimeographed and diffused throughout the Uriage network, contained twenty-three pages of Beuve-Méry's analysis and twenty-six pages of Péguy extracts and bibliography.

62 For more information on this session see the dossier "Stage d'information des 22–26 juin 1942: aumôniers" (102 J 80).

Father de Lubac liked to point out that while his hero Proudhon was a fierce anti-clerical and critic of the Church he had also been a traditionalist on questions of sexual morality and an admirer of certain "virile" Christian virtues. De Lubac also found much that was positive in the thinking of Nietzsche and, to a certain extent, of Marx as well.

63 Hubert Beuve-Méry, "Principes de la Révolution du XXe siècle" (mimeographed, no date) (102 J 15). Professor Comte cites this text as of "anonymous" authorship in "Uriage," 1002. This was also the thesis of Berdyaev's *Un nouveau Moyen-Âge* (Paris: Plon, 1927).

64 For more on this notion see F. Perroux, and J. Madaule, *La communauté française* (4e cahier d'études communautaires) (Paris: PUF, 1942), a text reviewed by Hubert Beuve-Méry as "Communauté et Économie," *Jeunesse ... France – Cahiers d'Uriage* 37 (December 1942).

65 "Jeunesse de l'Église," *Jeunesse ... France – Cahiers d'Uriage* 37 (à propos to the manifesto launched by the Jeunesse de l'Église group).

66 "Communauté et Religion," *Jeunesse ... France – Cahiers d'Uriage* 33 (July 1942).

67 P.H. Chombart de Lauwe, "Les communautés dans la nation," *Jeunesse ... France – Cahiers d'Uriage* 37 (December 1942), 12.

By earth and blood the community is incarnated in matter. On that land that moulds man and on which man works, the human group plunges its roots. His ancestors sleep there and his blood is mixed in with it. The village cemetery is the setting of that mysterious union.

Each family has its tomb and each village its cemetery. Each homeland has raised monuments to its heroes. "The Motherland," Jean Lacroix says, "is the earth infinitely fertilized by the tombs that ceaselessly give birth to cradles, in a sort of sacred rhythm." Earth and blood are necessary for the community to live.

68 *Journal ... Routiers*, cited in Delestre, *Uriage*, 179.

69 Paul Martin, "official liquidator" of the school, told Antoine Delestre that the closing had been demanded by Otto Abetz, Ambassador of the Reich in Paris. Delestre, *Uriage*, 179.

70 Letter of Segonzac to La Porte du Theil ("Mon Général") (102 J 12). Segonzac was specific about having the support of Pelorson to the end, and he seemed convinced that the Germans had not been behind the closing (see chapter 8, 1–2).

To hear the recollections of Segonzac and the Uriage alumni one would imagine that the Vieux Chef was considered a dangerous Resister, practically an outlaw, by Vichy authorities at the time of the closing of the school. He was also reported to have been horrified, later, on learning that the castle would be profaned by being turned over to the Milice. But the archives reveal a much more ordinary situation. Segonzac was informed in later January that his assigned functions at the SGJ had ceased but that he would be paid until the end of February, and that he would learn, soon, of his new status from the SGJ (letter from the "Service Administratif et Financier" of the SGJ, 19 January 1943) (102 J 12).

At the end of January Segonzac wrote Vichy to provide for the interim situation of the workers at the Château Bayard who would be assigned to the succeeding school. He asked to keep the place until 31 March so that the transfer might be orderly (a request that seems to have been honoured). He goes on record, however, against allowing the former Alleman family concierge (the same who aided the Countess to save some of the family art treasures?) to return to his old residence on the estate. ("Rapport sur l'état des opérations de liquidation au 31 Janvier 1943") (102 J 12).

71 In an interview years later Gilles Ferry said: "A little before the end of 1942 threats directed toward Uriage became more precise. Certain instructors were being prosecuted and Segonzac himself took refuge in a house at Vizille, a dozen kilometres from Uriage. Few people knew where he was living. For goodbyes, then, there was a large nocturnal ceremony." And Paul Reuter: "The dividing up of the flag was a very intense, poignant, and pathetic moment. We were intending to reconstruct it later. But we never did it and I ought to have a part in one of my drawers." Cited in Pierre Bitoun, *Les hommes d'Uriage* (Paris: La Découverte, 1988), 97.

CHAPTER EIGHT

1 Except one, the head of the Clerlande school, who reconsidered when cajoled and threatened. Riby was the spokesman for the regional school directors at this meeting.

2 Testimony of Georges Lebrec, then assistant to the head of the office of Cadres, responsible for the southern zone. Cited in Bernard Comte, "L'École Nationale des Cadres d'Uriage. Une communauté non-conformiste à l'époque de la révolution nationale (1940–1942)," Ph.D. thesis, Université de Lyon 2, 1987, 1050; Antoine Delestre, *Uriage, une communauté et une école dans la tourmente, 1940–1945* (Nancy: Presses Universitaires de Nancy, 1989), 185.

3 According to the testimony of Captain Louis Lanes, former trainee at the school (*stage* of 15 July to 3 August 1941), cited in *Journal de bord des Comédiens Routiers* (unpublished), Delestre, *Uriage*, 185.

4 Jean Le Veugle, *Journal d'un résistant* (unpublished), 66, cited in Delestre, *Uriage*, 186.

5 Text cited in Delestre, *Uriage*, 187. Professor Delestre remarks that "unfortunately we don't know where that text was published."

6 Letter of Segonzac to La Porte du Theil ("Mon Général") (102 J 12).

7 Testimony of H. Beuve-Méry, cited in Delestre, *Uriage*, 189.

8 Virieu, a cavalry officer wounded during the 1914 war, was taken prisoner in 1940. Repatriated, he took over the direction of the École régionale des cadres des Chantiers de la Jeunesse at Collonges in April 1941.

9 This information came via Yves Drapeau to J. Le Veugle; *Journal d'un résistant*, 65, cited in Delestre, *Uriage*, 191.

10 *Journal ... Routiers*, cited in Delestre, *Uriage*, 192.

11 Philippe Merlin established the semi-monthly magazine *Jeune Force de France* early in 1943 for a new generation of National Socialist French Youth. Many of the contributors came from Marcel Déat's RNP. Merlin, editor-in-chief, held a doctorate in jurisprudence, had been active before the war in the CLAJ (Centre Laïc des Auberges de la Jeunesse), and was a fervent disciple of the writer Jean Giono. The same romanticism that had oriented him to the rural outdoor life prescribed by Giono later led him to National Socialism and the Waffen-ss.

According to French ss lore, Merlin had doubts about the reality of Germany's "European" commitment and was disappointed in the real Waffen-ss: he went to Berlin to air his grievances personally before Himmler and came away deeply disappointed in the ss leader. Not long after his return, Merlin committed suicide. In remembrance of the ancient Vikings, he had willed that his body be cremated and the ashes scattered over the North Sea. Like many other middle-class Nazi sympathizers or fascists in interwar and wartime Europe, Merlin sought escape from the ambiguities and loneliness of modern urban life in a retreat to an atavistic, heroic, virile, tribal community. Bertram M. Gordon, *Collaborationism in France During the Second World War* (Ithaca & London: Cornell University Press, 1980), 272–4.

12 *Jeune Force de France*, bi-monthly, 3 (27 January 1943). Cited in Delestre, *Uriage*, 180.

13 According to the alumni of Dunoyer de Segonzac's Uriage, they were horrified to learn that their chateau would be "profaned" by the Milice. They professed outrage, years later, when in the controversy over Bernard-Henri Lévy's essay on Uriage a photo of the castle under the Milice was published, thus associating the two institutions. In his over-1200-page thesis on Uriage Professor Comte devotes one sentence to the school under du Vair, while Professor Delestre, in his book, offers an extended foonote. The idea that there could have been any parallels or continuity between the succeeding Uriage elite schools seems a taboo subject in the Uriage milieu.

14 Darnand emerged from the First World War a major war hero, later called by Poincaré an "artisan of victory," an accolade shared only with Foch and Clemenceau. In 1939–40 he fought alongside Dominican father R.-L. Bruckberger who, after the war, would employ his excellent resistance credentials to try to save Darnand's life. Cf. Gordon, *Collaborationism*, 149–50.

15 Darnand had been raised in a staunchly Catholic home and begun his education in a church school. At the age of ten he had been sent to board and study at the diocesan seminary at Belley. He was unable to complete his schooling there because of the insufficiency of family funds, but an interest in religion was kindled that never left him. Gordon, *Collaborationism*, 149–50.

16 Gordon, *Collaborationism*, 188–9.

17 Gordon, *Collaborationism*, 183.

18 W.D. Halls, *The Youth of Vichy France* (Oxford: Clarendon Press, 1981), 349; see also the remarks on the Milice at Uriage in H. Beuve-Méry, "École des cadres," *Esprit* (October 1945), 624–9.

19 A few families of instructors remained at St. Martin d'Uriage; in the fall of 1943 Mme Beuve-Méry was still there. Cf. Jacques Delperrie de Bayac, *Histoire de la Milice, 1918–1945* (Paris: Fayard, 1969), 190; Comte, "Uriage," 1049; Laurent Greilshamer, *Hubert Beuve-Méry* (Paris: Fayard, 1990), 193.

20 Comte, "Uriage," 1049.

21 Delperrie de Bayac, *La Milice*, 190. The most recent archival research on the Milice has been unable to come up with more information on how and why this eccentric Acadian came to be there (J-P. Azema).

22 Halls, *Youth*, 350.

23 Document cited in Delperrie de Bayac, *La Milice*, 191.

24 Ibid., 190–4.

25 This and the following material is taken from an unsigned report, dated the end of July 1943, found in the Uriage archives. It was attributed to a local *milicien* working for the Resistance (102 J 12).

26 Notably Lemaire, Mathourof, Roiron, and some others. People saw Madame Roiron imploring Darnand's guards, who were taking her husband away, and heard them promising her that he would be freed and she would see him again.

27 Halls, *Youth*, 350.

28 Unsigned note, dated the end of July 1943 in the Uriage archives (102 J 12).

29 Halls, *Youth*, 350.

30 United States Office of Strategic Services, Research and Analysis Branch, R and A No. 1694 "French Pro-Fascist Groups," an American intelligence report paralleling the *French Basic Handbook* and dated August 30, 1944, 12–13. The oss report is available in the Hoover Institution Library at Stanford University. It is cited in Gordon, *Collaborationism*, 169.

31 Bucard's Franciste movement modelled itself more on Italian or Spanish fascism than on nazism. Bucard fought bravely in both world wars, was wounded three times, and received eleven citations (cf. Halls, *Youth*, 331). The Franciste leader Bucard and his party's chief ideologist Paul Guiraud came from strong Catholic backgrounds: Bucard's peasant family had sent him to seminary; Guiraud's father was the prominent editor-in-chief of the Catholic daily *La Croix*, and he himself had a degree in philosophy. Although the Francistes were not openly clerical such as, for example, the Iron Guard, they referred more often than their collaborationist rivals (with the possible exception of Darnand's Milice) to French Catholic tradition. Thus Bucard and Guiraud had far less ground to make up in their approaches to the church and the faithful in France than did Déat or Doriot, and there was, accordingly, more traditionalist Catholic sentiment among the Francistes than in the RNP or PPF (cf. Gordon, *Collaborationism*, 223–4). (Professor Gordon seems more forthcoming and balanced in his treatment of the links between the Church and collaborationist forces than are the studies written by French scholars who, for whatever reasons, seem to want to avoid this issue.)

32 Gordon, *Collaborationism*, 189. Philippe Henriot had written several books of poetry during the early 1920s before he involved himself with the Catholic press and became committed to the interwar battle for greater freedom for the Church in France. In 1925 Henriot joined General de Castelnau, a pro-clerical war hero, and became a leading speaker for the Fédération Nationale Catholique, de Castelnau's political organization. Gordon, *Collaborationism*, 295.

33 Gordon, *Collaborationism*, 191. For example, trucks for the Milice in the spring of 1944 came from the supply of the Chantiers de la Jeunesse, who had been disbanded earlier that year by the Germans. (Professor Gordon gives a German archival source for this information.)

34 This is the opinion of Gordon, in his *Collaborationism*, 193.

35 Gordon, *Collaborationism*, 290.

36 Text cited in Gordon, *Collaborationism*, 296.

37 Suhard's gesture, so late in the war, was one of the factors that led de Gaulle to let it be known that the Cardinal Archbishop of Paris would not be welcome to preside at the Liberation Te Deum celebration in Notre Dame some months later.

38 Gordon, *Collaborationism*, 336–7.

39 Gordon, *Collaborationism*, 346.

40 For example, early Catholic Resistance leaders in North America Yves Simon and Jacques Maritain, who had wide contacts with anti-fascist Catholic intellectuals throughout the world, went so far as to estimate that the majority of the Catholics in the West were pro-fascist. The various factors that led them to form this judgment will be revealed in their unpublished correspondence, to be published soon. See John Hellman, "The Anti-Democratic Impulse in Catholicism: Jacques Maritain, Yves Simon, and Charles de Gaulle During World War II," *Journal of Church and State* 33, no. 3 (Summer 1991): 453–71.

41 Cf. Halls, *Youth*, 354; Comte, "Uriage," 1049.

42 Cf. Alban Vistel, *La nuit sans ombre* (Paris: Fayard, 1970), 476–7; M. Chanal, "La milice française dans l'Isère," *Revue française de la deuxième guerre mondiale et des conflits contemporains* 127 (July 1982): 1–42 (this article describes the closing of the Milice's Uriage and the execution of seven miliciens). Delestre, *Uriage*, 193.

43 Gilbert Gadoffre, cited in Delestre, *Uriage*, 197.

44 A much edited, and blander, text is reproduced as definitive in Pierre Dunoyer de Segonzac, *Le Vieux Chef. Mémoires et pages choisies* (Paris: Seuil, 1971), 241. A more interesting and complete version, "Décision No. 2, activités de l'Ordre" – a mimeographed text of 6 pages, undated (beginning of 1943?) and unsigned, probably written by Segonzac (from private archives) – is reprinted in Delestre, *Uriage*, 199–200. This text seems to be absent from the dossier on the Order in the Uriage archives (102 J 150).

Professor Delestre told me that several of the alumni of Uriage, including (uncharacteristically) Beuve-Méry, opposed his publication of this integral version of the Order's rules once he had discovered it – primarily because of the clause regarding the Jews. He secured their acquiescence for its publication with the argument (among others) that if this document subsequently came to light, as it likely would, the credibility of Professor Delestre's scholarship would be undermined.

45 Perhaps they belatedly realized this and hence the "heavy" passages of the Order's principles were edited out of the text in Segonzac's *Vieux Chef* (in another instance of Uriage people being a bit less than completely frank about their war-time positions).

46 Cf. M. Haedrich, "Antoine Mauduit, un fondateur de maquis," *Le Monde*, 21 August 1986 (cited in Comte, "Uriage," 1066).

47 According to a postwar opinion of one of its composers, the Summa was to constitute an overall plan in which would be integrated the diverse initiatives that the members of the team would take after the liberation, above all in the educational, social, and cultural areas. Gilbert Gadoffre, letter to Bernard Comte (25 October 1985), cited in Comte, "Uriage," 1065. A version of this Summa was published after the war, as we shall see.

48 "Procès-verbal de la seconde assemblée à Saint-Flour, avril 1943" (102 J 150), cited in Delestre, *Uriage*, 200.

49 J. Dumazedier, "Lettre à Berthier [Beuve-Méry]," 21 March 1944, mimeographed text of 12 pages, p. 9 (102 J 151); Delestre, *Uriage*, 200.

50 Delestre, *Uriage*, 200.

51 "Attitude vis-à-vis des mouvements extérieurs, Décision No. 2," 6 pages (Yves Jacquot papers), cited in Comte, "Uriage," 1071.

52 Roger Stéphane reported that Segonzac had a veritable phobia about masons, as we have seen. The strong anti-masonic bent of Uriage was confirmed by Paul de la Taille (interview with the author, June 1990).

53 "Décision No. 2, activités de l'Ordre," in Delestre, *Uriage*, 201. A document in the Uriage archives (102 J 150), "La politique de l'ordre" (no date), remarks: "à considérer les Français il semblerait qu'il y ait plusieurs France[s] ... Il y a ceux pour qui les intérets d'une internationale, soit capitaliste, soit juive, soit franc-maçonne, soit communiste, prime les intérets nationaux; ils ne sont pas nôtres."

In mid-July 1941, on the other hand, a collaborationist writer reproached Segonzac for a royalism devoid of the national-socialist impulse, and for an anti-semitism that was purely religious ("Jamais, dans ma famille, une de Segonzac n'aurait épousé un Juif." Yes, Augier responds, but what if the Jew converts?). He also reported that at the study day the previous May, preceding Darlan's visit, a delegate rose to protest the presence of the Jewish scouts (led by Hagueneau), but the Catholic scout leader defended the presence of the Jews. Clearly, the critic charged, Segonzac was contemptuous of anti-semitism and had not based the Uriage school doctrine on the important racial factor. Marc Augier, "Les Chevaliers sans armure," *La Gerbe*, 24 Juillet 1941, 1–3 (102 J 13).

54 Despite the Uriage inner circle's secret reservations about Jews the leaders of the only *corps franc juif* asked, in 1944, to put themselves under Segonzac's orders. Several Uriage instructors would marry Jewish women and a bright Jew with a strong personality and an important future, Simon Nora, who was introduced by Germaine Blum-Gayet, became a member of the "équipes volantes" of Uriage. Delestre, *Uriage*, 201 n.68.

55 "Décision No. 2, activités de l'Ordre", cited in Delestre, *Uriage*, 201–2.

56 Cf. Comte, "Uriage," 1072. Professor Comte hardly mentions this factor, which was probably more central to the Order's plans than he implies.

57 Henri Frenay, *La nuit finira* (Paris: Laffont, 1973), 419.

58 H. Noguères, *Histoire de la Résistance en France*, 5 (Paris: Laffont, 1981), 887.

59 "Organisation générale de l'Ordre," 4 pages, typed (Yves Jacquot papers), cited in Comte, "Uriage," 1068–9.

60 "Décision No. 2, activités de l'Ordre," and "Orientations politiques," p. 6, cited in Delestre, *Uriage*, 203–4.

61 Cf. Delestre, *Uriage*, 221–2.

62 "Journées des 2 et 3 Octobre (1943)" typed, one page, cited at length in Delestre, *Uriage*, 204–5.

63 H. Beuve-Méry, "Mise au point politique" (notes sur une conférence), 2 October 1943, mimeographed, 5 pages, cited in Delestre, *Uriage*, 206.

64 "Pour un rassemblement des volontés françaises," mimeographed text, 5 pages, unsigned but "doubtlessly by Segonzac," 30 November 1943 (private archives), cited in Delestre, *Uriage*, 206.

65 "Directives générales de notre pensée et de notre action," mimeographed text, 38 pages, unsigned, dated 30 November 1943. See also "Vers une politique et une force française," mimeographed text, 3 pages, unsigned, no date, cited in Delestre, *Uriage*, 243.

66 Delestre, *Uriage*, 243.

67 Interview cited in Pierre Bitoun, *Les hommes d'Uriage* (Paris: La Découverte, 1988), 146. Jean-Louis Lévy also noted that, after the war, for those closely associated with it, the newspaper *Le Monde* was "the values of Uriage incarnated in an organ of the press" (ibid., 179).

68 Delestre, *Uriage*, 210–11.

69 According to Henri Michel, the number of *insoumis* become fighting *maquisards* never surpassed 10 per cent. Henri Michel, "Les maquis au-delà de la légende," *Le monde d'aujourd'hui*, 30–31 December 1984. Cited in Delestre, *Uriage*, 211.

70 Bénigno Cacérès, *L'espoir au coeur* (Paris: Seuil, 1967), 51.
71 Cacérès, *L'espoir*, 55–6, 47–8.
72 Cited in Pierre Bitoun, *Les hommes*, 104, 115–16.
73 Delestre, *Uriage*, 214.
74 Cited in Bitoun, *Les hommes*, 116. Domenach remarked that his fiancée also belonged to the team, and was one of those who saw the fire that destroyed their Thébaïde from much closer than he himself did. Ibid., 110.
75 Cacérès, *L'espoir*, 63.
76 A-J. Maydieu, *Le Christ et le monde* (Paris: Paul Hartmann, 1946), 140–1.
77 Cited in Bitoun, *Les hommes*, 113–14, 107.
78 Cited in Bitoun, *Les hommes*, 124.
79 Beuve-Méry's differences with Vichy are amply (perhaps too amply) developed in Laurent Greilshamer, *Hubert Beuve-Méry* (Paris: Fayard, 1990), part 2, sections 2–3.
80 Cf. Xavier de Virieu, *Radio-journal Libre (juillet 1943–août 1944)* (Paris: Ed. Jean Cabut, 1947); Fabienne Coquet, "Le colonel Xavier de Virieu: un catholique dans la guerre (1939–1945)" (Mémoire) (University of Grenoble, 1984).
81 Pierre Bolle, ed., *Grenoble et le Vercors. De la Résistance à la Libération.* (Lyon: La Manufacture, 1985), 54; *Chronique des maquis de l'Isère*, 87, cited in Delestre, *Uriage*, 213.
82 According to Germaine-Gayet, (the Jewish) member of the Uriage team, interview cited in Delestre, *Uriage*, 213–14.
83 Bolle, *Grenoble et le Vercors*, 48, 238. As in the case of other negative things regarding the *équipes volantes* (or Uriage in general) it is the marginal figures of the Uriage group, or those who had contact with the Uriage people, who later gave the most persuasive accounts of the reality of the situation. It never seemed as if, in their subsequent reflections, Segonzac or Beuve-Méry – and certainly not Domenach, who always spoke of the *équipes volantes* as a mainstream Resistance institution – complained of the injustice of their being suspect as *pétainistes* by the *maquisards*. Moreover, given the real attitude of the Uriage Order toward the Communists in the Resistance, that they had to be combatted at all costs for they wanted power – or the free-masons, and even Jews (excluded a priori from the Uriage inner circle), or liberal democrats (objects of contempt) – the *maquisards'* mistrust was understandable.
84 Bitoun, *Les hommes*, 103; Delestre, *Uriage*, 217.
85 Germaine-Gayet interview cited in Delestre, *Uriage*, 213–14.
86 Testimony of Le Ray; Paul Silvestre, "STO, maquis et guérilla dans l'Isère," *Revue d'histoire de la deuxième guerre mondiale*, April 1983, 21,

describes the usefulness of the Murinais EVS to the Resistance morale.
Le Ray was the son-in-law of prominent Catholic novelist François
Mauriac.

87 Le Ray in Bolle, *Grenoble et le Vercors*, 55.

88 Le Ray in Bolle, *Grenoble et le Vercors*, 115–16; Delestre, *Uriage*, 229.

89 Cited in Bitoun, *Les hommes*, 126.

90 Delestre, *Uriage*, 251–2.

91 Testimony of P. de la Taille, cited in Delestre, *Uriage*, 255.

92 Daniel Lindenberg, *Les années souterraines* (Paris: La Découverte,
1990), 263.

CHAPTER NINE

1 Maurice Schumann, Catholic intellectual and voice of the Free French
on Radio London, had been active in the same periodicals and groups
as the best-known Uriage people. But he had very little knowledge of
Uriage's activities during the war and remembered them vaguely, in
retrospect, as "friendly" to the Free French (interview with the
author).

2 "La jeunesse française," anonymous, 37 pages, no date (c. June-July
1942), found in Lyon after the war and cited in Bernard Comte,
"L'École Nationale des Cadres d'Uriage. Une communauté éducative
non-conformiste à l'époque de la révolution nationale (1940–1942),"
Ph.D. thesis, Université de Lyon 2, 1987, 975–6.

3 Review of the meeting of the Conseil de la Jeunesse, 11 October
1943, cited in Comte, "Uriage," 1080.

4 His departure was after 6 January because he met Jean Le Veugle,
Hoepffner, and Stouff that day in Paris, according to Jean Le Veugle's
Journal d'un résistant (unpublished), 241, cited in Antoine Delestre,
Uriage, une communauté et une école dans la tourmente, 1940–1945
(Nancy: Presses Universitaires de Nancy, 1989), 262.

5 Pierre Dunoyer de Segonzac, *Le Vieux Chef. Mémoires et pages choisies*
(Paris: Seuil, 1971), 127.

6 Henri Frenay, *La nuit finira* (Paris: Lafont, 1973), 419.

7 Frenay, *La nuit*, 420.

8 Segonzac, *Le Vieux Chef*, 128–30.

9 Comments reported by Le Ray in Pierre Bolle, ed., *Grenoble et le Vercors. De la Résistance à la Libération* (Lyon: La Manufacture, 1985),
56–7.

10 Le Veugle, *Journal*, 256, cited in Delestre, *Uriage*, 256.

11 For example, Emmanuel Mounier's descriptions, some months later, of
the liberating American soldiers, is patronizing to say the least and
devoid of any sense of compassion for, or gratitude to, the Americans
who lost their lives in liberating France. After the war, *Esprit* under

Mounier and Domenach, and *Le Monde* under Beuve-Méry, were among the most prominent critics of American influence in France and in Europe, often from a perspective similar to the one Segonzac set out here. Cf. *Bulletin des amis d'Emmanuel Mounier* 7–8 (December 1955): 35, 58–9.

12 Segonzac, *Le Vieux Chef*, 131–5.

13 Comte, "Uriage," 1080.

14 "Note pour le Mouvement," mimeographed, 2 pages, unsigned, end April (?) 1944 (102 J 151); Delestre, *Uriage*, 266.

15 Comte, "Uriage," 1083.

16 According to Professor Delestre this was because the arresting of Resistance leaders (among whom some appreciated the activity of Uriage) suddenly multiplied. (Delestre gives no source but Uriage alumni he interviewed must have told him this.) Perhaps the attitude of de Gaulle, or that reported to be common among rank and file of the *maquis* by Fernand Rude, also helped block this initiative by the Uriage group. Cf. Delestre, *Uriage*, 226.

17 Testimony of A. Le Ray cited in Delestre, *Uriage*, 243–4.

18 Delestre, *Uriage*, 226 n.178.

19 Testimony of Le Ray, cited in Delestre, *Uriage*, 243.

20 Bénigno Cacérès, *L'espoir au coeur* (Paris: Seuil, 1967), 125.

21 According to Yves Drapeau, cited in Delestre, *Uriage*, 251.

22 Letter cited in Delestre, *Uriage*, 246–7.

23 "Libération-Révolution," NERF (May 1944?), mimeographed, 4 pages, "Manifeste" of the *équipe*, written by Dumazedier, 11 February 1944. Another, much longer version of the manifesto also exists in a 15-page mimeographed text (102 J 151); the manifesto is cited at length in Delestre, *Uriage*, 248–50.

24 "Décision No. 1," mimeographed, 5 pages, attributed to Segonzac, 1 June 1944 (102 J 151).

25 "Décision No. 11," 1 June 1944 (102 J 151).

26 Comte, "Uriage," 1081.

27 Delestre, *Uriage*, 276; on d'Aragon's Resistance activities see Charles d'Aragon, *La Résistance sans héroïsme* (Paris: Seuil, 1977).

28 Comte, "Uriage," 1081.

29 The Andrieux farm, "not far from the Vintrou dam": cf. *Les nouvelles compagnies franches du Tarn*, récit de Robinson (Rouchié), dessins de Michel Mare, carnets de route du 12ᵉ Dragons (Offenbourg [Bade]: Franz Burda, 1946); cited in Delestre, *Uriage*, 277.

30 Delestre, *Uriage*, 276. According to his secretary Paul de la Taille, this situation developed because of the way in which these groups of resisters approached Segonzac, rather than his imposing confessional distinctions on people (interview with the author, June 1990).

31 Comte, "Uriage," 1081.

32 L.M. Ardain, *Journal de guerre* (unpublished), 31, cited in Delestre, *Uriage*, 277.

33 Cf. Lucien Lazare in Anny Latour, *La résistance juive en France* (Paris: Stock, 1987), 322.

34 Jean Le Veugle (alias capitaine Le Brecq), *Du maquis de St-Marcel à la poche de St-Nazaire* (unpublished), 61–70, cited in Delestre, *Uriage*, 273–4.

35 "Positions à l'égard du communisme." Mimeographed, 12 pages, mimeographed, no date and unsigned, diffused by the Uriage network (102 J 151); Delestre, *Uriage*, 274–5.

36 Cf. Delestre, *Uriage*, 276.

37 L.M. Ardain, *Journal*, 32, cited in Delestre, *Uriage*, 278.

38 To Pierre Geny's fiancée, Melle Gaby Audibert (former secretary of Uriage), Segonzac wrote: "If you want, when we have had vengeance we will transport his body to Uriage to the feet of the three colours he served better than anyone." Cited in Delestre, *Uriage*, 281.

39 Delestre, *Uriage*, 269–70.

40 *Les nouvelles compagnies*; Delestre, *Uriage*, 282; Segonzac's final comment is cited by Anny Latour, *La résistance juive en France* (Paris: Stock, 1970), 230–1.

41 Testimonies cited in Latour, *La résistance juive*, 230–1.

42 Segonzac, *Le Vieux Chef*, 149.

43 Segonzac, *Le Vieux Chef*, 158; Comte, "Uriage," 1081; Delestre, *Uriage*, 294.

44 Testimony of Jean-Marie Domenach cited in Delestre, *Uriage*, 291.

45 Several projects for liberated Grenoble may be found in the Uriage archives (102 J 151); Delestre, *Uriage*, 291.

46 Interview with the author.

47 The name "Peuple et Culture" was not new; it was the name of the Collège du travail created in 1936 at Grenoble, in which Paul Lengrand participated and which was directed by Yves Farges, commissaire de la République at Lyon in 1944. Cf. Geneviève Carpier, *Fondation du mouvement national Peuple et Culture, 1944–1948* (Mémoire, Université de Paris 1, 1974); Delestre, *Uriage*, 292.

48 "Projet d'éducation à Grenoble," mimeographed, six pages, unsigned, 9 August 1944 (102 J 151); cited in Delestre, *Uriage*, 262.

49 "Allocution du commandant de Virieu" pronounced on 25 September 1944 on the occasion of the opening of the École militaire d'Uriage, mimeographed, two pages (102 J 111).

50 Testimony of General Le Ray cited in Delestre, *Uriage*, 293.

51 Lecture of Captain Poli (from private archives, cited in Delestre, *Uriage*, 294).

52 Le commandant Le Ray, chef départemental FFI de l'Isère, "Note pour le général Revers," Grenoble, 6 September 1944; Capitaine

Gadoffre, "L'École d'élèves officiers d'Uriage," article for the review *Aux Armes*, no date (102 J 11); Delestre, *Uriage*, 294.

53 Segonzac, *Le Vieux Chef*, 243.

54 Arrêté No. 308, appearing in the *Journal Officiel* 18 (4 October 1944). Cf. also Carpier, *Peuple et Culture*, 28, and Delestre, *Uriage*, 290.

55 Delestre, *Uriage*, 290. In 1945 Dunoyer de Segonzac participated in the liberation of Alsace, and then in mopping up operations in the Black Forest. At the armistice he was made "Officier de la Légion d'honneur à titre exceptionnel" and was distressed at the Left-ward political evolution of many in the Uriage Order (effectively being run by Beuve-Méry). From 1946 to 1951 he served with French forces in Morocco and from 1952 to 1957 in Germany, serving as chief of staff of the commander of the French occupation forces based in Baden-Baden. As things began to worsen for the French in Algeria, he became tank commander in the Oran area, was promoted Brigadier General, and then, from June 1959 to July 1961, served as "Directeur du Service de formation des jeunes" there – employing Uriage methods and spirit in an effort to transform Algerian young people. After retiring from the army he became director general of the "Union française des centres de vacances et de loisirs" from 1963 to 1968. He died in 1968 in the Val-de-Grâce military hospital in Paris.

56 As the publishing arm of the Catholic utopian Société de Saint-Louis, Seuil had published only three modest books before the war. Cf. the remarks on Éditions du Seuil in Michel Winock, *Histoire politique de la revue* Esprit, *1930–1950* (Paris: Seuil, 1975).

57 According to Michel Winock, this was because *Esprit* fit into the category of pre-war publications. Winock, *Esprit*, 240–1.

58 See John Hellman, *Emmanuel Moutier and the New Catholic Left, 1930–1950* (Toronto: University of Toronto Press, 1981), 207–8.

59 "*Esprit '40-'41*," *Esprit* 106 (January 1945), 303–4.

60 Cf. Hellman, *Mounier*, 207–8.

61 Cf. J-M. Domenach, "Le procés Angéli," *Esprit* 106 (January 1945); Jean Lacroix, "Charité chrétienne et justice politique," *Esprit* 107 (February 1945); J-G. Ritz, "Le seul procès," *Esprit* 110 (May 1945).

62 Winock, *Esprit*, 247.

63 Two currently prominent examples are European Community leader Jacques Delors and the former prime minister of Poland Tadeusz Mazowiecki. Delors took time off from his busy schedule to participate in a Round Table celebrating Mounier's thought on the fortieth anniversary of the death of Mounier at the Lycée Emmanuel Mounier at Châtenay-Malabry (30 November 1990). Mazowiecki, a scholar and a key figure in the life of Solidarnosc, was founder and manager of *Wiecz* (The Link), which was directly inspired by Mounier's review and often described as the "Polish *Esprit*." (Cf. John Hellman, "The

Prophets of Solidarity: Polish Left-Catholic Intellectuals Since the 1930s," *America* 147, 14 (6 November 1982): 266–9.

64 *Vers le style du XXe siècle*, by "L'équipe d'Uriage," directed by Gilbert Gadoffre (Paris: Seuil, 1945).

65 Bertrand d'Astorg, "Sur le style du XXe siècle," *Esprit* 120 (March 1946).

66 Winock, *Esprit*, 244.

67 Mme. Sauvageot was the mother of Jacques Sauvageot, the future co-director (after 1968) of *Le Monde* with Jacques Fauvet. Madame Sauvageot came from a *laic* family but converted to Catholicism in 1933 to become a very influential figure in Catholic publishing circles.

68 Laurent Greilshamer, *Hubert Beuve-Méry* (Paris: Fayard, 1990), 227–43; Pierre Bitoun, *Les hommes d'Uriage* (Paris: La Découverte, 1988), 176.

69 The last issue of *Jeunesse ... France – Cahiers d'Uriage* 37 was dated December 1942.

70 Bitoun, *Les hommes*, 176–7.

71 Beuve-Méry, cited in Bitoun, *Les hommes*, 178.

72 On 11 December 1944 the SARL (Société anonyme à responsabilité limitée) of the newspaper *Le Monde* was created. It was given a capital of 200,000 francs. H. Beuve-Méry, manager and director of the publication, invested 40,000 francs. René Courtin, a Christian Democrat professor in the law faculty of Paris and a faithful classical liberal, and Christian Funck-Brentano, charged with press relations by the Algiers government, did the same and made up the directing committee of the paper. Six other associates furnished the remainder. Courtin had reservations about the Pétainism of Beuve-Méry at the time. Bitoun, *Les hommes*, 176–7; Greilshamer, *Beuve-Méry*, 246–8.

73 Cited in Abel Chatelain, *Le Monde et ses lecteurs* (Paris: Armand Colin, 1962), 49; Greilshamer, *Beuve-Méry*, 262.

74 Jean-Louis Lévy, cited in Bitoun, *Les hommes*, 179–80.

75 Bitoun, *Les hommes*, 180.

76 Bitoun, *Les hommes*, 174–5.

77 Cited in Bitoun, *Les hommes*, 180–1.

78 Cited in Bitoun, *Les hommes*, 181–2. Jean Lacroix recalled how, often when he would arrive on the train from Lyon to Paris to work at *Le Monde*, "Beuve" would test him by asking him if he would like him to send one of the paper's limousines over to fetch him. Knowing he was being tested, Lacroix always refused. And Lacroix, too, was impressed by the fact that when, as an older man, Beuve broke a leg while climbing in the high Alps and could have been flown out with a helicopter, and transported to a Parisian hospital to assure that he would have the best of care, he insisted on being treated as if he were one of the local peasants (interview with the author).

79 Comte, "Uriage," 184.
80 Bitoun, *Les hommes*, 182.
81 *"D'Uriage à l'ENA"* (section of *La Somme* reprinted in Bitoun, *Les hommes*, 157).
82 Bitoun, *Les hommes*, 156.

Index

Abetz, Otto, 265n64, 300n69
Abresle, l', 125, 292n76
Académie française, 278n11, 289n19
Action Française, 7, 16, 38, 44, 64, 82, 142, 150, 155, 158, 198, 244n9, 246n35, 255n101, 276n90, 277n3, 287n60, 294nn1,2
Action Populaire, L', 113, 150, 279n25, 281n58
Agulhon, Maurice, 275n74
"Alain" (Émile-Auguste Chartier), 150
Alain-Fournier, 94
Alançon, Eric Audemard d', 20–1, 84, 122, 151, 194, 244n16, 258n132, 276n89
Alibert, Raphael, 17–18
Alleman (family), 26, 69, 244n19, 248n51, 270n7, 300n70
Alleux, o.p., Father des (R.P. Vandervoorde), 70, 154, 161, 167, 263n52, 293n96
alpinism, 42, 109, 231, 247n38, 312n78
Althusser, Louis, 48
"Amitiés scoutes," 128

Aragon, (Marquis) Charles d', 217
Aragon, Louis, 203–4
Ardain, Louise-Marie, 223
Ariès, Philippe, 275n74
Armée secrète (AS), 211
Aron, Robert, 149–50, 252n75
Association catholique de la jeunesse française (ACJF), 6, 7, 35, 44, 123, 126, 127, 129, 163
Astorg, Bertrand d', 54, 55, 70, 143, 154, 160, 170, 226, 263n47,n51
Atlantic Pact, 232
Auberges de (la) Jeunesse, "ajistes," 6, 47, 103, 111, 127, 137–8, 142, 203, 247n46, 301n11
Aubert, Jeanne, 112, 282n72
Aubert, Melle, 115
Auclair (ajiste), 103
Audibert, Melle Gaby, 310n38
Augier, Marc ("Saint-Loup" after the liberation), 142–3, 305n53

Baden-Powell, Robert, 130
Bainville, Jacques, 150
Balzac, Honoré, 113
Barrès, Maurice, 179

Barth, Karl, 150
Bastide, Roger, 151
Bataille, Georges, 66
Baudin, Louis, 151
Baudouin, Paul, 16, 62, 131–2, 283n86
Baum, Shirley (Mrs. Gregory), 258n132
Bayard, 26, 33, 64, 77
Beaussart, Msgr, 163
Becker, Raymond de, 61–2, 101, 267n91, 288n2
Beckett, Samuel, 66
Bédarida, François, 278n18
Bédarida, Renée, 296n26
Béguin, Albert, 54
Belin, René, 28–29
Belpeer, Jules, 80–1
Benjamin, René, 77–80, 85, 143, 272n35, 2273n36, 289n22
Berdyaev, Nicholas, 6, 7, 30, 38, 61, 86, 151, 175, 176, 275n71
Bergery, Gaston, 30, 32, 48, 104, 133, 139, 163–5, 246n36, 251n70, 252n75, 286n51, 294n4
Bergson, Henri, 7, 60, 81, 130, 151, 155, 177, 201, 219, 275n71
Bernadot, o.p., Vincent, 30
Bernanos, Georges, 3, 18, 92, 151, 276n90